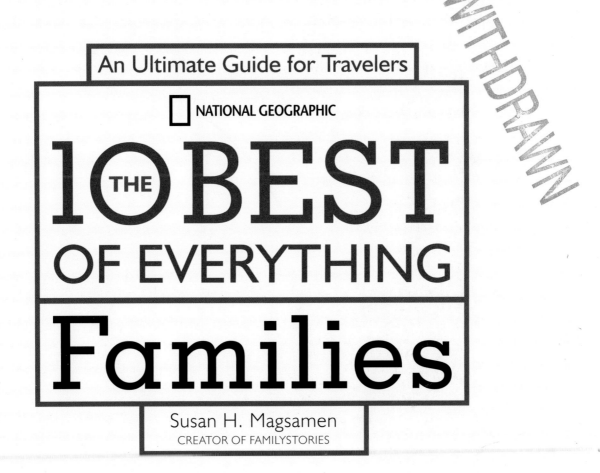

An Ultimate Guide for Travelers

NATIONAL GEOGRAPHIC

THE 10 BEST OF EVERYTHING

Families

Susan H. Magsamen
CREATOR OF FAMILYSTORIES

National Geographic
Washington, D.C.

foreword

When you have little kids, it's the little things that mean so much. Take, for example, playing in the snow, stomping in a puddle, or rustling in autumn leaves. Then, of course, there are the shapes, colors, and sizes of things to be understood. As our kids grow, we naturally connect the dots to unfold larger, amazing natural systems of life. Leaves are green (sometimes) and grow on trees that have roots in the earth, in forests all over the world. . . . How wonderful to be able to share the wonders in nature, cultures, and life with your children!

I am pleased to provide the foreword to this book because I believe it is a much needed resource for very busy parents like us, who know that little things matter and understand how they connect to make a very big thing—our families.

You will find that the information presented here is fresh, thoughtful, and invaluable. But perhaps one of the most important things you will appreciate is what a practical and easy-to-use tool you have available at your fingertips. It is

> There is no better way to see a new place than the way a child does, with open eyes, an open mind and an open heart.
>
> —Sven-Olof Lindblad,
> *President & Founder,*
> *Lindblad Expeditions*

chock-full of helpful ways to enrich a trip—whether it is around the corner or across the globe. Use it for ideas, inspiration, planning, and resources to enhance your family adventures.

Personally, I love the book and audio recommendations. I can't help thinking about my own childhood as I page through and remember the songs we sang in the car, the games we played, and the way my parents planned our vacations with an eye to finding something special for everyone.

Let's face it, so much of our busy lives are on-the-go. *The 10 Best of Everything Families* makes the BEST out of all of the moments we wander, explore, visit, or just find ourselves hopping in the car for a Sunday ride to get an ice cream cone! Every page is a reminder that adventure begins the moment we step out the door together.

Enjoy the trip.

Melina Bellows, Editor-in-Chief
National Geographic Kids

ten best
ways to use this book

1. Make it a family habit to think of yourselves as travelers. Chapter One is all about local destinations that spark interest in active discovery. Most are low cost and many are free.

2. The best vacations match up with your interests, time, and budget. Remember that kids are only little for a little while. Get away together to one of the Chapter Two vacation spots that families recommend and love.

3. Learning happens everywhere! Consider your child's educational level and interests as you read Chapter Three. It can help you plan trips that supplement school topics and introduce new ways of thinking. Connecting travel with learning is a great way to bring information off the page and to build lasting knowledge.

4. Use this book year-round. Chapter Four clues you in to seasonal celebrations, festivals, and annual events across the country.

5. Dream a little and make plans to see the world. Chapter Five shares favorite destinations and travel tips for family adventures on every continent.

6. Chapter Six is filled with real-world itineraries collected from families across the country. Read together and see what appeals to your gang.

7. Skip ahead to Chapter Seven and check out some of the ways families collect and share their travel memories. Build the art of "storykeeping" into your travel plans.

8. Make it your own! Copy the pages in Chapter Eight or write directly in the book to remember your own best trips or to plan future travel.

9. Use the Index to locate geographic listings of entries from all chapters. It's an easy way to mix and match your destinations.

10. Plan ahead and refer to websites included with most entries. At the same time, be flexible. The best adventures can take you by surprise. Celebrate serendipity. Take the backroads!

the adventure begins

When people ask me what I want for my children, I start with health and happiness. And right after that: a good education and lots of travel.

Family travel offers invaluable life experience to inform and inspire us all. Because we experience everything through our senses, we literally absorb something of every place we go. Experiencing new places and people lets us know one another in different ways. And the chance to talk about these unique moments helps everyone put life into a new perspective.

To know this country is to know ourselves a little better. There is so much to explore in every corner of America, from monumental national symbols like Mount Rushmore and Mesa Verde to its hundreds of small farms and backroad wonders. Our country is defined by these places: where we come from, who we are, and where we're going.

Traveling together we can experience history, science, art, and geography. We hear music in symphony halls, community bands, and backseat singalongs. We see the beauty of nature. We taste the special foods of a region and smell the distinctive air from seashores to mountains, cities to farms.

If we take care of the moments, the years will take care of themselves.

The 10 Best of Everything Families: An Ultimate Guide for Travelers is a book about great places to explore with your kids. We have talked with hundreds of people and researched thousands of places to share "in-the-know" recommendations on the best, most fun, and must-see places, for families and from families. The places that appear on these pages are only a small representation of what's out there.

The book starts with America's grassroots: playgrounds, foods, and farms that are distinctive to different regions. Chapters expand from there: to wonderful vacation destinations, places for eye-opening discovery, and even a few inspirations for international travel. It's all just a starting point. Every family has stories to share about its journeys. I hope you'll use this book to add to yours.

Susan Magsamen

contents

PART TWO

chapter three:

traveling to learn

8

chapter seven:

family memories

chapter eight:

resources

everyday travel in america

"They don't want to go to a theme park," said the wise old grandfather. "They just want you to push them on the swings at the park down the street." That's the idea for this chapter: For kids, exploration and curiosity begin at home, or in the car, or during a walk to the corner. Here we've gathered the inside scoop from families across the country: the parks and playgrounds where children are growing up . . . the places they stop for a treat after a trip to the library . . . the farms and markets where they learn the unique flavors and colors that define their corner of the country. What better way to get to know a place than to look up at its growing trees, kick the rocks, and eat the food that's made there?

Regions are defined by geographic characteristics and population diversity, and may overlap and blend at the edges a little—just like families themselves. To that end, these lists are meant to expand on our idea of borders and neighborhoods. While you're out and about, follow your nose to a local farmer's market. It's a living almanac where the first strawberries are a sign of summer and pumpkins often wind down the season. The best souvenirs might just be the ones you can smell and taste! Be an adventurous eater: Regional foods are a way to explore the cultural (and agricultural) history of a place. And while ice cream shops are everywhere, local favorites are hidden gems for traveling families.

Here are hundreds of ways to make exploration part of your everyday routine. And here are landmarks where you'll always feel at home, whether you're recognized as a local or welcomed as a visitor.

See you around the neighborhood!

- regional attractions:
  popular parks and playgrounds
- farms and markets:
  to discover what's grown close to home
- while you're here:
  places to find great ice cream
- regional specialties:
  foods inspired by culture and tradition

chapter one
the spirit of exploration

It is not down in any map;
true places never are.
—Herman Melville

northeast

Connecticut, Maine, Massachusetts, New Hampshire, New York, Rhode Island, Vermont

Tradition and excitement are always in season in America's Northeast. Each year, tourists come from all over the world to enjoy activities that are marked by varied climates and steeped in history.

Where else can you find fun-filled, world-class cities that never sleep and sleepy, pastoral towns that appear to be straight out of a Norman Rockwell painting?

For families that relish tracing the nation's roots, look no further: You can stand where the *Mayflower* docked, walk along Paul Revere's trail, or visit churches and meeting-houses that are virtually untouched by time.

Prefer modern pastimes? New York City is the nation's fashion, art, and theater capital as well as the birthplace of hip-hop music. If speed is your fancy, try watching souped-up race cars roar around the track at Loudon International Raceway in New Hampshire.

Consider New England's northernmost

> Let your walks now be a little more adventurous.
> —Henry David Thoreau

edges: New York and Ontario, Vermont and Quebec, Maine and New Brunswick. Touching on the Great Lakes and Canadian borders offers an international flavor for families and visitors alike.

Fall is for foliage: riding along New England's winding roads lined with trees whose leaves display different shades of orange, brown, red, and yellow.

Long winters offer endless opportunities to hit the ski slopes or to nestle around warm fires with candies made of Vermont maple syrup.

Spring marks the annual renewal of the most storied, pulsating rivalry in professional sports: Major League Baseball's New York Yankees and Boston Red Sox. Summers provide so many options that it's difficult to fit them all in one visit: basking along the shores of Cape Cod, hiking in the Adirondack Mountains, walking in Central Park . . . The list is as endless as your family's spirit of exploration!

ten best
parks & playgrounds

bug light park

South Portland, ME, 207-767-7670, www.southportland.org
Breakwater Light is a cute little lighthouse (pre–Civil War!) in Portland harbor, and it's the centerpiece of this oceanside park, known by locals as a great place for kite flying.

leddy park

Leddy Park Rd. & North Ave., Burlington, VT
802-864-0123, www.enjoyburlington.com
At the edge of Lake Champlain, this park is also home to a great indoor skating rink. This place is busy all year round, with a playground, tennis courts, and a seven-mile bike path along the lakeshore.

oakledge park

2 Flynn Ave., Burlington, VT 05401, 802-864-0123
www.enjoyburlington.com
A beautiful 500-square-foot treehouse is universally accessible for children in wheelchairs or with other needs. Other park highlights include a small beach, covered picnic areas, and tennis courts.

white park

Washington & Center Sts., Concord, NH
603-225-8690, www.ci.concord.nh
It's a popular year-round destination, but White Park is really hopping in winter with outdoor ice-skating and great sledding hills. A public pool and tennis courts make it a summer hot spot, too.

tadpole playground

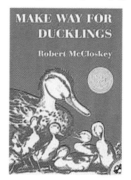

138 Tremont St., Boston, MA 02116, 617-635-4505 www.cityofboston.gov
It's a popular spot for children in the heart of the famous Boston Common, directly across from the Public Gardens. This is the oldest public park in America.

tip: Read *Make Way for Ducklings* by Robert McCloskey before you go.

❝ julie, massachusetts | **why i use mass transit** First on our list of "favorites" is public transportation, not only in Boston but wherever we go. We all have distinct memories of the commuter rail from Belmont to North Station going through the immense Boston Sand and Gravel facility, where all the concrete mixers would go to fill up. . . . I actually saw the world as a giant Richard Scarry book when the boys were little and hoped to present it to them that way.

gorham crosby park

Main St., Centerville, MA 02632
508-775-2201, www.hyannis.com

This playground is across the street from the Penny Candy Store, which has two benches out front on the porch. Sit here while eating your candy. The left bench is for Democrats, and the right is for Republicans. You are just one block away from the Craigville Beaches on Cape Cod.

impossible dream playground

575 Centerville Rd., Warwick, RI 02886
401-823-5566

Make-believe play gets a jump-start here, with a huge variety of play structures like castles, bridges, houses, and more. Designed especially to encourage side-by-side play for children of differing abilities.

compo beach playground

Compo Beach Rd., Westport, CT 06880
203-341-5090, www.westport.gov

Great new playground in a 29-acre park with basketball courts, softball fields, and skate park facilities. There's also a concession stand, and lifeguards are on duty for beach swimming from Memorial Day through Labor Day.

imagination playground

300 Parkside Ave., Brooklyn, NY 11226
718-287-3400, www.prospectpark.org

Encourage creative play near a water-spouting dragon statue or on a series of platform stages. Don't miss the statue of Peter and his dog, from

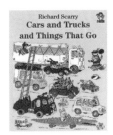

books | cars & trucks & things that go
by richard scarry

From the bananamobile to the giant grocery truck pileup, every kind of vehicle you've ever imagined turns up in the pages of this classic. hint: Look for Goldbug on every spread.

Ezra Jack Keats's classic "Whistle for Willie." Known as a bird-spotting location in Brooklyn, the playground is adjacent to the Audubon Center in Prospect Park. There are printable maps of the whole area on the park website, plus information about free parking on the grounds.

conservatory water

Central Park, East Side, 72nd to 74th Sts.
New York, NY, 212-360-3444
www.centralparknyc.org

Central Park covers 843 acres in Manhattan, but locals know where to find "parks-within-the-park." Here you'll find a model boat pond with radio-controlled miniature boats to rent and an ice-skating rink. Children clamber over statues of Alice in Wonderland and Hans Christian Anderson.

farms & markets

peace & plenty farm

1232 Reeds Mill Rd.
Phillips, ME 04966
www.organicblueberry.com

Maine is known for its wild blueberries, and this organic farm is a great place to pick your own by hand. Here you can pick Canadian sourtop blueberries, which ripen in hilly areas in late July and August.

farmers market at mill park

North Water St. & Northern Ave.
Augusta, ME, 207-549-5112
www.farmersmarketmillpark.org

Near the banks of the Kennebec River, a Maine farmer's market is held every Tuesday from May 1 through October 30. Look for fresh raw milk from Grassland Farm.

Enter a corn maze and follow the signs. You're sure to have fun along the way.

resource | the green guide

by mindy pennybacker

Local food is a growing trend nationally, as well. From 1994 to 2004 the number of farmer's markets nationwide grew from 1,755 to 3,706 according to the U.S. Department of Agriculture. *www.thegreenguide.com/doc/116/local*

burlington farmer's market

City Hall Park, Burlington, VT
888-889-8188
www.burlingtonfarmersmarket.org

Saturday mornings from Mother's Day weekend through Halloween weekend, families gather to shop for fruits, vegetables, crafts, and prepared foods. Farmers come from places with names like Dragonfly Sugarworks and Ladybug Herbs of Vermont.

apple hill farm

580 Mountain Rd., Concord, NH 03301
603-224-8862
www.applehillfarmnh.com

See this farm's website for an extensive "apple schedule" with picking dates for each of 24 varieties. Picking begins with berry season in June; it's closed during the winter months.

beech hill farm

Beech Hill Rd., Hopkinton, NH 03229
603-223-0828
www.beechhillfarm.com

Plan an afternoon of family activities including nature trails, seasonal corn mazes, and workshops. There's also a bakery and garden center. Don't forget the ice cream! They make their own here.

noto fruit farm

7539 E. Townline Rd., Williamson, NY 14589
315-589-8703, www.notofruitfarm.com.

Apple-picking season is August through October, and a variety of cherries is available in July and August. It's a short season for cherries, because birds like them, too!

tougas family farm

234 Ball St., Northboro, MA 01532
508-393-6406, www.tougasfarm.com

Strawberries and pumpkins are just a few of the pick-your-own offerings. There's also a farm kitchen with baked goods, a corn maze, and lots of sights and sounds for kids of all ages. It's worth the drive from Boston or Worcester.

copley square

St. James Ave. in front of Trinity Church, Boston, MA
617-635-4447, www.massfarmersmarkets.org

There are farmer's markets in Boston nearly every day of the week. This one, especially popular with

> New England is quite as large a lump of earth as my heart can really take in.
>
> —Nathaniel Hawthorne

city families, is held Tuesdays and Fridays from 11:00 a.m. to 6:00 p.m. Look for the monument in honor of the Boston Marathon finish line, located here. Fresh herbs and seasonal flowers abound.

spring rain farm

692 Caswell St., East Taunton, MA 02718
508-824-3393
www.springrainfarm.net

One of New England's very few true native crops, cranberries turn bright red when the fruit is ready for harvest in late fall. There are walking trails along the cooperative bogs about an hour outside Boston (for a map, go to www.cranberries.org).

Here you can see the bogs, visit farm animals, and choose self-serve fresh cranberries, October through December.

union square greenmarket

Union Square Park, 17th St. at Broadway, New York, NY 10003, 212-788-7476, www.cenyc.org/greenmarket

Browse alongside chefs, locals, and fellow families at New York's largest open-air market. This one operates year-round, Mondays, Wednesdays, Fridays, and Saturdays. See the Greenmarket website for other market locations around the city.

ten best
ice cream spots

ben & jerry's

I-89 Exit 10 to Rte. 100
North Waterbury, VT, 866-258-6877
www.benjerry.com

Come to the place where it all started. You can tour the factory on ice cream–making days and visit the sampling room! Check ahead for seasonal hours of operation. Closed in December.

New England is home to more than 1,300 dairy farms and a corresponding healthy appetite for ice cream.

serendipity 3

225 East 60th St., New York, NY 10022, 212-838-3531
www.serendipity3.com

Sit-down service only, strollers not allowed in the dining room, reservations not accepted for dessert-only seatings . . . but all that said, it's a quintessential Manhattan experience. Expect amazing and over-the-top ice cream creations and the occasional celebrity sighting.

arnie's ice cream place

164 Loudon Rd., Concord, NH 03301, 603-228-3225
www.arniesplace.com

The ice cream is 15 percent butterfat, and on Tuesday nights (before Columbus Day), fancy-pants cars parade in the parking lot for a weekly spectacular known as Cruise Night.

j.p. licks

352 Newbury St., Boston, MA 02116
617-236-1666, www.jplicks.com

With seven locations around Boston, this is a local institution. This Back Bay shop is in a bustling historic neighborhood within walking distance of bookstores, museums, and parks. Note the proximity to Emack & Bolio's. Try them both.

four seas ice cream

360 South Main St., Centerville, MA 02632
508-775-1394, www.fourseasicecream.com

Known for its charming staff, this Cape Cod favorite also offers sandwiches ranging from peanut butter and jelly to lobster salad. But start with the ice cream.

emack & bolio's

290 Newbury St., Boston, MA 02115
617-536-7127, www.emackandbolios.com

Everything old is new again: This place celebrates the rock scene of the 1970s with a psychedelic assortment of ice cream flavors. There are several locations; this one is adjacent to the New England Aquarium.

mt. tom's homemade ice cream

**34 Cottage St., Easthampton,
MA, 01027, 413-529-2929
www.mttoms.com**

At the foot of the Berkshires this confectionary shop makes ice cream right on the premises. If that's not enough, there's a dizzying array of candy jars, an espresso bar, and Internet access. Look for the famous reflection of Mount Tom in nearby Nashawannuck Pond.

spruce pond creamery

**370 King St., Franklin, MA 02038
508-520-7900, www.sprucepondcreamery.com**

Near picturesque Spruce Pond, where there's fishing in summer and ice-skating in winter, this is said to be a favorite ice cream spot of Patriots quarterback Tom Brady. There's also a selection of organic pizzas made in a wood burning oven. Carry out or eat in.

the ice cream machine company

**4288 Diamond Hill Rd., Cumberland, RI 02864
401-333-5053, www.icecreampie.com**

Considered by some to be the best ice cream in Rhode Island, wildly busy during summer months. Diamond Hill State Park is right across the road, and nearby you'll find an old monastery that's now home to the Cumberland Public Library.

newport creamery

**181 Bellevue Ave., Newport, RI 02840
401-846-6332
www.newportcreamery.com**

There are twelve locations for this Rhode Island institution, where everyone knows what you mean when you order an "Awful-Awful" (a shake made with ice milk, as opposed to a frappe, which is made with ice cream).

> **Hint:** Ask for a drop of marshmallow in the bottom of your cone to keep ice cream from dripping out, or ask for a cup and spoon for small children just in case.

Young or old, everyone loves a cone.

ten best
regional specialties

baked beans

Durgin Park, 340 Faneuil Hall, Boston, MA 02109, 617-227-2038
www.durgin-park.com

The traditional recipe is a time-intensive process involving dried navy beans that are soaked, simmered, and baked with salt pork and molasses. If you've only had the canned variety, you need to try Durgin's. This place boasts that "your great-grandfather ate here."

boston cream pie

Parker's Restaurant, 60 School St., Boston, MA 02108
617-227-8600, www.omnihotels.com

This custard and chocolate dessert was "invented" in the same Boston restaurant that introduced Parker House rolls. Both are still on the menu at this city landmark, a formal and expensive restaurant in the Omni Parker House Hotel, where a children's menu is also available.

buffalo wings

Anchor Bar Restaurant, 1047 Main St., Buffalo, NY 14209 716-884-4083
www.buffalowings.com

Legend has it that buffalo-style chicken wings were first made here in the

Try this "Yankee" tradition: Eat apple pie with a slice of sharp cheddar cheese.

mid-1960s. Today, it's a popular bar and restaurant with folks who want to see where it all started. Insiders recommend a lunchtime visit with children.

cheddar cheese

Smiling Hill Farm, 781 County Rd. Westbrook, ME 04092
207-775-4818, www.smilinghill.com

A dairy farm near Portland, Maine, is a favorite with local families. Award-winning cheese is available, along with ice cream and other dairy products. Each batch of cheese is distinct, reflecting the character and flavor of the land. The farm's been in the same family since the 17th century. Interesting extra: open for cross-country skiing in winter.

fried clams

Sea Swirl of Mystic, 30 Williams St., Mystic, CT 06355
860-536-3452, www.seaswirlofmystic.com

Folks who know their fried clams say that the very best are the whole belly variety, made from freshly shucked clams, not chopped. Clams are mollusks. They move with a single "foot" and suck in food through a kind of siphon. This casual clam shack is a local favorite that also serves wonderful ice cream. Open seasonally.

lobster roll

Waterman's Beach Lobster
343 Waterman's Beach Rd.
South Thomaston, ME, 207-596-7819
Chunks of fresh lobster are served on a center-sliced hot dog roll. They're available at many great spots in the region. Outdoor picnic tables and a beachfront location make this coastal location especially nice for families.

maple syrup

Kellerhaus, 259 Endicott St., Laconia, NH 03246
603-366-4466, www.kellerhaus.com
Among the many wonderful places to find maple syrup, candy, fudge, and more, this confectionary is a child's dream in a tiny town near Lake Winnipesaukee. During summer months there's a waffle buffet: "pure sticky joy."

spiedies

Pancho's Pit, 3537 Riverside Dr., Johnson City,
NY 13790, 607-798-0001
When a small city has its own signature sandwich, you've got to try it. Going north/south through the state of New York, schedule a lunchtime stop in Binghamton, just north of the Pennsylvania line. A spiedie is made with marinated and grilled chicken or lamb, served on a soft seeded roll.

roast beef sandwich

Charlie the Butcher, 1065 Wehrle Dr., Williamsville,
NY 716-633-8330, www.charliethebutcher.com
Beef on the Weck is the traditional name for this slow-roasted roast beef, sliced thin and served on a salty roll known as a kummelweck. Turkey and pork get the same treatment. Just outside the Buffalo airport, with other locations in the area.

pizza

Lombardi's, 32 Spring St., New York, NY
10012, 212-941-7994, www.firstpizza.com
America's first pizza oven is still in use here, in this little spot just north of famed Little Italy and Mulberry Street. It's definitely kid-friendly and a great, moderately priced family spot in the city. You can see the coal-fired oven, in operation since 1897, when pizza was a quick lunch for working folks.

> It is estimated that Americans consume more than 100 acres of pizza every day.
> National Association of Pizzeria Operators

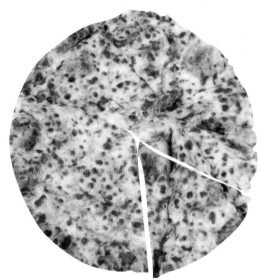

everyday travel
mid-atlantic

Delaware, Maryland, New Jersey, Pennsylvania, Virginia, Washington, D.C.

A wealth of history and diversity makes the Mid-Atlantic the hometown for much of American life. Living and visiting here, you're walking in the rich soil of America's roots. Among them: the first permanent English settlement (Jamestown, Virginia) and the site of the last battle of the Revolutionary War (Yorktown); the home of runaway slave turned abolitionist Harriet Tubman (Dorchester County, Maryland); the research lab of inventor Thomas Edison (Menlo Park, New Jersey); and the site where the Declaration of Independence and the U.S. Constitution were crafted (Philadelphia, Pennsylvania). At the center of it all is Washington, D.C., treasure trove of much of the nation's history and culture, encapsulated and displayed at the Smithsonian Institution. This family of museums lines the National Mall, an open-area national park that is the site of festivals, concerts, and civil demonstrations.

> I travel not to go anywhere, but to go. I travel for travel's sake.
> —Robert Louis Stevenson

Tourists can spend one day canvassing national landmarks in a busy, artsy granite-and-steel metropolis and the next singing jingles on a hayride at a nearby farm.

Because it lies between the Northeast and the Southeast, and also between mountain and ocean, weather can vary widely: Winter yields snow but rarely snows folks in. Summertime is hot and humid but seldom unbearably searing.

The Mid-Atlantic comprises a highly educated, transient population that is family oriented and friendly but fiercely proud and individualistic (Virginia leads the nation in personalized license plates). Folks crowd the region's fast-paced highways but also make time for sunset walks on friendly Virginia Beach or spend a day at the chocolate lovers' paradise, Hersheypark, in Pennsylvania. Here are just a few of the things that families find so appealing about the Mid-Atlantic.

parks & playgrounds

smith memorial playground

Philadelphia, PA 19121, 215-765-4325
www.smithplayhouse.org

The ten-kid seesaw and famous giant wooden slide are favorites at this landmark playground/playhouse near the Please Touch Museum and the Philadelphia Zoo.

van saun park

Forest & Continental Aves., Paramus, NJ 07652, 201-262-3771
www.co.bergen.nj.us

Walking trails and a bike path encircle this great destination playground, which is accessible for children of different abilities. Plan a whole day around a visit here. There are pony rides, a train, and a carousel just outside the Bergen County Zoo, which is also located in the park.

bellevue state park

Marsh & Carr Rds., Wilmington, DE 19809
302-761-6963, www.destateparks.com

Come for the great new playground, kids' climb-

Native Americans played pasuckuakohowog, which means "they gather to play ball with the foot."

ing wall, and preschool area. Stay to explore the former private estate with 300+ acres of woods, fitness track, catch-and-release fishing pond, horseback riding, and outdoor clay tennis courts.

federal hill park

Battery & Warren Aves.
Baltimore, MD, 410-396-5828
www.federalhillonline.com

From here, Union soldiers kept a lookout over this northern city full of Confederate sympathizers. Today there's a playground, where kids can see the whole of Baltimore, right out to the edge of Chesapeake Bay.

cabin john regional park

7400 Tuckerman La., Rockville, MD 20817, 301-469-7835, www.mc-mncppc.org

Ride a miniature locomotive train on a loop through the expansive playground and park grounds. Located about ten miles outside Washington, D.C.

“ **donna, washington, d.c. | parks** We love Wheaton Regional Park, Dumbarton Oaks, and the National Arboretum. Each is very different, and each has a lot to offer families. Our favorite, though, is the Bishop's Garden at the National Cathedral. Go when there's a full moon, and you'll never forget it.

bishop's garden

Massachusetts & Wisconsin Aves., NW, Washington, DC 20016, 202-537-6200
www.nationalcathedral.org

The National Cathedral formal garden includes acres of rolling woodland and paths of stone cut from George Washington's own quarries. It has a beautiful rose garden, too. It's a wonderful place for a quiet walk, and especially nice with strollers.

east potomac mini golf

Hains Point-Ohio Dr., SW, Washington, DC 20024 202-488-8087, www.golfdc.com

Beautiful views of Washington, D.C., are highlights of a round of mini golf. Open seasonally, on the south side of the Tidal Basin, site of D.C.'s famed cherry trees.

turtle park

4500 Van Ness St., NW, Washington, DC 20016 202-282-2198, www.turtlepark.org

Also known as Friendship Park, it's one of the best-maintained parks in D.C. Hang with local families and enjoy the proximity to Starbucks and Wagshal's—one of the city's best Jewish-style delis.

clemyjontri park

6317 Georgetown Pike, McLean, VA 22101 703-388-2807, www.fairfaxcounty.gov

A carousel is just one highlight of this inclusive Fairfax County playground. Playing here, kids also learn intuitively. Park layout and equipment are designed to encourage motor skills, coordination,

" kim, pennsylvania | parks

We have so many great memories of living in Pennsylvania. There are terrific state parks throughout the state—the best I have ever seen. Our gang has "graduated" from swings and slides to trails and challenging climbs.

and imagination with settings that showcase prism colors, telling time, roadway etiquette, and more.

east fairmount park

Forbes & Braddock Aves., Pittsburgh, PA 15218 412-422-6538, www.pittsburghparks.org

Bring your own cardboard for the concrete slide built into a hillside, with a fortress playground overlooking the rest of spectacular Frick Park. It has the only public lawn-bowling green in the United States and a 151-acre nature reserve.

There's nothing more fun than a fast sliding ride.

ten best
farms & markets

haddonfield farmers market

**Kings Hwy. & Chestnut St.
Haddonfield, NJ 08033
856-216-7253, www.
haddonfieldfarmersmarket.org**
Seven miles from Philadelphia is one of south New Jersey's most popular markets for families. Open Saturdays from May to November, with community programs and kids' activities plus an array of locally grown and made products. Ride here on the PATCO rail service.

To reach famed beaches of the Mid-Atlantic coast, families drive through traditional farming regions of New Jersey, Delaware, Maryland, and Virginia.

trax farms

**528 Trax Rd., Finleyville, PA 15332
412-835-3246, www.traxfarms.com**
Just outside Pittsburgh you'll find that all roads eventually lead to this popular family farm, with a busy fresh market and colorful fall events including hayrides and pumpkin picking.

clark market

**45th St. & Baltimore Ave., Philadelphia, PA
215-552-8186, www.clarkpark.info**
A nearby tot lot, playground, and outdoor tables make this an especially family-friendly weekend market. The park itself is a popular destination for families all week long.

donaldson farms

**345 Allan Rd., Hackettstown, NJ 07840, 908-852-9122
www.donaldsonfarms.net**
This busy working farm offers education programs and fresh produce available seasonally. It's located near the Delaware Water Gap, a historic area protected by the National Park Service.

bennet orchards

**30993 Armory Rd., Frankford, DE 19945, 302-732-3358
www.bennettorchards.com**
Less than ten miles from Delaware's famous Bethany and Rehoboth beaches, you can pick your own peaches and nectarines during the summer months. This farm has been family-run since 1867.

linvilla orchards

**137 W. Knowlton Rd., Media, PA 19063
610-876-7116, www.linvilla.com**
There's a year-round schedule of family activities, from picking fruits and vegetables to fishing in a stocked lake to cutting your own Christmas tree.

Peas are "fast food" at the Baltimore Farmers Market. Kids love to open the pods, count the peas, and eat them on the spot.

> A man's mind . . . stretched by a new idea . . . never shrinks back to its former dimensions.
>
> —Oliver Wendell Holmes

baltimore farmers market

Saratoga St. and the entrance to I-83
Baltimore, MD 21201, 410-837-4636
www.promotionandarts.com

Open on Sunday mornings from Memorial Day through mid-December, the bright and bustling market is tucked away near a highway entrance in the southeast corner of the city. Watch for the longest lines—a sign of a brief-season delicacy like sour cherries or the first fresh peas. It gets super-crowded beginning around 10:00 a.m., so backpacks are better than strollers for carting the youngest market-goers. Busiest day of the season: the Sunday before Thanksgiving.

event | pumpkin fun

The annual World Championship Punkin' Chunkin contest is held in Sussex County, Delaware, on the first weekend after Halloween. Competitors build contraptions to hurl pumpkins great distances. *www.punkinchunkin.com*

eastern market

7th St. & North Carolina Ave., NE
Washington, DC
www.easternmarketdc.com

Locals are deeply loyal to D.C.'s oldest continually operating market, predating grocery stores. Produce, fresh meats, and seafood are available during the week, and adjacent space opens for craft vendors and flea markets on the weekends.

williamsburg farmers market days

Duke of Gloucester St., Williamsburg, VA
757-259-3768, www.williamsburgfarmersmarket.com

Farmers and watermen bring their goods to the streets of Williamsburg on Saturdays from May through October, plus select dates during the winter. It's located between the College of William and Mary and Colonial Williamsburg.

homestead farm

15600 Sugarland Rd.
Poolesville, MD 20837
301-977-3761
www.homestead-farm.net

Here you'll find farm animals to pet and feed, pick-your-own apples, berries, and other in-season produce. Come for a hayride in the fall and pick your own pumpkin.

ten best
ice cream spots

dave & andy's homemade ice cream

207 Atwood St., Pittsburgh, PA 15213
412-681-9906, www.andrew.cmu.edu
Families can see ice cream being made on the premises, along with hand-shaped waffle cones. Try the signature malted flavors!

berkey creamery

Pennsylvania State University
119 Food Science Bldg., University Park, PA 16802, 814-865-7535
www.creamery.psu.edu
Line up with Penn State students for world-class ice cream. Much of the milk used here comes from the university's own Dairy Production Research Center. It's said that Ben & Jerry learned to make theirs from a PSU correspondence course.

bassett's

Reading Terminal Market, 45 N. 12th St., Philadelphia, PA 19107, 215 925 4315, www.bassettsicecream.com
The market is equal parts grocery store, craft market, and carryout, located right in the heart of Philadelphia. It's also home to the oldest ice cream shop in the United States. Bassett's has been in continuous operation since 1861.

In 1611, the first cow in America arrived in Jamestown, Virginia. So from the very start, dairy products have been a staple of the American diet.

denville dairy

34 Broadway, Denville, NJ 07834
973-627-4214, www.denvilledairy.com
Long lines and no seating at this Morris County favorite, but no one cares because the ice cream is so great! Families flock here on hot summer evenings, and there are usually 32 flavors available every day.

woodside farm

378 North Star Rd., Newark, DE 19711
302-239-9847
www.woodsidefarmcreamery.com
Wonderful ice cream about 15 miles off I-95, not far from Wilmington. There's live music on summer Saturday evenings, weather permitting. Visit the adjacent dairy farm, in business since 1796.

doumar's

1919 Monticello Ave., Norfolk, VA 23517
757-627-4163, www.doumars.com
Abe Doumar invented the ice cream cone at the 1904 World's Fair, and later started this place, complete with handmade ice cream and curbside service. Visit in the morning to see cones still being made by hand in America's first cone-making machine.

american city diner

5532 Connecticut Ave., NW
Washington, DC 20015, 202-244-1949
www.americancitydiner.com

Toy trains run around the ceiling, and free classic movies are shown every Friday night. Their shakes are highly recommended by D.C. families, along with classic diner food. Washington, D.C., is bordered by Maryland and Virginia. This place is located in the Chevy Chase neighborhood on the capital city's border with Maryland. The Friendship Heights Metro (subway) station is less than a mile away.

dolcezza

1560 Wisconsin Ave., Washington, DC 20007
202-333-4646, www.dolcezzagelato.com

Come to Georgetown for a walk along the C&O Canal (Georgetown is the start of the line for a historic waterway that ends nearly 200 miles away in Cumberland, Maryland). Then stop here for Argentinian-style gelato and sorbet. You can also try fresh churros—traditional South American fried pastries to eat plain or with creamy filling. It's a fashionable spot with cushioned benches inside or tables outside.

the dairy godmother

2310 Mount Vernon Ave., Alexandria, VA 22301, 703-683-7767
www.thedairygodmother.com

This D.C. suburban city is both quaint and sophisticated, and so is the frozen custard served up here. Locals rave about the Wisconsin style dense, creamy custard. There's also an imaginative array of sorbet in flavors that change regularly and have been known to include lemon lavender and pineapple with cilantro. Ask for some homemade marshmallows to go. No dogs allowed inside, but there's a dog "parking" space outside, and frozen pet treats are available to go.

dumser's dairyland drive-in

49th St. & Coastal Hwy., Ocean City, MD 21842
410-524-1588, www.beach-net.com/dumsers

Maryland's oceanside boardwalk favorite since 1939, with a casual menu and amazing sundaes. The orange ice cream soda is so refreshing! Tip for visitors: Ocean City's Coastal Highway buses offer all-day passes that make it easy to travel from one end of this bustling beachfront city to the other. A second Dumser's location is on 124th Street. The 49th Street spot is open year-round, along with other popular boardwalk shops and restaurants.

> The world's first ice cream soda was created in Elizabeth, New Jersey, in 1782.

ten best
regional specialties

Historic recipes are like little monuments to the culture of a place.

cheesesteak sandwich

Pat's King of Steaks, 1237 Passyunk Ave. Philadelphia, PA 19147, 215-468-1547 www.patskingofsteaks.com

Long lines seem to be a sign of good cheesesteaks. Pat's corner storefront claims to be Philly's oldest and best loved. Insiders report that two hungry children can fill up on a single sandwich.

blue crabs

Bo Brooks Restaurant, 2701 Boston St., Baltimore, MD 21224, 410-558-0202, www.bobrooks.com

Messy and fun to eat, blue crabs turn bright red when they're steamed. In Maryland they're covered with spicy Old Bay seasoning and dumped on the table for hours of cracking, picking, and eating. Waiters stand ready to show you how. Large male crabs (jimmies) are the easiest to eat.

peppermint lemon

Flower Mart Annual Event, Charles & Monument Sts. Baltimore, MD 21201, www.flowermart.org

A porous peppermint stick becomes an edible straw when it's stuck into a fresh lemon. It's a traditional treat available in early spring at the city's Flower Mart, celebrated for one day in early May at the foot of Baltimore's own Washington Monument (it's one of the first monuments in the country to honor George Washington). Ask for extra napkins.

virginia ham

The Cheese Shop, 424 Prince George St. Williamsburg, VA 23185, 757-220-1324

Ham making is an art in Virginia, with restrictions about where the hogs are raised, what they eat, and how the hams are cured. Look for this sweet, salty ham on menus throughout the state. This place in Merchant Square (adjacent to Colonial Williamsburg attractions) makes a wonderful Virginia ham sandwich. Ask for house dressing.

pretzels

Hammond Pretzel Bakery, 716 S. West End Ave. Lancaster, PA 17603, 717-392-7532 www.hammondspretzels.com

See pretzels being twisted by hand at the oldest family-run pretzel bakery in Pennsylvania. Look in from the factory store, or just pull into the parking lot and peer through the window here! Pretzels are a great travel snack.

nine layer cake

Classic Cakes, 1305 S. Division St. Salisbury, MD 21801, 410-860-5300
www.classicsmithislandcakes.com

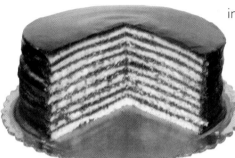

It's worth the all-day trip to remote Smith Island for a slice of yellow cake layered with chocolate frosting (see Chesapeake Bay Sites, page 260). The recipe goes back at least four generations. But the real thing is also available in some big towns along the Chesapeake Bay. Here they're made by a real Smith Islander who came to the mainland and opened this bakery in 2003. Maryland legislators recently made it the official state dessert.

senate bean soup

United States Senate Restaurant, Capitol Building Washington, DC, 202-224-4100, www.aoc.gov

How to get it:1. Call your Senator's office and request a letter of admission to the Senate Dining Room. 2. Check dress codes and be sure the Senate is in session. 3. Arrive after 1:30 p.m. and present your letter. You'll be seated based on availability. 4. Order the bean soup, on the menu here for more than a hundred years!

spaghetti & meatballs

Ferraro's, 8 Elm St., Westfield, NJ 07090
908-232-1101, www.ferrarosrestaurant.com

A side of meatballs is available as an entrée on the kids' menu of this friendly family-run restaurant in suburban New Jersey, about 25 miles from Manhattan. The kids' chicken parm is a generous portion of a traditional favorite.

world cuisine

Union Station, 50 Massachusetts Ave., NE, Washington, DC 20002, 202-371-9441
www.unionstationdc.com

The Union Station food court incorporates D.C.'s famous multicultural food offerings with family-friendly convenience. Everyone can try something different. There are individual stands and stalls with plenty of tables nearby. Choose Asian, Indian, Italian, Greek, Japanese, American Southwestern, Creole, and much more. Plus, it's housed in a world-famous station with trains, subway service, and colorful shops. Just take the escalator down from the grand main level of Union Station.

water ice

Rita's Ice, 1227 Bristol Pike, Andalusia, PA 19020
215-245-1782, www.ritasice.com

This is the original porchfront location of the ice-and-custard family business that is now a large franchise operation. Here it's called Italian ice, but the slushy concoctions are also known as water ice, snowballs, or snow cones (purists can tell you the differences). Make a summer event of comparing your favorites.

everyday travel
southeast

Florida (Atlantic Coast), Georgia, North Carolina, South Carolina

Warm smiles. Hot summers. Cool, starry nights and tall glasses of ice-cold sweet tea. There's something about the Southeast that says sit back, relax, and take it easy. It's a place where strangers still wave to one another as they pass along the main street. Youngsters still run through woods filled with tall pines and ride on the beds of their parents' pickup trucks. And, merchants say hello as if they're truly glad to see you—even if you're meeting for the first time.

Is it any wonder that Charleston, South Carolina, cornerstone of southern charm, opulence, and gentility, is annually voted by travelers as the nation's friendliest city? Truth is, there are plenty of runners-up in the area, from vast metropolises full of concrete-and-steel high-rises to white-sandy beachfronts to towns so small that, to coin a southern expression, "You've got to be going there to get there."

> This is my chance to do something. I've got to seize the moment.
>
> —Andrew Jackson

No trip to the Southeast would be complete without sampling (read devouring) its much-loved cuisine. Here, grits are not only a staple for breakfast, but with melted cheese and jumbo shrimp, they're a low-country lunch and dinner favorite. Ditto for pecan pies, peach cobbler, and banana pudding.

Indeed, the Southeast has never abandoned its hometown pride, even as it experiences unparalleled growth in its cities and towns. Here, family is everything, and waking up to watch the dew turn to vapors never grows old.

American culture owes much to the counties and cities, districts and neighborhoods of these savannah states. It's a region of famous birthplaces and hometowns for history-makers like Jackie Robinson (Cairo, Georgia), Dolley Madison (Guilford County, North Carolina), Gloria Estefan (Miami, Florida). Head to these places, mention the name, and someone will have a story to share.

ten best
parks & playgrounds

roanoke rapids lake park

145 Oakwood Ave.
Roanoke Rapids, NC 27870
252-410-6318
www.visithalifax.com

Known as a wonderful place to see a sunrise or sunset, this park also boasts a beautiful new playground, a nine-hole Frisbee golf course and concession stand, plus a fishing pier and public access for swimming. It's the head of the 7.5-mile Roanoke Canal Trail.

imaginon

300 E. 7th St., Charlotte, NC 28202
704-973-2780, www.imaginon.org

A joint venture of the Charlotte Mecklenburg Library system and Children's Theatre of Charlotte, this beautifully designed building features a youth library, two amazing theaters, computer labs, classrooms, a multimedia/animation studio, storytelling areas, a teen loft, and more.

The temparate climate makes the parks of the Southeast year-round destinations.

hampton park

55 Cleveland St., Charleston, SC 29403
843-724-7321, www.charlestoncity.info

A beautiful park designed for the 1902 World's Fair still feels like a place for celebration and exploration. Located near the Citadel, it has a famous rose garden and lagoon, and it's all across the street from McMahon Playground.

moultrie playground

41 Ashley Ave., Charleston, SC 29401
843-724-7398, http://sciway3.net

Located across the street from Colonial Lake near Charleston's historic district, with nice picnic grounds and fun playground equipment. Shaded pathways are great for walking, jogging, or strolling.

centennial olympic park

265 Park Ave., Atlanta, GA 30312
404-222-7275, www.centennialpark.com

On the site built for the 1996 Olympics, the park

> **maureen, florida** | **sunscreen** Right up there with brushing teeth is the habit of using sunscreen every morning, year-round. It's a way of life around here. It's important to remember it especially after the kids have gotten haircuts, since there's skin showing that wasn't showing before!

is as popular as ever, with a children's garden and two marvelous playgrounds scaled for children of different ages. Family Fun Days are specially planned for the afternoons of the fourth Saturdays of April through November.

Learn to do common things uncommonly well; we must always keep in mind that anything that helps fill the dinner pail is valuable.
—George Washington Carver

best friend park

6224 Jimmy Carter Blvd., Norcross, GA 30071
770-822-8000, www.gwinnettcounty.com

Cooling spray from play fountains and great digging equipment make this a favorite with Atlanta area families. The pay-by-the-visit pool is nice on hot days, and lifeguards are on duty.

metropolitan park: kids kampus

1410 Gator Bowl Blvd., Jacksonville, FL 32202
904-630-5437, www.downtownjacksonville.org

This free ten-acre water park and playground is complete with mini bicycles with training wheels and helmets to borrow. It's located within Jacksonville's biggest municipal park.

possum creek park

4009 NW 53rd Ave., Gainesville, FL 32653
352-334-2231, www.cityofgainesville.org

New playground equipment and a new skate bowl make this park great for kids of different ages and interests. Gainesville also has a number of historical and cultural events not to be missed.

a.d. barnes park

3701 SW 72nd Ave., Miami, FL 33150
305-666-5883, www.miamidade.gov

In the heart of Miami, this 49-acre park is a great place to see migrating birds. Families find inspiration at the Sense of Wonder Nature Center, and a park playground is part of the fun, too.

dante fascell park

8700 SW 57th Ave., Miami, FL 33143
305-666-8680, www.cityofsouthmiami.net

New playground equipment makes this a great destination—especially for families with preschool-age children in Coral Gables. Bring bread for ducks.

A family picnic in the park is fun for everyone.

ten best
farms & markets

beans 'n' berries

7155 Rhoney Rd., Connelly Springs, NC 28612, 828-403-6989, www.ncagr.com
This CSA farm offers tours and seasonal events. Blueberries and raspberries are available for the public to pick. Call ahead to find out about harvest schedules for crops ranging from pears and persimmons to corn and squash.

charlotte regional farms market

1801 Yorkmont Rd., Charlotte, NC 28266, 704-357-1269
www.ncfarmfresh.com
Open every day, this busy market is quite a neat place, and it's good for families who like to explore everyday places in fun ways. This is the neighborhood grocery store for folks who want to shop locally and in season—indoors, and featuring a huge array of fresh and prepared foods and dairy products.

matthews farmers market

105 N. Trade St. parking lot, Matthews, NC 28105
704-821-6430, www.matthewsfarmersmarket.com
A bonus at this market: It's right next to Renfrow Hardware—an old-fashioned real hardware store. Find produce, pottery, and chickens here, plus Middle Eastern breads, dips, and spreads.

Most pick-your-own places offer recipes plus ideas for freezing and preserving fruit.

charleston farmers market

Marion Square, Charleston, SC 29401, 843-724-7309
www.charlestoncvb.com
Pony rides and jumping castles are available for children visiting this friendly and colorful Saturday morning market that runs from April through December. This is a nice place to find souvenirs, since there's a great crafts area as well.

middleton place

4300 Ashley River Rd., Charleston, SC 29414, 843-556-6020, www.middletonplace.org
"Demonstration" rice crops are planted in May and harvested in September at this former plantation, now a historic landmark. Its Garden Center is open to the public free of charge, and families can learn more about the intertwined history of rice planting and slavery in the United States.

recipe | citrus peach cooler

Here's what you need: • 1 scoop lemon sherbet • 1 ripe peach • 1 cup fresh orange juice
Blend together and drink with a straw. Or put in the freezer for half an hour to make a slush to eat with a spoon.

the peach tree orchards

2077 Filbert Hwy., York,
SC 29745, 803-684-9996
www.thepeachtreeorchards.com
Pick your own peaches when weather allows. In 2007, there was no peach season at all because of a spring freeze in most of South Carolina. Call ahead to assure that fruit is ready to pick.

gardner farms

3192 Hwy 42, Locust Grove, GA 30248
770-957-4912
Waves of ripe fruit are available in June and July, including peaches, blueberries, raspberries, and blackberries. Bring your own containers or buy them there.

ridge island groves

6000 Old Polk City Rd., Haines City, FL 33822
863-422-0333, www.ridgeislandgroves.com
Pick your own oranges, grapefruits, or tangerines at this central Florida citrus farm. It's important to call ahead and be sure that fruit is in season and available, usually October to April. The harvest depends on weather.

Florida produces more than 80% of America's supply of citrus.

winter park farmers market

200 W. New England Ave.
Winter Park, FL 32789
407-599-3358
www.ci.winter-park.fl.us
Just north of Orlando, about five minutes off I-4, this Saturday morning market provides local farm offerings in an indoor/outdoor market that fills an old train depot with great sights, sounds, and smells. A nice alternative to commercial entertainment and franchises.

knauss berry farm

159880 SW 248th St., Homestead, FL 33031
305-247-0668
Tomatoes and strawberries flourish from mid-November to early April here in southern Florida just south of Miami. You can pick your own at this family-run farm, and also get a fresh mango or strawberry milk shake or homemade baked goods.

Community Supported Agriculture

About 400 farms across America work in cooperation with local communities. CSA farmers let individuals and families purchase farm shares and be a part of the work, harvest, and even risk of farm operations.

ten best
ice cream spots

calabash creamery

9910 Beach Dr., Calabash, NC 28467
910-575-1180, www.calabashcreamery.com
Stroll up to the wraparound porch of this
ice cream shop about 20 miles north
of Myrtle Beach—it looks like a beautiful Carolina-style home. Ice cream is
made daily.

mr. k's soft ice cream & drive in

2107 South Blvd., Charlotte,
NC 28203, 704-375-4318

Don't let appearances fool you. This has
been a family favorite for generations in
Charlotte. Locals have a real soft spot
for Mr. K's malted milk shakes.

*Everyone knows eating
ice cream too fast can
cause a headache. But
it's hard to slow down to
avoid "brain freeze."*

original painters homemade ice cream

2408 Hwy. 17 South
North Myrtle Beach, SC 29582
843-272-6934

Long lines are usually a sign of
good ice cream. Families find
this worth the wait. TV personality Vanna White has been
coming here for ice cream
since childhood. Closed in
winter months.

ye olde fashioned ice cream & sandwich cafe

474 Savannah Hwy.
Charleston, SC 29407, 843-766-485
Come for the sundaes, shakes, and
cones. But this is also a popular, family-
friendly eatery famous for a BLT with ten
slices of bacon.

nirvana

10930 Crabapple Rd., Roswell,
GA 30075, 678-277-2626
www.eatnirvana.com

Reserve online to join the free monthly
ice cream contest. Two locations are
just outside Atlanta: This one is open
for breakfast and lunch, and is not far from the
Native American and Civil War landmarks of Vick-
ery Creek Park.

brusters

3730 Carmia Dr., #340, Atlanta, GA 30331
404-349-5056, www.brusters.com

Yes, it's a chain (and pronounced BREW-sters, for the
record), but they do love this place in Atlanta, with
27 locations in and around the city. Bruce Reed,
the founder of Brusters, is a real ice cream guy. Kids
under 40 inches get free baby cones with candy
eyes and sprinkles.

jake's ice cream and muncheteria

515 N. McDonough St., Decatur, GA 30030, 404-377-9300
www.jakesicecream.com

Here, servers called Scoop Monkeys serve flavors including Nutter Nana Elvis, Diesel Fuel, and Devyn's Animal Cracker. Maybe you want to start with lunch; there's great chicken salad or grilled cheese. There are other locations in the city, but this East Atlanta spot shares a storefront with the family bookstore Little Shop of Stories (www.little shopofstories.com).

leopold's ice cream

212 E. Broughton St., Savannah, GA 31401, 912-234-4442
www.leopoldsicecream.com

This newly renovated confectionary is a Savannah tradition with recipes dating from 1919. Yet some current favorites are anything but traditional, like Girl Scout Thin Mints & Cream, Chocolate Chewie, and Rum Bisque. It's located in the city's beautiful downtown historic district.

> My advice to you is not to inquire why or whither, but just enjoy your ice cream while it's on your plate.
> —Thornton Wilder

old bridge ice cream company

2 Fairfield Blvd., Ponte Vedra, FL 32082, 904-273-0111

If you can finish the four-scoop Guana Monster, you get your picture taken for the "Guana Book" photo album. Then it's time for a hike. Old Bridge is a 15-minute drive from Guana River State Park, with beachfront trails between Jacksonville and St. Augustine.

scoops of cocoa beach

7 S. Atlantic Ave., Cocoa Beach, FL 32931
321-783-9446
www.scoopsflorida.com

If you're visiting Cape Canaveral Air Force Station, Kennedy Space Center, or just driving south on the famed A1A Highway, stop here for a beachfront scoop of homemade ice cream or gelato. Popular flavors include Garbage Can, Caramel Caribou, Bear Claw, and Moose Tracks. Interestingly, the city of Cape Canaveral is located at the northern tip of a barrier island on the Atlantic coast of Florida.

" john, florida | ice cream talk I'm not sure why, but when I was a kid, my older siblings spelled out the word *ice cream* instead of saying it. For the longest time, I thought the name for my favorite dessert was "i.c.e.c.r.e.a.m."

ten best
regional specialties

alligator nuggets

Joanie's Blue Crab Cafe, 39395 Tamiami Trail (US 41), Ochopee, FL 34141
239-695-2682

Drive across southern Florida through Everglades National Park and stop here for a "swamp lunch" featuring alligator tail, frogs legs, and fresh fruit milk shakes.

arroz con pollo

Cuban Café, 3350 N.W. Boca Raton Blvd. Boca Raton, FL 33431, 561-750-8860
www.cubancafe.com

Cuban food is an essential part of southern Florida cuisine, and rice with chicken is just one of the many traditional Cuban plates you can order here. It's tucked away in a small shopping center—no children's menu, but plenty that kids will love!

Traditional fried green tomatoes can be offered for breakfast, lunch, or dinner. Once you've tried them you'll agree that they're perfect for any meal.

recipe | ultimate fast food

Here's what you need:
- fresh-picked tomato
- 2 slices of good white bread
- salt, pepper, and mayonnaise (optional)

Cut the tomato in thick slices. Put two big slices on the bread. Add salt, pepper, or mayonnaise to taste. Eat outdoors if you can.

fried green tomatoes

Whistle Stop Café, 443 McCracken St. Juliette, GA 31046, 478-992-8886
www.thewhistlestopcafe.com

You'll find fried green tomatoes on menus all over the South, but it's fun to order them at this charming café, filming site of a 1991 film of the same name. About 90 minutes northeast of Atlanta, the town features outdoor movie nights on the second Saturday of each month.

fried peach pie

Chick-fil-A, Hapeville Dwarf House 461 N. Central Ave., Hapeville, GA 30354
404-762-1746, www.chick-fil-a.com

Peaches inspire countless desserts down South. This fast-food version is notable because of the source: served up just outside Atlanta at the original location of a now well-known chicken sandwich franchise.

frogmore stew

East Bay Crab Shack, 205 East Bay St. Charleston, SC 29401, 843-853-8600
www.crabshacks.com

Alert: There are no frogs in this stew! A beach feast or tailgate tradition, it's a bucketful of shrimp, potatoes, sausage, and fresh corn. You can get carryout from this casual, colorful spot, but families love the atmosphere here.

hoppin' john

Mary Mac's Tea Room
224 Ponce De Leon Ave., NE
Atlanta, GA 30308, 404-876-1800
www.marymacs.com

Spicy black-eyed peas cooked with bacon: It's a New Year good luck tradition, but yummy enough for every day all over the South. Fill out your own order right at the table at this charming place. It's the last of the original old tea rooms in Atlanta.

hush puppies

Price's Chicken Coop, 1614 Camden Rd.
Charlotte, NC 28203, 704-333-9866
www.priceschickencoop.com

Deep-fried, sweet, salty, and creamy, these corn-meal nuggets are perfect accompaniments to fried chicken, fried fish, and coleslaw. You can get them all here, in huge servings, at this much-loved local spot.

sweet tea

McAlister's Deli, 4950 Centre Pointe Dr.
Charleston, SC 29418, 843-725-3344
www.mcalistersdeli.com

Made in kitchens all over the South, you'll find it everywhere from convenience stores to fine dining establishments. This deli chain has locations all over the United States, and makes it the time-honored way: never chilled until it's poured over ice.

It seems as if there are as many recipes for grits as there are stars in the sky. Count (and taste) them for yourself and you'll see.

shrimp & grits

Jestine's Kitchen, 251 Meeting St.
Charleston, SC 29401, 843-722-7224

Any day but Monday (when it's closed), stop here for lunch or dinner. Traditional southern food includes collard greens, fried okra, and of course shrimp and grits, with or without gravy.

trout filet

South 21, 3101 E. Independence Blvd.
Charlotte, NC 28205, 704-377-4509
www.south21drivein.com

Kids love the fried trout sandwich—remarkable because it is whole fish, not minced or with filler added. Just outside Charlotte you can drive up, order from a carhop, and eat in the car.

Did You Know?
Baby trout are called troutlings or troutlets.

gulf coast

Alabama, Gulf Coasts of Florida and Texas, Louisiana, Mississippi

Families in the heart of America's most southern states have a secret. They know how to take the heat. Hot as in sultry climes, with temperatures sometimes climbing into the triple digits in summer. Hot as in piping, spicy food, most notably, mouthwatering Cajun cuisines throughout Louisiana, the place that produces Tabasco sauce.

Hot as in cutting-edge, trendy theater, unrivaled in its depth and variety, playing year-round and culminating in such annual events as the Sidewalk Moving Picture Festival in Birmingham, Alabama. Hot as in exciting outdoor activities, including America's most popular annual carnival, Mardi Gras, in New Orleans. And hot as in the newest stars from the nation's original music genres: blues, jazz, country, and gospel, much of which was either invented or influenced by life along the Mississippi Delta.

> There are many spokes on the wheel of life. First, we're here to explore new possibilities.
> —Ray Charles

Sports are big news here, especially high school and college football; during the season, it's easy to get swept up in the excitement that engulfs entire communities. Spring training for many pro baseball teams starts here too.

Here, history is an art, and art is a way of life. From the quilt makers of Gee's Bend, Alabama, to the International Museum of Muslim History in Jackson, Mississippi, you'll meet people who find unforgettable ways of looking back (and looking ahead) at the region's rich and dramatic cultural heritage.

The area is also well known for community rose garden exhibits, campgrounds, natatoriums, sport fishing, raceways, and farm mazes. Fold up your map and make a fan. Bring a sun hat and your comfortable shoes, and give yourself time to wander the byways of some of America's most tropical, welcoming cities and towns.

parks & playgrounds

el franco lee park

9400 Hall Rd., Houston, TX 77089
713-440-1587, www.co.harris.tx.us
Big like Houston, this multipurpose
park has six playground compounds,
all shaded and interconnected with
walkways. Located to the south of
the city, it's family central for recreational sports, nature trails, bird-
watching, and much more.

hermann park

6201 A Golf Course Dr.
Houston, TX 77030, 713-524-5876
www.hermannpark.org
Pedal boats and a summertime
water playground help families cool
off at this popular park, home to the Houston
Zoo, Museum of Natural Science, and other cultural attractions. There is a waterworks station
in the Playground for All Children, and a little-
known statue of the Dickens character Oliver
Twist. Check out the Kugel float-
ing granite ball, and
take a ride on the
mini train.

*Listen to a seashell
and hear whispers from
around the world.*

waddill refuge

4142 N. Flannery Rd., Baton Rouge,
LA 70814, 225-274-8192
www.wlf.state.la.us
Borrow a free cane pole if you'd like
to cast a line. You'll need to bring
your own fishing license for this
catch-and-release area—available
at any sporting goods store. This
former campground has 237 acres
of hardwood bottomland and wetland bordering on the Comite River
in Baton Rouge.

audubon park

6500 Magazine St., New Orleans,
LA 70118, 504-861-2537
www.neworleanscitypark.com
This classic metropolitan garden park is a thriving
destination within the city of New Orleans, with
a carousel, several playgrounds, walking paths,
and a tea room. The venerable Audubon Zoo and
new Insectarium are located on the grounds.

lefleur's bluff state park

2140 Riverside Dr., Jackson, MS 39202, 601-987-3985
This 500-acre park is home to the Mississippi Natural Science Museum and a nine-hole golf course.
There are seven nature trails, playgrounds, and
picnic tables, plus camping facilities.

mary, florida | naples In Naples, Florida, you can park your car in the local free garage off 5th Ave. and walk over to the family park, on the corner of 6th Ave. and 8th Street. There you'll find a large play area for ages 1-10. Older children, teens, and adults can use the adjacent baseball field; bring your own equipment, however. On a hot day, stand under the spray fountain; it cools instantly!

Slide down a plume of dragon flame at Storyland.

city park's storyland

Victory Ave. at City Park, New Orleans, LA
504-483-9356, www.cityparkkids.com

Explore 26 colorful storybook vignettes dating back to the 1950s. Look for a giant fire engine, wishing well, and open-mouthed whale. Since 2005, professional Mardi Gras decorators renovated them to "pre-K" quality (this is how locals refer to the time before Hurricane Katrina). Storyland is open Thursday through Sunday, with puppet shows daily.

langan park

4901 Zeigler Blvd., Mobile, AL 36601
251-208-1601, www.cityofmobile.org

Near the Mobile Museum of Art, it's a popular spot for families to feed ducks and geese. A pedestrian bridge connects the fully accessible playground with the rest of the 720-acre municipal park.

tom brown park

1125 Easterwood Dr., Tallahassee, FL 32311
850-891-3866, www.talgov.com

At the largest park in this capital city there are bike trails, tennis courts, soccer fields, disc golf, and shady places for picnics. Folks love the playground here, completely accessible for children of varying ages and abilities.

largo central park

101 Central Park Dr., Largo, FL 33771
727-587-6775, www.largo.com

It's in the heart of Tampa, with a beautifully accessible playground and plenty of shaded, grassy spaces. Fountains provide a cool mist if the breeze blows your way. This park is a nature preserve with a two-story observation tower and five miles of kayak and canoe trails.

bowmans beach playground

Bowman's Beach Rd., Sanibel, FL 33957, 239-472-3700
www.mysanibel.com

A shady playground is a beachfront bonus for families on the northwestern edge of the city of Sanibel, and a walking trail, restrooms, and kayak area add to the attraction. Sanibel is a barrier island sanctuary, with everything you could wish for, including a national wildlife refuge.

ten best
farms & markets

check virden's farm

West County Line Rd., Jackson, MS 39201, 601-362-8769

In late spring and early summer you can pick your own blueberries and blackberries. Figs and grapes come into season in late summer and early fall. While figs are not available for you to pick, you can buy a pre-picked basketful to take home.

red stick farmer's market

501 Main St., Baton Rouge, LA 70802, 225-267-5060
www.mainstreetmarketbr.org

Baton Rouge loves its markets! On Saturday mornings year-round, there's an open-air producer-only market. Nearby you'll find the larger Main Street Market, open six mornings a week and located under the cover of the Main Street parking garage. A monthly Downtown Arts Market is also held on the outdoor parking deck.

french market district

1008 N. Peters St., New Orleans, LA 70116
504-522-2621, www.frenchmarket.org

A combination of farm stands, restaurants, shops, and flea market, this is billed as "America's oldest city market," in business on the same site since

Berries, berries! Get your berries! Sure to put a sweet smile on anyone's face.

1791. It's a major destination for visitors, but also an essential shopping location for local families and chefs alike. Live music, guest chef appearances, and children's activities make it a perfect stop. The market is open year-round, seven days a week. The Farmer's Market is located outdoors.

houston farmers market

Saturday market: 3106 White Oak Blvd. Houston, TX 77007. *Tuesday market:* University Blvd. & Montclair, Houston, TX 77005, www.houstonfarmersmarket.org

Spring and summer seem to come early in Houston, with local summer squashes, fresh basil, and peaches available in May and June. Try red and green dandelion leaves in late spring—a bright and bitter salad flavor for adventurous eaters (the youngest and freshest shoots are nicest to eat).

mississippi farmers market

929 High St., Jackson, MS 392002, 601-354-6573

This state's farm landscapes influenced personalities ranging from Oprah Winfrey to Elvis Presley. Eat what they ate by shopping at the downtown market, open year-round on Tuesdays, Thursdays, and Saturdays beginning at 9:00 a.m. Arrive early, as farmers leave once they sell out.

ocean springs fresh market

1000 Washington Ave., Ocean Springs, MS 39564
800-683-4176, www.oceanspringsfreshmarket.com

A year-round Saturday morning tradition. All vendors sell homegrown or homemade produce, flowers, local honey, and Italian cookies made from a secret family recipe. Live music adds to the block party atmosphere.

mobile markets

Sat. market: Cathedral Square, 2 S. Claiborne St. *Thurs. market:* Mobile Museum of Art, 4850 Museum Dr. Mobile, AL 36608, 251-470-7730, www.ncsmobile.org

If you're lucky enough to be in town during market season, plan to take in one of the city's beautiful farmers markets. Market on the Square is a Saturday morning event held on Cathedral Square, with its cascading fountain. Market in the Park is a Thursday event near Langan Park.

aliyah acres

2030 County Rd. 23, Florence, AL 35633
256-766-1447, www.aliyah-acres.com

This small family farm offers fee-based workshops year-round. Make hominy from field corn in late fall, or start shítake mushrooms on a log to take home in early winter. Check their farming journal online to see what's fresh. It's way off the beaten path, about 1½ hours west of Huntsville.

betty's berry farm

3887 Driskell Loop Rd., Wilmer, AL 36587
251-649-1711, www.bettysberryfarm.com

About 20 miles from Mobile, Betty grows rabbit-

books | *roll of thunder, hear my cry*
by mildred d. taylor

A book for young adult readers about family life in rural Mississippi during the era of segregation and the Great Depression. Winner of the Newbery Medal in 1977.

eye blueberries, some nearly an inch in diameter! It's a short season in late spring and early summer. But while you're there you can also see the rabbits, emus, and peacocks that share the farm with the family.

naples farmers market

1220 3rd St., S, Naples, FL 34102
www.naplesfarmersmarket.com

This Saturday morning market is in season during "snowbird" months of October to April. You will find fresh citrus and fresh-squeezed juices and unusual offerings like pineapple plants, eggfruit, and bromeliads. It's a best-kept secret in Naples, located just three blocks from the beach. Arrive early, bring a cooler, and gather fresh ingredients for lunch on the beach. It can get pretty hot by 11:00 a.m.

ten best
ice cream spots

hank's

9291 S. Main St., Houston, TX 77025
713-665-5103, www.hanksicecream.com
They make their own ice cream and
bake their own cones. This location
is about two miles from the Houston
Zoo and Hermann Park playground.
For the record, Hank's also has a store
in Atlanta, Georgia.

la king's confectionary

2323 Strand St., Galveston,
TX 77550, 409-762-6100
An old-time soda fountain, candy shop,
and coffee bar serving ice cream made
here. Generations of customers are
loyal to this neighbor-

hood institution, where a
master candy maker cre-
ates saltwater taffy and
chocolates before your
eyes. Yes, saltwater taffy
is actually made with salt
water and sugar.

*Ride a bike to get great
ice cream on Sanibel's
east end.*

lsu dairy store

111 Dairy Science Building, South Stadium
& Tower Dr., Baton Rouge, LA 70810
225-578-4411, www.lsuagcenter.com
Louisiana State University's Agricultural
Center houses its own dairy store,
featuring campus-made ice cream and
cheeses. Purple-striped Tiger Bite is
a bestseller.

brocato's

214 N. Carrollton Ave., New Orleans,
LA 70119, 504-486-0078
www.angelobrocatoicecream.com
Take the Carrollton Spur of the Canal
Streetcar to reach the most authen-
tically Italian dessert treats in New
Orleans. There are rich gelatos, spumoni, and pas-
tries, but the best seller is refreshing lemon ice.

sugaree's bakery

110 W. Bankhead St., New Albany, MS 38652
662-534-0031
Famous for their layer cakes, the bakers here
also make wonderful ice cream sandwiches that

" **mark, florida | joke** Here is a good joke. The little boy walks into an ice cream store. He asks
for a sundae with extra hot fudge sauce. "I'm sorry," says the ice cream man. "Hot fudge only comes in
one temperature."

appear on the dessert menus of local restaurants. This wholesale bakery is open to the public and located just off highway 78.

buttercup on second street

112 N. Second St., Bay
St Louis, MS 39520
228-466-4930

Open for breakfast and lunch, this sandwich and ice cream shop was one of the first new businesses to open after the town of Bay St. Louis was devastated by hurricane Katrina in 2005. Indoor and outdoor seating.

cammie's old dutch ice cream

2511 Old Shell Rd., Mobile, AL 36607
251-471-1710

It's a Mobile institution with shakes, sundaes, and cones—located near some really popular casual barbecue spots. Try the Dusty Road hot fudge sundae, sprinkled with malt.

kitchen's ice cream company

543 Beckrich Rd., Panama City Beach, FL 32407
850-234-5423, www.kitchensicecream.com

With three locations in Panama City, this family-owned ice cream shop creates a multitude of unforgettable flavors ranging from Gator Stew to Down South Butter Pecan.

bo's ice cream

7101 N Florida Ave., Tampa, FL 33604
813-234-3870

Try the upside-down banana split. Or the shakes topped with cookie crumbs. Or even just a single scoop of really good vanilla ice cream. This is the place that locals have chosen to bring their children (and grandchildren) for more than 50 years.

pinocchio's original homemade italian ice cream

362 Periwinkle Way, Sanibel,
FL 33957, 239-472-6566
www.pinocchiosicecream.com

A Sanibel Island tradition for more than 30 years, located at the east end of the island. Take the bike path toward the lighthouse and stop here along the way. It's all handmade Italian-style ice cream with more than 130 flavors that rotate seasonally. A few that you'll only see here: World Famous Sanibel Crunch and Dirty Sand Dollar.

Top 10 Ice Cream Consuming Countries in the World:

1. United States
2. New Zealand
3. Australia
4. Sweden
5. Canada
6. Italy
7. Finland
8. Germany
9. Japan
10. United Kingdom

Euromonitor

ten best
regional specialties

beignets

Café du Monde, 1039 Decatur St.
New Orleans, LA 70116
504-525-4544, www.cafedumonde.com

Don't look for doughnuts in New Orleans. Here, a deep-fried square of pastry dough is served warm and dusted with powdered sugar. Families vouch for Café du Monde in the French Market (see page 48). Parents will want to try the house brew of café au lait with chicory.

You have not tasted the perfect pastry until you have had a warm beignet from Café du Monde.

cajun

Brunet's Cajun Restaurant, 135 S. Flannery Rd.
Baton Rouge, LA 70815, 225-272-6226
www.brunetscajunrestaurant.com

Immigrants from Canada's Acadia region arrived in southern Louisiana in the mid-18th century. They became a major influence on the Creole community, which was already a rich mix of European, African, and Native American cultures, and the word *Acadian* became *Cajun*. The influence remains; taste for yourself right here. This place is about 1.5 miles from the Waddill Refuge (see page 46).

grouper

Grouper & Chips, 338 Tamiami Trail North, Naples, FL 34102, 239-643-4577, www.grouperandchips.com

This places sells lots of grouper and only grouper, so they can offer decent prices and the freshest fish. It's all caught right in the Gulf of Mexico.

crawfish

Quarter View Restaurant, 613 Clearview Pky., Metairie, LA 70001, 504-887-3456, www.quarterviewrestaurant.com

Pull off the heads, crack the shells, eat the tails: Crawfish eating is a deliciously easy skill to learn. These bright red crustaceans are in season from early March through late June, and this is a wonderful place to bring kids to try them.

pecan pie

Camellia Grill, 626 S. Carrollton Ave., New Orleans, LA 70118, 504-309-2679

Note that pecan pie also appears as a regional specialty in the greater Texas region. Try it here, at this restaurant famous for the quality of this iconic dessert. Waiters wear tuxedos at this local institution, and the menu is packed with kid favorites.

pecan pralines

Molina's Cantina, 4720 Washington Ave., Houston, TX 77007, 713-862-0013 www.molinasrestaurants.com

Come for the great Tex-Mex food, and linger over

the complimentary pecan praline candies served after each meal. It's a nod to tradition, reminiscent of the open-air vendors who once sold these treats on the streets of Houston.

po-boys

Johnny's Po-Boys, 511 St. Louis St., New Orleans, LA 70130, 504-524-8129, www.frenchquarter.com/dining
The story goes that delicious sandwiches were made from meat scraps and gravy for "poor boys" in old New Orleans. Today they're made in endless lavish varieties, with anything from hot fried oysters to ham and cold cuts, all served on a long, thin French roll. Try one filled with French fries and beef gravy, harkening back to the original style of the New Orleans signature sandwich.

shrimp

Pass Christian Harbor, 106 S. Market St., Pass Christian, MS 39571, 228-452-5129, www.dmr. state.ms.us
Bring an ice chest and buy shrimp straight from the boats. Pass Christian (pronounced "Pass Krishty-Ann") is home to one of the country's most prolific shrimping communities. The season runs from June to December. Call ahead to find out the best times of day to meet the boats as they return with the day's catch. If you'd rather have someone else do the steaming, locals suggest that you try Kimball's Seafood and Deli, one block north of the harbor.

It's true: Everything tastes best right out of the sea, the fields, and the orchards.

sweet potato pie

Sweetie Pies, 109 S. McKenzie St., Foley, AL 36535, 251-943-8119
www.sweetiepiesfoley.com
Here in Alabama, Dr. George Washington Carver (born into slavery around 1864) invented more than one hundred ways to use sweet potatoes, including dyes, candies, flour, paste, sweeteners, and a coffee drink. About 25 miles from Mobile, you'll find wonderful sweet potato pie available seasonally (fall and winter). Tammy Mason, owner of Sweetie Pie, reports that she inherited her love of baking from her mother and grandmother. Pies are made fresh every day, and you can choose from 20 different varieties, depending on the season. It's hard to resist such a sweet slice of southern tradition.

key lime pie

Randy's Fishmarket, 10395 Tamiami Trail, Naples, FL 34108, 239-593-5555, www.randysfishmarket.com
This pie is not green. A pale, creamy yellow filling comes from the egg yolk that makes this dish so rich. This fish market makes it right on the premises. It has good kids' menu selections, too. Key limes are a prize fruit in southern Florida, and the trees grow in many backyards.

south central

Arkansas, Oklahoma, Tennessee, Texas

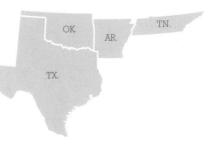

I t has storied history, scrumptious cuisine, and plenty of indoor and outdoor attractions. Yet what makes the South Central region so inviting for families is the abundant land. Even in the most developed areas, elbow room is scarcely a problem; its counties, cities, roads, facilities, parks, shopping centers, theme parks—most anything you can imagine—are built big and plentiful.

It's clear that the ambitious spirit among the region's residents echoes that of the cowboys, oil drillers, and frontier folk who preceded them. Look out, and you'll see so much built by nature and humankind, and still plenty of wide-open opportunities for exploration and creativity.

The area's outdoor life is rich and rugged, with rivers, lakes, prairies, and mountain ranges that are home to bison, wild turkey, longhorn steer, and armadillo. And it's been this way for millions of years: More than two dozen complete dinosaur

> Give me land,
> lots of land under
> starry skies above,
> Don't fence me in.
> —Cole Porter

fossils have been found in Texas. Tennessee is framed by the Blue Ridge and Appalachian Mountains and is home to cities like Nashville, Memphis, and Chattanooga, where annual festivals celebrate distinctive styles of food, music, and culture. Arkansas is the westernmost southern state, nicknamed Land of Opportunity because of its rich natural resources. Here you can dig for gems at Crater of Diamonds State Park or experience the steam and sights of Hot Springs National Park. State parks provide a wonderful introduction to the fascinating geography and cultural history of the region, once home to flourishing native populations.

The area is also well known for its space centers in Houston and Little Rock, its sports (the NFL Dallas Cowboys were once nicknamed America's Team), and its rodeo culture. Oklahoma's Elk City features a museum dedicated to famed Route 66, the traditional gateway to America's West.

ten best
parks & playgrounds

centennial park

West End at 25th Ave.
N. Nashville, TN 37203, 615-862-8431
www.nashville.gov/Parthenon
An exact copy of the Parthenon graces this popular park. It's also Nashville's art museum, where you can pick up a "family activities" scavenger hunt brochure to explore the building. On the park grounds are a duck pond, great playground equipment, and paths for biking and strolling.

charlie daniels park

1100 Charlie Daniels Pkwy., Mt. Juliet,
TN 37122, 615-758-6522
www.cityofmtjuliet.org/
charliedaniels.cfm
Named for one of Tennessee's best-loved musicians, this park and playground is consistently a Nashville family favorite. Kids love Planet Playground, a fenced-in, 9,000-square-foot play space. Check the website for information about frequent free music performances and family events.

It seems as if kids stand a little taller when they're wearing cowboy boots. Parents, too!

allsopp park

3200 Cedar Hill Rd., Little Rock,
AR 72201, 501-371-4770
www.littlerock.org/parksrecreation
More than 100 acres of forested parkland makes this one of Little Rock's most beloved parks. Families enjoy biking and easy hiking trails, playgrounds, and covered pavilions. It's a busy site for local sports. Chelsea Clinton played softball here as a child.

pinnacle mountain state park

11901 Pinnacle Valley Rd., Roland, AR 72223
501-868-5806, www.arkansasstateparks.com/
pinnaclemountain
Canoeing, hiking, fishing, and playground play are favorite activities at this beautiful park—the pride of the Arkansas state park system. The hike to the summit is manageable (and rewarding!) for families with active kids.

murray park

5900 Rebsamen Park Rd., Little Rock, AR 72207
501-371-4770, www.lrpr.org
Two playgrounds are located along the Arkansas River, along with docks and piers for fishing. Three soccer fields draw big family crowds on weekends.

zilker metro park

2100 Barton Springs Rd., Austin, TX 78704, 512-974-6700
www.austinparks.org

A wonderful Texas-style community park (350 acres!), also home to Austin's main cultural attractions, including the outdoor life-size dinosaur exhibits at the Zilker Botanical Garden.

playscape at central market

N. Lamar at 40th St., Austin, TX 78756, 512-206-1000
www.centralmarket.com

A gathering spot for families, this Austin grocery store has an outdoor dining patio and great play area for kids, all adjacent to the huge organic and natural foods market.

white rock lake

8300 E. Lawther Dr., Dallas, TX 75201, 214-670-4100
www.dallasparks.org

Families flock to this 1,015-acre lake, right in the heart of Dallas, with hiking and bike trails, bird-watching areas, and wetland exploration sites. You may see migrating flycatcher species in August and September or year-round inhabitants like ducks, woodpeckers, and double-breasted cormorants.

kid kountry

Andrew Brown Park East, 260 East Parkway Blvd. Coppell, TX 75019, 972-462-5100
www.ci.coppell.tx.us

The residents of this Dallas suburb built a creative

> Some folks look at me and see a certain swagger, which in Texas is called "walking."
> —George W. Bush

all-wooden playground. It's especially nice for preschoolers. Located within an expansive municipal park that includes rest rooms, a concession stand, walking trails, and paddle boats to rent.

martin park nature center

5000 W. Memorial Rd., Oklahoma City, OK 73142
405-755-0676, www.okc.gov/parks

Spot a deer, owl, or armadillo on a hike around the grasslands, streams, and forests of this popular urban park, located at the far northwest corner of the city. Call ahead about naturalist-led hikes and wildlife programs for children of all ages. It's adjacent to Pat Murphy Park (Hefner Road & Meridian), with a playground and mountain bike trails—a good place to spot migrating birds in the spring and fall.

> Armadillos dig for bugs that live in soil, making them lawn pests in Texas and Oklahoma. They migrate in search of diggable soil and won't settle where the earth is too dry and hard.

ten best
farms & markets

nashville farmers market

900 Rosa L. Parks Blvd., Nashville,
TN 37208, 615-880-2001
www.nashvillefarmersmarket.org
Sixteen acres of shops, farm
sheds, and eateries are open
every day in downtown Nashville. The market has been in
business since 1828 and in its
current facility since 1995. A flea
market space is open Friday to
Sunday, too, with occasional live
music on Saturdays.

*In 2007, watermelon was named the
official state vegetable of Oklahoma
(the state fruit is the strawberry).
State legislators observed that watermelons
are part of the gourd or squash family.*

memphis farmers market

Central Station Pavilion, G.E. Patterson & Front St.
Memphis, TN, 901-359-8441
www.memphisfarmersmarket.com
Spring and summer Saturday mornings, there's
live music on the schedule and great local produce and baked goods in the outdoor stalls. Check
ahead to find out about innovative kids' activities.
Get here by trolley, on the Main Street or Riverfront lines.

> Juice from the fruit of the prickly
> pear cactus is used to make sweet
> fruit drinks. Delicious!

river market

Oppenheimer Plaza
400 President Clinton Ave.
Little Rock, AR 72201
501-375-2552
www.rivermarket.info
Open Monday to Saturday,
Little Rock's favorite market
has been in business for more
than 30 years, with an open-
air pavilion, stalls, and shops.
Try online registration for kids'
cooking classes.

jones orchard

Singleton Market, 6850 Singleton Pkwy.
Millington, TN 38053, 901-872-0703
www.jonesorchard.com

There are two adjacent locations
for this farm, about 15 miles north
of Memphis. In late spring and
early summer you can pick your
own peaches, pears, berries, and
more. There's a farm market here,
too, in case you'd rather have someone else
do the picking.

cherry street farmers market

15th & Peoria Sts., Tulsa, OK
www.cherrystreetfarmersmarket.com
April through early October, the Saturday market

includes local and organic meats and cheeses, produce, crafts, and more. There's usually live music, too. Located along historic Cherry Street.

orr family farm

14400 S. Western, Oklahoma City, OK 73170
405-799-3276, www.orrfamilyfarm.com

There's an admission fee for this "agri-tainment" farm (adjacent to a horse-training farm). Hunt for semiprecious stones in a mining sluice, ride a pony, race pedal cars, and see a working farm in action.

osu/okc farmers market

OSU-OKC Horticulture Pavilion, 400 N. Portland Ave. Oklahoma City, OK 73107, 405-947-4421
www.osuokc.edu

At this state university campus, local growers gather inside the Horticulture Pavilion (November–April) on Saturday mornings. Many vendors offer certified organic produce; hothouse and hydroponics growers also set up shop. In summer, the market expands outside.

dallas farmers market

1010 Pearl Expy., Dallas, TX 75201
www.dallasfarmersmarket.org

In business seven days a week, this diverse 12-acre open-air market is a cornucopia of grocery, craft, and fresh food offerings. Look for Shed #1, which houses mostly local growers, and Shed #2 for specialty and prepared foods like fresh-made butter and cheese. Other sheds sell wholesale or grocery items to store owners who buy in big quantities. This is a busy place!

" **mac, tennessee | recycling**
I bring my own bags to the farmer's market since vendors like to reuse their pint boxes or baskets if they can.

austin farmers market

4th & Guadalupe (Saturdays), 46th & Guadalupe (Wednesdays), Austin, TX, 512-236-0074
www.austinfarmersmarket.org

Two locations operate on different days, allowing families to choose when to pick the freshest ingredients. Look for the vendor selling the distinctive organic prickly pear Pink Drink.

sweet berry farms

1801 FM 1980, Marble Falls, TX 78654-7384
830-798-1462, www.sweetberryfarm.com

"Walk across Texas" at the tremendous tall-grass maze. The Texas-shaped maze is one of many family attractions here, including pick-your-own strawberries plus other seasonal fruits and vegetables. Weekend pony rides.

ten best
ice cream spots

pied piper creamery

114 S. 11th St., Nashville, TN 37206
615-227-4114

Lounge around on the front porch or inside the children's book exchange area. The clever ice cream names are even a source of entertainment (My Cherry Amour, Strawberry Fields Forever, Banana Fanna Fo Fudding). Located in the Five Points District on the east side of the city.

dairyland drive-in

2306 Hwy. 161, North Little Rock, AR 72117, 501-945-4593

"Sooners" were the intrepid frontier families who tried to get a jump-start on the Oklahoma Land Run of 1889.

If you're driving north from Little Rock, plan to stop by the old-time family-run dairy bar with outdoor seating only. The Big Mike Special includes a hand-shaped ¾-pound burger, fries, and a soda. But you really arrive here for the milk shakes and sundaes, concocted with locally made ice cream and scooped fresh for your order. It's a fun trip for families.

sooner rocks

1127 Elm Ave., Norman, OK 73072
405-701-3036

Adjacent to Oklahoma University, this little shop opens at 2:00 p.m. and makes its own ice cream every day. It's a Sooner college hangout that stays open very late. Try the hot chili pies, also made fresh on the premises.

rusty's frozen custard

1000 E. Alameda St., Norman, OK 73071, 405-360-6177

Carryout and drive-through service in a neighborhood shopping center (there are three more Rusty's locations in the Oklahoma City area). Custard like this has less air and more milkfat than ice cream. They say it melts more slowly than ice cream as well. Visit on a hot day and find out for yourselves.

[
A la mode means "with the fashion." For generations, it's been very fashionable to serve a scoop of ice cream on anything, like slices of cake or pie or . . . more ice cream!
]

kaiser's ice cream

1039 N. Walker Ave., Oklahoma City, OK
73102, 405-236-3503

The Grateful Bean Café is located in the venerable Kaiser's building, home to the longest-operating ice cream parlor in Oklahoma. Much to the delight of midtown families, the coffee folks have recently restarted the ice cream tradition in this retro storefont with its original soda fountain.

amy's ice creams

5624 Burnet Rd., Austin, TX 78756
512-538-2697, www.amysicecreams.com

Weekly movies and fun play equipment make this a huge destination for Austin families (other locations are throughout Austin, San Antonio, and Houston).

purple cow ice cream

4601 West Freeway, Ft. Worth,
TX 76135, 817-737-7177

Try the purple vanilla shakes at this '50s-style diner and ice cream shop. This Fort Worth location is not far from the Fort Worth Stockyards.

blue bell creameries

1101 S. Bluebell Rd., Brenham, TX 77833
800-327-8135, www.BlueBell.com

This is the neighborhood ice cream brand for much of the region. A factory tour and tasting session is a fun family experience. Reservations are recommended. Highly recommended: Blue Bell's key lime pie ice cream. It has chunks of graham cracker crust. And it's only available in summer.

the chocolate bar

1835 W. Alabama St., Dallas, TX 75216, 713-520-8599
www.thechocolatebar.com

If you're a vanilla and strawberry type, try another place. But chocolate lovers will love the variety of cocoa and chocolate offerings on the ice cream menu here. It's a boutique-style fancy spot, where chocolate candies and desserts are treated like precious gems and fine art.

malcolm's ice cream & food temptations

2100 Paramount Blvd., Amarillo, TX 79109
806-355-3892

The sign outside just says "Malcolm's," and simplicity is what makes this place so charming. Half the menu is diner-style food. The other half is ice cream in sizes and servings for all tastes. Try a house specialty made with devil's food cake sandwiched with vanilla ice cream.

" **kim, texas | summer** I always looked forward to the summertime ice cream supper at Bullard United Methodist Church with all flavors of homemade ice cream and innumerable toppings. Favorites were pecan and peach since these came from local farms. I loved this because no one was really watching how many times you returned to the tables!

ten best
regional specialties

catfish

Catfish Platter Restaurant, Hwy. 377 & 99, Kingston, OK 73939 580-564-4204

Fish is fresh from the lake, deep-fried, and worth waiting in line for when this place is open—only on Thursday, Friday, and Saturday evenings. Lake Texoma, at Oklahoma's border with Texas, is a popular fishing and camping destination.

Friends of all ages come together to make lasting memories sharing seasonal goodies.

pecan pie

Mama's Daughters' Diner 2014 Irving Blvd., Dallas, TX 75207, 214-742-8646 www.mamasdaughtersdiner.com

The pecan is the state tree of Texas—so there's a plethora of great "peh-khan" treats to be found on menus here. There are five locations for this home-style diner in the Dallas area—this one is in the city's Market Center. They're famous for wonderful pies, made fresh every day.

chicken-fried steak

Chuck House, 4430 NW 10th St. Oklahoma City, OK 73107 405-942-0852

Oklahoma is known for cattle ranches and great meats. This might not be the purist's choice, but it's quite popular in the region and especially so at the colorful and time-honored sandwich spot, about five miles outside Oklahoma City. The steak comes with potatoes, or order it to replace ham in a chef's salad.

chocolate gravy & biscuits

P.J.'s Rainbow Cafe, 216 E. Main St., Mountain View, AR 72560, 870-269-8633

Chocolate gravy is a home tradition in Arkansas, served here as a weekly special on Saturday mornings only. This little spot is located not far from the closest big city of Clinton. It's actually a rich, hot chocolate sauce made in the consistency of gravy, and it's a real treat when poured over buttery, fresh-made biscuits. Definitely a special occasion menu item!

" **kevin, maryland | biscuits** We visited the Nashville area a few years back and really remember the amazing biscuits. They were served for every single meal, and at first we thought it was a little funny. Then we got kind of addicted to them. It's the first thing I think of when I remember that trip to Tennessee.

chili

Casa Rio, 430 E. Commerce St., San Antonio, TX 78205, 210-225-6718, www.casa-rio.com
Beans or no beans? Texans have strong opinions about chili, and you can make a family project of comparing favorites. San Antonio's Riverwalk has several places to try; this one is right on the water. Inside you can see elements of the 18th-century hacienda originally located here. For the record, the chili here has no beans, which is traditional in most parts of Texas.

red-eye gravy

Loveless Café, 8400 Hwy. 100 Nashville, TN 37221, 615-646-9700 www.lovelesscafe.com
There are lots of stories about how this salty, rich gravy got its name—ask around! Try it for breakfast, lunch, or dinner—over ham or biscuits. This spot is getting famous for its baked goods, jams, and other made-from-scratch offerings, and the consensus is that it's worth the 30-minute drive from Nashville. It's situated at the northern end of the historic Natchez Trace Parkway.

strawberry shortcake

Bulldog, 3614 Hwy. 167 North, Bald Knob, AR 72010 501-724-5195
It's the state's official dessert, and at this little hamburger spot near Searcy it's served only in-season (April to August). Try a biscuit-style shortcake with

> Before you eat, take a moment to thank the food.
>
> —Arapaho proverb

ice cream and lots of fresh strawberries and strawberry juice. There's a walk-up window for carryout, but it's best to eat your shortcake at an indoor table—with napkins!

tex-mex

Chuy's, 1728 Barton Springs Rd., Austin, TX 78704 512-474-4452
Spanish, Mexican, and American frontier ingredients and cooking styles is what Tex-Mex food is all about. Here the mix is compounded with over-the-top décor (velvet paintings and hand-carved fish hanging from the ceiling). Families love it.

sweet potato pancakes

Pancake Pantry, 1796 21st Ave., S, Nashville, TN 37212 615-383-9333, www.pancakepantry.com
Some say that a trip through the Nashville area isn't complete without a taste of sweet potato pancakes. There are lots of other pancake choices on the menu, but this recipe is especially loved here.

tacos

El Fenix, 1601 McKinney Ave., Dallas, TX 75202 214-747-1121, www.elfenix.com
In business for nearly one hundred years, it's a great place to get tacos for every taste. This is the original location of a popular regional franchise, with a great kids' menu and fast service.

everyday travel
midwest

Illinois, Indiana, Kentucky, Missouri, Ohio, West Virginia

From West Virginia's misty hillsides to the edges of the expansive American Plains, the Midwest—America's heartland—is a pleasure to behold. And seeing is just the beginning. The Midwest is rich in traditions and cultures that define the country's character and passion. Even if you're not a fan of a particular pastime, you know of its impact on the American psyche: Halls of fame abound, for football (Canton, Ohio), college football (South Bend, Indiana), college basketball (Kansas City, Missouri), and rock and roll (Cleveland, Ohio). West Virginia's known for traditions that have all but faded in many other parts of the country. Here, woodworking, quilting, and candle making still flourish. The state is also renowned for its county fairs and festivals celebrating commodities ranging from apple butter and chili to coal and dandelions.

The region is regarded as America's breadbasket, with corn and wheat fields blanketing

Twenty years from now you will be more disappointed by the things that you didn't do than by the ones you did do.

—Mark Twain

farmland like a down comforter. Yet it's also one of the nation's top destinations for outdoor recreational activities. Kentucky's known for thoroughbred racing and bluegrass music festivals. And Notre Dame football and Indianapolis 500 racing come to mind when we think of Indiana. Everywhere you go, it's ideal day-trip territory.

Ohio is home to protected water trails and historic canal lands, plus designated bikeways across the state. An hour, a day, a week—there's plenty to do here no matter how much time you have. Everything grows here—the state has more than a dozen wineries, including the award-winning Winery at Versailles in Darke County.

Missouri is largely shaped by two great rivers: the Missouri on the west and the Mississippi on the east, making it a true linchpin of American history and culture. Here are a few places to begin an exploration of the nation's remarkable Midwest.

parks & playgrounds

penguin park

**N. Vivion Rd. & N. Norton Ave.,
Kansas City, MO, 816-513-7500
www.kcmo.org**

Play inside a 23-foot penguin, climb over a giant elephant, slide down a 26-foot kangaroo slide, and much more. Penguin Park was named the favorite playground in Kansas City. This is one of Kansas City's older parks, but it's beautifully maintained and a favorite with locals and visitors alike. Bring the camera.

forest park

**Turtle Park, Oakland & Tamm Aves.
St. Louis, MO, 314-289-5330
www.stlouis.missouri.org**

"Meet me in St. Louis, Louis, meet me at the fair . . ." This park was originally home to the 1904 World's Fair, now one of the largest urban parks in the nation (500 acres larger than Central Park). A must-see: eight giant turtle sculptures— plus assorted sculpted eggs and a snake—perfect for climbing and picture taking.

In early September, Forest Park is the site of the annual Great Balloon Race.

forest park

**701 Cicero Rd., Noblesville, IN 46060
317-776-6350
www.cityofnoblesville.org**

Just a few of this park's attractions, about 25 miles north of Indianapolis: carousel rides for a dollar, a miniature golf course, well-maintained playground equipment, and the Indiana Transportation Museum with train excursions including Dinner on the Diner.

river promenade

White River State Park, 801 W. Washington St., Indianapolis, IN 46204, 317-233-2434 www.in.gov

A dramatic Indiana limestone walkway frames the outer edge of the famed Indianapolis Zoo near the banks of the White River. A minor league ballpark, Eiteljorg Museum of American Indians and Western Art, and the Congressional Medal of Honor Memorial are among the walking-distance attractions.

" nancy, missouri | **visit** I think the first place I would take a family visiting St. Louis is the top of the Gateway Arch at the Riverfront. It is a fantastic place to take in the whole city, the Mississippi River, and underneath the arch is a museum dedicated to the westward expansion and celebrating the stories of Lewis and Clark.

goodale park

120 W. Goodale Blvd.
Columbus, OH 43212, 614-645-3300
http://recparks.columbus.gov

Here's a great view of the Columbus skyline, with an expansive playground and pond, all encircled by the picturesque homes of the city's celebrated Victorian Village. It's an easy walk to the Short Norris arts district.

airport playfield

Beechmont & Wilmer Aves.
Cincinnati, OH 45226, 513-352-4000
www.cincinnati-oh.gov

Stroll, jog, or bike with locals along a 6.5-mile walking/biking trail and visit the Land of Make Believe children's playground, one of the city's nicest. Bike rentals are available, and there are also a driving range and a miniature golf course. For most families, though, the playground is the most popular attraction.

scovill zoo

71 S. Country Club Rd., Decatur, IL 62521
217-422-5911, www.decatur-parks.org/zoo

Overlooking Lake Decatur, this just might be the "children's capital" of the state. The zoo has a wonderful free playground outside the main entrance. A pathway leads visitors on an easy stroll to the castle-like Children's Museum of Illinois (there are separate entrance fees for each).

Play is the exultation
of the possible.
—Martin Buber

moreland park

W. Parrish Ave., Owensboro,
KY 42301, 270-687-8700
www.owensboro.com

A friendly playground and a short walking trail are here in the hometown of the International Bluegrass Music Museum and annual bluegrass and barbecue festival. Not far is the Owensboro Museum of Science and History, with a fun indoor interactive playground and motorsport display.

thoroughbred park

Main & Midland Sts., Lexington,
KY 800-845-3959, www.visitlex.com

Children climb over, under, and around monumental bronze sculptures depicting horses grazing, resting, and even racing! Also popular with visiting families: the cascading fountains of Triangle Park (at Lexington Center on Vine St.) providing a dramatic contrast with the city skyline.

ritter park playground

3th Ave. & 12th St., Huntington, WV
304-696-5954, www.ghprd.org

A creative playground for digging, climbing, and exploration. Toddlers love a sandbox nestled in a curved dinosaur tail. Nearby, the Heritage Farm Museum & Village offers hands-on explorations of Appalachian arts, traditions, and ways of life. Since 1934 this park has also maintained a 1,000 All American Rose Garden.

ten best
farms & markets

the city market

5th & Walnut Sts., Kansas City,
MO 64106, 816-842-1271
www.thecitymarket.org

Farmers come in on weekends to set up shop alongside a variety of daily merchants. It's open Saturdays and Sundays year-round, while the larger market itself is open every day. Brunch is available on Sundays at the farmer's market.

soulard market

730 Carroll St., St. Louis, MO 63104
314-622-4180
www.soulardmarket.com

Farmers from Missouri and Illinois stock the stalls of a historic market building with fresh in-season produce, meats, flowers, and more. Open Wednesday through Sunday year-round, it's located in a Victorian-era neighborhood that is the focus of a celebrated municipal renovation program.

the berry patch

22509 State Line Rd., Cleveland, MO 64734
816-618-3771, www.theberrypatchonline.com

Pick your own blackberries, blueberries, pumpkins, or raspberries, south of Kansas City. There's also honey from hives on the farm,

Fall is prime time for many farms and markets, with mazes, pumpkin picking, and hayrides.

and prepicked produce, a gift shop, refreshment stand, and picnic area. Kids can climb on giant bales of hay, and there's a tractor-drawn berry train.

indianapolis city market

222 E. Market St., Indianapolis, IN 46204
317-634-9266, www.indycm.com

Every Wednesday (May–October), Indiana farmers come to town for a vibrant open-air farmer's market established in 2008. One vendor sells hickory syrup, a prized natural sweetener for sauces, marinades, or desserts (www.hickoryworks.com). Follow your nose to the herb vendors, where you'll also find an assortment of rock salt, sea salt, and other flavors that delight all of the senses.

huber's orchard and winery

19816 Huber Rd., Borden, IN 47106, 800-345-9463
www.huberwinery.com

There's a small entrance fee to get into the Children's Farm Park ($5 in 2008), featuring mazes, slides, a pedal cart track, and a petting farm. Ice cream is made here and sold in the dairy shop, along with regional cheeses and other offerings. Pick your own strawberries beginning in spring.

findlay market

19 W. Elder St., Cincinnati, OH 45202
513-665-4839, www.findlaymarket.org
This is Ohio's oldest public market, located in the Cincinnati neighborhood of Over-the-Rhine. It's open Wednesday through Sunday, from April to November; an outdoor farmer's market is here on weekends. A diverse community of shoppers and merchants makes visitors feel welcome.

burnham orchards

8019 State Rte. 113, Berlin Heights, OH 44814, 419-588-2138
www.burnhamorchards.com
Not far from Sandusky, this village is home to the Berlin Fruit Box Company, maker of beautifully crafted boxes and baskets since 1858 (tours available: www.samuelpattersonbaskets.com). Fill your baskets at this family-run orchard at the outer edge of the village. Pick your own apples from late summer through fall.

jackson's orchard & nursery

1280 Slim Island Rd., Bowling Green, KY 40701
270-781-5303, www.jacksonsorchards.comSour
Just past Beech Bend amusement park (home of a classic wooden roller coaster, drag racing, and campgrounds) you can pick your own apples and peaches in the summer and early fall. Fall festivities include pumpkin picking, a corn maze, a straw castle, and wagon rides.

Today's farms and markets are reminders of the region's rich farming history.

orr's farm market

682 Orr Dr., Martinsburg, WV 25402
304-263-1168, www.orrsfarmmarket.com
This farm is uniquely situated close to the borders of Pennsylvania, Maryland, and Virginia. Strawberries, cherries, raspberries, and grapes are available to pick in-season.

lexington farmers market

Vine St. (between S. Mill & S. Limestone Sts.) Lexington, KY, 859-608-2655
www.lexingtonfarmersmarket.com
Come on Saturdays in early fall for pawpaws, also known as the Kentucky banana. At the market, folks will direct you to Mr. McIntosh, who offers them during pawpaw harvest season. Peel and eat them fresh, or use them to make puddings, sorbets, or other desserts.

recipe | kentucky banana pudding

- 1 cup white sugar • ¼ cup cornstarch • 1 egg
- 1 can evaporated milk (12 oz.) • 1½ cups milk •
2 tsp. vanilla • 1 package vanilla wafers (12 oz.)
- 4 Kentucky bananas (pawpaws), sliced

1. *In saucepan, combine sugar, cornstarch, egg, evaporated milk, and regular milk. Heat over medium heat, stirring until thick. Remove from heat, add vanilla, and mix well.* 2. *Arrange a layer of cookies in a large bowl or casserole dish. Pour mixture over cookies and top with a layer of sliced pawpaws. Refrigerate until chilled.*

ten best
ice cream spots

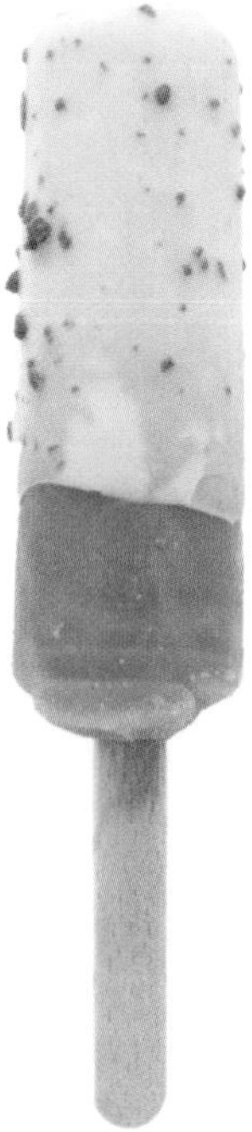

paleteria tropicana

19321 E. US 40, Independence, MO 64055, 816-795-0099
www.paleteriastropicana.com

Traditional Mexican *paletas* are frozen fruit confections on a stick, with flavors ranging from the familiar (strawberry, kiwi, and mango) to the amazing (avocado, cucumber-chile, and cactus pear). This shop is close to the Harry S. Truman Library and Museum.

serendipity homemade ice cream

8130 Big Bend Blvd., St. Louis, MO 63119
314-962-2700
www.serendipity-icecream.com

South of St. Louis in the suburb of Webster Groves you'll find ice cream made on the premises with scoops sold by size (as large or small as you like). Flavors invoke St. Louis specialties like Gooey Butter Cake and Gold Coast Chocolate.

oberweis dairy

951 Ice Cream Dr., North Aurora, IL 60542, 866-623-7934
www.oberweisdairy.com

This company makes great ice cream that you'll find all over the region. Go right to the source with a drive to their North Aurora production plant. Windows allow customers a view of ice cream being made. Insiders suggest that you order the turtle candy sundae.

krekel's dairy maid

2320 E. Main St., Decatur, IL 62521, 217-423-1719

Order at an outdoor window or indoor counter, and feast your eyes on the Chickenmobile, a converted Cadillac with a six-foot rooster head and an enormous tail. Expect great shakes, hot sandwiches, fries, and more. Close to the Scovill Zoo and Children's Museum of Illinois.

jeni's

59 Spruce St., Columbus, OH 43215
614-228-9960, www.jenisicecreams.com

On the first Saturday of every month, the Short Norris arts district hosts a "gallery hop," drawing folks of all ages. Everyone's favorite ice cream seems to be Jeni's, with flavors like Salty Caramel and Thai Chili. It's all not far from the Ohio State University campus. Other popular Jeni's locations are in the historic North Market, in nearby Grandview, and on Main Street in neighboring Bexley, Ohio.

beckie, missouri | ice cream Here's what I love about having my own ice cream shop. People eat ice cream in good times and in bad. No matter how people feel when they walk in here, they're always smiling when they leave.

chris' ice cream

1405 E. 86th St., Indianapolis, IN 46240
317-255-2156, www.indygreenways.org/monon
The Monon Trail is a 10.5-mile pathway stretching from 10th to 96th streets in Indianapolis. Near the north end you'll find wonderful ice cream, brownies, and more. See the link above to find out about accessing the trail and other city paths.

graeter's

8533 Beechmont Ave., Cincinnati,
OH 45255, 513-474-5636, www.graeters.com
Since the 1870s this ice cream has been made by the "French pot" method. Chocolate chip is remarkable: Chunky chips form when liquid chocolate is mixed into the swirling cream during preparation. This location is about four miles from the Airport Playfield.

chaney's dairy barn

9191 Nashville Rd., Bowling Green, KY 42101
270-843-5567 www.chaneysdairybarn.com
Ice cream is made on-site year-round, and seasonal events include winter dinner specials called Frosty Friday Buffets. Free movies are shown on alternate Friday evenings during the summer months. Local ingredients are used whenever possible, like Kentucky-grown pecans, strawberries, and peaches.

austin's homemade ice cream

1103 Centre St., Ceredo, WV 25507, 304-453-2071
They've been making their own ice cream here for more than 60 years. You can also order a great hot dog, but that's about all—because, as the owner points out, they need to devote most of their energy to making really great ice cream. Austin's is located about six miles from Huntington.

lic's ice cream & deli

2120 W. Parrish Ave., Owensboro, KY 42301
270-684-3571
If you're in Owensboro for great barbecue, a bluegrass festival, or a visit to one of the city's museums, make time for a stop at this local favorite for ice cream or picnic-perfect deli sandwiches. It's close to Moreland Park and Jack Fisher Park.

recipe | root beer float
(also known as a brown cow)

- vanilla ice cream
- chocolate syrup
- root beer

Scoop ice cream into glass. Pour root beer over the ice cream and drizzle chocolate syrup on top.

ten best
regional specialties

barbeque

Phils Bar B Que, 115 W. 5th St., Eureka, MO 63025, 636-938-6575

St. Louis is one of many places that is known for its fantastic barbeque, and folks say there is no better place than this one, 25 minutes from downtown. St. Louis–style barbecue is cooked plain, with sauce added afterward. Try it here, inside the only World War II–era Quonset hut in the region.

burgoo

Moonlite Bar-B-Q Inn, 2840 W. Parrish Ave., Owensboro, KY 42301, 800-322-8989 www.moonlite.com

Legend has it that the perfect bowl of burgoo must be cooked in an iron kettle and over an open flame. The stew of mutton, chicken, and vegetables is prepared that way here, just south of the Indiana state line. For the record, this place is even more famous for its own style of barbecue.

chili

Skyline Chili, 254 E. Fourth St., Cincinnati, OH 45202 513-241-4848, www.skylinechili.com

America's chili preferences are a great geographic indicator. Not to be confused with Texas chili, the Cincinnati variety is dark and slightly soupy in consistency, traditionally served over spaghetti and

You could plan a whole family vacation around the distinctive, unusual, and delicious favorite foods of America's Midwest.

topped with cheese. Onions or beans are added as extras (known as four-way and five-way chili, respectively).

concrete

Ted Drewes Frozen Custard, 6726 Chippewa, St. Louis, MO 63109 314-481-2652, www.teddrewes.com

When custard is so dense that it can't be eaten with a spoon, it's called concrete. Here's the Gateway City frozen custard stand where families with kids gather in the summer (shorter hours during the winter months). Banana chocolate chip is highly recommended. Flavors are mixed fresh for each serving.

fried chicken

Gray Brothers Cafeteria, 555 S. Indiana St. Mooresville, IN 46158, 317-831-7234 www.graybrotherscatering.com

This all-American dish makes its home in regions all across the country. At Gray Brothers, fried chicken is offered every day of the week: low on spices and simply prepared. The cafeteria is an Indiana institution, also known for homemade noodle dishes and great pie. Superconvenient for traveling families, about 30 minutes south of Indianapolis.

golden delicious apples

**Ridgefield Farm, 414 Kidwiler Rd.
Harpers Ferry, WV 25425, 304-876-3647
www.ridgefieldfarm.com**

Every apple has a story, and this is a great one. In the early 1900s, a sapling was found on a farm hillside in central West Virginia. By chance, it was not mown over and eventually began producing sweet yellow apples unlike any ever seen or tasted before. Today, golden delicious apples are grown all over the nation, but the very first came from this state. Pick your own here, at a family-run farm not far from the Harpers Ferry National Historical Park.

kentucky hot brown

**Brown Hotel, 335 West Broadway, Louisville,
KY 40202, 502-583-1234, www.brownhotel.com**

Open-faced turkey broiled with eggs, bacon, pimientos, and mornay sauce: This sandwich was created in the 1920s at Louisville's luxurious and historic Brown Hotel. Known for high-end accommodations, the hotel's more moderate café is a great place for families.

gooey butter cake

**Carondelet Bakery, 7726 Virginia Ave., St. Louis, MO
63111, 314-638-3519, www.carondeletbakery.com**

Legend has it that gooey butter cake was originally the result of a failed recipe, later replicated by bakers and celebrated as a St. Louis original.

> Tell me what you eat, I'll tell you who you are.
>
> —Anthelme Brillat-Savarin

Carondelet sells whole gooey butter cakes, since individual slices are so . . . well, gooey! It's the oldest bakery in the city. Its original ovens were buried in the yard for insulation, and though no longer in use, they're still there!

persimmons

**Annual Persimmon Festival, Main St., Mitchell, IN 47446
812-849-4441, www.persimmonfestival.org**

A late September community festival is timed to coincide with persimmon harvest season, when this Indiana fruit turns bright orange. Locals warn against eating a persimmon that is not completely ripe! They're most popular baked into sweet breads, or simmered to create uniquely flavorful jams and sauces. A festival highlight: the persimmon pudding contest.

toasted ravioli

**Farotto's, 9525 Manchester Rd., Rock Hill, MO
63119, 314-962-0048, www.farottos.com**

It all started in St. Louis (and it's not toasted at all). Ravioli, deep-fried and dipped in marinara sauce, is available at family restaurants all around the region. This location is just outside the suburb of Webster Groves, family owned and operated for more than 50 years.

> The city of Cremona, Italy, is said to be where ravioli was invented.

everyday travel
great lakes

Illinois (Chicago area), Michigan, Minnesota, Wisconsin

They are the largest collection of freshwater lakes in the world. They border eight U.S. states and the Canadian province of Ontario and at times have supplied water to one-third of Canadians and one-seventh of Americans. They're vaster than the entire New England region and define *beachfront* to many people who have never seen an ocean.

It is no wonder that the chain of five lakes in the upper Midwest region of the country have been aptly named the Great Lakes. Lakes Huron, Erie, Superior, Michigan, and Ontario and their adjoining waterways have long been renowned for shipping, water supply, and agriculture.

But what many vacationers don't know is that people from as far away as Washington, D.C., travel to the region for its pristine beaches, which are rarely overcrowded and generate waves that are safer to swim in than in oceans and gulfs. Still, waves can be dramatic enough for occasional surfing and bodyboarding expeditions.

That's not all. The lakes' four-season climate offers fun activities year-round, from skiing in the winter to golf in spring to fishing in the fall to swimming in the summer.

Moreover, one of the more popular pastimes is diving to explore more than 300 shipwrecks submerged in Lake Superior.

The lakes are bordered by areas that themselves make for great travel destinations, such as Chicago and Milwaukee (which border Lake Michigan) and national parks such as Isle Royale and Pukaskwa.

Many places retain the names bestowed on them by people who lived here hundreds, even thousands, of years ago. In the past two hundred years, they've become home to new Americans, many from northern Europe. Forget about long drives to getaway spots; in the Great Lakes the most remarkable sights, sounds, and tastes are often just a brisk walk away.

> Love many, trust a few, and learn to paddle your own canoe.
> —American proverb

ten best
parks & playgrounds

chutes & ladders playground

10145 Bush Lake Rd., Bloomington, MN 55438, 763-694-7687
www.threeriversparkdistrict.org

It's really called Hyland Lake Park Preserve, a 1,000-acre park located about 30 minutes from St. Paul. The town is also home to Mall of America. But towering slides and climbing equipment make this place the main attraction for active, outdoor family fun.

elliot park

1000 E. 14th St., Minneapolis, MN 55404
612-370-4772, www.minneapolisparks.org

In the heart of downtown Minneapolis, there's a popular park near North Central University. A new skate/BMX park, big playground, and wading pool make it a happy daytime attraction for local families.

There's no better place than a park to hang out, have fun, and enjoy nature.

wingra park

Wingra Canoe and Sailing Center, 824 Knickerbocker St., Madison, WI 53711
608-233-5332, www.wingraboats.com

Walk or cycle along the three-mile path around Lake Wingra, or play in the adjacent park playground. It's near the Henry Vilas Zoo, Vilas Park, and a host of other beloved Madison attractions. Rent boats and windsurf boards at a little pier that's open in the summer and fall.

margate park playground

4921 N. Marine Dr., Chicago, IL 60640
312-742-7522, www.chicagoparkdistrict.com

An innovative play space combining the best efforts of playground planners with community-based sculptors and artists. Decorative limestone walls double as seating, and a brick-paved decorative circle walkway graces the main entrance. There's great equipment here, including a three-kid seesaw, and it's all fenced in (adjacent to a really popular dog park).

" sue, minnesota | **my neighborhood** We live in an area that is just on the edge of the Boundary Waters Canoe Wilderness Area, which is totally untouched by development and into which no motorized vehicles can travel. It is covered with lakes, forest, and wildlife and is a wonderful place for solitude and reflection. In the mornings, we awake to the "alarm clock" of loons calling. In the winter, we often hear the howling of the wolves.

millennium park and grant park

**Welcome Center, Millennium Park,
201 E. Randolph St., Chicago, IL 60601
312-742-1168, www.millenniumpark.org**
A steel-and-wood bridge connects two of Chicago's most famous parks, offering spectacular views of the city skyline and Lake Michigan. Millennium Park has an interactive video fountain and "Cloud Gate," one of the world's largest outdoor sculptures. In Grant Park, stroll through flower gardens—inspired by the artwork of Mark Rothko and Peter Max in 2008.

Free admission to the Como Park Zoo means that St. Paul families make frequent quick visits to see favorite animals.

como park zoo and conservatory

**1225 Estabrook Dr., Saint Paul, MN 55103
651-487-8200, www.comozooconservatory.org**
Admission is free, but tickets are required for bumper cars or the little roller coaster in Como Town, a family-friendly amusement park located on the zoo grounds. The Marjorie McNeely Conservatory has outdoor attractions like the Como Ordway Memorial Japanese Garden, Enchanted Garden, and Frog Pond landscape.

bailey park

**166 Capital Ave., NE, Battle Creek, MI 49017
269-966-3431, www.bcparks.org**
Athletes flock here to play sports and to jog on the trails. But the crowning touch is the Any Bod-

ies Playground, offering a dynamic, active play environment for children with and without disabilities.

pine grove park

**1204 Pine Grove Ave., Port Huron,
MI 810-984-9760, www.porthuron.org**
This park and playground marks the starting point of a walkway that ambles along the banks of the St. Clair River to the base of the Blue Water Bridge and international border crossing. The park's softball stadium hosts exciting tournaments in summer months.

kensington park

**2240 W. Buno Rd., Milford, MI 48380
800-477-3178, www.metroparks.com**
Explore nearly 4,500 acres of woods, lakefront, bike trails, and a nature center. Best of all is the Farm Learning Center with hayrides or sleigh rides on weekends. A paved 8.5-mile trail circles Kent Lake.

4-h children's garden

**Michigan State University, Department of Horticulture
Bogue St., East Lansing, MI 48823, 517-355-5191
www.4hgarden.msu.edu**
Plan a foray to this university garden gem and delight in the Peter Rabbit Herb Garden, the Pizza Garden, and the Alice in Wonderland Maze. While you're on campus, get an ice cream cone at the MSU Dairy Store (see page 81).

ten best
farms & markets

st. paul farmers market

290 E. 5th St., St. Paul, MN 55101
651-227-8101
www.stpaulfarmersmarket.com

In and around St. Paul, there's a farmers market running every day of the week. This fun weekend market is open from late April to mid-November Saturdays and Sundays. The website lists dates and locations of 17 other SPGA markets.

minneapolis farmers market

Lyndale & Glenwood Ave., N, Minneapolis,
MN 612-333-1718, www.mplsfarmersmarket.com

Rooted in the city's tradition of vibrant farmers markets, this one is open daily (with slightly extended hours on weekends). The Lyndale market's signature red sheds house 170 vendors selling produce, cut flowers, baked goods, and prized local honey and wild rice.

> Over 20,000 farmers use farmers markets to sell directly to customers.

applewood orchard

Cedar Ave. & 225th St., Lakeville, MN, 952-985-5425
www.applewoodorchard.com

The juicy, sweet honeycrisp apple is the state apple of Minnesota. Pick your own (and several other varieties) at this farm just south of St. Paul. Most trees

Local markets are a great source of fresh baked goods.

are about eight to ten feet tall, making the harvest easy for young pickers. Kids love hayrides in big wagons pulled by antique John Deere tractors.

green city market

Lincoln Park, South & Stockton Sts.
Chicago, IL, 773-435-0280
www.chicagogreencitymarket.org

This is a great location for families visiting Chicago: In Lincoln Park, not far from the Lincoln Park Zoo and the Chicago History Museum, you'll find an awesome farmer's market in business on Wednesday and Saturday mornings. You can usually count on chef demonstrations or programs for children.

evanston farmers market

University Pl. & Oak Ave., Evanston, IL
847-866-2958, www.cityofevanston.org

Community supported agriculture (CSA) programs are available at many Chicago-area farms, and most have long waiting lists for CSA memberships. Seasonal markets like this one give everyone a chance to gather some of the best of locally grown produce. In business on Saturday mornings in summer and early fall, it's easy to reach from nearby Chicago (Evanston is the first suburb north of the Windy City).

hillsboro farmers market

Field Veterans Memorial Park, Hillsboro, WI
608-489-2521, www.hillsborowi.com
Watch for the horse-drawn buggies used by Amish farmers to bring their goods to market. Held on Saturday mornings, late spring through early fall, this market includes local produce, baked goods, preserves, and noodles. Hillsboro is known as the Czech Capital of Wisconsin.

dane county farmers market on the square

200 block, Martin Luther King Jr. Blvd., Madison, WI
608-455-1999, www.madfarmmkt.org
There are various locations for this year-round indoor and outdoor market, held in summer months on the state capitol's square. The Wednesday morning market on Martin Luther King Boulevard continues into early November, rain or shine. You'll find seasonal produce, award-winning cheeses, and a variety of meats ranging from beef and chicken to bison, venison, and emu. It's said to be the largest producer-only farm market in the whole country.

eastern market

2934 Russell St., Detroit, MI 48207, 313-833-9300, www.detroiteasternmarket.com
In the 19th century this site was part of the Underground Railroad, where slaves escaped along the Detroit River en route to Canada. Today it's a bustling Saturday morning market with 150 vendors from Michigan, Ohio, and Canada.

Soft concord grapes are the sweetest and juiciest. Hold with the stem end pointing to your mouth. Squeeze the grape near the smooth end and it will slip right out of its skin. Roll the grape around in your mouth and spit out the small seed inside. Remember to suck the juice out of the skin.

centennial cranberry farm

30957 W. Wildcat Rd., Paradise, MI 49768
877-333-1822, www.centennialcranberry.com
Explore the history of cranberry farming on Michigan's northern peninsula, along the shore of Lake Superior. This farm has been producing cranberries for more than one hundred years, and the original owner's hand-built, dovetailed timber home still stands on the property. Farm tours are free during harvest week (in October, depending on weather). Cranberry harvest is a sight to behold, as workers in hip boots wade through bright red flooded fields and mechanical pickers scoop up the ripe floating fruit.

carandale farm

5683 Lincoln Rd., Oregon, WI 53575
608-835-3979, www.carandale.com
Concord grapes have a distinctive sweet "jam" flavor. Pick your own during harvest season, in mid-October. Strawberries are ripe for picking in mid-June, and raspberries are available in the summer months.

ten best
ice cream spots

In Two Rivers, Wisconsin, you'll hear that the ice cream sundae was invented there. Folks in Ithaca, New York, make the same claim about their city's place in history.

izzy's ice cream café

2034 Marshall Ave., St. Paul, MN 55104
651-603-1458, www.izzysicecream.com
Plan to visit the first ice cream making shop that runs on solar power. So in addition to making amazing ice cream, Izzy's is also outfitted to produce clean energy and reduce demand on the municipal grid. Local dairies supply ingredients, and fresh ground coffee is delivered to the shop by bicycle. Recommended flavor: Norwegian Chai.

sebastian joe's ice cream café

1007 W. Franklin Ave., Minneapolis, MN 55405, 612-870-0065
Homemade sauces, baked goods, and ice cream are all available at this family-owned ice cream shop, located near Lake of Isles. It's a few blocks from the Walker Art Center and its free outdoor sculpture gardens.

babcock hall dairy store

1605 Linden Dr., University of Wisconsin-Madison, Madison, WI 53706
608-262-3045, www.foodsci.wisc.edu
Here is the first university-based dairy school in America. Its store has imaginative flavors that change monthly with names like School of Medicinnamon and Badger Blast. It's open every day but Sunday, and on Wednesday mornings there are free tours of the ice cream production and milk processing areas.

leon's frozen custard

3131 S. 27th St., Milwaukee, WI 53215, 414-383-1784
You can get hot dogs here, but families really come for the custard: chocolate, vanilla, and one or two additional specialty flavors that change daily. Built in 1942, Leon's neon-and-chrome exterior inspired the drive-in on the '70s TV show *Happy Days*.

" mary, wisconsin | **year-round** Depending on the season, plan to go hiking or cross-country skiing on trails in woods and prairies beginning around the University of Wisconsin Arboretum. There are great nature programs as well. Rent bikes and ride around Lake Wingra to any of the nearby attractions like the Henry Vilas Zoo, Vilas Park, Wingra Park, and Michael's Frozen Custard.

ella's

2902 E. Washington Ave., Madison,
WI 53704, 608-241-5291
www.ellas-deli.com

A Madison institution, where hundreds of animated circus displays compete with opulent deli and dessert menus for the attention of delighted customers. A famous sundae consists of a toasted slice of pound cake with frozen vanilla custard, hot fudge, and whipped cream.

michael's frozen custard

2531 Monroe St., Madison, WI 53711
608-231-3500, www.ilovemichaels.com

After enjoying Wingra Park, walk to Michael's for some frozen custard; it's what the local families do. There are five locations in town, and pints are available in grocery stores across the state. This one is the original location—and an easy walk after a visit to the lake.

> Wisconsin is home to more than 1.2 million dairy cows—that's as many cows as there are schoolchildren!
> Wisconsin Milk Marketing Board

original rainbow cone

9223 S. Western Ave., Chicago, IL 60620, 773-238-7075

One hand-packed serving is composed of five flavors: chocolate, strawberry, pistachio, cherry-nut, and orange sherbet. The family-run operation is in business at the original Chicago location. You can also get a Rainbow Cone at Millennium Park.

mario's italian lemonade

1068 W. Taylor St., Chicago, IL 60686

Get a slushy, frozen lemonade on a hot summer day. There is no telephone number or website for this tiny place in Chicago's Little Italy district, but anyone in the University Village neighborhood can point you in the right direction in the spring and summer.

the dairy store

Michigan State University, Dairy Foods Complex, 1120 S. Anthony Hall, Farm La. East Lansing, MI 48824, 517-355-7713
www.dairystore.msu.edu

On the MSU campus you can taste fresh ice cream and stroll along the dairy plant observation deck to watch it being made. You'll have the best chance of seeing the plant in operation if you plan your visit for a Tuesday, Wednesday, or Thursday.

moomers

7263 N. Long Lake Rd., Traverse City, MI 49684
231-941-4122, www.moomers.com

Visit near the end of the day and you may see the cows "come home" from the pasture at feeding and milking time. The ice cream shop and farm are about five miles outside Traverse City, where warm-weather visitors flock to the Sleeping Bear Dunes National Lakeshore and July's Traverse City Film Festival.

ten best
regional specialties

bratwurst

Charcoal Inn North, 1637 Geele Ave. Sheboygan, WI 53083, 414-458-1147
Go to Sheboygan and act like locals. Ask for a brat (rhymes with *hot*) on a crusty sandwich roll with brown mustard. Adding yellow mustard or ketchup might make you look like a tourist.

cherry pie

Grand Traverse Pie Company, 525 W. Front St., Traverse City, MI 49684, 231-922-7437, www.gtpie.com
Pie cherries are tart cherries, and more grow in Michigan than anywhere else in the nation (the Pacific Northwest is known for sweet cherries). Settlers first brought cherry pits to frontier Detroit from their gardens in France. This pie company has 14 locations around the state, and this is their flagship shop.

> Laughter is brightest where food is best.
> —Irish proverb

> **michael, wisconsin | every friday**
> In our town, just about every restaurant has a Friday Night Fish Fry. Everyone goes out and gets a fried fish platter for dinner.

cranberries

Glacial Lake Cranberries, 2480 County Rd. D, Wisconsin Rapids, WI 54495 715-887-4161, www.cranberrylink.com
"North America's native red fruit" flourishes in the expansive wetlands of central and northern Wisconsin. Call ahead to plan a visit any time of the year. Cranberry cultivation is a year-round effort, though the famous vistas of ripe red cranberry beds are most dramatic in late September and into October.

ginseng

Sprecher Brewing Company 701 W. Glendale Ave. Glendale, WI 53209, 414-964-2739 www.sprecherbrewery.com
Most ginseng grown in America comes from Wisconsin. This microbrewery uses Wisconsin ginseng in its popular soft drink Ravin' Red. With advance reservations, adults and children can visit their indoor beer garden on Fridays or Saturdays, when beers and non-alcoholic sodas are available.

squeaky cheese

Wisconsin Dairy State Cheese Company, 6860 State Rd. 34, Rudolph, WI 54475, 715-435-3144
Little Miss Muffet ate squeaky cheese. It's a

Wisconsin name for the first curds separated from milk at the beginning of the cheese-making process (the leftover milk is called whey). Bite into a fresh cheese curd and listen for the signature squeak.

chicago dog

Portillo's, 100 W. Ontario, Chicago IL 60610
312-587-8910, www.portillos.com

The history of the hot dog is linked to cities along the Atlantic coast, in the Midwest, and of course Chicago. Portillo's is the gold standard for hot dogs here. Ask for a "Chicago Dog" and get an all-beef frank on a poppyseed roll with a mix of savory toppings, but no ketchup.

pastie

Mackinaw Pastie & Cookie Company
117 W. Jamet at I-75, Mackinaw City, MI 49701
231-436-8202, www.mackinawpastie.com

It's a little hand-held pie with a meat and vegetable filling, pronounced POSS-tee. On the Upper Peninsula of Michigan, mine workers carried these traditional "sandwiches" in their lunch pails.

walleye

Betty's Pies, 1633 Hwy. 61, Two Harbors, MN 55616, 218-834-3367, www.bettyspies.com

When you peruse menus in the region, look for native species like lake trout, whitefish, burbot, and walleye. Near the shore of Lake Superior, this place serves a renowned walleye sandwich. Leave room for dessert!

wild rice

Minwanjige Café, 33287 County Hwy. 34, Ogema, MN 56569
218-983-3834
www.nativeharvest.com

In Minnesota, true wild rice can be harvested only when ripe, only from a canoe, using traditional beater sticks and using only a pole for navigation. You also need a license. Call ahead to visit this café, where Native American communities share in the work of harvesting, marketing, and serving indigenous foods (including wild rice, bison, and produce).

deep dish pizza

Uno Chicago Grill, 29 E. Ohio St., Chicago, IL 60611
312-321-1000, www.unos.com

Expect a big crowd at this bustling original location of the popular pizza chain, where deep dish pizza is said to have been invented in 1943. It's a great neighborhood for checking out turn-of-the-century architecture while you wait for a table.

The Great Lakes combined hold about 20 percent of Earth's fresh water. But at least 90 percent of their fish species are not native, but introduced by accident or intentionally.

plains

Iowa, Kansas, Nebraska, North Dakota, South Dakota

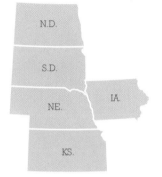

Come to the Great Plains and you'll find homes where the buffalo still roam—as do cattle, white-tailed deer, mountain goats, and burros.

The residents cannot help but follow suit. They roam along Kansas's rugged Gypsum Hills. They roam along terrain once canvassed by Lewis and Clark. They roam along fertile ground and plant seeds that sprout into much of the nation's wheat and sorghum, hay and corn. They roam in cars along Iowa's National Scenic Byways, while looking out for slow-moving Amish buggies. And they roam along the streets of busy cities like Lincoln and Omaha, Des Moines and Wichita.

These places are landmarks for the way the nation evolved in the 19th and early 20th centuries. From railroad expansion to copper mining to large-scale commercial farming and the cattle trade, American industry reshaped the landscape. The promise of opportunity was everywhere, turning hope-filled immigrants into determined pioneers.

> Where there is great love there are always miracles.
>
> —Willa Cather

The faces of America are literally carved into the plains, from Mount Rushmore National Memorial, in South Dakota, to the Crazy Horse Memorial, just 17 miles away, home to the world's largest mountain sculpture in progress, begun in 1948.

Everyday life means travel here: Wide expanses often separate home, school, work, and friends. Yet the fabric of community is still woven through cooperative programs for education, agriculture, athletics, and more. You'll likely recognize the phenomenon known as Nebraska Nice, where a spirit of friendliness and helpfulness prevail.

Indeed, much of the nation's frontier life is preserved in this region, where visitors can still watch a cowboy rodeo or trace the steps of such American legends as Gen. George Armstrong Custer or Native American Chief Sitting Bull. When you're here, you can walk age-old trails and paths and imagine what it was like to go west, in search of a new and promising way of life.

ten best
parks & playgrounds

double-ditch state recreation area

Hwy. 1804, Bismarck, ND
701-328-5357, www.ndparks.com
Hike along the Missouri River and explore the remains of a 16th-century Native American village. Close to Bismarck, the self-guided tour points out ditches, mounds, and traces of earth lodges to remind visitors about the rich history of the region.

storybook island

1301 Sheridan Lake Rd., Rapid City,
SD 57702, 605-342-6357
www.storybookisland.com
A must for families when traveling to or from famous Black Hills destinations. This free park is filled with vignettes from fairy tales and nursery rhymes, beautifully maintained and open Memorial Day through Labor Day. There are free plays presented in its nationally acclaimed children's theater, several times each day from Tuesday through Saturday.

mccrory gardens

6th St. & 22nd Ave., Brookings, SD 57007
800-952-3541, www3.sdstate.edu
On the campus of South Dakota State University

In parts of North Dakota, as much as 25 percent of annual precipitation comes down as snow.

you can explore 20 acres of formal gardens and a 45-acre arboretum. There's a Renaissance-style maze, with more than 1,100 square feet of hedges between three and six feet high—scaled just right for children. An elaborate rock garden includes 100 tons of quartzite rock with dramatic plantings.

big creek state park

8794 N.W. 125th Ave., Polk City,
IA 50226, 515-984-6473
www.iowadnr.gov
Just north of Des Moines, Big Creek Lake is a popular destination for a day trip, especially during warm-weather months. A lakefront playground is located on the beach and is fully accessible for visitors of all ages and abilities. The 26-mile paved trail is great for hiking and biking year-round.

sleepy hollow sports park

4051 Dean Ave., Des Moines, IA 50317
www.sleepyhollowsportspark.com
This outdoor family recreation park is designed to offer active fun year-round. Call ahead to find out about the warm-weather "do-it-all" pass with

tickets for go-karts, a climbing wall, mini golf, and more. In winter, there's snow tubing, skiing, and snowboarding.

gray's lake park

Fleur Dr. & George Flagg Pkwy.
Des Moines, IA 50309, 515-237-1386
www.dmgov.org

The lake is a wonderful place to see migratory birds in the spring and fall. But the best feature is the two-mile trail, which includes an illuminated ¼-mile pedestrian bridge with a beautiful view of the city in the distance. Paddleboats, kayaks, and canoes are available to rent. There are canoe basics and learn-to-sail classes on summer weekday evenings, offered through the city's park programs.

antelope park

1300 S. 27th St., Lincoln, NE 68501
402-441-6788, www.lincoln.org

This patchwork of gardens, walking paths, and play spaces is located seven blocks from downtown Lincoln. The indoor Ager Play Center has kid-powered ride-on vehicles and a track (small admission fee). Outdoors, the nearby Antelope Park playground is fully accessible. The Lincoln Children's Zoo (www.lincoln-zoo.org) is a real gem, with exhibits appealing to children's interests, abilities, and imaginations.

The world is a playground and life is pushing my swing.

—Natalie Kocsis

pioneers park

3201 S. Coddington Rd., Lincoln, NE 68522, 402-441-7895, www.lincoln.org

The park and nature center blanket more than 1,200 acres of gently rolling woodlands, prairie, and wetlands. Begin at the nature center's short driving paths for views of buffalo and bison.

lake shawnee park

3137 S.E. 29th St., Topeka, KS 66605, 785-267-1156
www.co.shawnee.ks.us

A seven-mile walking trail encircles Lake Shawnee, popular with walkers, bird-watchers, beachgoers, and boaters. Park at Ensley Botanical Gardens at Howey Road and 37th Street.

old dodge town

Antioch Park, 6501 Antioch Rd., Merriam, KS, 913-831-3355, www.jcprd.com

It's a wild West themed play space just outside Kansas City, Kansas. Generations of children have sauntered down its Main Street lined with child-size storefront, and have chased each other in and out of a child-size hotel, storefront, and more.

One Name, Two Cities

Kansas City, MO, and Kansas City, KS, share a border and are divided by the Missouri River. Both cities were named for the native Kansa people who originally lived here, around the confluence of the Kansas and Missouri Rivers.

ten best
farms & markets

gardendwellers farm

214 7th St., NW, Churchs Ferry, ND 58325, 701-351-2520
www.gardendwellersfarm.com
Go out of your way to visit this imaginative herb farm and flower garden. Custom-made scavenger hunt kits encourage kids to gather materials for a keepsake like a flower wristlet or a picture frame. Located west of Grand Forks, near Devil's Lake.

Summer in North Dakota brings intense bursts of color and fragrance in the forms of wildflowers, herbs, and cultivated blooms.

pipestem creek

7060 Hwy. 9, Carrington, ND 58421, 701-652-2623
www.pipestemcreek.com
This sunflower and grain farm is also a nationally known workshop for creating wreaths and other dried flower products, many intended as edible outdoor decorations to attract birds. You'll need to call ahead to schedule tours of their historic buildings, production areas, drying facilities, and private gardens. Pipestem Creek is located on a beautiful 5,000-acre farm.

wild rose berry farm

115 34th St., NE, Northwood, ND 58267, 701-587-5569
About 40 minutes from Grand Forks you'll find a family-run farm with strawberries to pick beginning in June. Ask about saskatoons, also known as Juneberries, which are native to Canada. It's far enough north that they ripen in June for picking.

sanderson gardens

47657 U.S. Hwy. 14, Aurora, SD 57002, 605-693-4871
Here's a fun stop near Brookings, South Dakota. At this family-run farm you can pick your own strawberries (in late spring) or raspberries (summer and fall). Wash them there and enjoy the perfect car snack as you continue your road trip!

black hills farmers market

West Omaha Park, Rapid City, SD 57701
605-923-4562, www.blackhillsfarmersmarket.com
This small market is a special treat if you're traveling

> ### Did You Know?
> The Native American Chippewa and Cherokee tribes made medicinal teas from the bark of the Juneberry bush used to treat digestive troubles.

near Mount Rushmore during the summer months. Rapid City is the nearest big town, and on Tuesdays, Thursdays, and Saturdays (July–October) you can meet local farmers and pick up fresh veggies.

lawrence farmers market

9th St. & Rhode Island St., Lawrence, KS, 785-331-4445
www.lawrencefarmersmarket.com

Upward of 80 vendors sell their own produce, meats, eggs, flowers, baked goods . . . the list goes on. On Saturday mornings, this all-Kansas market is a great destination for families, April through November.

des moines farmers market

Historic Court Avenue District, Des Moines, IA, 515-286-4928, www.desmoinesfarmersmarket.com
Kids love the weekly farming and nature-based crafts and activities that make this market especially memorable. The market is held on Saturday mornings May through October, and the earlier you can get there, the better.

omaha farmers market

11th & Jackson Sts., Omaha, NE, 402-345-5401
www.omahafarmersmarket.org
The Old Market historic district of the city has a rich tradition of farm commerce. Today it's the

Smells come from gas molecules that stimulate receptor cells deep inside your nose. The cells send messages to your brain, where the smell triggers ideas, memories, and opinions.

site of a thriving Saturday morning market, held from early May until early October. Try local cheese, honey, and dog biscuits.

haymarket farmers market

N. 8th St., Lincoln, NE 68508
402-435-7496
www.historichaymarket.com

A restored warehouse district is home to shops, galleries, and hotels. On Saturday mornings from early May to early October, it's also home to the state's biggest farm market. There's live entertainment most weekends in nearby Iron Horse Park, and in springtime there are University of Nebraska baseball games at Haymarket Park.

ames downtown farmers market

526 Main St., Ames, IA 50010, 515-232-5649
www.amesfarmersmarket.com
Thursday through Saturday, a year-round indoor market sells locally grown or made offerings ranging from meats and produce to wine, crafts, and baked goods. During warm weather, the bounty moves outdoors, with an open-air market held on Thursdays and Saturdays.

ten best
ice cream spots

dakota drug company

109 S. Main St., Stanley, ND 58784
701-628-2255

This pharmacy has been in business since 1911, and it still boasts its original soda fountain. Their antique WhirlaWhip machine creates thick blends of ice cream with add-ons of your choice. The nearest big city is Minot, home to the North Dakota State Fair every July.

fjord's ice cream factory

3606 Canyon Lake Dr., Rapid City, SD 57702, 605-343-6912

Pick up a picnic lunch or a good cup of coffee while you're here—there's a convenient drive-through. But Fjord's is best known for its homemade ice cream. It's about three blocks from the playgrounds at Canyon Lake Park.

the dairy bar

South Dakota State University, Dairy Science Building Room 101 A, Brookings, SD 57007
605-688-5420, www.sdstate.edu

This ice cream is so good that it's sold at restaurants

Around 1919, chocolate-coated ice cream bars were invented in Onawa, Iowa, so as not to have to choose between a candy bar and ice cream.

and in ice cream shops around the state. The on-campus store is only open on weekdays, and it's a great place to stop if you visit McCrory Gardens, also on the SDSU campus.

blue bunny ice cream parlor

16 5th Ave., NW, LeMars, IA 51031, 712-546-4522
www.wellsdairy.com

More ice cream is made here by a single factory than anywhere else on the planet. Tour Wells Dairy, explore an ice cream museum, and visit a 1920s-style ice cream parlor. It's a kind of ice cream mall, way out on the prairie in northwestern Iowa.

betty jane candies & ice cream

3049 Asbury Rd., Dubuque, IA 52001, 800-642-1254
www.bettyjanecandies.com

There are four Betty Jane locations, all serving hand-dipped chocolates. This location is the only one that also serves ice cream, made using an old family recipe. It's a few blocks from the Dubuque Arboretum and Botanical Gardens.

ted & wally's homemade ice cream

1120 Jackson St., Omaha, NE 68102, 402-341-5827

Look twice at the historic gas station in the colorful Old Market district. Here you'll find super premium ice cream made in old churning machines using rock salt and ice. They have a complete menu of more than 300 flavors; about 15 are available each day.

ivanna cone

701 P St., Lincoln, NE, 68508
402-477-7473, www.ivannacone.com

Witty flavors mingle with traditional favorites at this ice cream parlor and soda fountain in Lincoln's historic Haymarket district. Depending on the season you'll find flavors like Cornbread or Honey Custard along with wonderful chocolate, vanilla, and strawberry.

pop's place

301 Missouri Ave., Alma, KS 66401, 785-765-2500

In this suburb of Topeka, Pop's makes its own softserve ice cream in an old gas station. Chalk, bubbles, and checkers are always on hand, and families feel welcome to linger over their tornadoes: soft ice cream blended with an assortment of toppings.

Put the cream on a fire in a casserole, first putting in a stick of Vanilla. When near boiling take it off & pour it gently into the mixture of eggs & sugar. Stir it well . . . put it in moulds. Then put the mould into [a] bucket of ice.

—Thomas Jefferson
The first American recipe for ice cream

sylas and maddy's homemade ice cream

1014 Massachusetts St. Lawrence, KS 66044
785-832-8323

It's everyone's favorite ice cream shop, located in a converted blacksmith shop. Poet Langston Hughes spent his early childhood in this city, and his grandfather was part owner of a grocery store here on Massachusetts Street.

freddy's frozen custard

1050 S.W. Wanamaker Rd. Topeka, KS 66614, 785-783-3488
www.freddysfrozencustard.com

These franchises are convenient for travelers, like this one just off U.S. Route 70 in Topeka. It's known for its frozen custard, and kids love Dirt and Worms: crushed chocolate cookies and gummy worms.

recipe | peach melba • vanilla ice cream • peach • raspberries • 1 tsp. sugar
Mix raspberries and sugar and cook over heat. Cut peach in half and poach for 2 minutes in boiling water. Arrange peach halves on plate, scoop ice cream in middle, and pour raspberry sauce on top.

ten best
regional specialties

barbecue

**Rosedale Barbecue, 600 Southwest Blvd., Kansas City, KS 66103
913-262-0343**

Kansas City is known for barbecue, and you can get it in Kansas or Missouri. Rosedale comes highly recommended from folks in both states. It's a family operation, in business for more than 75 years, known for being very kid friendly. Expect pork, beef, turkey, and chicken varieties, with traditional sides like fresh slaw or corn.

kuchen

**Eureka Kuchen Factory, 1407 J Ave., Eureka, SD 57437
605-284-2838**

South Dakota is a wellspring of German tradition, fed by the recipes and appetites of the people who live here. Light yet rich, kuchen is a coffee-cake-style confection. Strudels, pfepperneuse, and homemade noodles are also available at this lakefront bakery.

sunflower seeds

Dakota's Best (in the Radisson Hotel lobby), 818 Main St. Rapid City, SD 57701, 605-348-3733, www.dakotasbest.biz

Seeds are the fruit of the sunflower, an indigenous American plant important in the diets of people

Experiencing new foods, new sounds, and new sights adds to the "memory bank" for kids and adults alike.

in this region for hundreds of years. This shop sells only products from North and South Dakota, especially fresh roasted sunflower seeds and other seed products like Lakota popcorn and flaxseed.

loose meat sandwiches

**Taylor's Maid-Rite, 106 S. 3rd Ave. Marshalltown, IA 50158
641-753-9684, www.maidrite.com**

This hot sandwich is made of seasoned ground beef served "loose" on a hamburger bun, unlike the patty shape of a traditional burger. You'll find it in several locations around Iowa. Here it's served with pickles, plus a spoon for easier eating.

ice water

**Wall Drug, 510 Main St., Wall, SD 57790, 605-279-2175
www.walldrug.com**

In the 1930s, the owner of a drugstore in Wall, South Dakota, wanted to attract customers. Free ice water sounded like a good idea—and it worked. Today, you can get bumper stickers, bobble-head dolls, posters, T-shirts, and much more. The best value might still be the five-cent cup of coffee, or that free cold water in a paper cup.

plum dumplings

Wilber Hotel, 203 S. Wilson St.
Wilber, NE 68465, 402-821-2020
www.megavision.net/hotlwil/

Nebraska is rich in Czech tradition, and you can taste for yourself at the Hotel Wilber. *Svestkove knedliky* (plum dumplings with melted butter and cinnamon) is just one of the choices in this authentic Czech restaurant, located in a bed and breakfast inn and near a museum celebrating Czech history and culture. Say "thank you" on your way out the door: *dêkuji*! (The *j* is pronounced like a *y.*)

bierocks

507 Ash St., Wamego, KS 66547, 785-456-9616
www.friendshiphouse.biz

Ground beef, onions, and cabbage, baked inside a golden yeast roll: It's called a bierock in Kansas. Here they're a weekly special, so call ahead for availability. Wamego is a mecca for fans of the 1939 film *The Wizard of Oz,* so check out the Oz-themed shops while you're in town.

kolaches

Verdigre, 405 Main St., Verdigre, NE 68783
402-668-2233, www.verdigrebakery.com

A *kolache* is a sweet pastry filled with poppyseed, prune, or apricot. At this bakery they're baked fresh every morning along with other Czech favorites like crescent-shaped *rohlicky* and seasonal *houska* sweet bread.

> Ponder well on this point: the pleasant hours of our life are all connected by a more or less tangible link, with some memory of the table.
>
> —Charles Pierre Monselet

muscatine melon

Schmidt's Farm Market, 5900 Grandview Ave., Muscatine, IA 52761, 563-263-6331

It is sweet, orange, and juicy inside, with deep ridges outside, as if inviting you to cut a slice. Muscatines are available only for a few weeks in the summer. Off U.S. Route 61, this farm stand usually has a great crop, plus a restaurant serving what's fresh and in season. Named Good Earth, the restaurant shares the same address and phone number as the farm stand and is known as a great place to take kids.

maytag blue cheese

Maytag Dairy Farms
2282 E. 8th St. N,
Newton, IA 50208
641-792-1133
www.maytagblue.com

It's the first blue cheese made in the United States. In the 1930s, microbiologists at Iowa State University created a Roquefort-style cheese with pasteurized cow's milk instead of the sheep's milk used in Europe. This farm ages its cheese in caves for twice as long as most other blue cheeses. Visit this factory store to sample and buy famous Maytag Blue.

everyday travel
rockies

Colorado, Montana, Wyoming

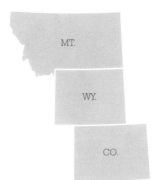

To live around the Rockies is to know snow. Folks here will tell you that the white stuff isn't just prevalent here; it's categorized: fresh powder, packed powder, hard packed, man-made, and springlike.

Such terminology comes in handy for a region where snow activities—skiing, sledding, snowmobiling, snowboarding, sleigh riding, and snowshoeing to name a few—make for an annual winter wonderland for tourists from around the world. But snow is only part of the draw. In fact, the region has a rich history steeped in the American West, with scenic prairies, mountain ranges, and trails that beckon to be explored on horseback.

And it still calls adventurers of all walks of life—fly-fishers, hikers, and sightseers, too. Montana, affectionately known as Big Sky country, has more than six dozen mountain ranges as well as the Battle of Little Big Horn site. Wyoming com-

> *Of all the memorable views, the best have been framed by Montana windows.*
> —William Hjortsberg

prises most of Yellowstone National Park. Colorado, the only U.S. state that lies entirely above 3,200 feet, is home to a portion of the Rocky Mountains, which greatly influences both weather and outdoor activity.

Here you can enjoy white-water rafting, mountain climbing, camping, hot-air balloon flights, and rodeos and see more than 600 wildlife species, many even from state highways. Then there's an activity that is growing in popularity here (and at other venues, too): soaring canopy tours. Featured in Colorado, tourists ride a single-person suspension harness along a cable that's attached to two high points in a forest or mountain range area. It's a fun way to see the sights while soaring through the air.

Families who make their homes here also make the most of the wide-open spaces. Here are some of the places they love in the northern and central Rockies.

parks & playgrounds

memorial park

1203 N. Last Chance Gulch, Helena, MT 59601, 406-447-8463
www.ci.helena.mt.us

This city's main street is Last Chance Gulch, site of a famous prospectors' camp more than 150 years ago. This park has swimming in the summer, ice-skating in winter, and hiking year-round, with a "warm house" open beginning in late December.

spring meadow lake state park

930 Custer Ave., West Helena, MT 59602
406-495-3270, www.fwp.mt.gov

Check out the park's website for a list of local and migrating birds spotted here throughout the year. An easy one-mile hiking trail circles the spring-fed lake. In early July it's the site of a cardboard boat regatta.

pioneers park

Virginia La. & Avenue D, Billings, MT 59102
406-657-8371, www.prpl.info/parks

Here's an ideal leg-stretching spot about 120 miles

northeast of Yellowstone National Park. This beautifully maintained municipal park has a playground, picnic areas, walking trails, and a wading pool—all welcome ways to experience the local views of Big Sky country.

kendrick park

830 Beaver St., Sheridan, WY 82801, 307-674-6483, www.sheridanwyoming.org

This northern Wyoming city is a popular stop for Wild West history enthusiasts. But children love the everyday appeal of a great local park with a seasonal ice cream stand and big playground, plus a public pool with a huge waterslide. It's adjacent to a refuge for elk and bison.

> "Getting there" can really be half the fun. Millions of people admire the landscape of the Rockies en route to famous destinations like Yellowstone National Park and Mount Rushmore.

" **diane, colorado | visitors** Where we take families in Denver depends on the ages of the children. Of course there's the Children's Museum, IMAX, and the National History Museum. There is so much more, though. The Butterfly Museum, the Aquarium, the Mint, wonderful art galleries, Buffalo Bill's grave, hiking—and teaching kids to hear the silence of the woods.

monument valley park

170 W. Cache La Poudre St., Colorado Springs, CO, 719-385-6550
www.springsgov.com

Monument Valley is the city's first park, comprising more than 150 acres divided into northern and southern portions. Each section includes playgrounds and rest room facilites. There's access to the Pikes Peak Greenway trail at the northern end of the park.

town square park

U.S. Hwy. 26-89, Broadway & Cache, Jackson, WY 307-733-7682, www.tetonwyo.org

Walk under huge arches made of elk antlers in this downtown Jackson park. It's a great place to stroll with an ice cream cone and enjoy the shade. It's walking distance to Moo's (page 100). Crowds gather around 6:00 p.m. on summer evenings, when a staged gun battle takes place. It's been a traditional Jackson event since 1957.

cheyenne botanic gardens

710 S. Lions Park Dr., Cheyenne, WY 82001 307-637-6458, www.cheyenne.org

Admission is free to the gardens and conservatory, located in Lion's Park. The surrounding municipal park includes walking and biking trails, playgrounds, mini golf, and cane and paddle boat rentals for exploring.

Colorado's Monument Valley Park provides access to one of many trails leading to Pikes Peak.

play grounds

4550 Broadway, Boulder, CO 80304, 303-442-1938
www.playgroundscafe.com

A great option for cold days: This café and creative indoor play space has a casual and healthy menu appealing to adults and small children alike. Kids love the construction zone, indoor tree house, and cozy reading nook. Admission fee for children under age seven.

belleview park

5001 S. Inca Dr., Englewood, CO 80110, 303-798-6927

From Memorial Day through Labor Day, there's a fee-based children's farm, miniature train, and Pirate Cove aquatic park with slides, pools, and floats. But the park's playgrounds, hiking trails, and picnic grounds are free and available year-round.

washington park

E. Virginia Ave., Denver, CO, 303-698-4962
www.denver.org

Washington Park was designed by German landscape architect Reinhard Schuetze. The 150-acre urban park has paths, lakes, and two playgrounds. Look for the "Dutch Lullaby" statue commemorating the famous poem about Wynken, Blynken, and Nod by Colorado poet Eugene Field. A famous tree in the park is a descendant of a Massachusetts elm under which George Washington took command of the Continental army in 1775.

ten best
farms & markets

helena farmers market

Fuller Ave., Helena, MT
406-449-7446
www.visitmt.com

Here's a Saturday morning gathering place, flanked on both sides by expansive public parks and held May–October. A nice coffee shop is nearby, and everything here is grown or made in Montana. It's one street away from Last Chance Gulch, Helena's historic main street.

Extreme Montana weather: from -45° to 49°F, January 14–15, 1972

sheridan farmers market

Whitney Commons
320 W. Alger St., Sheridan,
WY 82801, 307-672-8881
www.sheridanfarmersmarket.org

There's no vehicle traffic in the Whitney Commons park, so farmers cart in their goods each Thursday evening, mid-July through mid-September. This creates a great environment for kids—along with a playground, reflecting pond, and close access to downtown restaurants.

bogert farmers market

S. Church Ave., Bozeman, MT 59715, 406-539-0216
www.bogertfarmersmarket.com

Tuesday evenings, June through September, a farmer's market is held in Bozeman Park. Local artists and entertainers make guest appearances each week. The market helps to support the 6.8-acre park, which features a roller rink, picnic tables, and an outdoor pool. It's a nice way to meet local families.

rocky creek farm

34297 Frontage Rd., Bozeman, MT 59715
406-585-0225

Pick your own apples or try some hand-pressed cider here in southwest Montana. You can also purchase other fresh-grown fruits and vegetables, including raspberries in the summer and pumpkins in the fall.

" suzy, maryland | a trip to remember Another wonderful trip was Durango, Colorado, where we visited Silverton (an old mining town), took an amazing train ride, and went to Mesa Verde. My then third grader, Jack, even voluntarily did a picture report of Mesa Verde and the Indians.

virginia city market

405 W. Wallace St., Virginia City, MT 59755
406-843-5833, www.virginiacitychamber.com

This is an original intact gold-mining town with historic 19th-century buildings. The Adobe Town Schoolhouse hosts a small summer farm market on Saturday mornings; in winter months the market comes indoors with offerings from local artisans.

cheyenne farmers market

15th & Capitol Ave., Cheyenne, WY, 307-635-9291
www.calc.net/Farmers1.htm

August through October is harvest season for this Thursday and Saturday market held west of the Union Pacific depot in Cheyenne. Proceeds help support community action programs assisting low-income and homeless Laramie County residents.

highlands ranch farmers market

Highlands Ranch Town Center Square, 9288 Dorchester St., Highlands Ranch, CO 80129
www.denverfarmersmarket.com

This is one of several markets in and around Denver. They're held in spring and summer nearly every day of the week; this one is Sundays from 10 until 2. You can pick up a free newspaper and take advantage of kids' activities, along with fresh produce, breads, and cheeses.

berry patch farms

13785 Potomac St., Brighton, CO 80601
303-659-5050, www.berrypatchfarms.com

This certified organic farm is open for berry

picking in the spring and fall. Vegetables, cherries, and herbs are also available pre-picked. It's not far from Barr State Park, with a great nature center and nice picnic facilities.

ferrara's happy apple farm

1190 1st St., Penrose, CO 81240
719-372-6300, www.happyapplefarm.com

A "day-at-the-farm" kind of place close to Colorado Springs. Plan to pick your own apples or blackberries, then stay for an apple-smoked barbecue beef brisket (call ahead for availability). You can also purchase chilies, grown and roasted right here on the farm.

boulder farmers market

13th St. between Arapahoe Ave. & Canyon Blvd.
Boulder, CO 80301, 303-910-2236
www.boulderfarmers.org

This market has the longest-running season in Colorado: Saturday mornings from April through October, and early Wednesday evenings from May through September. It's truly a local gathering place, drawing families from all around the region.

books | stone fox

by john reynolds gardiner
Set on a Wyoming farm, it's an award-winning novel about a boy, his dog, and an epic sled race.

ten best
ice cream spots

the parrot

42 N. Last Chance Gulch, Helena,
MT 59601, 406-442-1470

In the heart of Helena, you can stop at this family-owned business and order a caramel cashew sundae from the original soda fountain. Then stroll over to the Lewis & Clark Public Library and explore the playground there (120 S. Last Chance Gulch).

big dipper ice cream

631 S. Higgins Ave., Missoula,
MT 59801, 406-543-5722
www.bigdippericecream.com

Each month the ice cream maker collaborates with local chefs and candy makers to come up with limited-time-only flavors. In the summer they celebrate Christmas in July, with holiday flavors like Candy Cane, Eggnog, and Pumpkin.

> July is National Ice Cream Month. And July 21 is National Ice Cream Day. To celebrate, have some with every meal, beginning with a spoonful in a mug of hot chocolate.

The average dairy cow produces 2,100 pounds of milk per month. It takes about 15 pounds of milk to make one gallon of ice cream.

bridger ridge homemade ice cream

2622 W. Main St., Bozeman, MT 59718
406-586-8810

This is located near the commercial and industrial end of town, near the Gallatin Valley mall and movie theater. Historic Main Street is located to the east of this location. They make their own great flavors and also supply local restaurants.

virginia city creamery

205 W. Wallace St., Virginia City,
MT 59755, 406-843-5513
www.goldwest.visitmt.com

See the ice cream being made right here, using a recipe from an old White House cookbook. The shop is located next to Elling Gold Exchange in a historic bank building, where they still buy and sell gold nuggets.

moo's gourmet ice cream

36 E. Broadway, Jackson, WY 83001, 307-733-1998

Ice cream here is made with no milk, only cream, for a 30 percent butterfat content. Sorbets are made with at least 99 percent fruit purees, so there's something for everyone. Flavorings are all natural: They even grind their own vanilla beans. Located on the south side of Jackson's town square.

bonnie brae

799 S. University Blvd., Denver, CO 80209
303-777-0808, www.bonniebraeicecream.com

Not far from famed Washington Park in Denver you'll find this locally owned ice cream shop. It's a bright, cheery place with indoor seating, plus an outdoor patio. Ice cream is made right on the premises.

bliss organic ice cream

2425 Canyon Blvd., Boulder, CO
303-443-9596, www.blissorganic.com

Try flavors like lychee or ice coffee milk. It's also a teahouse with Taiwanese pearl tea and an assortment of black and green tea. This is the retail shop for a line of ice cream available in regional groceries and markets. The café is attached to a knitting shop where you can pick up unique wools and a bit of free knitting advice.

glacier homemade ice cream

3133 28th St., Boulder, CO 80301, 303-440-6542
www.glacierhomemadeicecream.com

Here's the original location of a popular ice cream store that has expanded throughout the region and into California. As many as 80 flavors are available at a time, along with great coffee, non-dairy smoothies, and really wonderful hot fudge. People love their Coffee Caramel Crunch and Death By Chocolate ice cream.

recipe | **strawberry snow ice cream** You can make ice cream with stuff from a restaurant (except for the snow). You need: • 3 cups clean fresh snow • 2 individual half & half servings • 2 individual strawberry jam servings *Indoors, combine half & half and jam. Carry it outside and mix well with snow. Eat right away.*

josh & john's

111 E. Pikes Peak Ave., Colorado Springs, CO 80903
719-632-0299, www.joshandjohns.com

Since you're in the Rockies, you might want to try flavors like Colorado Cookies and Cream or Rocky Mountain Road. They blend it all right here in the store. The shop is walking distance to popular Acacia Park. This location is right next to the Peak Theater.

donell's

201 E. 2nd St., Casper, WY 82601, 307-234-6283
www.donellschocolates.com

This family-run confectionary has been in business since 1956, known all over the region for its handmade chocolates, candy canes, lollypops, fudges, popcorn, and candies. Their ice cream is made right here, too, a few blocks away from a convenient city park. Donell's has used fresh ingredients in every small batch for three generations.

ten best
regional specialties

beans

Homesteader's, 45 E. Main St., Cortez CO 81321, 970-565-6253
www.thehomesteaders.com

Dry beans were traditional frontier food, easy to carry and an important source of protein. A pot of beans is a basic side dish at this friendly restaurant just outside Mesa Verde National Park. Check out their collection of license plates from every one of the United States. Baked goods are made on the premises, including wonderful pie.

bread

Stella's Kitchen and Bakery, 110 N. 29, Billings, MT 59101, 406-248-3060

Wheat farming is big business in Montana. This place makes the most of it with aromatic homemade bread and "monster" pancakes. Get a free cinnamon roll if you can eat four monster cakes. It's open for breakfast and lunch only, with table service, a carryout bakery, and a very nice children's menu.

Nothing whets the appetite like a good long hike.

buffalo burgers

Log Cabin Family Restaurant, 102 S. Main Ave., Choteau, MT 59422, 406-466-2888

This casual restaurant has been a Montana favorite for generations, made famous in recent years by television personality David Letterman. Buffalo are farmed in Montana and Wyoming as a source of flavorful meat, more popular than beef for many families. Also on the menu: 25 to 30 different pies are made here each week, making this a dessert destination, too.

buffalo steaks

The Fort Restaurant, 19192 Hwy. 8, Morrison, CO 80465, 303-697-4771, www.thefort.com

This reproduction 1830s adobe fort is home to a fine restaurant that claims to sell more buffalo steaks than any other in America. There's a strong sense of Rocky Mountain drama here, with candles twinkling on the fort's outer walls and a beehive fireplace in many dining rooms. A children's menu is available. Dress to impress.

" sam, colorado | **mountain man toast** "Here's to the childs what come afore, and here's to the pilgrims what's come arter. May yer trails be free of grizzlies, your packs filled with plews, and may you have fat buffler in your pot. WAUGH!" *Adapted by Sam Arnold, founder of the Fort Restaurant.*

chiles

Pantaleo Produce and the Pueblo Chili Company, 39651 South Rd. Vineland, CO 81006, 719-948-4556, www.pantaleofarms.com

Try chile sausage, made right here. This place is a working family farm with seasonal roadside sales including roasted, dried, and fresh chile peppers. In October, they open a concession stand. Try roasted sweet corn, fresh tamales, and assorted hot sausage specialties.

chuckwagon

Moose Chuckwagon, Moose, WY, 307-733-2415 www.dornans.com

The chuckwagon was the food service operation for cattle-herding teams of the late 19th century. Try it for yourself at this resort inside Grand Teton National Park. Unlike the real thing, guests can choose from a menu (including children's options). But you can eat outside under the stars and talk about the day, as chuckwagon diners have done for more than a hundred years.

denver omelet

Sam's No. 3 Diner, 1500 Curtis St., Denver, CO 80202 303-534-1927, www.samsno3.com

When in Denver . . . try this! This really popular diner features a wonderful version, stuffed with ham, bell peppers, onion, chiles, and cheese. They open at 6:00 a.m. for breakfast on weekdays, 7:00 on weekends.

huckleberry candy

Yippy I-O Candy, 84 E. Broadway Jackson, WY 83001, 307-739-3020

Huckleberries are coveted fruit in the Rockies and the Northwest. At this over-the-top candy shop you'll find an unusual assortment of candies, syrups, and even chocolate—all flavored with this sweet, deep purple berry.

> The world's only public auction of elk antlers takes place at the Jackson Town Square on the third Saturday in May each year.

sourdough pancakes

Jedediah's House of Sourdough, 135 E. Broadway Jackson, WY 83001, 307-733-5671

Frontier families used sourdough starter to make breads and coarse cakes, keeping the yeast alive by adding flour and water. It's said that Jedediah's starter is more than a hundred years old. Prepare to wait for a table to get sourjack pancakes. Open for breakfast and lunch.

trout

Nora's Fish Creek Inn, 5600 W. Hwy. 22, Wilson, WY 83014, 307-733-8288

Varieties of trout are the state fish of Wyoming, Montana, and Colorado (and sixteen other states, too). Wilson is about six miles outside Jackson, Wyoming, and this very popular creekside spot is a great place to try it pan-fried.

northwest

Idaho, Oregon, Washington

Thinking about visiting the Northwest? Well, take a hike—literally! Talk about a hiker's haven. The states of Washington, Oregon, and Idaho beckon families who enjoy the great outdoors, with dense forest ranges (and some of the world's tallest trees), ice-capped mountains, lush hillsides, and winding water masses. Many, like Glacier Peak in Washington, are impassable by car, lending themselves to hiking through rough terrain in areas filled with wildlife like black bear, mountain goat, and lynx. Watch out! Mount St. Helens is among the state's active volcanoes.

Outdoor life typifies the area year-round. Idaho, named the Gem State because of its natural resources, is known for its ski resorts (Silver Mountain is among the most popular). It's also a draw for recreations like sport climbing in municipalities like the City of Rocks, a national

> Now I see the secret of making the best persons. It is to grow in the open air and to eat and sleep with earth.
>
> —Walt Whitman

reserve and state park. Not surprising, the region is home to ardent environmentalists (Greenpeace was founded in nearby Vancouver, BC). They encourage you to feast on wild berries, organic fruits, and vegetables grown locally. In addition to skiing and hiking, families here enjoy water sports, camping, and fishing.

That is not to say that there's not a great time to be had indoors. This is, after all, the area that produced grunge rock, Starbucks, Nike, and Microsoft. There are thriving arts programs including the Tears of Joy puppet theater in Portland, Oregon. The Idaho Falls Public Library showcases a life-size sculpture commemorating Billy Coleman and his hound dogs from the classic book *Where the Red Fern Grows*. And college and professional sports draw loyal fans all the way from Alaska. But remember when you're here: All roads lead back to the nature trail!

ten best
parks & playgrounds

alki beach park

1702 Alki Ave., SW
Seattle, WA, 206-684-4075
www.seattle.gov/parks

Remarkable for its views of the Seattle skyline, Puget Sound, and the Olympic Mountains, the playground here has updated equipment and nearby sports fields. Check out this park's miniature Statue of Liberty.

warren g. magnuson park

7400 Sand Point Way, NE, Seattle, WA 98115
206-684-4946, www.seattle.gov/parks

Situated along Lake Washington, this is a favorite spot for kite flying and bird-watching. Enjoy playground equipment outdoors, sports facilities indoors.

camel's back park

1200 Heron St., Boise, ID, 208-384-4240
www.cityofboise.org

This neighborhood park and playground is nestled at the edge of the Boise Foothills, where

At Idaho's Julia Davis Park, the Greenbelt pathway stretches more than 22 miles along beautiful Boise River.

the Rocky Mountains meet the Treasure Valley desert.

julia davis park

700 S. Capitol Blvd., Boise, ID
208-384-4240, www.cityofboise.org

Paying homage to Boise's heritage, this park includes Zoo Boise, a tree walk, and an awesome sculpture garden. Nearby is the Greenbelt, a 22.5-mile pathway along the Boise River.

washington park

S.W. Park Pl., Portland, OR, 503-797-1850
www.portlandonline.com

A true community gathering place, this park includes a fabulous playground area, a chiming fountain, and the city zoo. See a monument honoring the history of the Northwest Territory and the first U.S. statue to honor a woman, placed here in 1905. It depicts Sacajawea, the Shoshone girl who helped to guide Lewis and Clark's westward expedition.

> **jenny, oregon | car naps** For my son, a five-minute nap in the car was the ultimate "power sleep." It must have been something about the soothing sound of the engine, or the security of having his loved ones strapped in all around him. And once he woke up—watch out! He wouldn't need to sleep again for at least eight hours!

tryon creek state park

11321 S.W. Terwilliger Blvd., Portland, OR 97219
800-551-6949, www.oregonstateparks.org

Minutes from downtown Portland, this state park offers a taste of Oregon's natural beauty on accessible walking and hiking trails.

multnomah county library, central branch

801 S.W. 10th Ave., Portland, OR 97205, 503-988-5123
www.multcolib.org

Step inside to see sculptures of the Cheshire Cat, the White Queen, and the White Rabbit, originally built on the outer walls of this 1913 building. Also inside, the Beverly Cleary Children's Library is a premier draw for local families.

boise public library

715 S. Capitol Blvd., Boise, ID 83702, 208-384-4076
www.boisepubliclibrary.org

One Saturday each month, two certified therapy dogs are on duty to greet children. Each is trained to listen patiently to young readers. Check the library website for scheduled dates.

grant park

N.E. 33rd Ave. & U.S. Grant Pl., Portland, OR
www.portlandonline.com

Portland is the setting for many of Beverly Cleary's books, honored at this hospitable park with statues of Ramona, Henry Huggins, and Ribsy the dog. There are fun fountains and playground areas, too.

books | a girl from yamhill *by beverly cleary*

An autobiography from the legendary children's author (and Portland native), this is a wonderful read for young teens and parents. The sequel sees Cleary off to college. It's titled *My Own Two Feet*.

seattle children's playgarden

24th Ave., S, Seattle, WA 98144, 206-227-5458
www.childrensplaygarden.org

Sports facilities, playground, and garden are all accessible for wheelchairs and children of differing abilities. Shelters, gardens, and a rock scramble are the newest additions. There are scheduled free playdates each month, where parents and children can gather with facilitators to explore the best that the playgarden has to offer (picnic space, bunnies to see, a garden that needs tending by very willing little hands). Check the website for reservations. This place is a model for play programs across the country.

Playgrounds are a relatively new concept, emerging in late 19th-century American cities. The phenomenon is based on the understanding that play is a child's "work."

ten best
farms & markets

spokane farmers market

20 W. 2nd Ave., Spokane, WA 99201, 509-995-0182, www.spokanefarmersmarket.org
It's a collective effort of 35 local farms from the Spokane area. Open on Saturday mornings beginning in early May, there's also a Wednesday morning market each year beginning in June. Look online for a great seasonal listing of expected fruit, vegetables, and flowers.

A good rule of thumb is to choose the biggest pumpkin that the whole family can carve together.

capital city public market

8th St., Boise, ID 83702, 208-345-9287
www.capitalcitypublicmarket.com
Explore the wealth of produce and artfulness that is native to the Treasure Valley of Boise, especially cranberries, apples, nuts, and berries. Local chefs are featured each week

university district farmers market

N.E. 50th & University Way, NE, Seattle, WA
www.seattlefarmersmarkets.org
The bounty of the Northwest is at its freshest here at this year-round market. Identify different types of wild mushrooms, fresh oysters, and salmon, and plenty of wonderful prepared foods.

wilson banner ranch

16397 Hwy. 12, Clarkston, WA 99403, 509-758-2665
www.wilsonbannerranch.com
Pick your own apples, peaches, apricots, and more, depending on what's in season between June and December. Located near the Snake River and the Idaho border.

eugene farmers market

8th Ave. & Oak St., Eugene, OR 97401, 541-686-8885
www.eugenesaturdaymarket.org
Billed as the "oldest weekly open air crafts market in

amy, oregon | errands Going to farmer's markets instead of grocery stores turns a chore into an adventure. We go there for breakfast on Saturday morning, grocery list in hand, and the kids get to choose a treat to bring home for dessert.

the U.S." April through November, rain or shine, the market also has fresh local produce and prepared foods. It's more like a weekly block party than a shopping trip.

briggs family blueberry patch

5374 Greenlea Way, SE, Salem, OR 97301, 503-364-8222

Pick your own or pick up a pint of whatever's in season. Berries are ideal travel foods for healthy families—they're packed with antioxidants, fiber, and vitamins. And this organic farm doesn't spray.

portland farmers market

South Park Blocks, S.W. Harrison & Montgomery Sts., Portland, OR 97201 www.portlandfarmersmarket.org

Plan ahead and enroll in a Kids Cook at the Market program. They experiment with the farm-fresh foods that the Northwest is famous for.

idaho falls farmers market

501 W. Broadway St., Idaho Falls, ID 83402, 208-339-3230

Special events are scheduled during the season (Saturdays, May–October), including a summer Kids' Day and free slices of watermelon at the annual Watermelon Feed.

> You'll . . . be teaching your children that a carrot is a root, not a machine-lathed orange bullet that comes in a plastic bag. A lot more is going on at the farmers market than the exchange of money for food.
>
> —Michael Pollan,
> *"Six Rules for Eating Wisely,"*
> Time *magazine, June 11, 2006*

pike place market

Western Ave. & Pikes Market, Seattle, WA 98101, 206-682-7453
www.pikeplacemarket.org

It's worth the trip just to see the famous "flying fish" stand (Pike Place Fish Market). Stay for lunch, shop for dinner. At this spectacular market there are four berry vendors, five cherry vendors, six honey farm stands . . . and that's only the beginning. Specialty food vendors and two grocery stores make it convenient and delightful for families.

reed's dairy

2660 W. Broadway, Idaho Falls, ID 83402 208-522-0123, www.reedsdairy.com

This dairy still makes home deliveries of its own organic milk and cheeses, plus other basic refrigerated groceries. There's a petting area with small farm animals, and visitors are welcome to stroll the public areas of the dairy operation. Best of all, there's a dairy stand with homemade ice cream made on the premises.

recipe | watermelon limeade

Blend 2 cups of cut-up seedless watermelon, strain into a small pitcher, and add ½ tsp. fresh lime juice. Serve over ice.

ten best
ice cream spots

big apple diner

6720 Kitsap Way, Bremerton,
WA 98310, 360-373-8242

Old-fashioned ice cream bar with
tall glasses for ice cream sodas,
sundaes, and carryout cones, plus
great diner food.

comley's place

12622 E. Sprague Ave., Spokane
Valley, WA 99216, 509-924-5411

This is a great stop for a casual
lunch topped off with fresh pie a
la mode. It's all table service at this family-
oriented restaurant. By the way,
Comley's is known for
great pot pies, home-
made cornbread,
and a savory baked
spaghetti dish that is
a real local favorite.

ice cream renaissance

2108 Main St., Vancouver, WA 98660, 360-694-3092

A complete menu of ice cream concoctions, pies,
and coffees—and all ice cream is made on the
premises. Not sure what to order? Try the house
special, Indecision. Based on the size you choose
(Slightly Hesitant, Wavering, or Seriously Uncertain),

*Each American consumes a yearly
average of 23.2 quarts of ice cream.*

the staff invents an ice cream creation just for you.

eats market café

2600 S.W. Barton St., Seattle, WA
98126, 206-933-1200
www.eatsmarket.com

It's a market, a deli, a restaurant,
and an ice cream stand all rolled
together, and it's famously friendly
for kids. It's close to Fauntleroy Park,
with biking and hiking paths along a
forested creek.

husky deli

4721 California Ave., SW, Seattle, WA 98116
206-937-2810

Family run, with brown-bag lunches to go. Make
time for the great ice cream; they make their own
(and cones, too). When you're there, ask about the
stout ice cream they make for the brewery across
the street. In west Seattle, this place is close to Alki
Beach and Lincoln Park, and a real gathering spot
for city natives.

pick quick drive-in

4306 Pacific Hwy. E, Fife, WA 98424, 253-922-5599

Stop a few miles from Tacoma and have a made-to-
order shake with your burger and fries. Hang out
at the picnic benches in a small park space—very

nice for families. This walk-up stand has been here for more than 60 years.

staccato gelato

232 N.E. 28th Ave., Portland, OR 97232, 503-231-7100
www.staccatogelato.com

Gelato is made here every day, and donuts are fried up fresh on Fridays, Saturdays, and Sundays. There's a kids' area and outdoor seating ("if you're waterproof"). Be adventurous: try Fig, Earl Gray, or Baklava.

paulsen's pharmacy

4246 N.E. Sandy Blvd., Portland, OR 97213
503-287-1163, www.mygnp.com

Shakes, sundaes, and cones are served in a pharmacy that's nearly a hundred years old, located in Portland's historic Hollywood district. Try an ice cream soda made with "green rivers," a tart lemon-lime syrup.

goody's goodies

1502 N. 13th St., Boise, ID 83701
www.goodysgoodies.com

In a historic district at the end of the Boise Foothills Trail, this ice cream shop is a nice reward after a great hike. There are ten flavors available each day, made weekly. Located three blocks from the playground and playing fields of Camel's Back Park.

elk river lodge & general store

201 Main St., Elk River, ID 83827
208-826-3299, www.elkriverlodge.net

Go out of your way to try soft-serve huckleberry ice cream on the banks of the Elk River. Call ahead if you plan to camp overnight and forage for huckleberries while you're here! Just for fun, try a huck-a-fizzle, or maybe take home a huckleberry pie.

recipe | ice cream sandwich

Here's what you need:
- 2 leftover pancakes • 1 small scoop of ice cream • 1 teaspoon peanut butter

Spread a little peanut butter on one side of each pancake. Put the pancakes together with the ice cream in the middle, peanut butter on the inside. Eat right away!

regional specialties

coffee

My CoffeeHouse, 2818 E. Madison
St., Seattle, WA 98112
206-568-7509
www.mycoffeehouseseattle.com
Seattle is home to the concept
of coffee boutiques, and this
spot is known as the kid-
friendliest in Seattle. Located
in a great shopping area . . . and
excellent coffee, too!

Washington's San Juan Island was a setting
for the Free Willy films. Get here on the
Washington State Ferry and have a crabcake
or bowl of chowder for lunch.

chanterelles

Folks who harvest these wild mushrooms work
hard to protect the forests where they grow. Look
for them in local restaurants
and groceries along the
Oregon coast—it's the
official state mushroom.
Make a trip to a farmer's
market and ask about
how they're collected
and the best ways to
prepare them.

aplets

Liberty Orchards Company
117 Mission Ave., Cashmere,
WA 98815, 800-231-3242
www.libertyorchards.com
Sweet-tart apple candy
invented nearly a hundred
years ago by Armenian
immigrants after the failure of
their first venture—a yogurt
factory. Get the whole story
(and some aplets) during a factory tour.

marionberry pie

Larson's Bakery, 13411 S.E. Mill Plain Blvd., Vancouver,
WA 98684, 360-253-4555 www.larsonsbakery.net
Summer is marionberry season in Washington and
Oregon. Native to this area, the deep purple berry
is great for pies, jams, and more.

cherries

Smith's Hilltop Orchard, 9423 E. Green Bluff Rd., Colbert,
WA 99005, 509-238-4647
Rainier cherries, discovered in the 1950s, are a

❝ sara, oregon | **just a taste** The best way to get kids to try new foods is to make sure they're good
and hungry. I try not to have a ton of snacks in the car, and not fill up on crackers and such when we're waiting
in a restaurant. Then things like mushrooms, spinach, or a new kind of fish smell and taste extra wonderful.

hybrid of bing and Van cherries. Call ahead to this family-run farm and pick your own apples, nectarines, plums, or cherries depending on the season. By law, Rainier cherries must reach a certain point of sweetness (measured in degrees known as Brix) before they can be picked.

lavender

Hood River Lavender, 3801 Straight Hill Rd. Hood River, OR 97031, 541-354-9917 www.hoodriverlavender.com

A member of the mint family, lavender flourishes on sunny Oregon farms. See the beautiful fields, cut your own fresh blossoms, and find lavender honey, tea, and baked goods. There are wonderful views of volcanic mountains not far from the banks of the Hood River. This farm is part of the Hood River Fruit Loop, a 35-mile scenic drive about an hour outside Portland (www.hoodriverfruitloop.com). The route passes some of Oregon's friendliest farms, shops, and produce stands.

huckleberries

Wallace Heritage-Huckleberry Festival, 10 River St. Wallace, ID 83873, 208-753-7151 www.wallaceidahochamber.com

They're the state fruit of Idaho, but favorite picking spots are closely guarded secrets. At this annual event you can meet huckleberry enthusiasts and (if you're lucky) learn more.

> Seeing is deceiving. It's eating that's believing.
> —James Thurber

salmon candy

Whole Foods Market, Roosevelt Square, 1026 N.E. 64th St., Seattle, WA 98115, 206-985-1500

Try this Pacific Northwest twist, made by broiling fresh salmon with brown sugar, maple syrup, and honey. It's available in local groceries in the Seattle area.

potatoes

Idaho Potato Museum, 130 N.W. Main St., Blackfoot, ID 83221, 208-785-2517 www.potatoexpo.com

Blackfoot is known as the Potato Capital of the World. At this fun museum, explore farming, cooking, and the links between the potato and railroad industries.

hazelnuts

Holmquist Hazelnut Orchard, 9821 Holmquist Rd., Lynden, WA 98264, 800-720-0895 www.holmquisthazelnuts.com

Ninety-nine percent of all hazelnuts sold in the nation come from Oregon. Call ahead to visit this farm, or visit their stand at Seattle's Pike Place Market.

Did You Know?

Rainier cherries are the most difficult cherries to grow. If the wind blows too hard, the cherries bruise. If it rains for more than a single day, the cherries burst. On top of that, birds eat one-third of each crop!

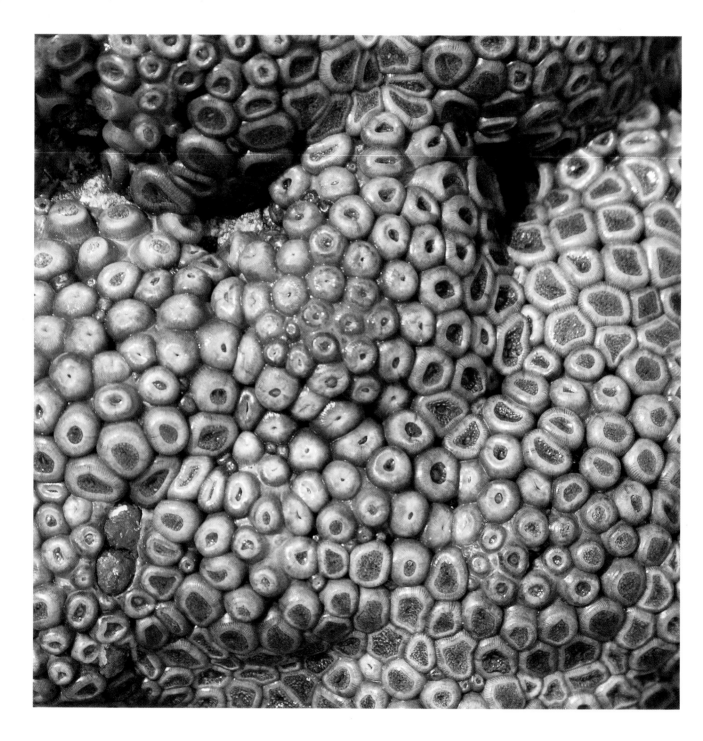

everyday travel
far west

California, Nevada, Utah

L os Angeles. Las Vegas. Salt Lake City. San Francisco. These are among the more popular tourist locales in the Far West. Yet some of the best times for families can be found in lesser-known venues.

Places like Sand Mountain, Nevada—a steep-hill haven for off-road vehicles about 85 miles west of Reno. Or the Thor's Hammer rock formation in Utah's Bryce Canyon National Park. Or the Hum-Boats of Humboldt County, offering kayaking along lagoons and lakes of the rugged area six hours north of San Francisco.

The Far West is home to a vast expanse of contrasts: mountains and valleys, wetlands and deserts, sun and snow, and superhighways like I-5 and the Nevada portion of Highway 50, coined in a 1986 *Life* magazine article as the "loneliest road" in America.

The area is so varied that most everyone seems to fit in, from transients to lifelong residents, beachcombers to mountaineers. Cultural diversity abounds, and big city ethnic communities are essential to the business of everyday life: San Francisco's Chinatown is equal parts tourism destination and preservation site for Asian traditions. Utah (named for the Ute people who originated here) is a hub of Native American historic sites and educational resources. The expanding Latino population in Nevada blends with age-old cowboy culture (and even older Native American traditions) for a unique influence on the region's foods, celebrations, and even politics.

In the Far West a friendly spirit prevails. The weather is usually beautiful. The lifestyle is free and easy. Local families have let us know about their favorite hiking trails, parks and playgrounds, farms and markets, ice cream spots, and neighborhood eateries, and they invite you to come visit soon!

> Ocean in view! O! The joy . . .
> —Capt. William Clark, November 7, 1805

ten best
parks & playgrounds

william land park

4000 S. Land Park Dr.
Sacramento, CA 95822
916-277-6060
www.cityofsacramento.org
www.fairytaletown.org

There is a nominal fee to enter Fairytale Town, a park-within-a-park featuring 25 different storybook-themed play sets in a lush 2.5-acre children's park. Or stroll to the zoo and monkey around on great playground equipment. There's a much-loved children's theater festival each September.

berkeley marina adventure playground

160 University Ave., Berkeley, CA 94710
510-981-6720 www.ci.berkeley.ca.us

A novel setting where kids sign in and get to work building, climbing, exploring, and creating. Materials, tools, and volunteer helpers are part of the experience. Popular in Europe, all three American Adventure Playgrounds are located in California.

The Golden Gate Bridge is one of the most distinctive landmarks in the world.

julius kahn playground

W. Pacific Ave. & Spruce St.
San Francisco, CA 94118, 415-292-2004, www.parks.sfgov.org

Great views of the city entertain adults while kids play on a climbing wall or in a water garden. It's close to the Presidio, a former military base and the nation's largest urban national park. The playground is managed by the city of San Francisco but located on the grounds of the historic Presidio. Locals refer to it as JK.

south beach playground

Embarcadero Pier 40 & AT&T Park
San Francisco, CA 94107

Children love the low-rolling climbing wall and climbing equipment. Water and marina views, plus proximity to two family-friendly coffee and sandwich shops make it nice for older visitors, too.

" **tom, california | outdoors** This happens all the time when we're hiking. On the trail we see adults decked out in the latest gear, special shoes, you name it. And here's my four-year-old, zipping up the hill in her sneakers and a windbreaker. That's all you need, really.

| **san francisco** Come to San Francisco! It's a great urban environment with diverse communities, easy public transportation (you don't need a car!), indoor and outdoor activities, and an unusual food and ethnic mix.

dennis the menace playground

Monterey Recreation Complex
777 Pearl St., Monterey, CA 93920
831-646-3866, www.monterey.org

Picture your family in the funny pages. Designed by comic creator Hank Ketchum, this playground has a famous hedge maze, great swings, and more. It's one of the most popular playground parks in California, drawing visitors from across the country. It's very close to the Monterey Bay Aquarium.

roxbury park

471 S. Roxbury Dr., Beverly Hills, CA 90210
310-285-6840, www.beverlyhills.org

Imagine mist rising among giant dinosaurs—that's the scene at the largest playground in the Beverly Hills area. Tennis and lawn bowling are nearby, so there's an activity for every age.

sand harbor

Lake Tahoe-Nevada State Park, 2005 Hwy. 28
Incline Village, NV 89450, 775-831-0494
www.aboutlaketahoe.com/beaches/sand-harbor.htm

It's the only state park on Lake Tahoe's Nevada side. Here families can picnic, hike, or go swimming and sunbathing in summer months.

. . . the play's the thing . . .

—William Shakespeare

mills park

IIII East William St.
Carson City, NV 89701

Everyone in the family can find something to do at Mills Park. There's an up-to-date playground, skateboard park, and, for a small fee, a miniature railroad train ride. Call ahead for train times. This is the site of the Pony Express Pavilion and its seasonal weekly farmers market.

sunset park

2601 E. Sunset Rd., Las Vegas, NV 89120
702-455-8225

Children under 12 do not need a fishing license to try for catfish or trout in this stocked pond (there is a three-fish limit, fishing in winter only). Playgrounds, a dog run, and picnic areas make it a great family spot.

liberty park

600 E. 1000 S. Salt Lake City, UT 84102
801-972-7800, www.slcgov.com

Especially for small children, the Seven Canyons water area is great for wading and splashing—located near the main playground. The Rotary Play area is especially designed for kids in wheelchairs, with water sprays and fountains.

ten best
farms & markets

apple hill family farm

2952 Carson Rd., Placerville, CA 95667, 530-622-5522
www.boavista.com

This working farm, located about an hour from Lake Tahoe, welcomes visitors year-round. A farm store offers baked goods and preserves, and you can pick your own fruit in season.

davis farmers market

Davis Central Park, 4th & C Sts., Davis, CA 95617
530-756-1695, www.davisfarmersmarket.org

There's live dancing at this farmer's market! There are also children's activities, cooking demonstrations, crafts . . . and lots of great farm vendors. Saturdays, year-round; Wednesdays, seasonally.

impossible acres

26565 Rd. 97D, Davis, CA 95616, 530-750-0451
www.impossibleacres.com

Northeast of the Napa region, this family-run farm has two locations: a pick-your-own stand and Grandpa's Barn, home to the farm's animals. There are hay rides, corn mazes, and other seasonal attractions.

When you start to open up a child's senses—when you invite children to engage, physically, with gardening and food—there is a set of values that is instilled effortlessly, that just washes over them, as part of the process of offering good food to other people. Children become so rapt . . . by being engaged in learning in a sensual, kinesthetic way.

—Alice Waters

aptos farmers market

Cabrillo College, 6500 Soquel Dr., Aptos, CA 95003, 831-728-5060, www.montereybayfarmers.org

Eighty-plus vendors, live music, and a close-to-the-beach location make this Saturday morning market a coastal California family tradition. There are four Monterey Bay Certified Farmers Markets; this website will link you to the others.

beverly hills farmers market

9300 block, Civic Center Dr., Beverly Hills, CA 310-550-4796, www.beverlyhills.org

Held on the second Sunday morning of each month, this market is close to neighborhood shops and restaurants, with pony rides and nutrition programs for kids.

day farms

500 W. Gentile St., West Layton, UT 84041
801-546-4316

April through October, Day Farms offers farm stand fruits and vegetables, plus pick-your-own

options in season. Honey is a natural resource in Utah, and this farm sells honey from local hives.

hillcrest farmers market

Normal St. between Lincoln & Cleveland Sts. San Diego, CA, 619-299-3330, www.hillquest.com

Families in San Diego go to Hillcrest Farmer's Market on Sunday mornings. Everything grows in San Diego, so everything seems to be in season. The kids can sit and watch a folk band play, and there's a fish stand, ethnic foods, jewelry and clothes vendors, local coffee, masseuse, and bread—a definite favorite.

salt lake city farmers market

Pioneer Park, 330 S. & 300 W., Salt Lake City, UT, 801-359-5118, www.slcfarmersmarket.org

Seventy farmers set up every Saturday morning June–October. You'll find bread, fish, meats, plants, and more. There's a bike valet to watch your wheels while you shop (located at the entrance to the market). It's a few blocks from the Discovery Gateway Children's Museum.

The central coast of California is called America's "salad bowl." Most of the lettuce (and broccoli, and artichokes . . .) eaten in the United States is grown here.

carson farmers market

Pony Express Pavilion, Hwy. 50, East Carson City, NV 775-746-5024, www.tahoe.com

On Wednesday evenings during the summer months, a miniature ride-on train travels around this local pavilion market (see the Mills Park listing on page 117).

lattin farms

1955 McLean Rd., Fallon, NV 89406, 866-638-6293 www.lattinfarms.com

Northern California, Nevada, and Utah are raspberry country. Pick your own here, where family events mark the changing seasons and a small petting zoo attracts the youngest visitors. September Goat Days include a goat obstacle course.

recipe | raspberry olives

Here's what you need:
• 12 fresh raspberries • 2 tablespoons soft cream cheese • 1 small plastic bag

Put the cream cheese in the plastic bag. Squish it toward one closed corner. Use scissors to snip away the point of the corner. Squeeze the bag to squirt a little cream cheese into the open end of each raspberry. Eat right away!

ten best
ice cream spots

screamin' mimi's

6902 Sebastopol Ave.
Sebastopol, CA 95472, 707-823-5902
www.screaminmimisicecream.com

Homemade, all natural ice cream is sold by weight at this Sonoma County favorite. Leave a tack on the map to show your own hometown. Parents appreciate the great cappuccino, by the way.

gunther's quality ice cream

2801 Franklin Blvd., Sacramento,
CA 95818, 916-457-6646

A small diner and ice cream parlor with a menu featuring sandwiches, soups, and (mostly) homemade ice cream. It's not far to William Land Park and the storybook settings of its fun Fairytale Town.

blenders in the grass

720 State St., Santa Barbara, CA 95101, 805-683-5858
www.drinkblenders.com

OK—there is no ice cream here. But creamy yogurt smoothies do the trick in beautiful health-conscious Santa Barbara, and this place has an ever changing rainbow of choices. Try anything with flavorful acai pulp, made from organically grown Brazilian

Food historians say that the Chinese created the first ice cream—possibly as early as 3000 B.C.

berries, or wheatgrass for an extra burst of energy.

hatch family chocolates

390 4th Ave., Salt Lake City, UT 84103
801-532-4912

Top your sundae with caramel made from a secret family recipe. This upscale confectionary also serves up coffee, plus plenty of candy for the ride home.

mootime creamery

1025 Orange Ave., Coronado,
CA 92118, 619-435-2422
www.mootime.com

Worth the trip by ferry or over the bridge from San Diego to the old-fashioned island town of Coronado. There are two locations here: one on lovely Orange Avenue, perfect for strolling and window shopping. The second is inside the historic Hotel del Coronado. Get a cone here and head out to the beach at sunset.

death valley nut & candy co.

900 E. Hwy. 95 N., Beatty, NV 89003, 775-553-2100
An incomparable road-trip stop on the highway between Arizona and California, this

over-the-top confectionery is just outside Death Valley National Park. Chocolate-covered gummy bears or homemade ice cream? You choose.

neilsen's frozen custard

570 West 2600, Bountiful, UT 84010, 801-292-7479

Utah-style custard is served as solid as possible, scooped into smooth creamy servings in a style called concrete (something like a super-thick shake). Chocolate and vanilla are available every day, plus an additional flavor that changes daily.

rosemary's family creamery

2733 F St., Bakersfield, CA 93301, 661-395-0555

This place does a big lunch business but is most famous for made-here ice cream and its own amazing sauces: chocolate, caramel, and much more. They even make their own whipped cream. It's not far from the Kern County Museum, which has a renowned children's discovery center and frontier life education program.

California is ranked #1 in the U.S. for the production of fluid milk, butter, ice cream, and nonfat dry milk.

mashti malone's ice cream

1525 N. La Brea Ave.
Los Angeles, CA 90028
866-767-3423
www.mashtimalones.com

After-school hangout for Hollywood preschool and elementary set with flavors like Herbal Snow or *Faludeh* (rose sorbet with sour cherry). In deference to the family's ice-treat making heritage, the owners are proud to announce that their recipes are "2,500 years in the making."

bi-rite creamery

3692 18th St., San Francisco, CA 94110
415-626-5600, www.biritecreamery.com

Try this place on weekdays, at midday. The lines on weekends can be intimidating for families. But once you're here, try the real fruit popsicles and an ice cream sandwich (or two). The menu changes regularly. They use local, organic ingredients.

" frank, virginia | **melting** On this day, I was driving our old white station wagon. Stopped for a "refreshing" cone. On the road again. Car windows open. No air-conditioning. Car up to speed on the highway. Looked in the rearview mirror. Hot-air wind from car motion blowing in. Ice cream melting. Children serenely licking cones. White coating of ice cream on all faces and also on shirts and seatbacks around their heads. Six blue eyes looking out from all white face coating. No expressions other than contentment with the ice cream and some (but not intense) effort to stay ahead of the melting process. Wish I had a camera. Hilarious to me at the time, but precious to me now in my memory.

ten best
regional specialties

asian food
**Eastern Empire, 460 Howe Ave.
Sacramento, CA 95825, 916-646-1698**

Parents love the Chinese and Polynesian menu offerings, and so do children. But at this place, atmosphere adds to the experience. You'll all remember the Buddha statue and fish fountain.

basque food
**The Star Hotel, 405 Silver St.
Elko, NV 89801, 775-738-9691**

Descendants of French and Spanish shepherds and farmers live in northern California and Nevada. Come here for large family-style servings of traditional Basque dishes

like cabbage and vegetable soup, lamb with chile and peppers, and the tenderest of steak sandwiches.

Asian cuisine is the umbrella term for a variety of South, East, and Southeast Asian dishes and fusion recipes. All will warm your soul.

bison burger
**Antelope Island State Park
4528 West 1700 South, Syracuse,
UT 84075, 801-652-2043, www.utah.
com/stateparks/antelope_island.**

Served at the café and food service stands of this spectacular state park, where the herds of wild buffalo are rounded up for observation every fall. There's also a great beach where kids can float in the Great Salt Lake.

fish stew
**Little Joe's, 50 Mission St.
San Francisco, CA 94103
415-433-4343**

Some call it cioppino. At Little Joe's it's caciuco—a spicy stew of shellfish, fish, and more. It's on the menu all year-round, but locals say it's best when crab is in season. There's a second location on 5th Street; reservations are recommended for either place.

❝ grace, california | car trips As a kid, I loved our Sunday afternoon drives. We'd head out toward the shoreline and my dad would narrate: There's a hawk on a branch overhead, a turtle by the side of the road! He'd notice that seagulls always face into the wind, or an osprey carries its catch face-forward. Now I do the same thing with my own family.

date shakes

Ruby's Shake Shack, 7408 Coast Hwy.
Newport Beach, CA 92657, 949-464-0100

Almost all of the dates grown in the United States come from southern California. Stop at a beachfront shack and try a creamy shake with dates and ice cream whipped together.

dungeness crabs

Captain Kidd's, 209 N. Harbor Dr., Redondo Beach,
CA 90277, 310-372-7703 www.captainkidds.com

Wait in line with local families for Dungeness crab when it's in season (September–March). You pick your own fresh seafood from a display case here

at this casual and affordable eatery. Even when Dungeness isn't in season, come for ocean views and terrific fish tacos. There's also a great "Kidd's" menu here.

fish tacos

Rubio's Fresh Mexican Grill, 4504 E. Mission Bay Dr.
San Diego, CA 92109, 858-272-2801, www.rubios.com

Southern California families love this fast-food chain (famous for fish tacos). You can order beer, and they usually have an aquarium. You'll get a kick out of watching fish while eating fish! They have kids' meals with a little toy. There are several locations for this popular franchise—this one is located in San Diego's Mission Bay.

fry sauce

Arctic Circle, 9th South, 135 East 900 South
Salt Lake City, UT 84111

Made famous during the 2002 Winter Olympics, this pink dipping sauce was "invented" at a popular Utah dining shop. This location is in the heart of Salt Lake City. It's used for dipping French fries and other fast-food menu items. The secret recipe is said to consist of ketchup and mayonnaise.

sourdough

Boudin's Demonstration Bakery, 160 Jefferson St.
San Francisco, CA 94133, 415-928-1849
www.boudinbakery.com

Miners and cowboys "stored" yeast in leftover dough. It was used to make bread that the region is famous for today. Here's a convenient spot to see, smell, and taste sourdough baking at its best. Legend has it that the foggy, hilly terrain of San Francisco traps yeast spores in the air—part of the city's "secret recipe" for great sourdough bread.

native american

Navajo Hogan, 447 East 3300 South, South Salt Lake
City, UT 84115, 801-466-2860, www.navajohogan.com

Try fry bread in savory or sweet renditions. The menu here is a mix of Native American, Mexican, and New Mexican offerings, and it's really popular with visitors and local families.

Fajitas are a great choice for sampling local produce with a regional flair.

everyday travel
southwest

Arizona, New Mexico

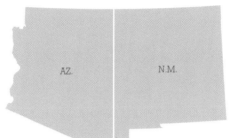

AZ.　　　N.M.

Think Southwest and two times of day come to mind: sunrise and sunset. Tourists flock to the spectacular views of both, particularly over Arizona's Grand Canyon and New Mexico's Sangre de Cristo Mountains, the southernmost portion of the Rockies. Yet families here know that there's much to be seen and explored anytime in the land of breathtaking landscapes.

The Southwest is rich in centuries-old Native American and Hispanic American culture. A must-see is the Aztec Ruins National Park, a preservation of ancient Pueblo structures that dates back to the 11th century.

Meanwhile, Santa Fe, New Mexico's capital, is well known for its diverse arts scene; a high concentration of artists captures the land's beauty in paint and clay. Undoubtedly, many draw inspiration from Chacon Canyon, a multicolored desert range.

> Yet America is a poem in our eyes; its ample geography dazzles the imagination . . .
>
> —Ralph Waldo Emerson

You'll discover that the region is a throwback to the Old West. Modern-day cowboys carry on traditions from that period with some of the world's most renowned rodeos, including the World's Oldest Rodeo in Prescott, Arizona (dating back to 1888).

But the focal point of this region is the Grand Canyon, the majestic gorge carved by the Colorado River that is one of the seven natural wonders of the world. At the foot of the canyon is Havasupai, the only place in the United States where mail is still delivered by mule.

The smells, sounds, and colors of this part of the country are truly remarkable. Once you have experienced the Southwest it becomes a part of you, and you will always long to go back someday. It goes with the territory: Folks here will tell you that unique sights, scenes, and sounds are something of an everyday occurrence in this remarkable part of the country.

ten best
parks & playgrounds

sahuaro ranch park

9802 N. 59th Ave., Glendale, AZ 85302
623-930-2820, www.glendaleaz.com

This 16-acre park sprawls across the grounds of an original ranch, with historic homes open for tours. Today it's also home to a nice playground, and original fruit orchards provide shade for picnics and playtime. Watch for the famous peacocks, rabbits, and chickens making their homes here, too.

red mountain park

7745 E. Brown Rd., Mesa, AZ 85307
480-644-2351, www.cityofmesa.org

Just off the Red Mountain Freeway, this park is popular for its playgrounds, lake, and lighted basketball court. Other accommodations include rest rooms and ramada shelters providing shade for picnics. It's clear how this place got its name. There are beautiful mountain views from here, and lots of community activity with recreation sports leagues.

posse ground park

525 Posse Ground Rd., Sedona, AZ 86336
928-282-7098, www.sedonaaz.gov

See the famous Red Rocks geological formations from the comfort of a friendly playground! Locals

You won't believe your eyes when you see Native American ruins for the first time. Architecture, art, and life take on new meaning.

report spectacular views from here. Extras are a skate park, batting cages, community pool, and natural foods store nearby. No signs at the entrance: Get there by heading up the road at the Ace Hardware sign. It's also the site of an annual Easter egg hunt and the Scrapture Festival, where sculpture is created from scraps. Watch for the occasional red dirt music festival, celebrating this increasingly popular contemporary country genre.

burton barr central library

1221 N. Central Ave., Phoenix, AZ 85004, 602-262-4636
www.phoenixpubliclibrary.org

Families are proud of the main library in downtown Phoenix. The exterior echoes a copper-colored mesa, and inside are glass elevators and a reflecting pool in the Crystal Canyon, a five-story atrium. The collection is fully integrated with Spanish

> Check the surface temperature of playground equipment before your child touches seats, handles, or bars. Look for playgrounds with water fountains, ramadas, or other shade shelters.

language materials, and the adapted computer equipment in the Special Needs Center makes it a model for libraries across the country.

salvador perez park

601 Alta Vista St., Santa Fe, NM 87505
505-955-2100, www.santafenm.gov

This park is memorable because of the enormous old coal-fired locomotive engine at the entrance. You'll also find a great playground, ball fields, and picnic facilities, plus a whimsical 15-foot giraffe sculpture.

los altos park

10103 Lomas Blvd., NE, Albuquerque, NM 87112
505-291-6239, www.cabq.gov

Just off I-40, this 32-acre park is a great place for traveling families to stop and stretch their legs. It's adjacent to a big municipal skate park that's open to BMX bikes, skateboards, and inline skates.

cox splash playground

Tempe Beach Park, 80 W. Rio Salado Pkwy., Tempe, AZ 85281
480-350-8625, www.tempe.gov

Free! One acre water playground filled with mist, "rain," and even a two-inch-deep ocean complete with ride-on whales. A second free water play-space, the Jaycee Park Splash Playground, is located near the Westside Community Center at 5th Street and Hardy Drive.

Weather is an adventure in itself. Notice clouds, heat-waves, breezes. Get umbrellas for everyone and use them.

twirl toystore & playspace

225 Camino de la Placita, Taos, NM 87571
575-751-1402, www.twirlhouse.com

This toy store has an imaginative outdoor play area with a pirate ship, playhouse, slide, and more. The shop also offers drop-in, fee-based activities for children of different ages, all housed in a lovely 150-year-old adobe building. Their website directs visitors to a host of fun Taos activities.

hyde memorial state park

740 Hyde Park Rd., Santa Fe, NM 87501
505-983-7175, www.emnrd.state.nm.us

This is a popular destination for local families, located 7.5 miles from Ski Santa Fe. It's a great way to explore the local terrain at an easier pace and away from crowds. Here you'll find a tube run, cross-country and hiking trails, and camping facilities in this beautiful Santa Fe state park.

carlsbad riverwalk

Carlsbad, NM 88220, 505-887-6516
www.cityofcarlsbadnm.com

A 6.5-mile pathway runs along both sides of the Pecos River. It's a place for family exercise or a refreshing rest stop just north of the Texas border and about 16 miles from Carlsbad Caverns. Cross the river at a floating bridge near a playground.

ten best
farms & markets

the farm at south mountain

6106 S. 32nd St., Phoenix, AZ 85042
602-276-6360
www.thefarmatsouthmountain.com

Three restaurants are clustered in this pecan grove, and families can eat outside and stroll the grounds of the small farm area. It's especially nice at lunchtime, with sandwiches and picnic fare available at the Farm Kitchen. Closed each summer.

downtown phoenix public market

721 N. Central Ave., Phoenix, AZ 85004
www.downtownphoenixpublicmarket.com

A year-round outdoor market offers a wealth of just-harvested and prepared foods almost exclusively from Arizona farms. The market focuses on food choices based on local availability, open on Wednesday evenings and Saturday mornings.

New Mexico's Rail Runner Express connects Albuquerque with Santa Fe's downtown Railyard and many other locations in the region: www.nmrailrunner.com

Giant saguaro cactus can grow up to 50 feet tall. They store enormous amounts of water for times of drought.

tolmachoff farms

5726 N. 75th Ave., Glendale, AZ 85303
623-386-1301, www.tolmachoff-farms.com

The farm welcomes visitors to pick vegetables depending on what's in season, usually beginning in early June. It's also a great play day destination for families, with seasonal children's events and "back of the farm" tours for a small fee.

schnepf farm

24810 S. Rittenhouse Rd.
Queen Creek, AZ 85242, 480-987-3100
www.schnepffarms.com

In the fall you can pick your own pumpkins and sunflowers; summer is peach season. This farm, restaurant, and gift shop is dedicated to sharing farm traditions with visiting families. It's open to the public October–December and April–June.

mother nature's farm

1663 E. Baseline Rd., Gilbert, AZ 85233, 480-892-5874
www.mothernaturesfarm.com

Introduce children to the work and wonder of growing fruits and vegetables. Apples, peaches, corn, and other vegetables are grown here. It's also a "dig-your-own" Christmas tree farm.

salman raspberry ranch

Junction NM 518 & 442
La Cueva, NM, 866-281-1515
www.salmanraspberryranch.com

Make a day of it and drive out to this historic district between Taos and Santa Fe. Call ahead to be sure that raspberries are in season—usually available for picking from August to October. A seasonal café features kid favorites like tamales and ice cream with raspberry topping.

los poblanos inn & cultural center

4803 Rio Grande Blvd., NW, Los Ranchos, NM 87107
866-344-9297, www.lospoblanos.com

Seven miles from Albuquerque, this resort is home to an organic farm, a lavender farm, and formal gardens, plus great accommodations for families. A weekly growers' market is held in town every Saturday morning.

santa fe farmers market

Railyard District
Paseo de Peralta, NM
505-983-4098
www.santafefarmersmarket.com

A brand new building houses an indoor/outdoor market (completely

Quien a buen arbol se arrima, buena sombra la cobija.

An old oak gives the best shade.

—Spanish proverb

outdoors in good weather). Located in the historic Railyard District, the facility was built to minimize environmental impact.

red willow farmers market

Red Willow Center, 885 Star Rd.
Taos, NM, 575-758-1028, www.taospueblo.com

Taos Pueblo was built more than 1,000 years ago by the predecessors of the people who live there today. There's a Sunday market from June through October, housed in a traditional native-built structure on the road to the historic pueblo. Only native vendors can sell here. Don't miss the horno-baked breads fired in outdoor clay ovens.

new mexico farm & ranch museum

4100 Dripping Springs Rd.
Las Cruces, NM 88011
575-522-4100
www.nmfarmandranchmuseum.org

Explore 3,000 years of farmwork, with daily demonstrations of milking, cattle herding, and crop tending. Call ahead for scheduled spinning and weaving, cooking, blacksmithing, and quilting presentations at this 47-acre hands-on museum.

ten best
ice cream spots

sugar bowl ice cream parlor

4005 N. Scottsdale Rd., Scottsdale, AZ 85251, 480-946-0051
www.sugarbowlscottsdale.com

Family Circus fans will recognize this as the local ice cream shop. Cartoonist Bil Keane was a neighbor of the original owner. The décor has lasted since 1958, with a pink checkerboard linoleum floor, marble tabletops, and an old-fashioned soda fountain.

gelato spot

3164 E. Camelback Rd. Phoenix, AZ 85016
602-957-8040, www.gelatospot.com

A sophisticated place to cool your heels with three other locations in southern Arizona. Older kids love the fancy lounge atmosphere. Everyone appreciates 150 rotating flavors: 36 available each day. Shaded patios are heated or misted (or both) to keep everyone comfortable, no matter what the weather.

[
Some ice cream shops in the Southwest keep a shaker of chile powder on the counter. Give it a try on a scoop of chocolate.
]

THE FAMILY CIRCUS   By Bil Keane

"Mmm! Mommy! I wish you could get a job in there!"

berry ocean gelato & espresso

4410 Wyoming Blvd., NE Albuquerque, NM 87111
505-294-5506, www.berryocean.com

Fresh-made gelato and soft-serve yogurt are made using only organic milk products. Organic coffee is brewed fresh all day.

mary coyle ol' fashion ice cream parlor

5521 N. Seventh Ave., Phoenix, AZ 85013
602-265-0405, www.marycoyle.net

Can your family polish off seven pounds of ice cream? This traditional ice cream parlor offers the Mountain, among other memorable sundae treats. Soups and sandwiches are also on the menu.

coldstone creamery

3330 S. McClintock Dr., Tempe, AZ 85282
480-491-1331, www.coldstonecreamery.com

Here's the one and only original location of this hugely popular franchise, now with locations all across the country. Choose toppings and mixers, and then servers will blend your own unique flavors. As always, the servers break into song when you leave a tip.

austin's old fashioned ice cream

6129 E. Broadway Blvd., Tucson, AZ 85711, 520-514-5132

Stop in for an inexpensive lunch and save room for the giant ice cream creations. A family reports that this place is virtually unchanged since it opened in 1959.

taos cow scoop shop & deli

Arroyo Seco, NM 87514, 505-776-5640
www.taoscow.com

This village is home to craftspeople and artisans, plus wonderful homemade ice cream. Stop here if you're driving anywhere near Taos Mountain (there's another location in Santa Fe). Flavors change regularly: try Piñon Caramel or Holstein Sunset.

paleteria michoana de paquim

6500 Zuni Rd., SE, Albuquerque, NM 87108, 505-266-3408

The Southwest celebrates refreshing fruit flavors at *paleterias* like these. If you can speak a little Spanish, try it here. Kids will love pondering the choices of these fruit, cream, and even vegetable-inspired frozen confections. You'll be ordering a *paleta*—frozen juice or pulp on a stick. In fact, the word paleta is rooted in *palo*, the Spanish word for "stick." Try cucumber chile or lime.

caliches

590 S. Valley Dr., Las Cruces, NM 88005, 505-647-5066
www.caliches.com

Try frozen custard from the retrostyle drive-through. This is a family-owned hometown favorite, and there are several locations in Las Cruces. Just so you know, it's pronounced ka-LEE-ches. The name comes from the Spanish word for "hard earth." It's a nod to the midwestern use of the word concrete to describe really dense frozen custard. They also offer their own style of Italian ice, called Desert Ice. Look for the retro-style neon signs and you're there.

tara's organic ice cream

1807 Second St., Santa Fe, NM 87507 505-216-9759, www.tarasorganic.com

It all started with a home ice cream maker. A young woman named Tara started making her own ice cream and then got the big idea to open Santa Fe's first organic ice cream store. Now, at any given time you can find an amazing variety of flavors like orange cashew, basil, lavender, a bunch of different chocolates, and vanilla. All products are certified organic. Insiders suggest you try an organic ice cream brownie sandwich. Tara's is served at restaurants across New Mexico, and there is another location in Berkeley, California.

ten best
regional specialties

agua fresca

Pro's Ranch Market, 4201 Central Ave.
Albuquerque, NM 87105
505-833-1765, www.prosranch.com

A traditional flavor is hibiscus flower (*jamaica* in Spanish). Other "refreshment waters" are made with watermelon, lemon, and even rice. This Hispanic grocery store chain is known for its variety of *agua fresca* (pronounced a-GWA FRES-ka) and its fun carnival atmosphere.

green chile cheeseburger

Michael's Kitchen, 304 N. Paseo Del Pueblo, Taos, NM 8757, 505-758-4178
www.michaelskitchen.com

Legend has it that chuckwagon chefs used hot chiles to hide bad food flavors. Today piles of chiles are the sign of a true southwestern burger. This spot is within walking distance of historic Taos Plaza.

horchata

Mosaic Café, 2455 N. Silverbell Rd., Tucson, AZ 85745
520-624-4512

A traditional Mexican drink made by soaking rice or melon seeds, then adding almond, sugar, and cinnamon—served over ice. Here it's made fresh

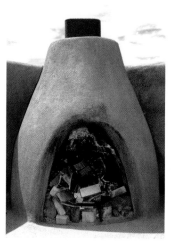

The kiva fireplace is true southwest design. These "beehive" ovens are perfect for baking and roasting.

every day along with homemade lemonade.

navajo taco

Arizona Native Frybread
1437 E. Main St., Mesa, AZ 85203
480-649-1314
www.aznativefrybread.com

Southwestern comfort food: fry bread topped with whole pinto beans, vegetables, and cheese (if the beans are mashed, it's an Apache taco). Native American–owned, this place has a great kids' menu (try a child-size bowl of hominy stew with a side of applesauce).

piñon nuts

Senor Murphy Candymaker, La Fonda Hotel, 100 E. San Francisco St., Santa Fe, NM 87501
505-982-0461, www.senormurphy.com

Piñon trees grow wild and produce nuts once every seven years. Piñoneros pick up the tiny nuts that fall to the ground, then sell them to a New Mexican roaster. Here they're turned into amazing candies like chile piñon brittle.

posole

Garduno's of Mexico, 8787 N. Scottsdale Rd., Scottsdale, AZ 85253 480-607-9222, www.gardunosofarizona.com

Made before the time of European explorers, this rich chile soup used to be made with a pig's head. Most places now use pork or chicken. The childrens' menu here comes highly recommended.

quesadillas

Dragonfly Café, 402 Paseo del Pueblo Norte, Taos, NM 87571, 505-737-5859, www.dragonflytaos.com

Now as familiar as grilled cheese sandwiches, quesadillas started in this region. They're on the kids' menu here, and there's an enclosed play space outside. Adults love the imaginative menu, adobe fireplace, and affordable prices.

sopaipillas

Macayo's Mexican Kitchen, 4001 N. Central Ave. Phoenix, AZ 85012, 602-264-6141, www.macayo.com

Fried pillows of dough are a special occasion food for local families. Here children can order beef-filled sopaipillas for dinner, then order another round drizzled with honey for dessert.

zuni bread

Paywa's Zuni Bread House, 11A Paywa Rd., Zuni, NM 87372 505-782-4849 www.zunitourism.com

Family bakers use outdoor ovens in the Zuni tradition (first introduced by Spanish explorers). Open on Wednesdays, Thursdays, and Fridays, this place makes breads primarily for Zuni, and nearby Navajo native communities.

tortillas

Phoenix Ranch Market 1602 E. Roosevelt St., Phoenix, AZ 85006 602-254-6676, www.prosranch.com

Corn and flour tortillas are the "bread" of southwestern pre-Columbian cultures. This market is a grocery store and carryout food court where you can see thousands of tortillas being made by hand. The Tortilleria has demo stations where you can taste regional cheeses, toppings, and breads that define this region.

[The Aztecs called their tortillas by the name *tlaxcalli*. The *maiza* (corn) version is the original North American tortilla.]

hawaii

Hawaii, Kauai, Maui, Oahu

Hawaii: The name is synonymous with sun, sand, surf, and sea. For the family that loves a day at the beach—and what family doesn't?—there is arguably no place in the country that is more inviting. But the seaside is just the beginning to exploring this land of 137 islands (only seven are inhabited), exotic sea life, and virtually every geographical terrain and climate. The Big Island (Hawaii) is home to not only the longest continuously erupting volcano in recorded history (Kilauea Caldera, which has been spouting lava since 1983), but also two of its mountain summits, snow-capped Mauna Kea and Mauna Loa. The island Kauai has rain forests, while Molokai comprises sea cliffs.

Then there's Diamond Head, the renowned, 760-foot volcanic crater on the island Oahu that features a 225-foot tunnel. It draws hikers and climbers from all over the world. For beach lovers, it scarcely gets better than nearby Waikiki, a neighborhood of the state's capital, Honolulu, that is the focal point of the state's tourism.

There's never a bad time to visit these venues. Climate is Hawaii's calling card: equal lengths of sunlight year-round, an average annual temperature of 75°F (slight variations depending on altitude), with intermittent showers and cooling trade winds.

And, despite being the most geographically isolated people on Earth—closer to the Marshall Islands (2,000 miles) than the nearest U.S. state, California (2,390)—Hawaii's residents are among the world's friendliest, welcoming visitors to their diverse cultures and cuisines. Among the more popular foods are *loco moco* (a hamburger patty on white rice with a fried egg and brown gravy) and *haupia* (a congealed coconut-milk dessert).

Here are some things to do in sunny Hawaii. Aloha!

HI.

> . . . the loveliest fleet of islands that lies anchored in any ocean . . .
>
> —Mark Twain

135

ten best
hawaii

poipu beach park, kauai

Poipu Rd. & Hoowi Rd., Kauai
South Shore, HI, 800-262-1400
www.kauai-hawaii.com

This beautiful destination is one of many beach areas on Kauai's south shore, a 30-minute drive from Lihue and the airport. It's on many "best beaches" lists for families, with boogie boards and snorkeling equipment available for daily rental.

Perhaps the most amazing thing you will ever see is a Hawaiian sunset over the ocean.

[When Hawaiian friends hang out and chat, it's called "talk story."]

waikiki beach, oahu

Pacific Soul Surfing, 2055
Kalia Rd., Honolulu, HI
96815, 808-942-4544,
www.pacific-soul.com

Visiting kids arrive at Waikiki eager to surf, and this shop and surf school is a great introduction to the beach and waters of the famous shoreline. You can also rent surfboards, learn more about water safety, and meet local surfers here.

baby beach, maui

Front St. & Puunoa Pl., Lahaina, HI 96761
808-270-7626, www.co.maui.hi.us

H. A. Baldwin Beach Park is one of east Maui's

most beautiful (and popular). At its west end, families bring kids to an area nicknamed Baby Beach for its protective reef and lagoon. Lifeguards are on duty, and public rest rooms are available.

'iao valley state monument, maui

End of Hwy. 32, 'Iao Valley,
HI, 808-984-8109
www.hawaiistateparks.org

It is a pretty well-known spot for tourists to visit, but that's for a reason. It is a beautiful place with waterfalls, little hikes (good for the kids), and little gardens. In 'Iao Valley, there is a bunch of koi ponds and bridges that children love to walk around and explore.

sunshine markets, kauai

Hanapepe Park, Kauai, HI 96716, 808-241-4946
www.kauai.gov

Wonderful farmer's markets are held in different locations each day but Sunday. Visit here on Thursdays for fresh produce, flowers, and other farm products. Look for tree-ripened bananas and fresh papayas. Bonus: It's not far from Salt Pond Beach Park. This is a quietly popular local beach where you

may see local families mining salt along the bay ponds. Mining rights are passed down from generation to generation.

tropical farms, oahu

49-227A Kamehameha Hwy., Kaaawa, HI 96730
808-237-1960

On the windward side of Oahu, this lovely local market offers the best of Honolulu County produce. On your way there you'll pass the Waikane Fruit Stand. If the Coconut Juice sign is up, stop for a chilled and fresh-drilled coconut and sip the milk through a straw.

matsumoto shave ice, oahu

66-087 Kamehameha Hwy., Haleiwa, HI 96712
808-637-4827, www.matsumotoshaveice.com

Locals and tourists alike line up for shave ice at this family-run operation, in business since 1951. Ask for azuki beans in the bottom of the paper serving cone. These sweetened red beans are reminders of the many Japanese influences on Hawaiian culture.

da kine 'ono grinds, all islands

Fran's Island Grill, 740 Lower Main St.
Wailuku, HI 96783, 808-242-8580

This Hawaiian phrase means "good food" or "delicious food," and usually refers to locally owned places with traditional foods. Here on Maui, this small place serves breakfast all day.

spam, all islands

7-11 Stores, www.7-eleven.com (check "store locator")

Hawaiians buy more of this pink canned meat than anyone in America. It's a popular breakfast ingredient, and also available in familiar convenience stores as *musubi*, a sushi-like presentation served cold with rice and seaweed.

dole plantation

64-1550 Kamehameha Hwy., Oahu, HI
808-621-8408, www.dole-plantation.com

This is an all-day adventure, with a train ride through the working pineapple fields, great North Shore views, garden tours, and the world's largest maze. Some say that it's worth the trip just for a taste of the famous pineapple Dole Whip. Insider tip: You can also get this treat at Honolulu International Airport.

" **karen, massachusetts | dole whip** It looks like soft-serve ice cream when it comes out of the machine topped on a simple cone. Pale yellow, silky in texture, just the right mix of tart and sweetness—as if a fresh pineapple had been pureed then frozen—I was eight and it was the best thing I had ever put in my mouth.

everyday travel
alaska

As its state motto says, Alaska is the United States' Last Frontier, a land that beckons those with a spirit of adventure.

It is an area nearly one-fifth the size of the rest of the country, mainly covered in ice, with bone-cold winters and hot summers. It is the only state that borders another country (Canada) but not another state. It has more coastline than all the other states combined. It is closer to Russia than any part of the United States, and many of Alaska's municipalities—including the state capital, Juneau—are accessible only by air or water.

Alaska is filled with some of the nation's most exotic wildlife. It is normal to spot a moose in a schoolyard, grizzly bear cubs in the woods, humpback whales along fjords, and sled dogs pulling a heavy load over frozen snow. Bald eagles, gray wolves, lynx, and polar bears roam like squirrels and pigeons in Central Park. Thus, Alaskans foster an appreciation for the

> To the lover of pure wildness, Alaska is one of the most wonderful countries in the world.
>
> —John Muir

environment that is passed from one generation to the next. Family activities are centered on nature, from fishing to hiking to wildlife viewing. Annual whale hunts preserve traditional ways of acquiring food, fuel, and other resources.

The state offers a cultural diversity not seen in many other states; it has America's largest Native American population (16 percent) and eleven cultural groups. An outpost of Russian influence exists at the far reaches of the Aleutian Islands, home to an Orthodox cathedral that holds one of the largest collections of religious artifacts in the United States. Traditional dance, woodcarving, and drumming are some of the many unique art forms found in the state. Alaska is a haven for ice art, and to many, Alaska is synonymous with some of the world's premier dogsled races.

Here are a few things to do when vacationing in Alaska.

ten best
alaska

north pole playground

City of North Pole, 125 Snowman La. North Pole, AK 99705, 907-488-2281
www.northpolealaska.com

It's actually 140 miles south of the Arctic Circle, but you can visit Santa Claus year-round in this small town near Fairbanks. Streetlights are painted like candy canes and a holiday mood prevails, even in summer when temperatures reach 95°F. You can be a landowner; buy one square inch of land, located near the playground within the town's popular Terry Miller Park on 5th Avenue.

pioneer park

2300 Airport Way, Fairbanks, AK 99701
907-459-1087, www.co.fairbanks.ak.us

Ride the Crooked Creek Railroad for a view of the whole historic park (including museums, restaurants, and shops), then try Red & Roela's Carousel. There's an information booth where you can borrow bocce balls or horseshoes.

valley of the moon park

1748 H St., Anchorage, AK 99501
907-343-4355, www.muni.org

A whale breaching out of the water will leave you speechless. Its huge size and beauty will astound you.

This playground park is near the Chester Creek Greenbelt trail (a four-mile pathway from Westchester Lagoon to Goose Lake Park). It's close to downtown, with a rocket-themed slide and plenty of places for a picnic.

light speed planet walk

Starting point: 737 W. 5th Ave. Anchorage, AK 99501
907-677-8629
www.anchorageplanetwalk.org

This 11-mile walk begins downtown at a giant tile mosaic representing the sun. From there you can follow a path representing a scale model of the solar system, traveling partway along the Tony Knowles Coastal Trail and ending 5½ hours later at Pluto (in Kincaid Park, known for views of Mount McKinley).

totem bight state historical park

9883 N. Tongass Hwy., Ketchikan, AK 99901
907-465-4563, www.dnr.state.ak.us

This state park, located on the Tongass Narrows, is a convenient stop for cruise ships. It's one of the state's best places to see totem poles, created by native clans to share the stories of their families.

tanana valley farmers market

2600 College Rd., Fairbanks, AK, 907-456-3276

Central Alaska has a growing season of only about three months, so families are eager to make the most of the chance to grow produce and flowers, then meet up at the market to sell, share, and meet visitors. This fun market is held on summer Saturdays and Wednesdays.

anchorage market & festival

300 C St., Anchorage, AK 99501, 907-272-5634
www.anchoragemarkets.com

Local youth set up shop in the Kids Market tent at this summer weekend market. Here they can sell their own homegrown or handcrafted goods. Look for the Eat Local section, with all-Alaska produce and prepared foods.

hot licks homemade ice cream

1521 S. Cushman St. (inside the Quality Inn), Fairbanks, AK 99701, 907-479-7813 • 1571 Nelchina St. Anchorage, AK 99501, 907-929-5425, www.hotlicks.net

Dairy cows are in short supply in Alaska. Hot Licks makes ice cream with hormone free cream from Oregon. One favorite flavor: Aurora borealis has cranberry and blueberry purees swirled in vanilla ice cream.

salmon bake

Alaska Salmon Bake, Pioneer Park, Fairbanks, AK 99701
907-452-7274, www.akvisit.com

Alaskan-caught salmon, halibut, and cod are cooked outdoors over wood-burning grills. This place is open from mid-May through mid-September—one of the many visitor attractions of Pioneer Park (see page 140). It's an easy and fun way for families to enjoy fresh seafood in an inviting outdoor setting.

wild berries

Alaska Wild Berry Park, 5225 Juneau St. Anchorage, AK 99518, 907-562-8858
www.alaskawildberryproducts.com

Wild blueberries, raspberries, and even watermelon berries can be found in summer months, but pickers should educate themselves about toxic look-alikes. Here's one safe alternative, where visitors can see jam, jelly, and candy being made from locally picked wild fruit. This small amusement park is a fun setting for families with young children.

" judith, alaska | **getting around** One very useful product here in Alaska that we use as a travel bible/survival info is the Milepost. It comes out every year and describes everything on the road system in great detail. www.milepost.com

family vacations

ime to pack the bags; a world of family travel awaits. There are mountains to climb, slopes to ski, double-decker buses to ride, and roller coasters to scream upon.

Need a reason to get going? Try an anniversary, a birthday, a graduation. Or perhaps the simplest, and maybe the best, reason of all: because it's been a while since the family has vacationed together.

By stepping away from everyday schedules and responsibilities, parents and kids can turn their attention and energy to one another. And what can be more memorable for a child than seeing dad perched on a carousel pony or mom on a snowboard?

There's a plethora of entertainment options, and of course many "brand name" sites come to mind: Disney, Six Flags, Carnival. But that's just a small sampling of what's out there. And this does not even begin to account for all of the amazing back roads adventures, tours, and expeditions. The great outdoors can provide a

You'll always be glad you had this time together.

backdrop for vacations of a lifetime, where families can take a collective deep breath as they explore mountains, forests, and wide-open coastlines.

Vacations can also serve as opportunities for extended families to get together, including aunts, uncles, cousins, and in-laws. Nowadays, many vacation packages include family reunions and family heritage destinations. It is such a pleasure when families come together to catch up, meet one another for the first time, or simply gather to listen to all of the stories.

This chapter is divided into sections appealing to different tastes, interests, reasons, and seasons for vacations: family reunions (including great places to hold them), shorelines and beaches, sports, great outdoors, wheels and rails, arts, theme parks, and health. Mix and match with places you'll find in other chapters, and do a little exploring of your own to get ideas for more stops along the way. True to the nature of family life, no two vacations are alike!

chapter two
getting away together

The less routine
the more life.

—Amos Bronson Alcott,
father of Louisa May Alcott

family reunions

family reunions & family heritage

You can pick your friends, but you can't pick your family, goes the old saying. And despite some rocky patches, in most families we wouldn't want it any other way.

Our families are where our stories begin and take shape. Our family histories matter to our health, our happiness, and our sense of self.

Regardless of where you go there is sure to be big excitement when everyone is "back together." Family reunions have historically been a popular means of bridging gaps of time and distance among families, a way to bond and reconnect with relatives, and a way to learn more about one's unique heritage.

In past years families planned reunions or vacations on their own. Today family gatherings and getaways are big business. Organizations nationwide can make the experience a fun-filled excursion for the whole gang. Agencies offer travel packages complete with family-friendly hotels, dining discounts, and tours. There's help to be found in creating a family tree and locating faraway relatives. And these days it is easy to trace your personal history through digital records, websites, or even DNA analysis.

Children love to be involved in planning and carrying out plans for reunions. From counting down dates on a calendar . . . to surfing the Web for fun activities and destinations . . . to creating invitations, handling correspondence, and more. After all, anticipation is part of the fun of a big family get-together.

Remember that the youngest and oldest members of the family can be the most important folks at a reunion. Maybe it's because they're often the best storytellers—and story listeners. Take your cues from the family members who are sitting in the shade, holding hands, or want to slow down and linger over a glass of lemonade. Moments like these are a sign that memories are in the making.

> If you look deeply into the palm of your hand, you will see your parents and all generations of your ancestors. All of them are alive at this moment. . . You are the continuation of each of these people.
>
> —Thich Nhat Hanh

ten best
reunion locations

town/city parks

Parks are a popular choice because they can accommodate large crowds and offer picnic tables (often covered), barbecue grills, playground equipment, open green spaces for games, and easy access to water and rest rooms. Plan to visit a nearby museum, garden, or monument.

Reunions offer living links to our past and hopeful views of our future.

state and national parks

Pitch a tent or tow an RV to a state or national park. Or, stay in rental cabins or lodges. Families can hike and boat together, little ones can frolic in the playground, and everyone can share a favorite family story around the evening campfire. The National Park Service offers free, kid-friendly Junior Ranger programs.

hotels

A weekend reunion at a hotel offers restaurants, spas, banquet rooms, pools, gyms, game rooms, and more. Most hotels offer group discounts, off-season rates, and other special offers. Additional activities can include visits to local parks, museums, and gardens.

family heritage sites

Spend the night on or near an ancestor's homestead, or visit the family cemetery to repair and rub tombstones. An old B&B or historic spot is a popular choice for heritage reunions.

theme parks

Amusement parks with wildlife safaris, marine attractions, or thrill rides can be the right destination for active families. Wisconsin Dells, SeaWorld, and many other large parks help families plan their reunions.

beaches and lakefronts

For an unforgettable reunion recipe, combine shoreline fun with flexible lodging. Choose from hotels, motels, rental homes, or camping and mix in biking, hiking, fishing, swimming, surfing, and building sand castles.

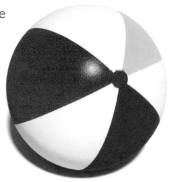

cruises

Cruises offer all-inclusive packages appropriate for all generations, budgets, food tastes, and departure points. Stop-off locations provide families an opportunity to take in local attractions, shop for mementos, and more.

ranches

Take in a day-long horse ride, help the youngest tie a fly, or swap family stories on the porch of a stone lodge. Organize small or extended family gatherings with the help of ranch staff. The YMCA of the Rockies is a top reunion destination and holds its Family Reunion University in the fall.

resorts

All-inclusive resorts are ideal for family reunions because entertainments, accommodations, recreation, and meal planning is onsite and pre-planned. Prices may be prohibitive, however, so look for special group rates, off-season rates, and other special offers.

home

When it comes to gathering for a family reunion, an intimate event in the house or backyard can be ideal. In fact, that's where more than 50 percent of family reunions take place. Why? Easy advanced planning and family-friendly amenities. Forget the camera? Not a problem. It's in the house!

activity | planning a reunion

A reunion will be as wonderful and unique as your family. A few basic ideas help to ensure that everyone shares in the planning and the fun.

who's your family? From siblings and grandparents to distant cousins and dear friends, collect contact information and family details.

communicate: Set up a basic website with a message board so everyone gets the same information. Maybe send regular postcard updates.

define the event: An afternoon cookout? A long weekend at a resort? Four days in the old hometown? Think about shared interests, resources, and family ages.

choose a date: Start up to a year in advance. Try to accommodate school and work schedules so that everyone can be there.

think small: Be inspired by the youngest folks. Their needs for regular meals, rest, and play time set a natural pace for reunion activities.

record the event: Schedule a family photo. Create a collage of everyone's fingerprints. Invent a family song with new words to an old tune. Share the results.

Check this website for more helpful information: *www.familystories.org*

ten best
family heritage

the new york public library's irma and paul milstein division of united states history

**Fifth Ave. & 42nd St., New York, NY 10018
212-930-0800, www.nypl.org/research**

This is one of the largest genealogical and local history collections open to the public in the country. Plan to explore the library's extensive children's books on heritage holidays and celebrations.

ellis island

Statue of Liberty National Monument & Ellis Island New York, NY 10004, 212-363-3200, www.nps.gov/elis/index.htm

Almost half of the American population can trace a relative that came through Ellis Island, once a place where Indians gathered oysters for food. Today, families can interactively search for names, dates of arrival, and even photos of their ancestors' passenger ship. You can search records online at www.ellisisland.org.

At Ellis Island you can research immigration records. It's adjacent to Liberty Island, home of the Statue of Liberty.

friends historical library

Swarthmore College, 500 College Ave., Swarthmore, PA 19081, 610-328-8493, www.swarthmore.edu

Located on the campus of Swarthmore College, this library maintains either in manuscript or microfilm the largest collection of Quaker records in the world. Open to the public, it houses over 60,000 photographs and other audio and visual resources that document the history of the Society of Friends from the 17th century to the present.

library of congress

101 Independence Ave., SE, Washington, DC 20540, 202-707-5000, www.loc.gov

Jump back in time and meet famous Americans or find out what happened on your birthday. Explore Colonial America or the Civil War. Visit the Local History and Genealogy Reading Room where records of more than 50,000 genealogies and 100,000 local histories are stored.

national archives and records administration

700 Pennsylvania Ave., NW, Washington, DC 20408 202-357-5000, www.archives.gov

Long considered "the nation's attic," this is a great place to research family heritage. Family genealogy, American Indian documents, wartime records, and more are housed here. Don't miss seeing the original Declaration of Independence, the

Constitution, and the Bill of Rights. Regional branches throughout the country.

general society of mayflower descendants

4R Winslow St., Plymouth, MA 02361
508-746-3188
www.themayflowersociety.com
Located in Plymouth, the society's library maintains a collection of Pilgrim genealogy and history in the form of books, periodicals, microfilms, and manuscripts. The library is adjacent to the Mayflower House Museum. Their helpful website lists May-flower societies in all fifty states.

national society of the daughters of the american revolution

1776 D St., NW, Washington, DC 20006
202-628-1776 www.dar.org
Families with young children can explore colonial America, and Girl Scouts can research antique objects and make a family tree. Learn the identi-ties of more than 6,600 African Americans and American Indians who contributed to American independence. Bible records, cemetery records, birth, marriage, death records, and more offer families a chance to explore their roots.

A person is a person through other persons.

—African proverb

There were 103 passengers on the Mayflower—a ship that was 106½ feet long.

the newberry library

60 W. Walton St.
Chicago, IL 60610, 312-255-3506
www.newberry.org
This independent research library is free and open to the public, with especially good resources on African-American genealogy. Reference materials are available only to visitors over the age of 16. Begin with a free tour of the collection, offered two days each week (call ahead for dates).

family history library, church of jesus christ of latter-day saints

35 N.W. Temple St., Room 344, Salt Lake City, UT 84150
866-406-1830, www.familysearch.org
More genealogical records are stored here than at any other site in the world. Located in Salt Lake City, this library is open to the public and has more than 3,400 branches around the globe.

los angeles public library

630 W. 5th St., Los Angeles, CA 90071, 213-228-7000
www.lapl.org
The history and genealogy department offers records, telephone directories, and an extensive collection of historical photos of the Los Angeles region. Nearly one-fifth of its collection is not found elsewhere.

shorelines & beaches

oceans, rivers & lakes

Water is the main ingredient in the human body, and maybe that's why we're so drawn to the oceans, lakes, and rivers that shape and reshape our land. Esteemed biologist Loren Eisley pondered its importance in his 1959 classic, *The Immense Journey.* "If there is magic on this planet," he wrote, "it is contained in water."

And so water makes the United States an especially amazing place. Nearly half of the 50 states border one of the country's three shorelines (Pacific and Atlantic Oceans and the Gulf of Mexico). Others border rivers, lakes, bays, falls, creeks, reservoirs, and ponds. It's not surprising that a country with so many bodies of water has so much to offer in waterside activities and excursions. In fact, 75 percent of our recreation takes place along a waterway.

Water keeps us moving, from surfing along the shore's high waves and white-water rafting in strong currents to still-water rafting, canoeing, or sailing in lakes with light currents. Some people prefer not to move at all; they fish at quiet ponds,

By the sea,
by the sea,
by the beautiful sea
. . . how happy
we will be!

—Harold Atteridge

camp along the beach, or watch misty falls from lookout perches.

Water activities and excursions are synonymous with family getaways. After all, an aquatic vacation is at most only a few hours away from most places in the United States. From the broad savannahs of the south Atlantic to the steep slopes of the Pacific coast, from the placid beauty of cool lakes to the invigorating rush of rivers and streams, America's shoreline landscapes inspire a welcome feeling of slipping away from the solid ground of everyday life.

Scientists study why we feel so great when we're near water. Is it because we feel more hopeful when we can see a wide-open horizon? Is it the smell of the sea, the sound of crashing surf, the taste of salt in the air? Is it the nature of coastal air itself, charged with negative ions that are said to make us feel better?

The simplest answer is probably the most obvious: It's just wonderful to be together, to float, to swim, and to be carried away together by a stream, a wave, or a breeze. Here's to the refreshing power of water in all its forms!

northern shorelines

lake champlain

Burlington, VT 05401
877-686-5253, www.vermont.org
Blue waters, miles of shoreline, and enticing bays make this a popular spot for families who enjoy boating, fishing, swimming, waterskiing, and windsurfing.

mackinac island

Mackinac Island, MI 49757
877-847-0086
www.mackinacisland.org
Situated on the Straits of Mackinac between Lakes Michigan and Huron, Mackinac Island provides the charm of vintage America. Fudge, ice cream, and plenty of walking, carriage rides, and biking. Rich in Native American, voyageur, missionary, and military history.

golden crescent

Lake Ontario & St. Lawrence River, Chaumont, NY
A cool summer playground comprises the waterfront areas of Chaumont, Guffin, and Black River Bays, as well as the towns of Sackets Harbor and Henderson Harbor. Sailing, boating, and fishing are all popular activities. Nearby, the Black River is ideal for kayaking and white-water rafting.

Kids feel empowered when parents get buried in the sand!

indiana dunes national lakeshore

1100 N. Mineral Springs Rd., Porter, IN 46304, 219-926-7561, www.nps.gov/indu
Karner blue butterflies and bank swallows greet you. There are eight beaches here, including West Beach, Porter Beach, and Dunbar Beach. West Beach offers rest rooms, showers, a picnic shelter with grills, swimming, and lifeguards.

sleeping bear dunes national lakeshore

9922 Front St., Empire, MI 49630, 231-326-5134
www.nps.gov/slbe
Walk the sands of this 35-mile stretch of spectacular beach, huge dunes, winding trails, and shady forests. Spectacular beaches include D. H. Day Park in Glen Haven, North Bar Lake, Good Harbor Bay, and Manitou Island.

lake michigan

1 South Harbor, Grand Haven, MI 49417, 800-303-4092
www.visitgrandhaven.com
Endless water, ribbons of shoreline, and wonderful outdoor adventures. For small-town charm, visit Grand Haven. Ride the trolley and stroll the boardwalk. Beautiful sunsets and sand dunes.

john, new york | surfing the great lakes One of my favorite surf movies is *Step into Liquid,* with scenes of the Great Lakes. I never knew you could surf Lake Michigan, but I want to give it a try. It's warm in summer, but some of those guys surf in cold weather, too.

kenai fjords national park

Seward, AK 99664, 907-224-7500
www.nps.gov/kefj

It's a different kind of beach adventure! From the waters of Resurrection Bay, see the blue-white tidewater glaciers. Guided tours are recommended, and rustic public-use cabins are available during the summer months. The nearby town of Seward offers additional accommodations.

oval beach area

Perryman St., Saugatuck, MI 49453, 800-506-1299
www.saugatuck.com/beaches.asp

Saugatuck and Douglas are Michigan's premier beach towns. Both exude a warm, small-town feel. Lovely parks dotted with Victorian-style gazebos are perfect spots for picnicking, reading, or sailboat gazing.

traverse city

101 W. Grandview Pkwy., Traverse City, MI 49684
800-940-1120 www.visittraversecity.com

Miles of Lake Michigan shoreline and turquoise lakes offer locals and visitors a wide range of beaches. Bayside Park offers a bathhouse, plenty of picnic areas, and a playground area. The water here is shallow with a sandy bottom, perfect for little ones.

pictured rocks national lakeshore

N8391 Sand Point Rd., Munising, MI 49862
906-387-2607, www.nps.gov/piro

A 40-mile stretch of sandy beach on Lake Superior can feel positively tropical in the summer months, with temperatures over 90°F. There are famous cliffs, a hundred miles of trails, spectacular waterfalls, and campgrounds: an all-in-one vacation experience.

Average Vacation Days,
Per Year, Around the World:

Italy 42 days
France 37 days
Germany 35 days
Brazil 34 days
United Kingdom 28 days
Canada 26 days
Korea 25 days
Japan 25 days
United States 13 days

World Tourism Organization
www.unwto.org

---

ten best
east coast beaches

old orchard beach

Old Orchard Beach, ME 04064
207-934-2500
www.oldorchardbeachmaine.com

This seven-mile-long stretch of wide, sandy beach has drawn families each summer for generations. Enjoy its beachfront amusement park and Thursday night fireworks.

coast guard beach

Cape Cod National Seashore, 99 Marconi Site Rd., Wellfleet, MA 02667 508-349-3785, www.nps.gov/caco

Located in Eastham along the seashore's 44,600 acres, this beach has long been a family favorite. A prime swimming destination during the summer season, it has bodysurfing, nature, and the nearby educational site, the *Mayflower's* landing.

ocean city

861 Asbury Ave., Ocean City, NJ 08226
609-399-6111, www.ocnj.us

Located on an island between the Atlantic Ocean and Great Egg Harbor, this family landmark offers swim and surf beaches stretching over eight miles. Each Thursday on the Boardwalk in July and August is Family Night, with classic, pop, and oldies bands, strolling barbershop quartets, face painters, roving magicians, and more.

cape may

Cape May Welcome Center, 405 Lafayette St., Cape May, NJ 08204, 609-884-9562, www.capemaychamber.com

Cape May is the oldest seashore retreat in the United States. Located at the southernmost tip of the state, the town's known nationally for its huge collection of Victorian-era architecture and the popular Wildwood Boardwalk. Surfers will like Cove Beach. Search for the fabled Cape May diamonds along Sunset Beach.

lewes, rehoboth, & bethany beaches

Rte. 1, DE, 866-284-7483, www.visitdelaware.com

These beach towns retain the small-town flavor that defines mid-Atlantic beach resorts. Lewes has quiet beaches and gentle waves, Rehoboth offers upscale shopping and dining, and Bethany remains a family favorite with its cottage rentals and natural beauty. Watch for migratory birds along this eastern flyway.

hilton head island

Hilton Head VCB, 1 Chamber Dr., Hilton Head Island, SC 29938, 800-523-3373, www.hiltonheadisland.org

Luxurious and subtropical, Hilton Head offers the

active family plenty of recreation: golf and tennis, bike rides, and fresh- and saltwater fishing. Lifeguards, rest rooms, a bathhouse, and a playground can be found at Coligny Beach. Loggerhead turtles emerge from the sea at night to lay their eggs.

the outer banks

Outer Banks Chamber of Commerce, 101 Town Hall Dr., Kill Devil Hills, NC 27948, 877-629-4386 www.outerbanks.org

Small-town charm, protected beaches, warm water, and wild horses makes Corolla a family favorite. For lifeguarded beaches, visit Nags Head, Kill Devil Hills, or Kitty Hawk, also home of America's first air flight. The world's longest stretch of barrier islands, Cape Hatteras National Seashore, has three noted historic lighthouses, dunes staked with sea oats, a graveyard of shipwrecks, and wild surf.

cumberland island

St. Marys, GA 31558, 912-882-4336, www.nps.gov.cuis

Known for its well-preserved habitat and more than 17 miles of sugar-white beaches, this barrier island is part of the world's largest undeveloped barrier islands. Collect sharks' teeth and unoccupied seashells in the morning. In the afternoon, go bird- and wildlife watching, and at night, pitch the family tent and look up at the dazzling display of stars.

There is a summer pony roundup each year at Chincoteague, but some families report that it's nicer to visit at a less crowded time.

assateague & chincoteague islands

Assateague Visitor Center, 7206 National Seashore La., Berlin, MD 21811, 410-641-1441, www.nps. gov/asis • Chincoteague Visitor Center, 757-336-6577, www. chincoteaguechamber.com

Assateague and Chincoteague islands are linked by a short causeway. While Chincoteague offers no beachfront, it does have restaurants, bike rentals, a museum, and more. Cross over to Assateague to see its famous wild horses.

books | misty of chincoteague

by marguerite henry

This is the fact-based 1947 Newbery Honor book. Set on the Virginia island of Chincoteague, the book tells the story of a family's efforts to raise a pony born to a wild horse.

bathtub reef park

Stuart/Martin County Chamber of Commerce 1650 S. Kanner Hwy., Stuart, FL 34994 772-287-1088, www.goodnature.org

This lovely beach, located in southeast Florida, is ideal for young families. Small children can enjoy the gentle surf with the protection of an offshore reef.

ten best
west coast shorelines

san juan islands

San Juan Islands Visitors Bureau
P.O. Box 1330, Friday Harbor,
WA 98250, 888-468-3701
www.guidetosanjuans.com
Fly from Seattle or take the
Washington State Ferry from
Anacortes. For orca viewing,
plan to stay on San Juan Island.
Beachcombing fun, bike rent-
als, and sea kayak tours are
plentiful on Lopez Island.

*Rent a board and plan to take a lesson when
you're ready to try surfing for the first time.*

seaside

Seaside Visitors Bureau, 7 N. Roosevelt, Seaside, OR
97138, 888-306-2326, www.seasideor.com
Since the 1800s, visitors from around the world
have been coming to Seaside. A three-mile ocean-
front promenade is ideal for strollers, bike riders,
and skaters. Visit the end of the Lewis and Clark
Trail statue and the Seaside Aquarium.

cannon beach

Cannon Beach Chamber-Commerce, 207 N. Spruce
St., Cannon Beach, OR 97110, 503-436-2623
www.cannonbeach.org
Located west of Portland, these waters are often
too cold for swimming, but kids can enjoy exploring
the tide pools and building sand castles. Fly a kite
on the wide beach.

point reyes national seashore

1 Bear Valley Rd., Point Reyes
Station, CA 94956, 415-464-
5100, www.nps.gov/pore
Point Reyes National Sea-
shore is a place where
children can discover the
wonders of wildlife watching,
hike along a variety of trails,
build sand castles, watch for
whales, seals, and sea lions,
and discover the lighthouse
(and its 308 steps!).

golden gate national recreation area

Golden Gate National Parks, Fort Mason, Bldg. 201
San Francisco, CA 94123, 415-561-4700
www.nps.gov/goga/
This 60-mile swath of coastal lands has rocky
coasts and shelter tide pools. For families, the sandy
beaches provide playgrounds for all ages as well as
homes to many plants and animals. Many ranger-
led programs are available.

big sur

Big Sur Chamber of Commerce, Big Sur, CA 93920
831-667-2100, www.bigsurcalifornia.org
From the annual migration of California gray

whales to the ever present elephant seals and the soaring California condors, Big Sur is the best way to see the highlights of the western coast. Dotted along the famous highway are coves, beaches, redwood stands, and stunning views of the blue Pacific.

carpinteria state beach

Visitors Bureau Santa Barbara 1601 Anacapa St., Santa Barbara, CA 93101, 805-966-9222 www.santabarbaraca.com
Carpinteria State Beach offers a mile of beach for swimming, surf fishing, tide-pool exploring, and camping. With its calm water and small waves, West Beach attracts families with young kids. Tide pools contain sea stars, sea anemones, crabs, snails, octopuses, and sea urchins.

santa monica beach

Santa Monica Visitor Center, 1920 Main St., Ste. B, Santa Monica, CA 90405, 800-544-5319 www.santamonica.com
Located along scenic Santa Monica Bay, this broad stretch of sand defines classic California beach living. Dolphins swim offshore while kids frolic in the

Sea lions use their front flippers to move on land, and they have ears that you can see. That's how you can tell them apart from seals.

gentle, sparkling surf. Relax on the clean, raked sand or play volleyball. Known for its healthy lifestyle, Santa Monica's beach has bike trails and an array of many outdoor activities.

la jolla cove & la jolla shore beach

La Jolla Visitor Center, 7966 Herschel Ave., La Jolla, CA 92037 858-456-1700, www.sandiego.gov
La Jolla Cove is a jewel of a beach, with a narrow staircase along sandstone cliffs that leads to soft sand and a gentle surf. A popular spot for families, La Jolla Shores is a clean beach with gentle swimming and surfing. Nearby, visit the Scripps Institute of Oceanography.

coronado beach

Coronado Visitor Center, 1100 Orange Ave. Coronado, CA 92118, 866-599-7242 www.coronadovisitorcenter.com
With its wide expanse of sturdy sand and mild surf, this beach will suit active beachgoing families. Kids can swim, sail, and surf, while little ones can explore tidal pools or bike along flat pathways.

" fran, washington, d.c. | vacation Don't take these family vacations for granted because they don't go on forever . . . children become teenagers who have other summer jobs and commitments. Enjoy this very special time in your lives.

ten best
gulf shore beaches

sand key park

1060 Gulf Blvd., Clearwater, FL 33767
727-588-4852, www.pinellascounty.org/
park/15_Sand_Key.htm

Near Clearwater Beach and located on a
barrier island, Sand Key Park
welcomes families with its
beauty and amenities, including
a playground and picnic area.
Discover its artificial reef
program and sea turtles.

fort myers beach

8700 Estero Blvd., Fort Myers
Beach, FL 33931, 239-463-4588
www.fortmyerssanibel.com

Choose from more than 30
access points along this beach.
From restaurants and cafés to secluded, pristine
stretches of beachfront, this shoreline has something for everyone.

sanibel island

Sanibel Island & Captiva Island Chamber of
Commerce, 1159 Causeway Rd., Sanibel Island,
FL 33957, 239-472-1080, www.Sanibel-Captiva.org

Considered the shell-collecting capital of the world,
this peaceful coastline boasts warm weather, white
sands, manatees, and sea turtles. Visitors are welcome to use the wonderful public library, and local

*Water is a natural magnifier. Put a little shell
in a bucket and see how it looks larger when
it's covered with an inch of water.*

museums and restaurants are
famously family-friendly.

bonita beach park

27954 Hickory Blvd., Bonita
Springs, FL 34134, 800-237-6444
www.leeparks.org

Located on the northern tip of
Bonita Beach, this beautiful park
features a boardwalk and a swimming area. Walk the sand dunes, pack
a picnic, and enjoy the views from the
gazebo. Restaurants and shops
are close by.

siesta county beach, florida

Official Sarasota Visitor Information Center, 800-522-9799, www.sarasotafl.org

Clear water and fine, white sand make this a favorite for beach lovers. For active kids, there's plenty
of volleyball, biking, and picnicking. Listen to the
rhythms of the Siesta Key Drum Circle every Sunday evening.

emerald coast

Emerald Coast Convention & Visitors Bureau, Inc.
1540 Miracle Strip Pkwy., Ft. Walton Beach, FL 32548
800-322-3319, www.destin-fwb.com

Located between Destin, Ft. Walton Beach, and

Okaloosa Island are 24 miles of stunning coast-line and white sands. Sea oats, sand pines, gentle dunes, and blossoming magnolias alternate with six miles of park beaches. Enjoy the pavilions, gazebos, and easy beach access.

gulf shores

Gulf Shores Welcome Center, 3150 Gulf Shores Pkwy. Gulf Shores, AL 36542, 800-745-7263 www.gulfshores.com

This stretch of small beach towns, with its sugar-white sand and brilliant blue and swimmable water, is a popular and affordable beach destina-tion. Within Gulf Shores is Gulf Coast State Park, containing 6,000 acres of land with 2.5 miles of beach, a freshwater lake, nature trails, and a beach pavilion.

gulf islands national seashore

1801 Gulf Breeze Pkwy., Gulf Breeze, FL 32563, 850-934-2600; Mississippi District: 228-875-9057 ext. 100 www.nps.gov/guls

Enjoy this park's sparkling waters, bayous, historic forts, and recreational opportunities. Open year-round, the seashore has more than 80 percent of its land submerged and is teeming with marine life. After a morning paddling and sunbathing, learn about breezes, tides, and hurricanes on a ranger-guided tour.

padre island national seashore

Malaquite Visitor Center, Corpus Christi, TX 78480-1300, 361-949-8068, www.nps.gov/pais

Padre Island National Seashore is the longest remaining undeveloped stretch of barrier island in the world. In spring or early summer, children can watch the release of the endangered Kemp's Ridley turtle, which nests on the island. It's known also for great bird-watching and big dunes.

quietwater beach, florida

800-874-1234, www.visitpensacola.com

Known as a wonderful spot to swim because of its calm waters, Quietwater Beach is on the sound side of Pensacola Beach. The sand here is ideal for castle building.

The Kemp's Ridley is the only sea turtle that nests predominantly during daylight hours.

ten best
hawaiian beaches

hanalei bay

Kauai Visitors Bureau, 4334 Rice St., Ste. 101, Lihue, HI 96766, 800-262-1400 www.kauaidiscovery.com

This half-moon-shaped beach on the North Coast will have kids paddling the beginner waves in no time. Little ones will splash and wade in the warm, placid waters.

po'ipu beach park

Kauai Visitors Bureau, 4334 Rice St., Ste. 101, Lihue, HI 96766, 800-262-1400 www.kauaidiscovery.com

Located on the sunny south shore of Kauai, this beach has picturesque crescent shores rimmed with blue water. Younger kids will love swimming in the naturally formed wading pool. Older kids will like surfing and snorkeling nearby in the open ocean. Lifeguards, showers, rest rooms, a grassy expanse, and picnic tables.

kailua beach park

www.visit-oahu.com

Kailua Beach Park has beautiful sand, dunes, shade trees, and lovely views. Families like the small pocket beach where children can play in the sand and swim in calm waters. Excellent windsurfing, kayaking, and swimming for older kids.

Hawaii is famous for breezy coastlines and crashing surf. You'll find windsurfers in the more protected bays and inlets.

ala moana beach park

www.visit-oahu.com

An ideal spot on Oahu for families, offering parking, large grassy areas, and a wide sandy beach. Picnic under a shade tree and then splash into calm, clear waters.

waikiki beach

www.visit-oahu.com

It's not just the safe water and wide white sand beach that make this the most famous shoreline in the world. Waikiki offers plenty of amenities, including lifeguards, rest rooms, a shaded pavilion, and plenty of grills and picnic tables. Just a short stroll to favorite Oahu attractions like the Waikiki Aquarium.

kapalua beach

Maui Visitors Bureau, 1727 Wili Pa Loop, Wailuku, HI 96793, 800-525-6284, www.visitmaui.com

Located in west Maui and situated between two lava outcrops, this beach has beautiful golden sand, palm trees, and calm water. Families with small children find the shallow waters ideal, and snorkelers of any age will enjoy the underwater attractions.

music | for the love of hawaii

by linda yapp

Spring 2008 Music Parents Choice Award; Ages: 1–18 yrs. Producer: Yapp Music

Vocalist/musician Linda Yapp's tender songs are a loving tribute to the people, flora, fauna, sea, land, and legends of Hawaii.

kamaole I, II, & III

South Kihei Rd., Kihei, HI 96753, 808-879-4364
www.co.maui.hi.us

Three beaches stretch along South Kihei Road, and each one is great for kids. Here they can play volleyball, rollerblade, and play basketball as well as swim and surf. All three beaches have lifeguards. Snorkelers will see parrotfish and sea turtles.

samuel spencer beach park

Akoni Pule Hwy. (HI-270), between mile markers 2 & 3
www.gohawaii.com

On the northwestern Kohala coast, this popular beach is known for its sandy stretch and calm, reef-protected water. Shaded grassy areas and showers/rest rooms are available. It's within walking distance of Puukoholoa Heiau National Historic Site, home to ancient temples and an August Hawaiian cultural festival.

hapuna beach state recreation area

www.gohawaii.com/big_island/learn/quick_guides

Surrounded by landscaped grounds, this Big Island beach park has nice swimming and bodysurfing areas during calm seas. Pack a picnic and enjoy this half-mile-long crescent beach that slopes down to crystal-clear waters. Lifeguards are on duty here. They can't chat while they're watching the surf, but between shifts you can ask them for tips about water safety.

anaehoomalu beach

www.bigisland.org

On the Kohala coast of Kona, on the Big Island, this spot is a favorite for active ocean lovers and families who picnic. Rent glass-bottom boats, kayaks, hydro bikes, or boogie boards nearby. Snorkel, scuba dive, or windsurf. Children can safely swim along the gently sloping shore. Walk inland to see historic fish ponds that hug the beachfront.

"

karen, massachusetts | i remember hawaii . . . Driving to the North Shore with my parents and getting a glimpse of the places they visited when newlyweds . . . Having my dad let me wade in Waimea Bay, the famous surfing mecca, as I was too afraid of the big waves but wanted to say I had been in the water!

moving water

kennebec river, maine

Kennebec Valley Chamber of Commerce
800-345-6246, www.mainewhitewater.com
This 150-mile-long river offers one of the most popular white-water rafting adventures in New England. Combine the excitement of a roller-coaster ride with stretches of gentle water to get a perfect family ride.

youghiogheny river, pennsylvania

Pennsylvania Tourism Office, 800-VISIT-PA
www.visitpa.com/visitpa/home.pa
(It's pronounced yock-a-GAIN-y.) The Middle Yough is an ideal family float trip. Its calm and scenic Class I and II rapids are perfect for young kids. Arrange to throw in a fishing line along the way or watch wildlife. The Upper and Lower Yough offers challenging rides for more experienced rafters.

new river gorge national river

Glen Jean, WV 25846, 304-465-0508, www.nps.gov/neri
Located in West Virginia, the New and the Gauley Rivers' rocky terrain and rough water make this a celebrated rafting destination. Guided trips with licensed outfitters ensure a safe and exuberant trip for thrill-loving families.

Rafting, canoeing, or sailing together is a wonderful exercise in family cooperation.

suwannee river

3900 Commonwealth Blvd., Tallahassee, FL 32399, 800-868-9914
www.floridastateparks.org/wilderness
Paddle a canoe from Fargo, Georgia, to Big Shoals State Park, Florida, to see nature's beauty. Big Shoals features the largest white-water rapids in Florida, so novices will want to portage to the smaller rapids, called Little Shoals.

guadalupe river

Guadalupe River State Park
3350 Park Rd., 31, Spring Branch, TX 78070, 830-438-2656
www.tpwd.state.tx.us
Tubing the Guadalupe is a favorite Texas Hill Country water sport. Canyon Lake is festive, while Guadalupe River State Park is quiet. Here, families can also swim, picnic, hike, and mountain bike.

flathead river

Flathead National Forest, 650 Wolfpack Way, Kalispell, MT 59901, 406-758-5204, www.fs.fed.us/r1/flathead
One of the best ways to view northwest Montana's vast beauty. Located on the borders of Glacier National Park, this wild and scenic river offers a mix of smooth stretches, giddy thrills, and truly heart-racing rapids.

colorado river, grand canyon, arizona

928-638-7888
www.nps.gov/grca/planyourvisit/
whitewater-rafting.htm

At this famous site, the Colorado River offers both challenging white-water rapids and serene, calm waters. Launch a half-day or full-day trip from the northern or western end of the canyon. Start with a one-day guided (commercial) trip. Some longer trips require permits and are scheduled a year or more in advance.

green river, desolation canyon, utah

Moab Area Travel Council, 800-635-6622
www.utah.com

Located in a deep gorge, this river has 84 miles of calm water with some Class III rapids scattered throughout. Along the way, see abandoned frontier homesteads and prehistoric Indian petroglyphs. Sandy white beaches are beautiful to explore.

snake river, oregon & idaho

509-758-0615, www.fs.fed.us/hellscanyon

North America's deepest river gorge, Hells Canyon is a dramatic, remote region in the Northwest. Rapids here range from relaxed to extremely rough, so allow for a multiday trip with an experienced outfitter.

Unforgettable: the sight of your dad in an orange life vest

american river, california

www.theamericanriver.com

A great place for families to start out before trying more challenging rivers. The South Fork is great rafting for ages six and above, offering the scenery of the Sierra foothills, narrow rocky gorges, and placid stretches —it's a nice day trip from the Bay Area. The Middle Fork is more challenging and the North Fork is famously wild and rough. All three forks offer beautiful foothills and swimming holes for resting and enjoying the scenery. This website includes a helpful white-water outfitters directory.

River Records

largest: The Mississippi has the greatest volume of water—593,000 cubic feet per second at its mouth. It's also the widest—about one mile across near Alton, Illinois.

longest: The Missouri is about 2,500 miles long. For comparison, the distance between New York and Los Angeles is about 2,700 miles.

shortest: The Roe in Montana and the D River in Oregon are each just over 200 feet long, depending on water flow.

ten best
lakes

lake champlain

Lake Champlain Regional Chamber of Commerce, 60 Main St. Burlington, VT 05401, 877-686-5253, www.vermont.org
Blue waters, miles of shoreline, and enticing bays make this a popular spot for families who enjoy boating, fishing, swimming, waterskiing, and windsurfing.

otsego lake, new york

Cooperstown Chamber of Commerce, 607-547-9983 www.cooperstown.net
The Baseball Hall of Fame is located a few blocks from the shore of this glassy lake. The area is a haven for fans of history, sports, and outdoor activity. Especially recommended for families is a day at the nearby Farmer's Museum, plus plenty of time for canoeing, hiking, and swimming.

lake george, new york

800-958-4748, www.visitlakegeorge.com
Located in the Adirondacks, this 32-mile-long lake is a family favorite. In addition to wide stretches of undeveloped shoreline, the area has charming communities with welcoming restaurants, mini-golf courses, local festivals, and weekly fireworks. Hike the local trails for blueberries. Nearby, find

A lake is the landscape's most beautiful and expressive feature. It is earth's eye; looking into which the beholder measures the depth of his own nature.

—Henry David Thoreau

regional attractions such as Fort Ticonderoga and Whitehall, birthplace of the U.S. Navy.

lake michigan

1 South Harbor, Grand Haven, MI 49417, 800-303-4092 www.visitgrandhaven.com
Endless water, ribbons of shoreline, and wonderful outdoor adventures. For small-town charm, visit Grand Haven. Ride the trolley and stroll the boardwalk. Beautiful sunsets and sand dunes.

lake of the ozarks

Missouri Division of Tourism 573-751-4133, www.visitmo.com
With more than 1,100 miles of shoreline, this is one of the largest man-made lakes in the world. In addition to secluded coves and gorgeous scenery, the lake offers mini golf, indoor and outdoor water parks, and the Main Street Opry Music Show. Houseboat rentals are a novel option for families.

jackson lake

Grand Teton National Park, Moose, WY 83012 307-739-3300, www.nps.gov/grte
Located in Wyoming's stunning Grand Teton

National Park, this lake is a wonderful place to view wildlife and take in the sweeping vistas. Visit the Jenny Lake Lodge for a meal or enjoy the Grand Teton Music Festival that's held here every summer.

lake powell, utah

928-608-6200
www.go-utah.com/lake-powell
Formed in 1965 by the creation of the Glen Canyon Dam, this huge lake is ringed by deep-red sandstone canyons. Rent a houseboat to see the uncanny rock formations, and later anchor in a sandy cove. Let the kids build sand castles, and after the family cookout, watch for the flicker of campfires that spark around the lake at night.

lake washington & lake union, washington

www.seattle.gov/html/visitor/location.htm
Lake Washington is the second largest natural lake in the state of Washington and the largest lake in King County. Joining it is Lake Union, a popular Seattle recreational spot. Take a cruise,

There are 41 million acres of lakes and reservoirs in the United States.

look out for famous houseboats and yachts, and enjoy the scenic skyline.

lake mead national recreation area

601 Nevada Way, Boulder City, NV 89005, 702-293-8990
www.nps.gov/lame
The man-made lake in the Mojave Desert is one of the largest in the world. It offers active families ample boating, fishing, swimming, and white-water rafting opportunities. Snorkeling and scuba enthusiasts can view striped bass, rainbow trout, and other aquatic life from October to April.

lake tahoe

Lake Tahoe Chamber of Commerce, 169 Hwy. 50 3rd Fl., Stateline, NV 89449, 775-588-1728
www.tahoechamber.org
Known for its intense blue color, Lake Tahoe offers great fishing, kayaking, biking, and hiking opportunities. Ride the Heavenly Gondola in South Lake Tahoe for views of the Sierra Nevada range.

"

mary, maryland | lake story There are so many great books about kids taking lakeside vacations. *Magic By the Lake* was my favorite, about siblings who discover a speaking turtle during a summer full of magical happenings. It's second in Edward Eager's *Half Magic* series.

sports

skiing, fishing, skating, biking, tennis, riding, racing, and more

So much of today's recreation is geared toward the indoors. State-of-the-art video and Internet games scarcely stimulate the mind and do virtually nothing for the body. Our younger generation is barely familiar with four words that yesteryear's youth heard from their parents daily: Go outside and play.

Consider the limitless options—bike trails, fishing adventures, driving ranges, and batting cages. Playing together offers hands-on methods for learning a particular sport, as well as means of discovering untapped abilities and passions. And sitting together to cheer on favorite sports heroes has an amazing ability to meld a family's sense of identity and shared interests.

Legendary television personality Howard Cosell once said, "Sports is human life in microcosm." It's a lesson in hope when you bring a baseball glove to sit in the outfield seats at a Major League game—just in case a home run ball comes your way. It's a nod to tradition when you stand to stretch together in the seventh inning. And when it's hard to find common ground on

It is a happy talent to know how to play.

—Ralph Waldo Emerson

other subjects, most parents and kids can chat together about spring training, hall of fame records, and home team schedules. In fact, a team's "away" games can be the ideal incentive for planning a trip.

Creative vacations can appeal to everyone's varied interests. For example, does someone you love dream of a trip to the Indy 500, while others crave exercise and the great outdoors? Consider all the options, and while you're in Indianapolis, rent some bikes and follow the Monon Trail through the city.

Family psychologists often encourage families to try out a new sport or outdoor activity together. It's great for children to see their parents learning a new skill like handling an oar or saddling up a trail pony. And everyone wins when they experience the teamwork, communication, and mutual encouragement that happens when they board a ski lift, bait a fish hook, or set out on a challenging hike . . . together. The sights and sounds and smells of these new experiences become part of your family's story forever.

ten best
ski spots

okemo, vermont

800-228-5830

www.okemovalleyvt.org

This ski spot is located in the Green Mountains of south-central Vermont. Okemo Resort offers one of the best kids' skiing programs in the country. Budget-minded families will like the "kids six and under ski free" program. For a change of pace, take a ride on the Green Mountain Railroad (www. rails-vt.com).

smugglers' notch

4323 Vermont Rte. 108 South
Smugglers' Notch, VT 05464
800-419-4615, www.smuggs.com

Located in the heart of Vermont's Green Mountains, "Smuggs" features mountainside lodging, three big mountains with 1,000 acres of terrain for every ability, award-winning children's programs, and comprehensive vacation packages.

[Cross country skiing has been a Special Olympics winter event since 1977. Athletes compete in distance challenges and team relays.]

Call resorts to ask about learn-to-ski packages for parents and children together.

copper mountain

Copper Mountain Resort Chamber
760 Copper Rd., Frisco, CO 80443
970-968-6477

www.copperresortchamber.com

This area is only 75 minutes from Denver's airport. Enjoy beginner to advanced trails, with a snow-skate park, a beginner terrain park, and kid-friendly trail maps.

steamboat springs, colorado

877-237-2628, www.steamboat.com

Seven thousand feet up in the Colorado Rockies, Steamboat Springs offers kids-only terrain and lifts, night tubing, and a terrain park in an Old West setting.

aspen/snowmass, colorado

800-525-6200, www.aspensnowmass.com

In the heart of the Rockies, this famous resort offers all levels of skiing, and one lift ticket buys access to four different mountains. Along with an admired children's ski program, Snowmass has the new Treehouse Kids' Adventure Center, with playrooms for children as young as eight weeks, a climbing gym, and space for teen dances and movie nights.

vail

Vail Chamber of Commerce, 241 S. Frontage Rd. E #2, Vail, CO 81657 970-477-0075, www.vailchamber.org

The second largest mountain ski and snowboard complex in North America, Vail is a favorite for slope-bound families. The trails are divided equally among beginner, intermediate, and advanced terrain. For variety, try snow tubing, ski biking and snowmobiling.

breckenridge, colorado

877-251-2417, www.gobreck.com

It's the centerpiece of the Colorado Rockies, with an altitude of 9,600 feet. This spot offers fun for all ages. Glide powder slopes, night ski, ride the scenic gondola, and rip at the terrain parks and pipes. See the annual Snow Sculpture Championships.

sun valley, idaho

866-305-0408, www.visitsunvalley.com

Stay in Ketchum and take the free KART shuttle bus to the ski area. Great hills for novice skiers and lots of other winter activities like tubing,

Powder skiing is not fun. It's life, fully lived, life lived in a blaze of reality.

—Dolores LaChapelle

ice-skating, and cross-country exploration. The resort itself has a rich winter sports history, and the first chairlift was invented here!

salt lake city area, utah

800-200-1160, http://utah.travel/attractions/12-skisnowboard/

Known as one of the country's best ski areas and located just an hour's drive from Salt Lake's airport. The Deer Valley Resorts kids' program is highly acclaimed, and teens and parents can carve graceful turns in deep powder there or at any of the area's seven ski locations.

lake tahoe, california & nevada

www.tahoechamber.com

Surrounded by the Sierra Nevada, this ski area has a sweet spot for everyone. Try Northstar-at-Tahoe's wonderful children's program, ride Heavenly's new gondola, or visit any of the nearby small and large resorts, all with top notch trails, some with interchangeable passes and hot chocolate to boot.

john, maryland | snowboarding We made a big snowboarding trip to Killington, Vermont, last year. It was a long weekend trip. A good idea is that we rented an SUV to get there, which made driving a lot easier in the winter weather.

ten best
fishing adventures

trout fishing, maine

866-624-6345, www.visitmaine.com/fishing/
species/brook_trout
Brook trout is a Maine favorite, and kids
can catch a brookie with worms and a
bobber off a dock or bank. Or, fly cast
tiny dry flies on the Kennebago River, the
Roach River, or the Rapid River. Book a
cabin along pine shores and cast a line
for lake trout in the cold, deep waters of
Sebago or Moosehead Lake.

surf casting, massachusetts

800-227-MASS, www.massvacation.com/
outdoor
Try Nantucket, a beautiful former whal-
ing port, in early June for striped bass
around Madaket Harbor. Go off-road, through the
gorgeous wild dunes for false albacore in Great
Point. Pack a beach picnic and surf cast virtually
any shoreline for bluefish.

bass fishing, new york

405 Riverside Dr., 315-686-3512, www.townofclayton.com
The Thousand Lakes region is a favorite for walleyes, pike, panfish, and muskies. Grab the tacklebox,
pole, and a lunch. Here a bridge system connects
the U.S. and Canada over the St. Lawrence River.

*What do fish eat? What
eats fish? Use quiet fishing time to ponder the
food chain and other big
thoughts about life.*

kayak fishing, the everglades, florida

40001 State Rd. 9336, Homestead, FL
33034, 305-242-7700, www.nps.gov/ever/
Paddle, pause, and cast for grouper,
snapper, and snook. Both experienced
and novice family fishermen will love this
fishing trip in Everglades National Park.
Before you go, read *Hoot*, a young adult
novel by Carl Hiaasen, a lively mystery set
in this very area.

deep sea fishing, florida

www.visitflorida.com/fishing
For a family fishing trip, try a deep-
sea charter boat in the Gulf of Mexico
going after tarpon. Half-day options are
a great choice, departing in early morning hours
and avoiding the effects of the midday sun.

freshwater fishing, minnesota

800-877-7281, www.ely.org
Fish for walleye in Ely, the gateway to one of the
most pristine water regions in the world: the
Boundary Waters Canoe Area Wilderness. Plan to
visit during the Blueberry/Art Festival, a three-day
July tradition with children's activities and a wealth
of regional art offerings.

holly, washington | cookout Nothing tastes better than a fresh trout that I caught myself. We take our golden retrievers hiking and fishing and share our fun with them—they are our kids.

ice fishing, minnesota

888-350-2692, www.millelacs.com
In the winter, pop up an ice hut on Mille Lacs and settle in. This Minnesota lake is well known for perch and walleyes. This website lists several resources for ice house rental and guide services. The name means "thousand lakes," and well describes the seemingly endless waterways of the region.

fly-fishing, montana

Missoula Area Chamber of Commerce
825 E. Front St., Missoula, MT 59802
406-543-6623, www.missoulachamber.com
Known as the setting for Norman MacLean's novella *A River Runs Through It*, this city offers fishable waters just a step off the road. Or take a float trip to find a deep, quiet canyon. Some of the most difficult fly-fishing in the world is found along the Middle Fork of the Flathead. Fish for fresh river trout and enjoy the beautiful Montana

Luck affects everything. Let your hook always be cast; in the stream where you least expect it, there will be a fish.

—Ovid

landscape and wildlife, including moose and bighorn sheep.

wade fishing, texas

800-45-COAST, www.fishporta.com/about_port_a.htm
Port Aranas is known as the fishing capital of Texas, great for shallow wade fishing. It's about three hours from San Antonio. Sandy beachfront, resort attractions, and cabin rental availability make it a great vacation destination. There are four lighted piers to fish from day or night. Red fish, flounder, black drum, and trout can be found in these waters.

halibut fishing, alaska

907-235-7740
www.homeralaska.org/visitHomer/fishing.htm
Kachemak Bay in Homer, Alaska, is considered the halibut fishing capital of the world. Here, the family can fish from a bank or a boat. Fly in, then float out or hike to get to where the fish are.

activity | make a fish print Try *gyotaku*, big in ancient Japan. You need a fresh-caught fish, a sheet of blank paper (bigger than the fish), and some nontoxic tempera paint. Wipe off the fish and use your fingers to cover one side of it with paint. Press the painted side against the paper, including the fins, tail, and head. Carefully lift away to reveal a fish print. Wash off the paint, and then cook and eat the fish.

ten best
sports shrines

lake placid olympic region, new york

800-447-5224
www.lakeplacid.com

Home of the 1980 Winter Olympics, this is a wonderful family attraction. See the famous ice rink, site of the famed U.S.–U.S.S.R. ice hockey matchup, and enjoy year-round athletic attractions indoors and out. The setting is a very quaint alpine-style town, almost a throwback to the glorious 1980s.

fenway park

4 Yawkey Way, Boston, MA 02215, 877-733-7699
http://redsox.mlb.com

Fenway Park is the home field of the Boston Red Sox baseball team. Opened in 1912, it's the oldest of all current Major League Baseball stadiums. Baseball greats Cy Young, Babe Ruth, Ted Williams, and many others played here. Call to find out about stadium tours and rare day-of-game ticket availability.

boston marathon, massachusetts

617-236-1652, www.bostonmarathon.org

Begun in 1897, the Boston Marathon is the world's oldest annual marathon and ranks as one of the world's best-known road-racing events. It's held on

Patriots' Day, the third Monday of April, and attracts tens of thousands of participants each year.

national baseball hall of fame

25 Main St., Cooperstown, NY 13326, 607-547-7200, www.baseballhalloffame.org

Located in the charming village of Cooperstown, this museum is popular with both players and spectators. Learn everything there is to know about baseball cards, great pitchers, women in baseball, and more. Doubleday Field is home to lots of exhibition games, especially in the summer. Many exhibits change annually. Each month baseball legends visit Cooperstown for Voices of the Game, an exclusive interactive event.

basketball hall of fame

1000 W. Columbus Ave., Springfield, MA 01105
877-4HOOPLA, www.hoophall.com

Plan a trip here to celebrate basketball's greatest moments and people. The first floor is an official-size college court, with interactive displays to try out basketball moves or play-by-play broadcaster announcing. Kids love the gallery of jerseys and sneakers from current and past players, and the third-floor hall is an awe-inspiring gallery focused on the masters of the game.

churchill downs

700 Central Ave., Louisville, KY
40208, 502-636-4400
www.churchilldowns.com
The Kentucky Derby, considered
the "most exciting two minutes in
sports," is held the first Saturday in
May at Louisville's Churchill Downs.
Inveterate horse-race fans will enjoy strolling through the racetrack's historic grounds.

spring training,
florida & arizona

www.visitflorida.com, www.arizonaguide.com
Fans watch their favorite teams practice and play
exhibition games during the warm weather over
spring break. In March, Florida's baseball stadiums
host the Grapefruit League's spring training camps
and Arizona welcomes the Cactus League.

pro football hall of fame

2121 George Halas Dr., NW, Canton, OH 44708
330-456-8207, www.profootballhof.com
Located in Canton, this museum offers fans and
novices a great experience to learn about football.
Fans can relive football history by viewing the large
collection of memorabilia, video, and audio records
from 1892 to 1992. Or, find out more about the

current 32 clubs and highlights of
recent NFL record holders.

indianapolis 500
motor speedway

4790 W. 16th St., Indianapolis, IN 46222
800-822-4639, www.indianapolis
motorspeedway.com
Every Memorial Day weekend, racing fans flock to Speedway, Indiana, to watch the
Indianapolis 500 race. On the grounds is the Speedway's Hall of Fame Museum. Here you can purchase advance tickets for the very popular seasonal
Ground Tour, which include a bus ride around the
famed racetrack.

wrigley field

1060 W. Addison St. #1, Chicago, IL 60613
773-404-2827, http://cubs.mlb.com
Baseball fans love to visit Wrigley Field, the
second oldest ballpark in the league and home of the
Chicago Cubs. Its grassy expanse recalls the game's
most historic moments, like when Babe Ruth pointed
to the bleachers before he launched a home run in
the 1932 World Series. Tours are available during
baseball season, though some areas are restricted if
you visit on game days. Batting practice begins when
gates open, two hours before game time.

" **jeff, massachusetts | hall of fame** My dad took me to see Cal Ripken inducted into the
Baseball Hall of Fame in 2007. It was like a big street party right in the little village of Cooperstown!
I'll always remember it.

ten best
skate parks

rye airfield

170 Lafayette Rd., Rye, NH 03870
603-964-2800, www.ryeairfield.com
This is New England's largest skate park and BMX track, created by the designers of the Gravity Games. Highlights include three concrete bowls (including a beginner bowl) and a 1,300-foot outdoor downhill BMX track. There are daily or weekly passes plus year-round memberships available.

woodward skateparks

1943 Franklin Mills Cir., Philadelphia, PA 19154, 215-612-8170
www.woodwardskateparks.net/philly
This massive state-of-the-art facility attracts skateboarders from all over the mid-Atlantic area. You can skate for a few hours, get a monthly

Many cities have free municipal skate parks. Check "parks and recreation" on city websites for details about required safety equipment, hours of operation, and parent supervision.

Most large private skate parks offer summer camps and discounts for parents who want to skate with their kids. Bring a helmet, required at most public or commercial skateparks. Add stickers for a mod look.

membership, or just drop in to watch some of the region's best skaters. There are other locations in Dallas, Denver, and Atlanta.

kona skatepark

8739 Kona Ave., Jacksonville, FL 32211, 904-725-8770, konaskatepark.com
A Saturday lesson led by trained park riders is great for first-time visits to the park. Admission is free for parents who check their kids in to skate (and for visitors over 65!). This is the oldest continually operating skate park in the world.

vans skateparks

5220 International Dr., Orlando, FL 32819, 407-351-3881, www.vans.com
Vans has two skate park locations: one here in Florida and another in Orange County, California. Each one is situated in a shopping center, and a great place to see the latest skate clothes, boards and equipment. You can rent equipment and take lessons from expert skaters at this skating mecca.

athens skate park

701 E. State St., Athens, OH 45701, 740-592-3325
www.athensskatepark.com
This Ohio park is part of the community's parks

and recreation system, with free admission, a great outdoor setting, and seasonal contests and challenges for skaters of varying abilities. It's illuminated for skating until 11:00 p.m. most nights. Their website offers skaters tools to communicate with follow skaters.

ranney park

3201 E. Michigan Ave., Lansing, MI 48912, 517-483-4277
www.cityoflansingmi.com
Managed by the city's parks and recreation system, this free outdoor park is well maintained and popular with local skaters and rollerbladers. The course of half-pipes, rails, and boxes was designed and built by skateboarders.

mat hoffman action sports park

1700 S. Robinson St., Oklahoma City, OK 73103, 405-297-2211, www.okc.gov/Parks/skatepark/index.html
This free outdoor park has a flow course with bowl combinations of varying shapes, depths, and heights, plus a well-equipped street course. The two areas are connected with a 20-foot-wide obstacle-course sidewalk. It's open till 11:00 p.m. nightly for BMX freestyle riders, skateboarders, and inline skaters.

alamosa skate park

6900 Gonzeles Rd., SW, Albuquerque, NM 07121
505-836-8760, www.cabq.gov/recreation/skate/html
Also known as West Side Skate Park, it's been celebrated by architects and skaters alike for the way it blends design with cutting-edge skating challenges. The layout of the park echoes the forms of New

Skateboard artists design and paint amazing images, symbols, and scenes on the bottoms of boards for others to see.

Mexico's arroyos, as well as the steps, curbs, and rails of some of Albuquerque's most popular street skating locations.

skatelab

4226 Valley Fair St., Simi Valley, CA 93063
805-578-0040, www.skatelab.com
The Skateboarding Hall of Fame is located here, in a museum showcasing more than 2,000 vintage skateboards along with many highlights in the history of the sport. The park hosts weekend Skate Schools on a first-come, first-serve basis, and has a dedicated group of talented local skaters who are fun to watch. It's part of the regional SoCal Skateparks Network (www.socalskateparks.com).

louisville extreme park

Clay and Franklin Sts., Louisville, KY
502-456-8100, www.louisvilleextremepark.org
This gigantic concrete park is nationally known for its 24-foot full pipe and great outdoor location. From Lousiville's Riverwalk pathway you can walk past Slugger Field and follow a walking path under the expressway to reach the skate park. It's open 24 hours a day, year-round.

ten best
bike trails

cape cod rail trail, massachusetts

www.mass.gov/dcr/parks/southeast/ccrt.htm

You can rent bikes (including hand-pedal bikes for visitors with disabilities) at different points along 22 miles of flat path framed by sea oats, dunes, and quaint towns. The path traces the old railroad lines that once connected Boston with the Cape Cod seaside.

charles river reservation, massachusetts

www.mass.gov/dcr/parks/metroboston/charlesR.htm

Explore the historic Boston area, enjoy the sparkling Charles River, and plan to stop for a relaxing lunch in family-friendly Cambridge around the hub of Harvard University.

c & o canal trail, maryland & washington, d.c.

www.nps.gov/choh

This 184.5-mile flat trail parallels a historic waterway that begins in Georgetown and ends in Cumberland, Maryland. For a great short family ride, start in Georgetown and pedal to Fletcher's boathouse. Picnic along the Potomac. Families come from all over the country to make the entire trek.

Teach your kids to ride a bike because it's true that they will never forget.

manasquan to matawan, new jersey

www.bikely.com/maps/bike-path/Manasquan-to-Matawam-New-Jersey

Bike along old rail lines from Matawan, just south of Raritan Bay, to the Atlantic beachfront at Manasquan, near Jersey Shore resorts. The ride combines stretches of the Henry Hudson Rail Trail and the Masaquan Rail Trail.

the virginia creeper

www.vacreepertrail.com

The Virginia Creeper, great for easy-going mountain biking, runs from Whitetop to Abingdon, Virginia. The former rail bed passes through the back country of southwest Virginia, through rhododendron glades and across swift, winding streams.

the greenbrier river trail, west virginia

www.greenbrierrivertrail.com

This is a great flat rails-to-trails route for families. It follows the rushing Greenbrier River and offers an unspoiled glimpse of the Allegheny Mountains, routing riders from Caldwell to Cass, West Virginia. The 78-mile trail is also a destination for cross-country skiing. Rental cabins are located along the route.

syllamo mountain bike trail, arkansas

Green Mountain Rd., Mountain View, AR 72560, 870-757-2213
www.fs.fed.us/oonf/ozark/recreation/syllamo_bike.html

This famous mountain biking trail is part of the million-acre Ozarks-St. Francis National Forests system. If you're new to the park (or the sport), start with the Bad Branch Loop, a scenic 12-mile trail. There are 51 trail miles in all. Rent bikes in Little Rock, about two hours away. The Ozark Folk Center State Park is not far from here (www.ozarkfolkcenter.com).

mission trails regional park, california

www.mtrp.org

This San Diego park offers 40 miles of natural and developed hiking and biking trails. Families can explore the cultural, historical, and recreational aspects of this sunny, friendly city apart from the crowds at Balboa Park. The visitor's center boasts a 94-seat theater where guests explore and learn about the wonders of nature and the people who once lived on the land. It's just eight miles from downtown San Diego.

I started out to seek adventures. You don't really have to seek them . . . they come to you.

—Mark Twain

stub stewart state park, oregon

www.oregonstateparks.org/park_255.php

Gentle rolling hills, lush forests, and deep canyons just 31 miles outside of Portland. Picnic with a view of the Coast Range.

the george s. mickelson trail, south dakota

www.sdgfp.info/parks/regions/northernhills/mickelsontrail/index.htm

This 110-mile rail-to-trail winds through the heart of the beautiful Black Hills. Its gentle, accessible path has bridges and four hard rock tunnels. Bike rentals available.

Teach Your Child These Basic Safety Rules:

1. Keep your bike in good repair.
2. Wear a helmet.
3. Ride on the right side, with traffic.
4. Use appropriate hand signals.
5. Obey traffic signs and signals.
6. Keep both hands ready to brake.
7. Make eye contact with drivers.
8. Never ride with headphones.
9. Don't pass on the right.
10. Use lights at night.

tennis resorts

gunterman tennis school at stratton mountain resort

5 Village Lodge Rd., Stratton Mountain, VT 05155, 800-426-3930
www.greattennis.com

Nestled within southern Vermont's beautiful mountains, this resort pairs its top adult program with a highly rated junior day camp. Tailored instruction, seven hard courts, eight Har-Tru courts, video analysis, 4–5 hour lessons, small student-teacher ratios. Hiking, soccer, swimming, and more. Kids under 21 love the Wreck, with the billiards and a climbing wall.

The origins of tennis are still a bit of a mystery. Some people believe the game is a variation of different ancient ball games played by Egyptians, Greeks, and Romans.

wintergreen resort

Wintergreen Resort, Rt. 664
Wintergreen, VA 22958, 800-926-3723
www.wintergreenresort.com

Located in the heart of the Blue Ridge Mountains, this top-ranked resort offers 19 clay courts and 3 indoor deco-turf courts. Little ones are called Mighty Mites here, and they learn tennis while having fun. Older kids can hone their skills in clinics, drills, and competitive play under the guidance of supportive staff. It's a year-round program with two state-of-the-art tennis centers. The resort itself is world-renowned for golf and other outdoor sports.

sea colony resort

Bethany Beach, DE 19930, 888-500-4254
www.resortquestdelaware.com

This resort offers five highly rated teaching professionals who lead stimulating clinics, camps, and personal instruction for tennis players of all abilities. There are 34 courts, including four indoor and 14 Har-Tru. Off court, kids can build sand castles, swim in the ocean or pool, enjoy arts and crafts, and learn lifeguarding skills. The resort is adjacent to Bethany's small-scale boardwalk with games, shops, frozen custard, pizza, and colorful summer evening crowds.

kiawah island golf resort

One Sanctuary Beach Dr., Kiawah Island, SC 29455
800-654-2924, www.kiawahresort.com

Located along the shores of Kiawah Island, South Carolina, this resort is perfect for families. Clinics and drills are offered daily. Kids can learn the basics at the Stroke-a-Day Clinics. The Tiny Tots Program serves 4–6 year olds, Junior Tennis Camps offers extended play, and Junior Tournament Tough Workout provides competitive tennis for ranked juniors ten and older. Custom tennis vacation packages include clinics or drills plus accommodations.

palmetto dunes resort

4 Queens Folly Rd., Hilton Head Island, SC 29928
800-827-3006, www.palmettodunes.com

This top-ranked tennis program offers 23 clay and 2 Nova ProBounce courts (8 of which are lighted for night play). Group and private lessons, stroke clinics, round robins, and competitive play for adults. Short Shot Clinics help little ones learn tennis with motor skill development. Older kids will enjoy improving their strokes while participating in a variety of fun games and activities. The resort is a vacation mecca in famous Hilton Head.

colony beach & tennis resort

1620 Gulf of Mexico Dr., Longboat Key, FL 34228
800-282-1138, www.colonybeachresort.com

Beautifully located on Florida's central west coast, this resort offers a sweet spot for every family member. Choose from adult, junior, and kids' tennis clinics and more on 21 tennis courts and 10 soft-surface courts with two lighted for night play. The resort offers programs for tots as young as three. Friendly staff offer innovative lessons for children and teens. Look for value packages.

rancho valencia resort and spa

5921 Valencia Cir., Rancho Santa Fe, CA 92067
050-756-1123, www.ranchovalencia.com

Located outside of San Diego in lovely citrus-scented hills, this secluded resort offers summer and holiday tennis camps for juniors and two-hour clinics specifically tailored for the family. It's about five miles from the pretty beaches of Del Mar.

ponte vedra inn & club

200 Ponte Vedra Blvd., Ponte Vedra Beach, FL 32082
904 285-1111, www.pvresorts.com

Located in northeast Florida, beside the Atlantic Ocean, Ponte Vedra's Racquet Club hosts Leach at the Beach Summer Tennis Camp, which offers nine adult camps held in both morning or evening sessions and four junior camps for children. The Club has five Har-Tru clay courts and eight courts lighted for night play.

the broadmoor

1 Lake Ave., Colorado Springs, CO 80906
866-837-9520, www.broadmoor.com

Built in 1918 and located in Colorado Springs, this Rocky Mountain landmark has a popular Family Tennis Package that offers instruction and fun for parents and children. While parents are on the court, kids have a pool party, take a trip to the zoo, and more. Three-day junior camps focus on tennis fun and skill improvement. The all-new tennis center opened in 2009.

tops'l beach & racquet resort

9011 US Hwy. 98 W, Santa Rosa Beach, FL 32459, 850-267-9211, www.topsl.com

Located on 52 acres in the Florida Gulf, this top-ranked tennis resort has pristine courts, daily and weekly clinics, and weekend round robins. Choose from over ten tennis packages. The Kids' Club offers outdoor and indoor play for children.

ten best
horseback rides

carriage roads

Mohonk Mountain House, 1000
Mountain Rest Rd., New Platz,
NY 12561, 845-255-1000
www.mohonk.com

Ride Western-style along Mohonk's lovely carriage roads. Hour-long rides are led by experienced Mohonk trail guides.

atlantic coastal trail

Deep Hollow Ranch, Rte. 27
Montauk, NY 11954, 631-668-2744
www.deephollowranch.com

A 1½-hour guided horseback ride takes you along Block Island Sound to the beach (shorter scenic trips are also available). This is known as "America's oldest cattle ranch," on the easternmost tip of Long Island. It's said that pirate loot is buried somewhere along the shores here.

shenandoah valley, virginia

www.visitshenandoah.com/activities/family-programs.cfm
View the blue mountains and green lush valley of the Shenandoah by horseback. Trails reveal what makes this area famous: waterfalls, wildflowers, mountain summits, abandoned homesteads, and rocky streams.

Riding a horse is a wonderful childhood experience.

mackinac island, michigan

www.mackinacparks.com
During summer months, visit this beautiful island, home to more than 600 horses. Take a guided or unguided ride through wooded trails or sit back and enjoy the views from a carriage.

cowboy for a day, low country, texas

800-364-3833, www.banderacowboycapital.com
Local stables in the town of Bandera offer daily horseback riding through the beautiful Hill Country. At night, see nightly rodeo shows at area ranches. In this cowboy capital, little ones will be "skippin' rocks" and "washer pitchin'" in no time.

rocky mountain ride, colorado

www.nps.gov/romo
Just a nod outside of Denver is Rocky Mountain National Park, gateway to wonders. For the youngest rider, a gentle hour-long ride in the smooth valleys makes sense. For older kids, an alpine trip is a winner. Take a pole and sign up for

a guided ride that allows time for fishing for brown, brook, rainbow, and cutthroat trout.

zion, utah

435-679-8665, www.nps.gov/zion
View beautiful dripping springs, forested glens, and high-walled canyons by horseback. Guided tours in Zion National Park are available from March through October. More than 285 bird species have been spotted here.

yellowstone national park, wyoming, montana, idaho

307-344-7381, www.nps.gov/yell
Established in 1872, Yellowstone is America's first national park. It's located in three states and has one of the largest varieties of wildlife, including bison, elk, and grizzly bears. Leave the crowded footpaths and ride horseback on a guided tour of wildlife and waterworks—a classic way to see famous sights.

grand canyon, arizona

www.nps.gov/grca/planyourvisit/mule_trips.htm
One of the best ways to explore the Grand Canyon is by mule. For a half- or full-day exploration, try the North Rim. To reach the bottom, you must take a two-day trip from the South Rim. Sheer cliffs, stunning panoramas, and sure-footed animals make this a favorite adventure for families with older children.

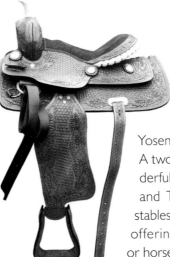

tuolumne meadows, california

www.yosemitepark.com/Activities_MuleHorsebackRides.aspx
Take a horseback trip through Yosemite with licensed park outfitters. A two-hour or half-day ride offers wonderful views of the Sierra high country and Tuolumne Falls. There are three stables within the park boundaries, each offering breathtaking views by mule or horseback.

books | the black stallion

by walter farley
Walter Farley's love of horses started when he was a little boy in Syracuse, New York. His interest continued as he grew up in New York City, where his family moved. Farley never actually owned a horse. But his uncle, who was a professional horseman, spent a lot of time at the stables with him. This family influence shaped his understanding of the equestrian world. Farley's uncle changed his interest in horses from runners to jumpers to show horses to trotters and pacers, then back to runners again. This provided Farley with a great background on many different types of training and trainers.

ten best
auto raceways

new hampshire motorspeedway

1122 Rte. 106 N., Loudon, NH 03307, 603-783-4931, www.nhms.com

This speedway hosts the only NASCAR Sprint Cup Series, NASCAR Nationwide Series, and NASCAR Craftsman Truck Series events held in the New England region. Racing schools are conducted throughout the year by the Richard Petty Driving Experience and Penguin School.

bristol motor speedway

151 Speedway Blvd., Bristol, TN 37620 423-989-6933, www.bristolmotorspeed way.com

Track tours include Thunder Valley, the home of Bristol Dragway, cruising its quarter-mile, and then a view overlooking the course, plus a lap around the track.

lowe's motor speedway

5555 Concord Pkwy., S., Concord, NC 20027 704-455-3200, www.lowesmotorspeedway.com

Tour the racetrack and explore the racing gift shop. Several driving schools are nearby, including the Richard Petty Driving Experience. The Auto Racing Hall of Fame is in Mooresville.

Bring earplugs—the noise level at races can reach 110 decibels. Earplugs can reduce the effect by up to 30 decibels.

atlanta motor speedway

Hwy. 19-41, Hampton, GA 30228 770-946-4211, www.atlanta motorspeedway.com

Twice a year, this is the site of the popular NASCAR Sprint Cup Series. But, for the rest of the year, the Atlanta Motor Speedway is open to the public for speed-way and behind-the-scenes tours. Friday night drag racing sparkles with a "show & shine" contest.

daytona international speedway

1801 W. International Speedway Blvd. Daytona Beach, FL 32114, 386-254-2700 www.daytonainternationalspeedway.com

Located an hour from Disneyworld, this legendary speedway is a must-see for NASCAR fans. For budding racers, try the Richard Petty Driving Experience. Visit Daytona US, where guests can pilot a stock racing car, design a car, or practice pit crew skills.

sebring international raceway

113 Midway Dr., Sebring, FL 33870 863-655-1442, www.sebringraceway.com

Located among the orange groves and cattle

ranches of central Florida, Sebring is the oldest permanent road-racing track in the United States. Its annual 12 Hours of Sebring endurance race is part of the American Le Mans Series and includes tours, amusement rides, and automobile displays.

talladega superspeedway

3366 Speedway Blvd., Talladega,
AL 35160, 877-462-3342
www.talladegasuperspeedway.com
NASCAR's Most Competitive Track offers visitors a ride on the tracks or a tour of the speedway's hall of fame, featuring stock race cars, Indy cars, drag racers, and motorcycles. Visit nearby Birmingham for southern comfort food, or take a short hike in the Talladega National Forest.

indianapolis motor speedway

4790 W. 16th St., Indianapolis, IN 46222, 317-492-6700,
www.indianapolismotorspeedway.com
Visit the extensive Hall of Fame Museum, a national historic landmark, to see approximately 75 vehicles on display, including the Marmon Wasp, which won the inaugural Indianapolis 500 in 1911. See (but don't touch) Brickyard bricks.

rocket | going fast
An NHRA Top Fuel dragster leaves the starting line with a force nearly five times that of gravity, the same force of the space shuttle when it leaves the launching pad at Cape Canaveral. **National Hot Rod Association:** *www.nhra.org*

texas motorplex

7500 W. Hwy. 287, Ennis, TX 75119, 972-878-2641
www.texasmotorplex.com
Located in Dallas, this is a favorite for drag racing fans. It's the site of a Guinness Book of World Record winner: the Fastest Speed in Top Fuel NHRA Drag Racing (Female) was 330.31 mph in 2005. In September it's the site of the world-renowned Fall Nationals. Reserve in advance for the best grandstand seats.

infineon raceway

Hwys. 37 and 121, Sonoma, CA 95476, 800-870-RACE
www.infeonraceway.com
Formerly known as Sears Point Raceway, this site is host to one of only five yearly NASCAR races that run on road courses. Known for its complex, twisting route, it also offers kids eight and older a chance to get behind the wheel at the Jim Russell International Karting Centre.

Quarter midgets are race cars driven by kids between five and sixteen years old. Parents are really involved in the sport, with races held on tracks across the nation: www.quartermidgets.org.

great outdoors

resorts, campgrounds, hikes, national parks, climbing, ranches, geocaching, extreme adventures, road trips

Few places make sights, sounds, and smells come alive like the wilderness. The rays of sunlight streaking through tall trees with a dozen shades of green; the crumpling of fallen leaves underfoot and echoes of birdsongs overhead; the aroma of wildflowers and high grass.

Be it hiking trails, rock climbs, ranches, or national parks, outdoor vacations offer wonders that few human-made ventures can. There is a virtual learning experience in every step. Below and above ground, there are hundreds of insect and animal species, plant life, and rock formations. The night sky, undisturbed by light pollution, is filled with starry constellations.

Vacationing in the outdoors is a valuable learning experience as well. It is arguably the best way for families to learn about the environment and the importance of preserving it. In fact, it's essential to human health. Views of mountains and greenery and the sounds

. . . we contemplate the whole globe as one great dewdrop, striped and dotted with continents and islands, flying through space with other stars all singing and shining together as one, the whole universe appears as an infinite storm of beauty.

—John Muir

of crashing surf are proven to improve moods, reduce stress, and increase a sense of well-being.

The National Park System was founded to preserve some of our most beautiful wild places. Many include well-informed tour guides that convey the history of a national park and how its species thrive year-round. Others have markers that tell of famous battles fought or sojourns that paved the way for modern-day cities and towns. And most have Junior Ranger programs to intrigue and educate young visitors.

Campgrounds and all-inclusive resorts enable families to rest and relax in the outdoors and take part in age-old rituals such as telling stories and roasting marshmallows around campfires. These are essential childhood experiences, helping young people to think of wilderness as "home," and to establish lifelong habits of enjoying, protecting, and respecting wild places.

ten best
all-inclusive resorts

the balsams grand resort hotel

1000 Cold Spring Rd., Dixville
Notch, NH 03576, 877-225-7276
www.thebalsams.com

Set on 15,000 acres in the
mountains of New Hampshire,
this grand, old-fashioned place
runs Camp Wind Whistle, with
activities day and night, seven
days a week in the summer, for
kids age five to ten-plus.

Resorts can be a great deal when you factor in the value of children's activities.

smugglers' notch resort

4323 Vermont Rte. 108 S., Smugglers' Notch, VT 05464
800-419-4615, www.smuggs.com

The resort's Snow Sport University is world-
renowned and caters to all levels. Other outdoor
activities include cross-country skiing and snowshoeing, dogsledding, and snowmobile touring.

mohonk mountain house

1000 Mountain Rest Rd., New Paltz, NY 12561
800-772-6646, www.mohonk.com

Built on Lake Mohonk in 1869, this 265 room Vic
torian castle is one of America's oldest family-owned
resorts. Mohonk has over 85 miles of hiking trails,
tennis, midweek golf, lake swimming, boating, ice-
skating, cross-country skiing, and snowshoeing. Its
children's programs are especially popular.

the homestead

1766 Homestead Dr., Hot Springs,
VA 24445, 866-354-4653
www.thehomestead.com

Founded ten years before
the American Revolution, this
historic luxury resort draws
visitors to its hot springs. For
preschoolers to 'tweens: The
Homestead Kids' Club has
games, hikes, crafts, stories and
plays, swimming, and homemade popsicles in summer
(ice-skating and cocoa in the winter).

the greenbrier

300 W. Main St., White Sulphur Springs, WV 24986
800-453-4858, www.greenbrier.com

A national historic landmark, the Greenbrier was
built in 1778 and is nationally known for its golf
courses. The resort offers full-day and evening
programs for ages 6–12 that combine artistic and
intellectual enrichment with physical and outdoor
activities.

the sanctuary

One Sanctuary Beach Dr., Kiawah Island, SC 29455
800-654-2924, www.kiawahresort.com

Housed in a grand mansion, the resort includes
255 spacious rooms and suites. Its Kiawah Kids

Program (for ages 3–11) is located at the 21-acre Night Heron Park, with sports, crabbing, face painting, crafts, environmentally sensitive nature hikes, and scavenger hunts.

hawks cay resort

61 Hawk's Cay Blvd., Duck Key, FL 33050
305-743-7000, www.hawkscay.com
This 60-acre resort is nestled in the heart of the Florida Keys and surrounded by the only living coral reef in the continental United States. Water activities are the main attraction at Hawk's Cay, where families can sail, scuba dive, and snorkel, deep-sea and fly-fish, water ski, and join ecotours.

grand traverse

100 Grand Travese Blvd., Acme, MI 49610
800-236-1577, www.grandtraverseresort.com
Golf, sailing, cross-country skiing, and tennis are just a few outdoor activities with extra programs for families. The resort has a range of restaurants, plus the Cub House (caring for children under age six), hiking, nature programs in Camp Traverse, and special weekend Kids' Night Out offerings. Kids love the treehouse at the Indies Club.

hyatt regency hill country resort

9800 Hyatt Resort Dr.
San Antonio, TX 78251
210-647-1234
www.hillcountry.hyatt.com
This resort is convenient to San Antonio attractions including Six Flags, Sea World, Natural Bridge Caverns, and the Alamo. Camp Hyatt is available for children ages 3 to 12. Go wild with a cowboy-and-Indian motif: rodeo, totem poles, arrowhead searching, and nature hikes and coyote-spotting are all part of the fun.

sunriver resort

17600 Center Dr., Sunriver, OR 97707
800-801-8765, www.sunriver-resort.com
With nearly 300 days of sun, the resort exudes the ambiance of the Pacific Northwest. Sunriver excels at everything, from service to dining to recreation and spa. The Sunriver Nature Center & Observatory offers education and insight into the natural world of the surrounding Cascades mountain landscape. Fort Funnigan is base camp for kids' adventures, arts, and crafts.

"

fran, washington, d.c. | siblings Some of our best vacations happened when we brought cousins along with us. Everyone got along so well. Maybe it was a case of "the more the merrier," or children being on their best behavior when others were around. I'd encourage other families to do this!

ten best
campgrounds

chippokes plantation state park

695 Chippokes Park Rd. Surry, VA 23883, 757-294-3625, www.dcr.virginia.gov/state_parks/chi.shtml
Fifty beautiful campsites surrounded by leafy trees, rolling farmland, historic buildings, and the James River. Programs include Chippokes at Play, featuring colonial and Native American children's games, family-friendly canoe trips, group campfires, and more.

nickerson state park

Rte. 6A, Brewster, MA 02631, 508-896-3491
www.mass.gov/dcr/parks/southeast/nick.htm
Camp surrounded by woods that slope down to the banks of eight crystal-clear, freshwater ponds.

[
Try this: A great thing to do around a campfire with kids is to start a story and have everyone go around and add to it. You will be amazed at the tale you can spin!
]

Every child should sleep under the stars at least once before he grows up!

Cape Cod Bay is within walking or bicycling distance. Swim and canoe at Flax Pond, bird-watch, or catch and release fish at Higgins Pond.

wildwood state park

North Wading River Rd. Wading River, NY 11792 631-929-4314, http://nys parks.state.ny.us/parks/info.asp?parkID=52
An hour and a half drive east of New York City, this campground has deep forests and sits on the high bluff overlooking Long Island Sound. Pitch a tent in one of the 322 campsites, go for a swim in the Long Island Sound, and lunch under shady trees.

first landing state park

2500 Shore Dr., Virginia Beach, VA 23451, 757-412-2300, www.dcr.virginia.gov/state_parks/fir.shtml
A traditional family campground offering historical, cultural, and natural attractions. More than 220 campsites and some cabins situated among oaks near the dunes of the Chesapeake Bay. Sand-castle building, swimming, crabbing, and more. You'll see (and hear) Navy training jets overhead.

petersburg park

3998 Petersburg Rd., Appling, GA
30802, 706-541-9464
www.sas.usace.army.mil/lakes/
thurmond/campinginfo.htm
Petersburg Park is located on Thurmond Lake near Augusta. This popular, family-friendly park has 86 lakeside campsites, clean rest rooms, and hot showers. Beaches, hiking trails, and more. It's managed by the U.S. Army Corps of Engineers.

roche-a-cri state park

1767 Hwy. 13, Friendship, WI 53934
608-565-2789 www.dnr.state.wi.us
A quiet family campground with 41 rustic campsites—and playgrounds, too. The park's centerpiece is a 300-foot rock formation with stairs to climb. See petroglyphs and pictographs. An annual Pumpkin Walk is held before Halloween, and naturalist programs are held on weekends during the summer.

boyd lake state recreation area

3720 N. County Rd. 11-C, Loveland, CO 80538, 970-669-1739, http://parks.state.co.us/Parks/BoydLake
If you're looking for plenty of activities, head to this park in Loveland. Families return year after year to enjoy its playgrounds, beaches, fishing, and numerous campsites. Boyd Lake is a premier recreational facility of the Front Range area. Make reservations up to 180 days in advance.

In wilderness is the preservation of the world.

—Henry David Thoreau

apgar

Glacier National Park Headquarters,
West Glacier, MT 59936
406-888-7800, www.nps.gov/glac
On the west side of Glacier National Park, next to Lake MacDonald, this family-friendly campground is the largest in the park. Its proximity to the lake offers tired hikers a chance to cool off. Also located close to Apgar Village and visitors center. Ranger programs are conducted nearby.

jenny lake

Grand Teton National Park, Moose, WY
83112, 307-739-3300, www.nps.gov/grte
Private campsites nestled between pines and rocks at the base of the Tetons, located inside Grand Teton National Park in northwestern Wyoming. In 1972 Congress dedicated 24,000 acres as the John D. Rockerfeller Jr. Parkway, recognizing his generousity and foresight. This parkway is a link between two national parks—Grand Teton and Yellowstone.

takhlakh lake

Gifford Pinchot National Forest, 10024 US Hwy. 12
Randle, WA 98377, 360-497-1100 www.fs.fed.us/gpnf
Rustic camping facilities are available in one of America's most beautiful settings. In this forest you'll see lakeside views of Mt. Adams, a volcano located east of Mt. St. Helens.

ten best
national parks

acadia national park

Bar Harbor, ME 04609
207-288-3338
www.nps.gov/acad

View this park's stunning ocean shoreline by driving the 27-mile Park Loop Road. On the eastern edge of the island is Sand Beach, the perfect spot to view a sunrise, spread an afternoon picnic, and explore tide pools teeming with barnacles, sea stars, and crabs. The Junior Ranger program offers boat tours.

isle royale national park

800 Lakeshore Dr., Houghton, MI 49931
906-482-0984, www.nps.gov/isro/

Located on Lake Superior, this wonderful, wild park is a maritime adventure. Hike its many trails, explore its rugged coast, listen to wolves. Arrive by ferry or plane, and plan to pitch a tent or stay at Rock Harbor Lodge, the park's only lodge.

bryce canyon national park

Bryce Canyon, UT 84764, 435-834-5322
www.nps.gov/brca

The rim of Utah's high plateau dazzles with pastel-colored stones in fantastic shapes called

Gray wolves were reintroduced to Yellowstone National Park after a seventy-year absence.

hoodoos. Hunt for favorites: Queen Victoria, the Sinking Ship, and the Alligator. At night, budding astronomers stargaze through park telescopes into one of the best dark skies on Earth.

gateway arch/ jefferson national expansion memorial

11 North 4th St., St. Louis, MO 63102, 314-655-1700
www.nps.gov/jeff

For a stunning view of St. Louis, ride the tram to the top of the tallest monument in America, the soaring 630-foot stainless steel arch. Afterward, explore the lives of Lewis and Clark, sodbusters, cowboys, American Indians, and more in the underground Museum of Westward Expansion.

mount rushmore national memorial

Hwy. 244, Bldg. 31 Suite 1, Keystone, SD 57751
605-574-2523, www.nps.gov/moru

This 5,725-foot-tall granite landmark is an engineering feat in the remote Black Hills. Each nose is 20 feet long, and each pupil is carved to bring sparkle and life to Presidents Washington, Jefferson,

Lincoln, and Theodore Roosevelt. Visit the sculptor's studio or detonate dynamite at one of the exhibits.

yellowstone national park, wyoming, montana, idaho

307-344-7381, www.nps.gov/yell

In 1872, Congress established the world's first national park here in Earth's greatest geyser area, with more than 10,000 geysers. Watch Old Faithful spew, see bison herds in Lamar Valley, climb over weird rocks in Mammoth Hot Springs, and don't miss the Grand Canyon of the Yellowstone.

john day fossils bed national monument

32651 Hwy. 19, Kimberly, OR 97848
541-987-2333, www.nps.gov/joda

Journey to ancient Oregon. Look at fossils in the museum, explore hands-on activities in the classroom, work on a Junior Ranger badge, or watch actual paleontologists at work in the lab.

grand canyon national park

Grand Canyon, AZ 86023, 928-638-7888
www.nps.gov/grca

Known worldwide for its geological grandeur, this

> *The national park is the best idea America ever had.*
>
> —James Bryce
> *British Ambassador 1907–1913*

park is a great destination for families with older kids. Try the Junior Ranger Adventure Hike down the strenuous South Kaibab Trail or, for kids seven and up, hitch a mule ride at the North Rim. Tykes in tow? Rangers read fun books, hand out condor tattoos, and administer the Junior Ranger Oath.

walnut canyon national monument

6400 N. Hwy. 89, Flagstaff, AZ 86004, 928-526-3367
www.nps.gov/waca

Here's a hint from a family in the know. This is a wonderful canyon alternative for families with small children. Less crowded, it's also a smaller canyon with easier, more manageable hikes and views of cliff dwellings built by the Sinagua people 800 years ago.

zion national park

Springdale, UT 84767, 435-772-3256, www.nps.gov/zion

Grand Canyon in reverse: sheer cliffs of colored sandstone rise to the blue sky. Along the Virgin River a short and popular hike called Riverside Walk boasts small rapids and pools, hanging wildflower gardens, and an ever narrowing rock corridor. Horseback tours are available.

"

brendan, pennsylvania | national parks I am 8 and my sister is 11. We pick up our Junior Ranger programs at the visitor center and fill in the answers with things we learn at the park. When we finish, an actual Park Ranger swears us in and gives us badges! We earned our first badges at Death Valley in 2006.

rock climbing

the chelsea piers sports complex

Pier 60, 23rd St. & the Hudson River New York, NY 10011, 212-336-6000 www.chelseapiers.com

Step into a harness and learn safety knots at this popular New York City gym. Discover rappelling and belaying on the 30-foot-high rock-climbing wall, designed specially for children and youth.

ems climbing school

White Mountain Exploration, 151 Tenney Mountain Rd., Plymouth, NH 03264, 888-289-1020, www.white mountainexploration.com

Located near the White Mountains, this climbing school offers half- and full-day family climbs. Gear up for an outdoor, hands-on experience as you decend the spectacular Tenney Mountain Gorge.

rei outdoor school

1790 Expo Pkwy., Sacramento, CA 95815 916-924-8900, www.rei.com/outdoorschool

Three levels of climbing classes are offered, beginning with practice at the store's indoor climbing wall and (eventually) culminating in challenging local rock climbs. This outfitter offers classes in outdoor

Prepare for a climbing adventure with a few trips to a climbing gym.

arts and sciences through most of its locations (including Boston, Philadelphia, D.C. area, and coastal California).

carderock

Georgetown Visitors Center, 1057 Thomas Jefferson St., NW, Washington, DC 20007, 202-653-5190 www.nps.gov/choh

Located in C & O Canal National Historic Park, this craggy spot is just minutes from the District of Columbia. A popular climbing destination since the 1920s, Carderock has routes for newbies as well as advanced climbers.

seneca rocks

Monongahela National Forest, 200 Sycamore St., Elkins, WV 26241, 304-636-1800, www.fs.fed.us/r9/mnf

Located in the Monongahela National Forest, this is a challenging rock climb. Dramatic views, trails abound. Local mountaineering guides offer family classes.

rocky mountain national park

1000 Hwy. 36, Estes Park, CO 80517, 970-586-1206 www.nps.gov/romo

Climbing has been popular here since the 1800s, and the park offers a range of opportunities: rock, big wall, snow and ice, bouldering, and mountaineering. For guided climbs, contact the park's licensed climbing concessionaire, the Colorado Mountain School: www.cmschool.com.

grand teton national park

Jackson, WY, 307-739-3300, www.nps.gov/grte

This beautiful park offers rock climbers a bit of everything. Families with young children like the four-day climbing camp or day-long parent/child classes offered by the park's concessionaires. Guides provide hands-on practice in the middle of the Tetons.

yosemite

Yosemite Mountaineering School, Yosemite, CA 95389 209-372-1000, www.nps.gov/yose

Yosemite is considered one of the world's greatest climbing areas. The Yosemite Mountaineering School offers climbing classes for all ages as well as guided climbs. Tuolomne Meadows is a wonderful place for rock scrambling for those too young to scale a sheer wall.

joshua tree national park

74485 National Park Dr., Twentynine Palms, CA 92277 760-367-5500, www.nps.gov/jotr

This is where the Colorado Desert's vast emptiness abuts the Mojave's giant yucca plants and rock piles. Start at the Oasis Visitor's Center, stop

Sneakers are the basics for kid-friendly scrambles. Rappeling requires more stuff, more skill and preparation.

at Jumbo Rocks and Skull Rock, and be sure to explore the scenic Hidden Valley, popular with both climbers and spectators.

smith rock state park

Redmond, OR 97756, 800-551-6949 www.oregonstateparks.org/park_51.php

Located in central Oregon's dry desert, this park offers hundreds of climbing routes. For guided climbs, First Ascent (www.goclimbing.com) provides family climbs, as well as kids' camps and classes. Ask about special programs for guests at nearby resorts.

rock-climbing glossary

bouldering: climbing on big rocks without equipment.

carabiner: a spring-loaded ring for attaching rope to a other tools.

chock: a tool that wedges anchors into crevices in rock.

piton: a spike to help with climbing, hammered into a crack or crevice.

rappel: to descend by rope after a climb.

scramble: a casual climb without equipment, on low-lying rocks.

scree: piles of broken rock, often at the bottom of a cliff.

ten best
ranches

rocking horse ranch

600 Rte. 44/55, Highland, NY 12528
800-647-2624
www.rhranch.com

Created in 1958, the Rocking Horse Ranch is located in the Hudson River Valley. Families enjoy kayaks, paddle boats, and fishing on the ranch lake. There's an indoor "fun barn," workout room, miniature golf, beach volleyball, tennis, heated pool, and more on 500 mountain and orchard acres.

ymca ranch

Silver Bay YMCA of the Adirondacks, 87 Silver Bay Rd.
Silver Bay, NY 12874, 518-543-8833, www.silverbay.org

Located in the heart of the Adirondacks on beautiful Lake George, Silver Bay is an all-family resort with year-round activities like boating, hiking, swimming, crafts, and campfires. Your local YMCA membership gets you a discount here.

horseshoe canyon ranch

3900 Lochridge Rd., Jasper, AR 72116
800-480-9635 www.gohcr.com

Next to the pristine Buffalo National River wilderness near Jasper you can explore caves, catch a glimpse of local elk, and enjoy a barbeque cookout before tucking in at nightfall. Sleep well in your

Put on a cowboy hat and suddenly the world looks like a very adventurous place.

comfortable, rustic log cabin with its spectacular views of rolling meadows and high cliffs.

mountain sky guest ranch

Big Creek Rd., Emigrant, MT 59027
800-548-3392, www.mtnsky.com

Well-trained counselors supervise dress-up, plays, skits, campfires, and fun playtime. Adults can ride or hike in to a stream-side, authentic cowboy breakfast. The kids take the ranch van! Kids have their own dinners, followed by nightly s'mores.

twin peaks ranch

Salmon, ID 83467, 800-659-4899
www.twinpeaksranch.com

Located near Salmon, Idaho, on the River of No Return, this 29,000-acre working ranch offers families an authentic wild West experience. Families can pack into the ranch's wilderness tent camp in an elk preserve. Or overnight at Rams Head river camp on the Salmon while white-water rafting. Participate in a cattle roundup and drive, team penning, or trap and target shooting on the ranch. Look forward to nighttime line dancing instruction, sing-alongs, and live western bands.

tanque verde guest ranch

14301 E. Speedway, Tucson, AZ 85748, 800-234-3833, www.tvgr.com
Come to the foothills of the Rincon and the Catalina Mountains between the Coronado National Forest and Saguaro National Park. Tanque Verde provides hiking, horseback riding, and mountain biking with experienced trail guides, wranglers, and bikers. The fully supervised children's program provides ranch experience for kids ages 4 through 11.

burnt well guest ranch

399 Chesser Rd., Roswell, NM 88203
866-729-0974, www.burntwellguestranch.com
This is a family-owned and -operated cattle and sheep ranch in sunny southeastern New Mexico. Small guest capacity makes this a personal, tailored ranch experience. It's an active vacation, too, since this is a working cattle and sheep ranch. You check more than 50 miles of fence or just ride on the well-trained ranch horses (no nose to tail horses here).

To make the best s'mores, start with marshmallows roasted over an outdoor campfire and add your imagination.

rock springs guest ranch

64201 Tyler Rd., Bend, OR 97701
800-225-3833, www.rocksprings.com
A highlight here is the youth program. Guests ages 4 to 12 have a staff of youth counselors, on duty from 9 a.m. to 8:30 p.m., who put together fun, flexible programs.

bar m ranch

58840 Bar M La., Adams, OR 97810,
888-824-3381 www.barmranch.com
Tucked away on the Umatilla River in the Blue Mountains of eastern Oregon, this 3,000-acre ranch has miles of scenic mountain and river trails to ride on. Kids fish the stocked pond or catch and release rainbows on the river. Shoot hoops in the log barn. There's outdoor dining on the deck and campfires at night under the stars.

spanish springs ranch

530-234-2050, www.spanishspringsresort.com
Step into this High Sierra lodge in California and smell a heady mix of leather, coffee, flowers, and pies. Ages five and up can learn to ride in a serious but varied horseback-riding program and more.

"

danielle, virginia | wild west My best vacation ever was at a dude ranch in Wyoming. "Dudes" are the guests, and pretty much all ranch activity centers around each one. I loved riding horses and rafting on some of the fastest water I'd ever seen. Guests come from all over the world.

ten best
extreme adventures

hot air ballooning albuquerque, new mexico

www.newmexico.org/play/air/index.php

Unique weather and wind patterns make this city the balloon capital of the world. Visit the International Balloon Museum and then take a hot air balloon ride into Albuquerque's wide, blue skies. This city is home to the annual Balloon Fiesta, held each October.

treasure hunting yosemite, california

www.nps.gov/yose

Don't forget to take your technology into the wilderness! But this time, let it be a GPS unit. At Yosemite, kids enter latitude and longitude coordinates into their hand-held units and search for a cache of fun treasure hidden in various waterfalls, vistas, and special sites. Top it off with a half-day rock-climbing class and a tram ride to Upper Grove for a top of the world view.

alpine rides, utah

www.utah.com/parkcity/alpine_slide.htm

Try a luge-style ride on one of the world's longest

GPS unit for treasure hunting in Yosemite National Park

slides, located at Park City's Utah Olympic Park. The 3,000-foot narrow course ends at the base of the K-64 ski jump. Don't forget to try the World's Steepest Zipline: The Xtreme Zip goes 50 mph. Take the slower Ultra Zip along the winter freestyle hill.

kayaking, san juan islands, washington

www.experiencewa.com

Take a three-hour kayak trip around these beautiful Pacific Northwest islands. Licensed guides give paddling lessons, as well as safety and equipment tips to the whole family. Then push off and paddle through ever-green-shaded coastlines. Great seal- and whale-spotting opportunities.

surf's up, santa cruz, california

www.richardschmidt.com/www.beachboardwalk.com

Before summer heats up, think surfing. And Santa Cruz, just south of San Francisco, is the perfect place to go. Sign up for surf camp, where beginners can take up a board and hang ten. Visit the Surfing Museum nearby. In the evening, stroll the Santa Cruz boardwalk and take a ride on that classic wooden roller coaster, the Giant Dipper.

snorkeling, the keys, florida

www.nps.gov/bisc

Explore this beautiful underwater wilderness (where only five percent of the park is land) with fins, snorkel, and mask. At the Dante Fascell Visitors Center, sign up for a reef cruise in a glass-bottom boat or join a snorkel and dive excursion.

packtrip into "the bob," montana

www.fs.fed.us/r1/flathead/

Customize a family pack trip and head into the Bob Marshall Wilderness. Kids as young as six can ride horseback deep into the scenic, wild backcountry where moose, bear, trout, and silence reign supreme. At night, snuggle around the fire and hear backcountry tales under the stars.

heli-skiing, alaska

www.winterinalaska.com

Would your family like to plunge out of a helicopter onto the edge of a snow-clad mountain? Plan to visit Valdez, Cordova, Girdwood, Haines, or Juneau from February to April. Just want to watch?

Excitement releases adrenaline, boosting heart rates and making you feel breathless. It's a good thing!

Visit Valdez's ten-day Chugach Mountain Festival for an extreme sports and film fest.

rock climbing, jackson hole, wyoming

www.nps.gov/grte

Harness up for a day of rock climbing in the middle of Grand Teton National Park. Kids learn hands-on during day-long classes or four-day camps administered by the park's licensed concessionaires. In the evening, roast s'mores by campfire or dine in comfort at Jenny Lake Lodge.

dogsledding days, alaska

www.winterinalaska.com

Whether the family wants to learn to mush or simply to ride a sled, Alaska offers the real bark. In Fairbanks, you can try a short, 15-minute sled trip or longer. Or, experience Denali West Lodge's multiday trip: From Fairbanks fly to Lake Minchumina, and step off the plane and onto the runners of a dogsled.

"
anna, oklahoma | fear I remember looking at my son and husband's faces—white as ghosts—thinking the same thing they were thinking. "There is no way I am jumping out of this helicopter." But we did it and then skied down the most beautiful mountain in our lives.

ten best
famous road trips

covered bridges, vermont

www.bennington.com

See five covered bridges on one drive through Vermont's Bennington County: Silk Bridge, Paper Mill, Village Bridge, Henry Bridge, and West Arlington Bridge. Autumn is the best time to go, but it's also lovely in late spring.

lighthouse tour, maine

www.visitmaine.com

There are 65 lighthouses still standing in Maine. Today, about ten light stations include museums; others are bird sanctuaries, wildlife refuges, or a nature preserve; and a few house research facilities. Drive from Frazer Point Picnic Area and Winter Harbor Light to Prospect Harbor and Prospect Harbor Light, Maine, in one day.

skyline drive, virginia

www.nps.gov/shen

The 105-mile parkway along the crest of the Blue Ridge mountains starts in Front Royal, Virginia, and winds above the Shenandoah River valley, where early American Indians lived and where Daniel Boone and settlers passed through on their

Notice how the scenery changes around every bend, hill, and fork in the road.

way to the western frontier. The mountains here are smooth and low, and famed for the blue mist created by foliage.

a1a scenic & historic coastal byway, florida

www.byways.org/explore/byways/2477

Allow two hours to drive this byway, which lies between the Atlantic Ocean and the Intercoastal Waterway on a narrow barrier island. Along with breathtaking views, you'll see the Gulf Coast, flora and fauna, resorts, and art deco architecture.

michigan's peninsulas

www.michigan.org/partners/North-Coast/

See the iconic dunes, shoreline, waterfalls, pines, and famed cherry orchards. The road stretches from Sleeping Bear Dunes to Petoskey to St. Ignace to Sault Ste. Marie to Munsing.

san juan skyway, colorado

http://ouraycolorado.com/San+Juan+Skyway

Travel the "road to the sky," which offers views of the towering 14,000-foot San Juan Mountains to rolling hillsides speckled with ancient Pueblo Indian ruins. It's a 236-mile route from Durango to Ouray, through Telluride and Mancos, back to Durango.

albuquerque to taos, new mexico

www.turquoisetrail.org

Explore the Southwest through its fabled history and figures. Drive the Turquoise Trail from Albuquerque to Santa Fe to Taos, then back to Albuquerque to discover the culture of the Pueblo Indians, Georgia O'Keeffe, mountains, canyons, cliffs, cliff paintings, ghost towns, and artist colonies.

going-to-the-sun road, montana

www.nps.gov/glac

Lake McDonald is Glacier National Park's largest lake, at ten miles long. Driving along the McDonald Valley provides a history of the glaciers that carved the U-shaped valley. Families can park at the visitor's center at Logan Pass, the top of the Continental Divide. The road leads to the Going-to-the-Sun Mountain, at 9,642 the highest in this area of the park.

> Look for chances to take the less-traveled roads. There are no wrong turns.

HIGHWAY 1

pacific coastal highways, california

www.byways.org

Take in the West Coast in its entirety or in manageable short jaunts. The first section begins in Portland, passing the Willamette River, early pioneer settlements, stunning waterfalls, rugged coastline, weird monoliths, and towering redwoods. The second section from San Francisco to L.A. features the Golden Gate, Big Sur, wine country, Hearst Castle, Spanish missions, Hollywood, mountains, beaches, surfing, and harbors.

chain of craters, hawaii

www.nps.gov/havo/planyourvisit/craterdr.htm

Chain of Craters Road, located in Hawaii Volcanoes National Park, is a 20-mile journey that showcases a natural landscape shaped by volcanoes. Whether driving or hiking, visitors can see craters, lava flows, tropical rain forests, mountains, and coastal areas.

> " **amy, florida | out for a drive** I always say that my car has better upholstery than most of the furniture in my house. No wonder we all love leisurely sightseeing drives, with time to talk, look out the window, maybe stop for ice cream . . .

wheels & rails

trains, buses, transportation museums

Vacations are the perfect time to try new things: unusual food, "resort wear," novel surroundings like a beach house or a hotel room. The same goes for transportation—when you're on the road, it's the perfect time to try out a new way of getting around.

Add to that the sheer fascination we all have with stuff that moves: Powerful trains, sleek race cars, and indefatigable buses are iconic objects in the life of a child. Playthings on a grand scale, they can be both vacation destinations *and* the means of getting there!

Consider the sense of anticipation that comes with having a ticket in hand—and maybe a picnic lunch, too. Peruse a route map and think about the stops along the way. Practice etiquette by giving a seat to an elderly passenger, or making appropriate small talk with someone across the aisle. A simple train ride is packed with opportunities to learn . . . and moments to remember.

Everything changes when the parent's not in the driver's seat. On a long train ride there are card games to play and books to read.

> There is more to life than increasing its speed.
>
> —Mahatma Gandhi

On a bus trip there's the passing view from a big window, with running commentary that you make up together as you go. Along the way you might try needlepoint, magic tricks, palm reading, origami—fun and easy activities with materials (if any) that fit in your pocket, ready to pull out at a moment's notice.

Tour buses are staffed with knowledgeable guides, gifted at sharing the stories of their cities and byways. "Theme" trains are a return to the time mentioned in grandparents' anecdotes, when railcars were the primary source of mass transit. And thanks to America's major rail and highway systems, getting there is half the fun of a family journey. Your imagination goes along for the ride when you visit museums that showcase innovative examples of engine power and travel.

So take a cue from the childhood obsession with wheels, rails, and all things that go. There's a world of adventure waiting, and your family would love to get there—fast!

All aboard!

big train trips

adirondack:
montreal–albany–
new york city

Leave the skyscrapers of New York City for views of the lush, color-suffused Hudson River Valley. Military buffs will like seeing West Point Military Academy and Lake Champlain, home of Fort Ticonderoga. The Adirondack hugs the shoreline for 50 miles and comes to a stop in charming Montreal.

Who knows where the tracks will take you?

lake shore limited:
chicago–albany–
new york city

Along the shore of Lake Michigan and the Erie Canal, follow a famous Native American highway. In New York State, pass through the Finger Lakes region, where Harriet Tubman, founder of the Underground Railroad, lived.

cardinal: manhattan–chicago

See rolling horse country, the Blue Ridge and Allegheny mountains, the Shenandoah Valley, and the white-water rapids of West Virginia. Heading westward, continue to Indianapolis and then northward to Chicago.

capitol limited:
washington, d.c.–
pittsburgh–chicago

Travel through the history of American democracy. Pass the capital and travel through historic towns, including the site of John Brown's 1859 raid at Harpers Ferry. The route passes famous Civil War battlefields and offers mountain views. At nightfall, the train arrives in Pittsburgh, crosses into Ohio, and ends in Chicago.

texas eagle:
chicago–san antonio

Explore the Land of Lincoln, cross the mighty Mississippi, and take in views of the Ozarks. Go from Little Rock to cosmopolitan Dallas, through bat-friendly Austin, and finally to San Antonio, site of the Alamo.

empire builder: chicago–
seattle–portland

West from Chicago, see the sandstone formations of the Wisconsin Dells. In Montana (during summer months), the train stops at a log cabin station in Glacier National Park. In Spokane, the route splits. The Seattle destination passes through the seven-mile Cascade Tunnel. The Portland route follows along Lewis and Clarke's expedition, past waterfalls and majestic scenery.

california zephyr: chicago–san francisco

One of the most beautiful train trips in the country, the *Zephyr* traverses much of the West's spectacular scenery. Tracing the route of early pioneers, the *Zephyr* crosses the Rockies, taking numerous switchbacks as it gains altitude. The route has 29 tunnels and crosses the Continental Divide, at 9,000 feet above sea level. Along the way is Grand Mesa, the world's largest flat-topped mountain. Cross the Utah desert to Salt Lake City. From there, the colorful Nevada desert leads to the High Sierra and California's infamous Donner Pass. At route's end is magical San Francisco.

coast starlight: seattle– sacramento–los angeles

See the country's most dramatic natural vistas, from Puget Sound to the densely forested Cascade Range, where the railroad's 22 tunnels and hairpin turns will thrill kids of all ages. Traverse northern California's legendary gold country. Then ride alongside the sparkling Pacific Ocean to Los Angeles—100 miles of palm tree–lined beaches.

For all these trips, call 800-USA-RAIL (www.amtrak.com)

southwest chief: chicago–los angeles

Known as the journey of elevations, this route goes from the shadows of the highest peaks in Colorado to the Grand Canyon. Guides join the trip at Bent's Old Fort National Historic Site, the Pecos National Historic Park, and Petroglyph National Monument.

cascades: eugene– portland–seattle–vancouver

Known for panoramas of the Pacific Northwest, this route is a train lover's favorite. Passes Oregon's Mount Hood, the Columbia River, and southern Washington's rolling hills. The train hugs Puget Sound's deep blue waters and showcases the Olympic Mountains. The beautiful San Juan Islands, volcanic Mount Baker, and towns north of Seattle lead to Vancouver, with its waterfront charm and green parklands.

books | the little engine that could
by watty piper

First printed in 1930, this title and its theme of "I think I can" have become part of the American psyche. Over the last hundred years there have been many versions of this story. Piper's retelling has sold millions of copies and is a childhood classic.

ten best
touring trains

mount washington cog railway

Base Rd., Bretton Woods, NH 03575, 800-922-8825
www.thecog.com

This popular train climbs some of the steepest railway tracks in existence. And from the top of Mount Washington, passengers can view four states, Québec, and the Atlantic Ocean. On the way down, learn about the machinery's toothed cog gears, rack rails, and tilted boilers.

strasburg railroad

Rte. 741 East, Lancaster County, PA, 717-687-7522
www.strasburgrailroad.com

This 45-minute steam train ride travels through Pennsylvania Dutch countryside. Visit the Railroad Museum of Pennsylvania and the National Toy Train Museum nearby.

boone & scenic valley railroad

Iowa Railroad Historical Society, 225 10th St. Boone, IA 50036, 800-626-0319
www.scenic-valleyrr.com

Ride through the picturesque Des Moines River valley from Boone to the old mining town of Fraser

The sounds of a train whistle will bring back great memories for years to come.

in 1920s-era coach cars. Look for turkey, deer, and bald eagles along the way. Families with little ones will like to take the 25-minute Thomas the Tank Engine ride.

durango & silverton narrow gauge railroad

479 Main Ave., Durango, CO 81301, 877-872-4607
www.durangotrain.com

This coal-fired, steam-operated narrow-gauge train takes passengers on a 90-mile round-trip journey through remote wilderness, including the spectacular Animas Canyon of the southern Rockies. Kids will love to follow the tracks that miners, cowboys, and settlers of the Old West took over a century ago.

georgetown loop railroad

Interstate 70, Georgetown, CO 80444, 303-569-2888
www.georgetownlooprr.com

Located in the Rockies, near the historic Lebanon Silver Mine, this steam-powered train travels between the towns of Georgetown and Silver Plume. A highlight of the trip: crossing over the nearly 100-foot-high Devils Gate High Bridge, an engineering feat of the 1880s.

manitou and pikes peak railway

515 Ruxton Ave., Manitou Springs, CO
80829, 719-685-5401
www.cograilway.com

Rushing streams, blue spruce, and giant boulders line this train's route. It's the world's highest cog train, the highest Colorado train, and—at its 14,110-foot summit of Pikes Peak—the highest train in the United States. In the winter, a giant snowplow clears the tracks to keep the bright red Swiss trains on schedule.

cumbres and toltec

Antonito, CO, and Chama, NM, 888-286-2737
www.cumbrestoltec.com

America's highest and longest narrow-gauge railroad. This 64-mile, narrow-gauge train winds through the spectacular mountains and valleys of southwestern Colorado and northern New Mexico. Kids will love how the steady train hugs the sheer cliffs and climbs to an altitude of 10,115 feet. The historic route dates back to the 1880s, when these trains served the silver mining district of the San Juan Mountains.

grand canyon railway

233 North Grand Canyon Blvd., Williams, AZ
86046, 800-843-8724, www.thetrain.com

First opened in 1901, this 130-mile train trip takes passengers down through pine forests and up to high desert as it winds to the South Rim of the Grand Canyon. Along the way, watch for mountain lions, elk, and California condors.

mount hood railroad

110 Railroad Ave., Hood River, OR 97031
541-386-3556, www.mthoodrr.com

Climb aboard these historic trains and enjoy the scenery at the base of Mount Hood. Try a themed ride, such as the Western Train Robbery Excursion Train. Or, let the kids wear pj's and drink hot cocoa on the Polar Express.

white pass & yukon route railway

231 Second Ave., Skagway, AK 99840, 800-343-7373
www.whitepassrailroad.com

Designated an International Historic Civil Engineering Landmark, this narrow-gauge railroad follows the original Klondike Gold Rush Trail, from sea level to 2,800 feet. See the steel cantilever bridge, which was the tallest of its kind in the world when it was constructed. Take in panoramas of mountains, glaciers, gorges, waterfalls, tunnels, and trestles.

Some Tips For Avoiding Motion Sickness

- Place your child in the middle of the vehicle, facing forward.
- Have her look out the window in the distance.
- Avoid heavy meals up to two hours before traveling.
- Distract him by listening to a CD, the radio, or by talking.

The Children's Hospital of Philadelphia
(www.chop.edu)

ten best
transport museums

mystic seaport

75 Greenmanville Ave., Mystic,
CT 06355, 860-572-5315
www.mysticseaport.org

Maritime history snaps to life here, where kids can climb aboard a historic tall ship or watch a wooden boat being constructed in the working shipyard. In town, antique boats fill the harbor.

Transportation museums explore the historic and the scientific.

b & o railroad museum

901 W. Pratt St., Baltimore, MD 21223
410-752-2490, www.borail.org

This is the largest railroad museum in the Western Hemisphere. The Baltimore & Ohio Railroad company once ran trains from the Ohio River to Baltimore. Watch as locomotives are moved in and out of the 1884 roundhouse.

the smithsonian national air and space museum

Independence Ave. at 6th St., SW, Washington, DC 20560, 202-633-1000, www.nasm.si.edu

This is the most visited museum in the world. Hundreds of original, historic artifacts are on display—some suspended from the ceiling, some open for a walk-through. Be sure to see the Wright 1903 *Flyer,* the *Spirit of St. Louis,* and the *Apollo 11*

command module *Columbia.* A favorite gallery for children is How Things Fly—the place for hands-on action including fascinating science demonstrations and paper airplane contests.

henry ford museum & greenfield village

20900 Oakwood Blvd., Dearborn, MI 48124, 800-835-5237
www.hfmgv.org

Exhibits include presidential limousines of the 20th century and the Wright Brothers' Bicycle Shop, where the men built their first airplane. Kids can ride the historic Suwanee Riverboat, a historic steamboat.

steven f. udvar-hazy center

14390 Air & Space Museum Pkwy., Chantilly, VA 20151, 202-633-1000, www.nasm.si.edu

Stroll through three levels to see displays of small and large aircraft, including the Lockheed SR-71 Blackbird, the fastest jet in the world; the Boeing B-29 Superfortress *Enola Gay;* and the deHavilland Chipmunk aerobatic airplane. Many engines, helicopters, ultralights, and experimental flying machines are on display in a museum setting.

national corvette museum & factory tour

350 Corvette Dr., Bowling Green, KY 42101
800-53VETTE, http://corvettemuseum.com

See more than 50 Corvette models and one-of-a-kind concept cars spanning the history of Corvette. Fans can see photos, movies, rare memorabilia, and dioramas, as well as the historic one-millionth Corvette.

museum of transportation

2967 Barrett Station Rd., St. Louis, MO 63112
314-965-6885, www.transportmuseumassociation.org

This museum has a unique 1919 panel truck made in St. Louis and a Bobby Darin Dream Car—a one-of-a-kind custom-made auto. Kids can learn all about transportation at the Creation Station, a hands-on learning center for ages five and under.

the national automobile museum

10 S. Lake St., Reno, NV 89501, 775-333-9300
www.automuseum.org

Located in Reno, Nevada, this museum is a step back in time. A century of automobiles are here, with more than 200 antique, vintage, classic, and special-interest autos displayed. Recent exhibits include Porsche Power and the 100th anniversary of the 1908 New York to Paris Automobile Race.

northwest railway museum

38625 S.E. King St., Snoqualmie, WA 98065
425-888-3030, http://trainmuseum.org

Located east of Seattle, this charming museum showcases Northwest railroading. Kids will love the steam locomotives, passenger and freight cars, and special right-of-way equipment. Don't miss the beautifully restored Snoqualmie Depot and its excursion train ride.

the california state railroad museum

111 I St., Sacramento, CA 95814
916-445-6645, www.csrmf.org

The California State Railroad Museum (CSRM) in Old Sacramento showcases the role of the "iron horse" in connecting California to the rest of the nation. This museum features 21 lavishly restored locomotives and cars, some dating back to 1862. There is a full-scale diorama of an 1860s construction site.

> **michael, virginia | supersonic** I'll never forget walking into the hangar at the Air & Space Center in Virginia, where the enormous stealth jet sits. Everyone gets very quiet and just looks. You could spend a whole day here. Younger kids think the gift shop is one of the exhibits.

arts

museums, festivals, camps, and movie houses

Families look forward to vacation as a time to refresh, renew, and rejuvenate relationships. It's a time to take the long view of family life—and the world in general. That's why the arts factor in to so many family adventures. When we make travel plans, we look for moments that pique all of our senses. Innately, we know that this is how we create moments to remember forever.

Set aside a day or a week to celebrate your family's creative side. Art museums, children's museums, festivals, and workshops all offer opportunities for creative expression. Together, adults and children have a chance to see how others see and to experience new ways of listening, looking, and communicating. Marvel at masterpieces that you might only get to see once in a lifetime, or roll off your blanket laughing at a few lines from Shakespeare performed on an outdoor stage. When you ponder an artist's work, you all might discover a little more about yourselves!

Bring along a sketchbook or notepad to write a comic strip about your adventure, or create a masterpiece of your own. Because great art inspires great art! Use artful moments to prepare for your vacations, too.

Heading to the beach? Download old surf music and sing along while you drive there. Going hiking? Before you head out, read the poetry of Mary Oliver or *My Side of the Mountain* by Jean Craighead George. On your way to the Baseball Hall of Fame? Rent DVDs like *Damn Yankees* or *The Jackie Robinson Story*.

Best of all, art gives each child and adult in the family a chance to voice an opinion or to tell a unique story. While you're away from everyday routine, try a new art or hobby. Pick up a paintbrush, invent a funny puppet voice, try your hand at the kettle drums. Together, you can encourage, admire, or even laugh off the results. When you're on vacation, you can conspire about how you'll describe the experience once you get back home. Vacations are meant for exploring, and you might each discover new gifts or talents that will mean a lot more than just another store-bought souvenir.

> The beginning is the most important part of the work.
>
> —Plato

ten best
art museums

peabody essex museum

161 Essex St., Salem, MA 01970
866-745-1876, www.pem.org

A hands-on, interactive arts program for kids makes this a wonderful, engaging museum. Yin Yu Tan is an actual Chinese home, rebuilt here for a view of architecture and art traditions that were part of everyday life in China.

metropolitan museum of art

1000 Fifth Ave, New York, NY 10028
212-535-7710, www.metmuseum.org

One of the largest art museums in the world. Children love the Egyptian rooms, with their mummies, and the Costume Institute, with its gowns and flourishes. Spend the whole day.

winterthur museum

Rte. 52 (5105 Kennett Pike), Winterthur, DE 19735
800-448-3883, www.winterthur.org

Located in the Brandywine Valley, this house museum has everything for the young and the young at heart. The "Troll Bridge," a fairy house, and more are outside in the Enchanted Woods. Inside the museum, the "Touch-It Room" lets kids be kids. Child-friendly food in the restaurants and changing tables in the cheery rest rooms.

Classic art may have a wealth of small details. Play "I Spy."

carnegie museum of art

4400 Forbes Ave., Pittsburgh, PA 15213
412-622-3131, www.cmoa.org

This kid-friendly museum goes out of its way to give kids an appreciation for art and imagination. Drop-in programs feature treasure hunts and art making, wonderful storytelling events, and more. Admission includes the Carnegie Museum of Natural History, another family favorite.

dayton art institute

456 Belmonte Park North, Dayton, OH 45405, 937-223-5277
www.daytonartinstitute.org

Founded in 1919, this museum has a great family program. Its exuberant Experiencenter orients first-time visitors with fun, educational programs. The museum offers tours for preschoolers. Museum Tuesdays explore themes in art through viewing and art making.

art institute of chicago

111 S. Michigan Ave. #1, Chicago, IL 60603
312-443-3600, www.artic.edu

At the entrance of the museum you can get an attention-getting audio guide, the "Lions Trail Family Tour" for families with children between five and ten. The Kraft Education Center has special publications for school-age children, encouraging a closer look. Check out "Mini Masters," where parents and little ones can explore the museum with educators who engage kids with stories, games, and art activities in a guided gallery visit.

joslyn art museum

2200 Dodge St., Omaha, NE 68102
402-342-3300, www.joslyn.org
This museum has a broad collection of European and American art and is chock-full of fun for kids. A great tour begins with SmART Start cards—colorful, engaging cards that help families find and learn about some of the museum artworks. In the Scott EdTech Gallery, kids can also use computers, video, and games to learn more about art.

dallas museum of art

1717 N. Harwood St., Dallas, TX 75201
214-922-1200, dallasmuseumofart.org
During the summer, this museum has monthly Late Nights, festive events that bring out the whole family. The museum stays open until midnight and offers performances, concerts, readings, and more. Recent offerings: Kids bring pillows, wear pj's, and listen to wonderful bedtime stories.

It seems that the best art is one person's creation that makes everyone else feel creative, too.

de young fine arts museum

Golden Gate Park, 50 Hagiwara Tea Garden Dr., San Francisco, CA 94118
www.famsf.org/deyoung/
Founded in 1895, The de Young museum has been a cherished part of the city for over a hundred years. Located in Golden Gate Park, this gem offers a fun program called Doing and Viewing Art and Big Kids/Little Kids—tours of current exhibitions followed by professionally led studio workshops. In the summer, kids can explore galleries and do hands-on art. Kids stay up late during Friday Nights, a museum event that includes live music, poetry, and art projects for kids.

los angeles county museum of art

5905 Wilshire Blvd., Los Angeles, CA 90036
323-857-6000, www.lacma.org
This museum has a free kids and youth membership program called NexGen, which includes admission to family programs and events. Sunday is family time at this exciting museum: A recent program explores how artists in Africa have found new ways of seeing and making art. Each spring there is a free opening night event for teens only, with live music and artmaking activities.

" jill, delaware | washington, d.c. For me, memories of the nation's capital are about monuments like I. M. Pei's National Gallery of Art with Calder's mobile sculpture inside and Henry Moore's giant monoliths outside.

ten best
children's museums

the boston children's museum

300 Congress St., Boston, MA 02210, 617-426-6500
www.bostonchildren museum.org

There are two goals here: engaging families and building communities to help kids become creative, curious, global, green, and healthy. At "Boats Afloat," kids can sail an assortment of boats and barges while controlling the current in an amazing 28-foot, 800-gallon tank. Come for the wonderful climbing structure!

Most children's museums offer workshops and hands-on events, especially on weekends.

strong national museum of play

1 Manhattan Square, Rochester, NY 14607, 585-263-2700
www.strongmuseum.org

Home to the National Toy Hall of Fame and the world's largest collection of toys, dolls, games, and other items that celebrate play. The indoor butterfly garden is a great place to walk among approximately 800 brilliantly colored butterflies. Don't miss the craft stations.

brooklyn children's museum

145 Brooklyn Ave., Brooklyn, NY 11213, 718-735-4400
www.brooklynkids.org

The first museum created especially for children, this museum has engaged children and their families since 1899. Exhibits include "Totally Tot" and "World Brooklyn." In "Neighborhood Nature" you can visit a freshwater pond, a beach, a garden, and an urban woodland.

port discovery children's museum

35 Market Pl., Baltimore, MD 21202, 410-727-8120
www.portdiscovery.org

A "ginormous" slide and climbing structure is the

> ### Not to be Missed:
> please touch museum, pa
> www.pleasetouchmuseum.org
> kidspace children's museum, ca
> www.kidspacemuseum.org
> childrens museum of pittsburgh, pa
> www.pittsburghkids.org
> a great resource to find a children's
> museum near you:
> association of children's museums
> www.childrensmuseums.org

centerpiece of this interactive museum. "Wonders of Water" is the museum's newest exhibit.

the children's museum of indianapolis

3000 N. Meridian St., Indianapolis, IN 46208, 317-334-3322
www.childrensmuseum.org

The largest children's museum in the world lets kids explore physical and natural sciences, history, world cultures, and the arts.  Immerse yourself in three environments—a brightly colored underwater coral reef, a dinosaur discovery area, and an Egyptian tomb.

madison children's museum

100 State St., Madison, WI 53703
608-256-6445, www.madisonchildrensmuseum.org

A cool "green" exhibit, "First Feats" and its child-centered activities support the healthy development of infants and preschoolers. Adults can compare notes with other caregivers, find out more about infant brain development, or tap in to community resources. In 2010, new location is 100 N. Hamilton.

discovery center museum

711 N. Main St., Rockford, IL 61103
815-963-6769 www.discoverycentermuseum.org

Explore Rock River Discovery Park, the first community-built outdoor science park in the U.S.

> Children's museums put learning into the hands of children and make learning empowering, creative, and fun.
>
> —Janet Rice Elman,
> *Association of Children's Museums*

Design a Mars Rover or space station in "Robotics Lab." "Air & Flight" teaches the four basic principles of flight, demonstrates aerodynamics, and promotes principles of scientific inquiry.

the children's museum of houston

1500 Binz, Houston, TX 77004, 713-522-1138
www.cmhouston.org

"Yalálag, A Mountain Village in Mexico" replicates a real Oaxacan village. See live chicks hatch at "Farm to Market," solve mental mind benders in the "Think Tank," chase dragonflies, scoop pond water, and make animal tracks in "My Home Planet Earth."

minnesota children's museum

10 W. Seventh St., St. Paul, MN 55102, 651-225-6000
www.mcm.org

Visit "Rooftop Art Park," where art and nature converge with a great view of St. Paul. Kids scramble up to a 12-foot tree fort and dance under the shadow dome, mimicking tree shapes and shadows.

children's discovery museum of san jose

180 Woz Way, San Jose, CA 95110, 408-298-5437
www.cdm.org

The striking 52,000-square-foot purple building explores themes of community, connections, and creativity. In "Alice's Wonderland," kids step into a fairytale that exercises math, science, and literacy.

ten best
theater festivals

berkshire theatre festival, new york

413-298-5576
www.berkshiretheatre.org
Standing tall in the western corner of Massachusetts, the Berkshires offer a lovely backdrop for the oldest performing arts venue in the country. The festival's Theater for Young Audiences recently showcased *Around the World in Eighty Days*.

international festival of arts & ideas, connecticut

888-278-4332, www.artidea.org
Located on the Yale University campus, this event showcases international theater; classical, jazz, and popular music; visual arts; poetry; street theater; tours of historic spaces; dance; literature; conferences; and discussions and interactive activities for children and families.

---

resource | one minute theater
Check out this international website featuring one-minute videos made by kids. They range from the dramatic or choreographed to the spontaneous and hilarious.
www.theoneminutesjr.org

the pittsburgh international children's festival, pennsylvania

412-321-5520
www.pghkids.org
Celebrate children's creativity and discover performing arts traditions from around the world at this renowned Pittsburgh-based festival for families. Recent performances included the Mimbre Acrobats from the U.K. and an adapted Grimm fairy tale from Joyful Theatre—a puppet and multimedia theater from South Korea.

the national storytelling festival, tennessee

800-952-8392, www.storytellingfoundation.net
Located in Jonesborough, 90 minutes north of Knoxville, this festival has a special tent that features storytellers and stories suitable for families. At the Youthful Voices concert, young storytellers share their finest tales. Ghost tales at night, in the open air.

puppetry arts institute

11025 E. Winner Rd., Independence, MO 64052
816-833-9777, www.hazelle.org
A year-round destination for fans of puppetry and puppet making. In summer, there are expanded

schedules of performances. A hallmark of the institute are the great puppet-making programs, beginning with hand-painting clay-headed puppets in an inspiring workshop environment.

illinois shakespeare festival

309-438-8974, www.thefestival.org
Visit this open-air, Elizabethan-style theater in Bloomington midsummer. Entertainment for kids of all ages takes place on the Festival Courtyard Stage several evenings a week.

utah shakespearean festival

351 West Center St., Cedar City, UT 84720
800-752-9849, www.bard.org
Within a day's drive of seven national parks, this festival features costumed actors, musicians playing Renaissance instruments, and Shake-spearean plays.

oregon shakespeare festival

15 S. Pioneer St., Ashland, OR 97520, 541-482-2111
www.orshakes.org
Located in Ashland, the Oregon Shakespeare Festival is the largest theater in rotating repertory in the United States. Each year from February through October, it presents 11 plays (more than 770 performances) in three theaters. Performances are suitable for families with older children who are middle school age and above.

san francisco theater festival

415-291-8655, www.sftheater festival.org/festival/childrensfest.htm
This is a one-day summer extravaganza. More than 75 performance troupes act, sing, and dance. Some are children's shows performed by adults; others are performed by young people and are intended for all ages. A highlight is "The Best of the Buddy Club," hilarious for kids. Recent performances included a magic show by Robert Strong, the Golden Thread's Fairytale Players, and the Oakland Public Conservatory of Music.

toy theatre festival

111 South Grand Ave., Los Angeles, CA 90012
213-972-7211, www.musiccenter.org
This event is located at the Los Angeles Music Center during the summer. The Toy Theatre Festival brings together acclaimed puppetry artists who work in a genre of puppetry that enacts plays using two-dimensional rod puppets in miniature theaters. Family-friendly professional productions are presented in repertory over the two days in various spaces throughout Walt Disney Concert Hall. Expect small-scale (but powerful) versions of an eclectic range of stories, poems, and wild inventions. Performances and workshops vary from year to year. Reservations are recommended.

ten best
music festivals

tanglewood music festival

297 West St., Lenox, MA 01240, 413-637-1600
www.tanglewood.org

This summer-long event in the Berkshires features top-notch artists from around the world. Hear a variety of musical performances from the Lawn, a great place to spread out a blanket and enjoy an evening picnic.

international children's festival

1645 Trap Rd., Vienna, VA 22182, 703-255-1900
www.wolf-trap.org

Located twenty minutes outside of the nation's capital, this annual festival offers children a colorful showcase of musicians, dancers, and artists from around the world. From multiple indoor and outdoor stages, kids can listen to Chinese opera, watch masterful martial artists, or twirl to Finnish music. Hands-on arts projects, too.

music | listen up!

Parents Choice is trusted for family evaluations of children's products. Their website lists recordings that earned top marks:
www.parents-choice.org

austin city limits festival, texas

www.aclfestival.com

At the end of September, visit this festival in Austin's Zilker Park, where kids can enjoy a wonderful area devoted to family-friendly music. Recent acts have included the Sippy Cups and Ziggy Marley.

fiddler's grove, north carolina

828-478-3735, www.fiddlersgrove.com

Located an hour north of Charlotte, in Union Grove, North Carolina, this festival has kids moving to the energetic fiddling. The Fiddles of the Festival competition is a popular event.

jazz and heritage festival

336 Camp St., New Orleans, LA 70130
504-410-4100, www.nojazzfest.com

For ten wonderful days in April and May, this festival celebrates the rich music and culture of New Orleans and Louisiana. Find the family tent to hear performers such as the Brass Band Throwdown and Native American Lore and Tales.

grant park music festival, illinois

www.grantparkmusicfestival.com

Located in downtown Chicago, this festival is the nation's only free outdoor classical music series.

Bring the kids to an afternoon performance and then enjoy Millennium Park (and try a Rainbow Cone; see page 81). Even better: Head to a free open rehearsal, where whispered conversation is not frowned upon. If you have a group of ten or more, you can request a free docent tour.

Music is the poetry of the air.

—Jean Paul Richter

Families love the Kids Pavilion. When you arrive, head to a safety tent to register children with ID bracelets and make "lost and found" plans in case you're separated at this huge event.

aspen music festival and school, colorado

970-925-9042
www.aspenmusicfestival.com
This lovely classical music festival is nestled among soaring mountains, within a wildflower meadow. Each summer, locals and visitors bring a blanket and picnic basket and stretch out on the lush grass. Children relax or scamper in the nearby stream and sloping lawn.

bumbershoot, washington

Seattle Center, 206-281-7788
www.bumbershoot.com
Located in Seattle, this is one of the largest urban music and arts festivals in the world. Enjoyed every Labor Day, Bumbershoot highlights a range of music, including zydeco, jazz, and classical guitar.

kidzapalooza, california & illinois

www.kidzapalooza.com
Held in Chicago and Los Angeles, this three-day, interactive music festival offers rock-and-roll fun for families. Recent performers include the Paul Green School of Rock All Stars and Tiny Masters of Today. Between sets, tease up a punk rock hairdo or create your own hip-hop rhymes and moves.

appel farm arts & music festival

457 Shirley Rd., Elmer, NJ 08318
800-394-8478, www.appelfarm.org
The Children's Village is a prime destination at this annual festival, held on the first Saturday of June. Puppetry, crafts, and children's music spill out from this tented area, and a creative spirit pervades the southern New Jersey countryside. The festival celebrates the craft of the songwriter.

kevin, maryland | car music My kids are plugged into their own MP3 players when we travel. I got an adapter for the car radio, and every once in a while we play their music through the car's speaker. It can be an eye-opening (or ear-opening) experience!

ten best
family art camps

medomak

178 Liberty Rd., Washington, ME 04574, 866-Medomak
www.medomakcamp.com

Families nestle into cabins along Medomak Lake. Photography, jewelry and mask making, and yoga. Sport activities include rowing, sailing, kayaking, and canoeing.

common grounds center

473 Tatro Rd., Starksboro, VT 05487, 800-430-2667
www.cgcvt.org

This 700-acre farm in Starksboro offers music, crafts, dance, and yoga, as well as group sports, hiking, and more. Vegetarian and organic meals are served family-style. In September the Lost Arts Week is for families to make rope, candles, paper, quilting, and other materials that children might not otherwise recognize as handmade.

chautauqua institution, new york

800-836-2787, www.ciweb.org

This camp is located in western New York and features a range of activities for family members. Outdoor sports, including swimming, golf, and

Hands-on activity leads to improved communication and cooperation.

tennis, are combined with lectures on theater, ballet, and the symphony.

know theater summer educational program, new york

www.knowtheatre.org

Summer educational workshops are designed for individuals to learn and practice page-to-stage skills required for producing a theatrical performance. There are two-week programs for students age 8–80, who are divided into three specific age groups. The Binghamton, New York, theater is housed in a historic fire house, converted into a black-box staging and performance area.

concordia language villages

901 S. 8th St., Moorhead, MN 56562, 800-222-4750
www.concordialanguagevillages.org

Concordia focuses on the art of language— German, French, Finnish, Spanish, Danish, or Swedish, to be exact. Families immerse themselves in the language, art, music, and cuisine of the culture of their choice. Culture-specific art projects, architectural design and construction, science experiments, and dramatic performances are just a few of the language-building activities.

lark camp, california

707-964-4826, larkcamp.com
Located in Mendocino Woodlands State Park, this camp offers music and dance from around the world. Workshops in Middle Eastern drumming, jazz singing, accordion, and more. English country dancing to belly dancing.

berkeley tuolumne family camp, california

510-981-6717, www.berkeleycamps.com
Located in Stanislaus National Forest, this camp offers watercolor and pottery workshops for adults. Kids can learn the art of stilt walking and magic shows. Classic camp arts like lanyards, bottle art, and jewelry making add to the creative spirit of the place.

feather river camp

5469 Oakland Camp Rd., Quincy, CA
530-283-2290, www.featherrivercamp.com
This camp is located in Quincy, in the Plumas National Forest. Family camps are offered in the summer with a variety of weekly arts themes. Choose from garage band week, folk dancing, or an entire week devoted to storytelling, puppetry, and magic. Arts workshops include paper making and gourd painting, with after-dinner flashlight tag.

montecito sequoia family vacation camp

64410 General's Hwy., Kings Canyon National Park, CA 93633, 800-227-9900, www.mslodge.com
For starters, this is a classic all-around family camp, with an emphasis on outdoor adventure, riding, and water sports. But it also encourages the performance artist in each family member, with morning sing-alongs, artists of the week, a staged variety show, and hilarious open-mike nights.

cazadero performing arts camp

5385 Cazadero Hwy., Cazadero, CA 95421
707-632-5159, www.cazadero.org
Relax together in Sonoma County's Russian River Valley. This all-inclusive camp has two summer sessions especially for families. Programs encourage confidence in creative self-expression.

> **lisa, maryland | knitting camp** My grandmother was famous in our family for knitting comfy slippers. One year she made a project of passing along her gift, teaching all of us kids how to make them ourselves.

ten best
movie houses

weirs drive-in

76 Endicott Rte. 3, Weirs Beach, NH, 603-366-4723
www.weirs-beach.net/drivein
The largest drive-in movie theater in New Hampshire, about 45 minutes northeast of Concord. Arrive early and use your ticket stub for discounted admission at the mini-golf course next door.

Get on an e-mail list for historic movie houses. You'll receive advance notice about special screenings. Plan a trip around your favorites!

brattle theater

40 Brattle St., Harvard Square, Cambridge, MA 02138, 617-876-6837, www.brattlefilm.org
Many New England schools are on break during President's Day week, and that's when this place presents an annual Bugs Bunny Film Festival. Check their website for an extensive schedule of classic films and watch for Cinema Circus in January, with family discussions of intriguing short films, held in partnership with the Cambridge Center for Adult Education.

commodore theatre

421 High St., Portsmouth, VA 23704 757-393-6962, www.commodoretheatre.com
Monday and Tuesday are slower nights, so they're often a better time to bring children to this popular movie house and restaurant (age eight is the young-est admitted). Huge fun: Your table is equipped with a phone to call the kitchen with your order. Enjoy the luxurious surroundings and first-run feature films.

colonial theatre

227 Bridge St., Phoenixville, PA 19460, 610-917-0223
www.thecolonialtheatre.com
Laurel and Hardy, Abbott and Costello, and Harold Lloyd. . . weekly classic films are screened with families in mind. Just outside Philadelphia, this glamorous old movie house features Monday Baby Nights when parents with really little ones can enjoy first-run feature films. It's also a destination for live music performances.

fabulous fox theatre

660 Peachtree St., NE Atlanta, GA 30308, www.foxtheatre.org
One of the oldest and largest grand theaters still in operation, it also features Broadway plays and stage shows. Its schedule of first-run and classic films includes an annual gala screening of *Gone with the Wind* and summer sing-along events accompanied by music from the giant organ. This place sells 4½ tons of popcorn a year.

beach theatre

315 Corey Ave., St. Pete Beach,
FL 33706, 727-360-6697
www.beachtheatre.com

This historic deco-style theater shows free movies for kids on Saturday mornings. It's been in continuous operation here since 1939, except for an 18-month hiatus during WWII, when nightly blackouts were ordered after German submarines were spotted off the coast.

warren theatre

11611 E. 13th St., Wichita, KS 67206, 316-691-9700
www.warrentheatres.com

This 20-screen theater has lots of old-fashioned glamour plus modern comforts like wide seats, cutting-edge sound and projection systems, and a Cry Room in some auditoriums (with separate seating and sound systems for families with small kids). It's known for great food, too.

stars & stripes drive-in

5101 Hwy. 84, Lubbock, TX
79416, 806-749-7469
www.driveinusa.com

Drive-in movies, Texas-style, with three outdoor screens showing a first-run double feature on each. Their website lists showings, so check ahead for features suitable for kids. A

Everyone remembers the first movie they ever saw in a real movie theater!

complete menu is available in a 1950s-style café with nearby picnic tables and a playground.

the loft cinema

3233 E. Speedway Blvd.
Tuscon, AZ 85716, 520-795-7777
www.loftcinema.com

A great entertainment resource, home of the International Children's Film Festival in the summer, plus classic family movies shown outdoors on Thursday nights, May through October, at nearby La Placita Village. It's a real favorite with local families. The concession stand sells pizza, popcorn, and vegan cookies.

grauman's chinese theatre

6925 Hollywood Blvd., Hollywood, CA 90028
323-464-8111, www.manntheatres.com

This L.A. landmark has been a mecca for movie lovers since it opened in 1927. Chinese artifacts grace the iconic entrance, and the handprints and footprints of film stars are embedded in the sidewalk outside. Reserve ahead to buy tickets for first-run feature films, or try to be in town during one of the red-carpet premieres scheduled so often at this site.

[
free outdoor movie night
Call visitor centers or chambers of commerce to find out if there's one on your summer travel route. Two musts: folding chairs and early arrival times.
]

a day in the park

parks, roller coasters, carousels, kiddie parks

How will the fun begin? With high-pitched screams while roaring downhill on a roller coaster? With the scrumptious tastes of funnel cake, hot sausages, and cotton candy? With games of chance that seem so likely to assure the winner an oversize stuffed toy?

The truth is, amusement parks can bring out the optimist in each of us. It's a family-size fantasy world where you can let your imagination take over for the day. Fly on a rocket ship or a pony with wings. Ride a log down a whitewater chute, then grab a front-row seat for a stage show featuring Broadway songs or Irish step dancers. Reality disappears for a day, and a perfectly acceptable lunch might include corn dogs and ice cream sodas followed by a giant lollipop. For start-to-finish and over-the-top family fun, there's nothing quite like a vacation day at an amusement park. It's been an American family vacation tradition for nearly 200 years.

Amusement park creators can't wait to impress you with their creativity, engineering skills, and sense of drama and design. Each season brings a new crop of superlatives: roller coasters that are higher, faster, or more terrifying than any that have come before . . . shows that tap into the fascination with the latest musicals and dance trends . . . water features that splash, roll, and rush in ways you never imagined. At the same time, the classics will bring you back again and again, from the carousel horse your child rides every summer to the bumper cars that look and sound and smell exactly the same year after year. The formula works, blending novelty and nostalgia to create the ideal family getaway experience.

Here is an interesting fact: Research shows that when it comes to spending time with their families, kids want most of all for their parents to be less stressed. A day at an amusement park can go a long way toward making that wish come true. For parents, the greatest pleasure comes in simply seeing the elation in a child's eyes, or joining the young ones for a jolting ride in bumper cars or an inflatable tube race. And for kids, there's nothing better than to see parents whoop and holler along with them on the rides of a lifetime.

> Dignity is in leisure.
>
> —Herman Melville

ten best
amusement parks

coney island

1208 Surf Ave., Brooklyn, NY
11224, 718-372-5159
www.coneyisland.com

Coney Island is one of our great old amusement parks, with a famous Ferris wheel, as well as the Spook-a-Rama and about twenty other rides. The New York Aquarium and Coney Island Museum are also here.

The landscape of an amusement park makes a permanent imprint on the imagination of a young visitor.

hersheypark

100 W. Hersheypark Dr., Hershey, PA 17033
800-242-4236, www.hersheypa.com

On 110 acres with more than 60 rides and attractions, the park hosts seven-foot-tall costumed characters dressed as Hershey products. Tour Chocolate World and the Hershey Museum, see how chocolate's made, and sample the free chocolate. Don't miss the Hershey Kiss–shaped lights!

idlewild park

P.O. Box C, Rte. 30 East, Ligonier, PA 15658
724-238-3666, www.idlewild.com

Main attractions include historic Olde Idlewild, which is the original amusement area, the Raccoon Lagoon, Storybook Village, Jumpin' Jungle, and Mister Rogers' Neighborhood children's areas, Hootin' Holler mining town, and Soak Zone water park.

kennywood amusement park

4800 Kennywood Blvd.
West Mifflin, PA 15122
412-461-0500
www.kennywood.com

Opened in 1899, Kennywood is known as one of America's great traditional parks because of its rare, historic amusements. A single-track roller coaster, the Racer, is considered the fastest of its kind in the country. The park has shady, garden-like grounds and classic carnival food.

busch gardens europe

1 Busch Gardens Blvd., Williamsburg, VA 23187
757-872-8100, www.buschgardens.com

This 17th-century Europe–themed park is separated into six "countries," each featuring its own music, foods, and thrills. Visit Corkscrew Hill for a magical and mystical Celtic journey. Try the Griffon, the world's tallest—and the first floorless—dive coaster. The park is just minutes from Colonial Williamsburg.

walt disney world

1675 N. Buena Vista Dr., Lake Buena Vista, FL 32830, 407-936-6244, http://disneyworld.disney.go.com/wdw/index
The world's most popular resort has four themed parks. For young and old, Magic Kingdom's Cinderella's Castle, Mad Tea Party, and Splash Mountain are timeless favorites. Celebrate culture and world wonders at Epcot. Disney's Hollywood Studios offers Broadway-style stage spectaculars, and Animal Kingdom's Kilimanjaro Safari gives kids the chance to see up to 1,700 animals.

wisconsin dells

1410 Wisconsin Dells Pkwy., Wisconsin Dells, WI 53965, 608-254-6351, www.noahsarkwaterpark.com
Known for its sandstone cliffs and restored WWII Duck vehicles, the Dells also has more than 20 water parks. Kids love the new Flash Flood, where boats plunge down a 50-foot hill. Popular too is Dark Voyage, a 600-foot-long dark tube ride. Tour the park by horse-drawn wagon or explore the circus museum.

cedar point

One Cedar Point Dr., Sandusky, OH 44870
419-627-2350, www.cedarpoint.com
Located on a Lake Erie peninsula, it is the second oldest amusement park in the nation and home to the most rides (75) and roller coasters (17) in the world. Older kids love the thrilling Wicked Twister coaster. Just for kids: four park areas and the Jr. Gemini, a starter coaster with a top speed of six mph. Planet Snoopy has a family center with chang-ing stations and private areas to feed children in a quiet atmosphere. Three antique carousels, as well as an authentic steam locomotive ride, bumper cars, spinning rides, and more.

legoland

One Legoland Dr., Carlsbad, CA 92008
760-918-5346, www.legoland.com
Here interactive attractions are "kid powered." They push, pull, steer, pedal, squirt, climb, or build their way through a day of adventure. Pirate lovers can glide in Captain Cranky's Challenge, and the youngest can venture into the wilds of Africa on Safari Trek, where Explore Village offers life-size giraffes, zebras, lions, and more  made of LEGO bricks. New in 2008 is the 1920s, Egypt-inspired Land of Adventure where kids ride an all-terrain roadster on a journey to recover stolen treasure.

disneyland resort

W. Ball Rd. & S. Disneyland Dr., Anaheim, CA 92802
714-781-4565, www.disneyland.com
This is the smaller of the Disney parks. Once divided into four parks, today it is now Disneyland Park, where kids can wander down Main Street, visit Mickey's house, and wield light sabers at the Jedi Training Academy. Costumed characters are everywhere. The popular Heimlich's Chew Chew Train (an adventure on the back of a hungry caterpillar) is in the California Adventure area.

ten best
roller coasters

superman: ride of steel

Six Flags New England, Rte. 159
1623 Main St., Agawam,
MA 01001, 413-786-9300
www.sixflags.com/newEngland
Thrill seekers love the Ride of Steel, considered to be the best steel coaster in the world. Climbing to 208 feet and reaching speeds of 77 mph, this superman goes up, up, and away. Features a mile-long track of twists and turns.

boulder dash

Lake Compounce, 822 Lake Ave., Bristol, CT 06010
860-583-3300, www.lakecompounce.com
The longest and fastest wooden coaster on the Eastern seaboard and the only ride built into a mountain. The Boulder climbs Southington's face and then drops over a cliff, hitting 65 mph on the way down.

the cyclone

Coney Island, 1208 Surf Ave., Brooklyn NY 11224
718-372-5159, www.coneyisland.com
First opened in 1927, this famous and influential coaster is 85 feet tall and has a track 2,640 feet long. A compact wood twister, Long Island's land-

Save the roller coaster for last. It can take a whole day to work up the nerve to ride one for the first time.

mark is located on the site of the world's very first roller coaster, the La Marcus A.

kingda ka coaster

Six Flags Great Adventure & Wild Safari, 1 Six Flags Blvd.
Jackson, NJ 08527, 732-928-1821
www.sixflags.com/greatAdventure/index.aspx
Thrill-seeking kids will love the 456-foot straight-up incline and the lung-wringing descent that reaches speeds of 128 mph. And some may be glad the ride's over in 59 seconds.

lightning racer

Hersheypark, 100 W. Hersheypark Dr., Hershey,
PA 17033, 800-242-4236, www.hersheypa.com
This beautiful dueling wooden coaster was the first of its kind built in America. Fast, smooth, and thrilling, the twin woodies race and come within feet of each other during the zigzagging journey.

dueling dragon coaster

Universal Orlando Resort, 1000 Universal Studios
Plaza, Orlando, FL 32819, 407-224-4233
www.universalorlando.com
Located in Universal's Islands of Adventure, the

Dueling Dragon Coaster is the world's first set of inverted, dueling roller coasters. Hold on tight as it soars 125 feet in the air and reaches speeds of 55 mph. Ride either the Fire Dragon or the Ice Dragon as they narrowly pass within inches of each other throughout the ride.

the barnstormer

Walt Disney World, 1675 N. Buena Vista Dr. Lake Buena Vista, FL 32830, 407-939-6244 http://disneyworld.disney.go.com/wdw/index
Located in ToonTown, this is a great coaster for young children. Hop aboard Goofy's crop-duster plane for a ride around the farm. Hold on as it zips through a fun-filled course and then returns home for a landing—but watch out!

millennium force

Cedar Point, One Cedar Point Dr., Sandusky, OH 44870, 419-627-2350, www.cedarpoint.com
This super-fast ride takes thrill seekers on an unforgettable 92-mph journey along 6,595 feet of track that winds its way through the center of the park, crosses a lagoon, and dives onto an island. Try the Top Thrill Dragster, too.

the roller coaster at new york-new york

New York-New York, 3790 S. Las Vegas Blvd., Las Vegas, NV 89109 800-NY FOR ME www.nynyhotelcasino.com
The casino is a grown-up attraction, but visiting kids love this ride, right up and over the Las Vegas Strip. There's a 144-foot drop at 67 mph, spinning out to a 180-degree barrel role. Check out your photo, which is captured when your car reaches top speed. Daredevils like to sit in the very back.

giant dipper

Santa Cruz Beach, 400 Beach St., Santa Cruz, CA 95060, 831-423-5590, www.beachboardwalk.com
For a classic coaster experience, this beautiful red-and-white coaster is a must for the whole family. The sixth oldest roller coaster in the United States, the Giant Dipper offers a ride that starts with a startling dip, then a climb to the sky with a spectacular view of the ocean below, and stomach-churning turns to the end. The rattle of the wood coaster is unforgettable. Lines are shortest when the coaster first opens at 11:00 a.m.

" **scott, maryland | setting a goal** My kids and I try to ride the roller coaster as many times as possible in a day! Our top number of rides so far is ten. Our favorite parks have timed ticket options so we don't have to wait in line so long, just show up at the assigned time and get as many rides as we can. We take turns waiting in line.

ten best
carousels

crescent park carousel

700 Bullocks Point Ave., Riverside,
RI 02915, 401-435-7518
www.eastprovidenceri.net/
boards/CrescentPark
Carousel.php

Ride the flying steeds or
magical chariots and capture the
brass ring. Beautiful decorative
panels, beveled mirrors, faceted
glass jewels, and colored sandwich
glass windows make this 1895 Looff
carousel a masterpiece.

flying horse merry-go-round

Bay St., Westerly, RI 02891, 401-348-6007
www.visitrhodeisland.com

This Watch Hill, R.I., carousel is the oldest in the
country. Only children are permitted to ride these
horses, which are hand-carved from a single piece
of wood and feature authentic tails, manes, leather
saddles, and agate eyes. Try to grab the brass ring!

trimper's rides

South First St. & the Boardwalk, Ocean City, MD
21842, 410-289-8617, www.beach-net.com/trimpers

This is one of the oldest operating carousels in the
country. Children love to choose from its menagerie of animals, including a cat, dog, frog, rooster,

You've got to be quick to pick your favorite ponies. Outside horses are always the most popular.

deer, goat, lion, tiger, ostrich, pig,
and dragon.

glen echo park

7300 MacArthur Blvd., Glen Echo,
MD 20812, 301-634-2222
www.glenechopark.org/kids.htm

Located in the suburbs of the
nation's capital, this beautiful menagerie Dentzel carousel is a wonderful place to ride a tiger or giraffe.
And, under the canopy of a thousand lights, within the circle of animals,
a horse leads. Which one is it?

midway carousel

Cedar Point, One Cedar Point Dr., Sandusky,
OH 44870, 419-627-2350, www.cedarpoint.com

Built in 1912, this park classic takes riders on
a gentle ride up and down and around on a
beautifully carved steed. The ride includes sixty
horses and four chariots, four abreast.

cedar downs racing derby

Cedar Point, One Cedar Point Dr., Sandusky,
OH 44870, 419-627-2350, www.cedarpoint.com

Who will cross the finish line first? Sixty-four horses
race four abreast around the track, with each horse
seeming to gallop independently. The momentum

of the ride increases to reach a thrilling 15 mph.

kiddy kingdom carousel

Cedar Point, One Cedar Point Dr. Sandusky, OH 44870, 419-627-2350 www.cedarpoint.com

For little ones only. This finely crafted Dentzel carousel boasts 16 standing and 36 jumping animals, two chariots, and a menagerie consisting of bears, rabbits, ostriches, a lion, a tiger, and a donkey.

1909 looff carousel

Riverfront Park, 507 N. Howard St. Spokane, WA 99201, 509-625-6600 www.spokaneriverfrontpark.com

A 1909 Looff, this beautiful and well-preserved hand-carved wooden carousel is on the National Register of Historic Places. It features 54 horses, a giraffe, a tiger, and 2 Chinese dragon chairs. A favorite horse, Miss Liberty, is adorned in red, white, and blue and has a lunging, outstretched neck, giving her the look of speed.

santa monica pier carousel

1600 Ocean Front Walk, Santa Monica, CA 9029 301-458-8900, www.santamonicapier.org

Located on the Santa Monica Pier and housed in a historic Moorish-style shelter overlooking the ocean, this beautiful 1920s-era indoor carousel is gaily painted, with prancing horses, ponies, and

The famous San Francisco carousel includes hand-painted images of the city, located on the first level at the bay end of Pier 39.

chariots. Gleaming brass poles, festive lights, and mirrored panels evoke an earlier time. One hundred years old in September 2009, the Pier is a classic "SoCal" destination.

1911 looff carousel

Santa Cruz Beach, 400 Beach St. Santa Cruz, CA 95060, 831-423-5590 www.beachboardwalk.com

Designated a National Historic Landmark, this 1911 Looff carousel features a working ring dispenser and boasts 73 uniquely hand-carved wooden horses. Interestingly, some smile and show their teeth, while others are more serious. Some are flower-draped; all have real horsehair tails. Located in Santa Cruz's Beach Boardwalk. The distinctive carousel music is produced by antique band organs, including the Boardwalk's original (and recently restored) 1894 organ.

books | the brass ring *by nancy tafuri*

This beautifully illustrated book evokes the sights and sounds of a peaceful beach vacation through the eyes of a young child. Activities are fun and familiar, culminating in a ride on a carousel inspired by the Flying Horse in Watch Hill, Rhode Island.

ten best
kiddie parks

kiddyland, playland

Playland Pkwy., Rye, NY 10580
914-813-7000, www.ryeplayland.org
This classic amusement park in Rye offers a special area for pint-size park goers. Kiddyland boasts the Mini Scrambler, Slime Buckets, and the Kiddy Coaster. Cool off at the sandy beach or pool.

wiggles world: six flags great adventure & wild safari

1 Six Flags Blvd., Jackson, NJ 08527
732-928-1821, www.sixflags.com/greatAdventure/index.aspx
For families with kids ages 2–6, Wiggles World offers themed rides and attractions. The littlest thrill seekers will enjoy the Big Red Car Ride, Dorothy the Dinosaur's Rosy Teacup Ride, and the S.S. *Feathersword* Pirate Ship.

sandcastle cove

Hersheypark, 100 W. Hersheypark Dr., Hershey, PA 17033, 800-242-4236, www.hersheypa.com
Located within Hershey's new water-park (Boardwalk) is Sandcastle Cove, a great place for young guests to cool down. This giant sand castle has waterslides, cannon,

It's nice to find familiar playground equipment in the "parks-within-parks" at major attractions.

water curtains, and a shallow, nine-inch-deep surrounding pool.

raccoon lagoon, idlewild park

Rte. 30 East, Ligonier, PA 15658
724-238-3666, www.idlewild.com
Raccoon Lagoon is a lovely nine-acre area located within Idlewild. It offers pint-size classics such as Cattail Derby (a miniature version of bumper cars) as well as pony rides, a shaded outdoor eating area, and a lagoon with fountains.

water country usa

176 Water Country Pkwy., Williamsburg, VA 23187, 800-343-7946
www.watercountryusa.com
This park is located just three miles from its affiliated park, Busch Gardens. Attractions for the younger set include the Minnow Matinee Theater and Kid's Kingdom, which has pint-size pools, fountains, and waterslides.

cedar point

Cedar Point, One Cedar Point Dr., Sandusky, OH 44870, 419-627-2350, www.cedarpoint.com
This famous Sandusky park has four play areas

just for kids. Planet Snoopy has seven rides, including a mini-tea cup, rocket, and train ride. The J. Gemini ride is a starter coaster with a top speed of six mph. Ample amenities, including changing and feeding areas.

nickelodeon universe, kings island

6300 Kings Island Dr., Kings Island, OH 45034, 800-288-0808, www.pki.com

Within this 364-acre amusement park is Nickelodeon Universe, the children's play area. Young kids enjoy the 18 rides and attractions that feature characters such as the Backyardigans, Blue's Clue's, and SpongeBob SquarePants.

playtown, legoland

One Legoland Dr., Carlsbad, CA 92008 760-918-5346, www.legoland.com

The Playtown area within Legoland is geared toward young children and offers buildings, slides, activities, and more. Kids can ride the Legoland Express or glide in a leaf-shaped boat on Fairy Tale Brook, sailing through different fairy tale scenes built from Legoland bricks. This is located about 30 minutes north of San Diego, not far from the innovative Museum of Making Music (www.museumof makingmusic.org).

sesame street at seaworld

500 SeaWorld Dr., San Diego, CA 92109, 800-257-4268 www.seaworld.com

The Sesame Street play area at SeaWorld is a new attraction for families with young children. Enjoy breakfast with Elmo, a 4-D movie (*Lights, Camera, Imagination!*), and the Bay of Play, with its three soaring and spinning rides.

six flags

www.sixflags.com

In California, Georgia, and Massachusetts, these Six Flags theme parks offer the new Thomas Town children's play area. Little ones enjoy the mythical Island of Sodor setting with familiar Thomas the Tank Engine entertainments. Sir Topham Hatt is often on hand to greet visitors and pose for photos.

> **cindy, north carolina | small children** How great to be able to slow down in a big park for little kid stuff. It's such a sweet surprise to turn the corner from the large-scale hustle and bustle and find child-scale equipment, free play areas, and little spots to cool your jets for a while (nice for parents, too!). It's usually the shadiest place in the park.

health

cooking, workouts; mind, body, and spirit

Getting away from it all—isn't that the biggest benefit of a family vacation? A rested body is better able to stave off illness and rise to the challenges of everyday life. So travel and togetherness is actually a prescription for the good life in the most literal sense!

Health-conscious families have plenty of options, many of which can be tailored to fit busy schedules. They can make for rewarding and guilt-free ways for families to learn about good nutrition and physical fitness. Training, weight loss, and fitness programs are currently offered at vacation sites nationwide. Some are virtual fitness centers, with spas; basketball, tennis, and squash courts; and state-of-the-art exercise equipment.

Pick almost any spot in the country and find out about sports, training, and fitness camps. They offer exercise in a structured atmosphere, where participants can learn more about particular sports or activities as well as improve their skill levels. In summer programs, instructors may be coaches, college athletes, or educators who are willing to share nuanced skills in their favorite sports. When they sign up together, families discover the thrill of skilled competition, all while working up a healthy glow.

And what better way to learn about the importance of good nutrition than taking a cooking class? Even the most versed culinary connoisseurs could benefit from a course in making traditional family food classics healthier without losing taste. Experimenting with food introduces you to new ideas about culture, history, agriculture, and even table manners. So every taste is really an adventure in itself.

There's a quieter side to health, too. Think about exploring the benefits of meditation, reflection, and personal faith when you're planning a family trip. From famous old cathedrals to the silence of a deep forest, you can discover your own important places to find a sense of quiet, of wonder, and of reflection. Here's to your family's health—inside and out!

> Your thoughts become actions.
>
> Your actions become habits.
>
> Your habits shape your character.
>
> Your character becomes your destiny.
>
> —Proverb

ten best
cooking programs

stoweflake mountain resort

1746 Mountain Rd. (Rte. 108), Stowe, VT 05672, 800-253-2232
www.stoweflake.com

Its annual Vermont Chocolate Show has educational programs, chocolate sculpture displays, and a children's chocolate land.

culinary institute of america, new york, texas & california

www.ciachef.edu

The whole family can explore culture and cuisine at this famous professional cooking school, with programs for enthusiasts held in New York, Texas, and California. Try the Comfort Food Favorites class from the Cooking with Your Teen series. Hands-on cooking and plenty of sampling make these day-long classes utterly delicious.

culinary arts center, the greenbrier

300 W. Main St., White Sulphur Springs, WV 24986
800-228-5049, www.greenbrier.com

These gourmet cooking classes are great for both children and adults. Parents learn the latest trends in gourmet food. For budding chefs, the Children's

You'll make the most of your vacation when you discover cooking techniques to try at home.

Gourmet Cooking Classes offer single-day, hands-on lessons taught by Greenbrier culinary staff.

charleston cooks! at maverick south kitchens

194 E. Bay St., Charleston, SC 29401, 843-722-121
www.mavericksouthernkitchens.com

Offers a full schedule of cooking classes, including the popular Taste of the Lowcountry, which explores the secrets of Lowcountry cuisine. During school vacations, Charleston Cooks! offers a selection of classes for children.

wahoo's wilderness discovery

1780 Nelson Siding Rd., Cle Elum, WA 98922, 888-235-0111, http://highcountry-outfitters.com/3_1.html

Located in the beautiful Cascade Range just two hours from Seattle, this backcountry camp teaches leadership skills, horsemanship, and outdoor living skills, including Dutch oven cooking. Wranglers and Adventurer campers plan, pack, and prepare all their own meals on the trail. Parents can pack in for an overnight with their kids, or assist as cabin counselors or kitchen helpers during special Home School programs.

the jekyll island club hotel

371 Riverview Dr., Jekyll Island, GA 31527
800-535-9547, www.jekyllclub.com

The Jekyll Island Club Hotel is a four star resort and national historic landmark. During the year, a number of multiday cooking schools are offered, featuring hands-on cooking classes. During the summer there are lunch cooking sessions for children.

viking cooking school

325C Howard St., Greenwood, MS 38930
662-451-6750, www.vikingcookingschool.com

Cooking is cool at Viking Cooking School, where young cooks learn in classes designed especially for them. In some classes adults join in the fun for a unique bonding experience, gaining life skills like teamwork, applied math and science, and creativity.

chefs, inc.

10955 W. Pico Blvd., Los Angeles,
CA 90064, 310-470-2277, www.chefsinc.net

This cooking school in Los Angeles offers Kids Cooking Camp, one-week sessions throughout the summer. A sample camp menu includes regional and world cuisine, sweet and savory foods, and how to cook like a Food Network star. Youth and adult classes are scheduled as well. During the year, there are four-week series for teens and younger children, often concurrent with adult programs.

santa fe school of cooking

116 W. San Francisco St., Santa Fe, NM 87501
800-982-4688, http://santafeschoolofcooking.com

This renowned cooking school offers seasonal, hands-on classes for families to make quesadillas and other Sante Fe specialties. While here, you get to learn about the way food is grown, harvested, and prepared in the region, plus experiment with food flavors and colors. It's a memorable part of a Southwest adventure.

royal tine camp cook school, montana

800-400-1375, www.campcookschool.com

Located in the backcountry bordering the Anaconda Pintlar Wilderness, this outdoor cooking school teaches campers how to make delicious dishes with bare essentials and Dutch ovens over wood heat. A main focus is on learning to clean and cook what you catch in the wild. Children ages ten and older can attend with adults.

books | salad people
by mollie katzen

Look for great "portable" food in this fun book, most notably chewy energy circles. Kids can follow illustrated instructions on their own (with a little help, sometimes, from adults). It's a follow-up to the classics *Pretend Soup* and *Honest Pretzels.*

ten best
workout vacations

maine golf & tennis academy

35 Golf Academy Dr.
North Belgrade, ME 04917
800-465-3226, www.golfcamp.com/
golf_camp-tennis_camp/family.htm
Nestled along the shore of beautiful Lake Salmon, 20 minutes north of Augusta, this popular camp offers a week-long golf and tennis family program. In the morning, parent and child enjoy instruction from PGA pros and then play together. Choose from an array of afternoon activities, and at night, sing songs around the campfire. Water sports and local outings.

wrightsville beach surf camp

530 Causeway Dr., Suite B-1, Wrightsville Beach,
NC 28480, 866-844-7873, www.wbsurfcamp.com
Located in several warm-water regions, this camp offers a five-day learn-to-surf program and an overnight camp program. The camp teaches to all levels and is staffed by professional instructors, with a student-to-teacher ratio of 3:1.

windells camp, oregon

800-765-7669, www.windells.com
With facilities at Timberline Resort and Mt. Hood

Kids learn personal health habits from the adults in their lives.

Meadows, Windells is the official camp of the U.S. Snowboard Team. For ages six to adult, Windells offers family instruction, accommodations, and a skiing and skateboarding camp.

wellspring family weight loss camp

Pinehurst Resort, 1 Carolina Vista Dr., Village of Pinehurst, NC
28374, 866-364-0808, www.wellspringfamilycamp.com
Health and weight management are approached in a positive, active way in a fun family vacation environment for parents and kids to experience together. The one-week (or more) program include personalized fitness plans plus nutrition and culinary training at a resort location best known for its outstanding golf facilities.

the jekyll island tennis center

400 Captain Wylly Rd., Jekyll Island, GA 31527
912-635-3154, www.jekyllisland.com
Located on beautiful Jekyll Island, this top-ranked municipal tennis facility offers 13 clay courts and tennis clinics for every level. During the summer, parents can enjoy personal or group lessons while kids drill and strategize in junior camp.

img academies

5500 34th St., W., Bradenton, FL 34210, 800-872-6425
www.imgacademies.com

Located in sunny Florida, this multi-sport camp, training, and education facility is one of the largest of its kind in the world. The 300-acre campus offers tennis, golf, soccer, softball, baseball, basketball, and swimming training. While the younger ones practice afternoon drills, parents can enjoy the Wellness Spa after they've finished their workouts.

mt. hood summer ski camps, oregon

503-337-2230, www.mthood.com

Located in Mount Hood's 12-month ski area, this camp offers ski, snowboard, and rock-climbing sessions throughout the summer. MHSSC has hosted campers between the ages of 5 and 84.

richard schmidt surf camp

1186 San Andreas Rd., La Selva Beach, CA 95076, 831-423-0928, www.richardschmidt.com/surfcamps.html

Nestled in one of California's most beautiful coastlines, this surf camp offers weeklong, overnight surf camps in Santa Cruz during the summer months.

There are adult and mixed-age sessions for surfers of varying abilities.

brady tennis camps

310-798-0333, www.southbaygrandprix.com/shared/bradycamp/index.cfm

Located in southern California, these camps offer adult and junior weekend and weeklong tennis camps. Family camp is available for one week in June at the University of California, Santa Barbara. Other locales include Indian Wells, Los Angeles, and La Costa. All programs include personalized on-court instruction and organized match play.

canyon creek sports camp

41600 Lake Hughes Rd., Lake Hughes, CA 93532 661-724-9184, www.canyoncreeksportscamp.com

Located an hour from West Los Angeles in the Angeles National Forest, this camp is a completely self-contained sports complex offering one- and two-week sports camp for kids 7 to 14. For adults, there's Ultimate Fantasy Sports Camp, a three-day camp that lets participants choose up to fifteen sports and competitions, including soccer, street hockey, tennis, swimming, and more. It's at the edge of Lake Castaic.

rick, pennsylvania | playing together It is such a pleasure to play tennis with my daughter. We use the time as a way to hang out and just enjoy each other. Sometimes we don't even keep score, just volley and count how long we can go without missing a beat.

firsthand knowledge

The more senses you involve in a learning experience, the deeper and richer the memory becomes.

Books, magazines, and electronic media can go only so far in conveying the dimensions and depths of various cultures and faraway places. Often, nothing beats seeing for oneself, which is why a well-traveled person is most often a broad-minded person. Experiencing different locales and meeting different people not only foster an appreciation for diversity, but also show how people of many backgrounds bring their own unique strands to the fabric of the human experience.

Traveling as a family instills a love for discovery and a deeper understanding of science, history, and culture. It broadens family discussions about world events and can promote a greater appreciation for one's own family heritage, as well as instill a new level of curiosity, attentiveness, and respect.

Check your child's reading list and school curriculum. It can help you plan your travel in the days ahead. Match up destinations with classroom topics and current events. Ask your child's teacher about upcoming learning units. Students experience a thrill of recognition at school when they've already explored the topic with family. The world is your family's classroom when you use these pages as a starting point to explore the elements (earth, air, water, and green destinations), technology and science (places of discovery and inventiveness), applied arts (including architecture and artists' homes), history (from the prehistoric to the present), culture (a view of six different influences), creatures (protected and endangered), and values (including civil rights landmarks and opportunities for family service).

There are endless ways for traveling families to open their hearts and minds. Millions have gazed up at the Rocky Mountains, walked Civil War battlefields, visited a wildlife preserve, and taken snapshots at the birthplace of Martin Luther King Jr. Each family comes away with an experience that's uniquely its own.

traveling to learn

Tell me and I hear.
Show me and I understand.
Involve me and I remember.

traveling to learn
nature & science

wilderness, natural phenomena, animals, discovery, technology

Learning happens everywhere. When children read, they absorb the story, as well as the habit of sitting in light, turning pages, and tracking the sequence of letters on a page. The more they read, the more their bodies and minds become attuned to the act of reading.

We enhance our children's receptiveness to learning about science and nature by helping them to practice the habit of discovery. We begin, of course, by modeling it ourselves: with interest in news about our changing environment, or with curiosity about the things we see on a walk.

Science is essentially a sensory experience, a way of measuring the things we see, hear, touch, taste, and smell. It's rooted in observation and conversation, and it often depends on our human ability to notice the way things grow and change. It's only natural that children ask a million questions, savor and repeat facts, and occasionally test your patience with their own seemingly infinite interest in dropping things from a high chair, rolling marbles across the floor, or watching water swirl down a drain. Science is in their nature.

> The universe is wider than our views of it.
> —Henry David Thoreau

A child's ability to understand scientific ideas takes a giant leap when you step outside together. What will those birds eat when the weather gets colder? Why do the clouds seem so low in this valley? How can we tell the difference between planets and stars in the sky?

The best answers to questions like these come from direct experience. Visit a wildlife preserve and look under the leaves on a forest floor. Hike up a hill and see what happens to clouds as the sun rises and the air gets warmer. Spend a few nights in a row looking at the sky, giving your eyes time to adjust and observing the fixed and changing patterns. What's going on here? The world is full of marvels, and so is the open and observant mind of a child.

Along the way there will be a place for expert commentary, for textbooks and references, for classroom instruction and science fair projects. But all of these will hold much more meaning and interest for a child who has experienced the wonder of science and nature firsthand, becoming adept at "reading" the world on her own.

ten best
peaks

What makes a mountain? Glaciers sliding, volcanoes erupting, and shifting plates of the Earth's surface create bumps, piles, and bubbles that eventually become mountains.

sun mountain

Bromley Mountain Ski Resort, 3984 Vermont Rte. 11 Peru, VT 05152, 802-824-5522, www.bromley.com

Southern exposure means that Bromley Mountain (aka Sun Mountain) has sun all day long, bringing welcome light and warmth to the northern stretch of the Appalachian Mountain chain. The resort is known for great family programs in winter and summer.

adirondack state park

High Peaks Information Center, 102 Adirondack Loj Rd. Lake Placid, NY 12946, 518-523-3441, www.adk.org

The highest peak in New York is Mount Marcy (5,343 feet), and the trailhead to get there is in

Lake Placid, New York, is a gateway to the Adirondacks.

Lake Placid, home of the 1980 Winter Olympic Games. It's a great village with year-round activities for families. Families enjoy the 2.3-mile hike to Marcy Dam, with 187 feet of elevation.

shenandoah national park

3655 U.S. Hwy., 211 E., Luray, VA 22835 540-999-3500, www.nps.gov/shen

Hawksbill is the highest peak here, but the most ambitious hikers choose the longer and more challenging climb up Old Rag (3,268 feet) with a breathtaking view of surrounding mountains and valleys. Driving through the park is half the fun; Skyline Drive is one of the nation's most scenic roadways. And the famous Luray Caverns are located near the central part of the park.

grandfather mountain

U.S. 221, two miles north of Linville, NC 28646 800-468-7325, www.grandfather.com

Grandfather Mountain has great views from the Linville Peak vantage point. Get there by walking across an 80-foot chasm on the Mile High Swinging Bridge. This mountain has the highest peak in the Blue Ridge mountain range (5,964 feet).

rocky mountain national park

1000 Hwy. 36, Estes Park, CO 80517, 970-586-1206 www.nps.gov/romo

At 14,259 feet, the Rockies' Long's Peak is the

highest point in a national park known for its magnificent heights. Its summit is described as the size of a football field, and the climb to get here is for experts only. Instead, try the Gem Lake Trail, a rocky pathway great for kids to climb.

leadville, colorado

Visitor Center, 809 Harrison Ave., Leadville, CO 80461, 888-532-3845 www.leadvilleusa.com

This former mining town has the distinction of being situated at the highest altitude of any town in America, near the top of the Continental Divide. It's nearly 2 miles above sea level. A national historic landmark district, it's known for its charming Victorian architecture and wealth of winter athletic activities, all set against a dramatic mountain backdrop.

olympic national park

800 E. Park Ave., Port Angeles, WA 98362 360-565-3130, www.nps.gov/olym

The west side of the mountain range includes Pacific beachfront and rain forest, with around 144 inches of rainfall each year (the most in the continental U.S.). The east side receives as little as 16 inches annually. This is the range's "rain shadow" effect on

[All the world's major rivers are fed from mountain sources.]

Mountains are Earth's undecaying monuments. They must stand while she endures . . .

—Nathaniel Hawthorne

the surrounding terrain. Mount Olympus is the highest point, at 7,980 feet.

heavenly mountain

Heavenly Mountain Resort, corner of Wildwood & Saddle, South Lake Tahoe, CA 96150, 775-586-7000 www.skiheavenly.com

Here's a great way to scale a mountain in the summer: Take the resort's gondola to an observation deck 9,123 feet above sea level and admire the view of Lake Tahoe and the Sierra Nevada. Try the dramatic zipline ride.

denali national park

Denali National Park, AK 99755 907-683-2294, www.nps.gov/dena

Here's the highest peak on the continent: Mount McKinley stands 20,230 feet tall. Working sled dogs are part of the ranger team at Denali. In summer the park hosts sled dog training demonstrations. In winter, the same dogs aid rangers in patrolling.

hawaii volcanoes national park

Hwy. 11, HI 96718 808-985-6000, www.nps.gov/havo

Mauna Kea is 13,796 feet tall. Its "sister" peak, Mauna Loa, is about 115 feet lower—and also the center of attention because it's an active volcano. Visit at night for the best views of bubbling lava. Because of the volcanic activity, the air can seem smoggy at times. Wear shoes!

ten best
depths

Water swirls deep below the Earth's surface, carving out caves and creating underground pools and waterfalls.

rock of ages granite quarry

Rock of Ages Granite Quarry, 558 Graniteville Rd., Barre, VT 05641
866-748-6877
www.central-vt.com/web/roa

On summer and fall weekdays you can take a shuttle 600 feet into the working quarry and see how blocks of cool gray stone are located and cut from layers of earth and other minerals. There's also a self-guided factory tour where you can see stone artisans at work, and a unique "cut-in-stone" activity for visitors to try.

luray caverns

U.S. Hwy. 211 W, Luray, VA 22845, 540-743-4531
www.luraycaverns.com

Mineral deposits in water drip inside the cave for thousands of years. As they do, piles of deposits start to build up from the cavern's floor and ceilings. They turn into powerful mineral "drip castles" that we recognize as stalagmites and stalactites. Dramatic interior lighting makes this a memorable East Coast cavern visit. One way to get there, albeit not the fastest, is via beautiful Skyline Drive.

Luray Caverns is located about 90 minutes from Washington, D.C.

pioneer tunnel coal mine

19th & Oak St., Ashland, PA 17921, 570-875-3850, www.pioneertunnel.com

Refitted coal cars carry passengers on a horizontal journey straight into the side mountain to the site of a former coal mine. Once inside, you're guided on a walking tour to discover the history and science of anthracite coal mining.

devil's millhopper

4732 N.W. 53rd Ave., Gainesville, FL 32653, 352-955-2008, www.floridastateparks.org/devilsmillhopper

A naturally formed sinkhole gives way to a rain forest environment 120 feet below the surface of the sandy Florida terrain. Boardwalk-style steps and platforms allow visitors to notice unusual plants, tree frogs, and small waterfalls during the descent.

Bring a flashlight if you're planning an underground adventure. Bring some extra batteries, too! Most important: Check safety guidelines and consult a professional guide if you're exploring new territory.

carlsbad caverns

3225 National Parks Hwy., Carlsbad, NM 88220
505-785-2232, www.nps.gov/cave

The deserts of New Mexico are above, and below are caves and caverns where the temperature is 56°F year-round. Call ahead for ranger-guided tours to the more challenging or fragile areas, like Spider Cave. A self-guided tour along the Big Room route is a great introduction to the caverns.

mammoth cave national park

Mammoth Cave Pkwy., Cave City, KY 42259
270-758-2180, www.nps.gov/maca/index.htm

The cave system is the world's longest. The Frozen Niagara tour is best for new cave explorers. Eight-to twelve-year-olds can try the Trog Tour—some crawling required.

wind cave national park

26611 U.S. Hwy. 385, Hot Springs, SD 57747
605-745-4600, www.nps.gov/wica

This park is in the Black Hills, located about 40 miles from Mount Rushmore. There's a great driving tour of the cave area's geologic history, tracing

books | journey to the center of the earth

by jules verne

This early work of science fiction tells the wild story of a professor and his nephew whose exploration into the depths of the Earth is also a kind of journey back in time.

rock formation that began as long as one billion years ago.

death valley

Furnace Creek Visitor Center, Rte. 190, Death Valley National Park, CA, 760-786-3200, www.nps.gov/deva

In the Badwater region of this park, you're at the lowest point in the United States, 282 feet below sea level. Look to the mountain above for a sign that shows the height of sea level. Visit Mosaic Canyon, and ask about the mysterious moving rocks of the Racetrack. Death Valley is the hottest, driest place in the country.

black chasm canyon

15701 Volcano Pioneer Rd., Volcano, CA 95689
209-736-2708, www.caverntours.com

This cave is famous for helectite crystals, with formations that look like bright white coral. It's considered one of the most beautiful canyons in the world. There's also a gem-mining area for kids, plus a geode-cracking station where visitors can find crystal formations inside rocks.

waikiki bay

Atlantis Adventures, Hilton Hawaiian Village All'I Tower Oahu, Honolulu, HI 96815, 800-548-6262

Here's a pricey but memorable way to get deep below sea level without a mask and snorkel. A spacious submarine cruises the waters of Waikiki Beach for an up-close look at fish, coral, undersea wrecks, and the ocean floor. Diamondhead Crater is located at the southeast end of the Waikiki area.

ten best
deserts & dunes

A desert is defined as a region that receives less than ten inches of rainfall a year. Deserts, like other land forms, can change substantially over time.

desert of maine

95 Desert Rd., Freeport, ME 04032, 207-865-6962
www.desertofmaine.com

It's the easternmost desert region in the United States, formed by the passage of a glacier more than 11,000 years ago. The sand and dunes are remnants of the original ancient desert. It's all open for tours, with marked nature trails and a small convenience store.

nebraska sand hills

Nebraska National Forest, Bessey Ranger District
Halsey, NE 69142, 308-432-0300
www.thenebraskasandhills.com

This is a paleodesert, where ancient sands lie beneath the grassy prairie. This region covers more than 23,000 square miles in the state. Highway 2 travels through it along grass-covered dunes leading to the Nebraska National Forest. There are 720 different species of plants growing in the sandhills, the large majority of which are native.

franklin mountain state park

1331 McKelligon Canyon Rd., El Paso, TX 79930, 915-566-6441

Just outside the city limits you can explore the wilds of the Chihuahuan Desert. Try the Wyler Arial Tramway for a bird's-eye view all the way to Mexico. If you're visiting in spring, watch for golden poppies in bloom.

great sand dunes national park

Visitor Center, 11999 Hwy. 150, Mosca, CO 81146
719-378-6300, www.nps.gov/grsa

Kids can bring snowboards to slide down any of the unvegetated dunes in the park. The best conditions are just after some rainfall. In early summer, the snowmelt waters of Medano Creek are fun for wading and paddling.

tohono chul park

7366 N. Paseo del Norte, Tucson, AZ 85704
520-742-6455, www.tohonochulpark.org

This "secret garden" is a 49-acre park that celebrates desert nature and culture. It's also the site of great festivals, concerts, and the Santa Fe County Fair (in early August).

> **paul, delaware | adventure** The first time we went to Red Rock Canyon we could not believe our eyes. We still look at our photos and remember what a great time we had.

albuquerque biological park

2601 Central Ave., NW, Albuquerque,
NM 87104, 505-768-2000
www.cabq.gov/biopark

A study in contrasts, this park is home
to Albuquerque's zoo and aquarium
near the banks of the Rio Grande.
Here you'll also find the Rio Grande
Botanic Garden. The Children's Fantasy Garden is full of gigantic garden
stuff, offering a bug-eye view of vegetables, flowers, and garden tools.

One is a cactus. Two are cactuses.

bonneville salt flats

Visitor Center, 2370 South 2300 West, Salt Lake City,
UT 84110, 801-977-4300, www.utah.com/playgrounds/
bonneville_salt.htm

About 15,000 years ago, this region was covered by a giant freshwater lake. The Great Salt
Lake is a shrunken remainder, though ancient
shoreline markings can still be seen around the
edges of the flats. Home to record-setting car
races, but you can visit and see the incredibly flat
landscape for yourself.

books | dune
by frank herbert

This is the first in a series set on
the planet of Arrakis, where a
stark desert environment plays
an important role in the elaborate
unfolding of the story.

desert botanical garden

1201 N. Galvin Pkwy., Phoenix, AZ 85008
480-941-1225, www.dbg.org

Try a Flashlight Tour and see flowers
that bloom only at night and creatures
that avoid the light and heat of day.
By day, the garden's outdoor exhibits
introduce visitors to the variety, beauty,
and color of desert plant life. There
are more than 300 animal species and
1,200 types of plants.

arizona sonora desert museum

2021 N. Kinney Rd., Tucson, AZ 85743, 520-883-2702
www.desertmuseum.org

This is a great starting point for learning about plant
and animal life in the Sonoran Desert regions of
Arizona, California, and Mexico. The Arizona-
Sonora Desert Museum combines a zoo and
natural history museum, and it's known for its raptor shows, where falcons and hawks fly free in the
open desert.

red rock canyon state park

Hwy. 14, Cantil, CA, 661-942-0662, www.parks.ca.gov

The canyon is located where the Mojave Desert
meets the Sierra Nevada. It's famous for its colorful
rock formations and beautiful landscapes, just two
hours from Los Angeles. Guided tours are available, and a visitor center is located in the nearby
town of Lancaster.

ten best
rocky places

Rock is the construction material of America's coastlines, canyons, and cliffs. Learn to identify it: sedimentary, metamorphic, or igneous.

beavertail state park

Beavertail Rd., Jamestown, RI 02835, 401-884-2010
www.riparks.com

This rocky shoreline is composed of ancient stone that is upward of 500 years old. It is much older than any other local rock, but similar in age and composition to geologic "puzzle pieces" along the African coast, illustrating the effects of continental drift. A popular Narragansett Bay hiking and sightseeing area, the park has an aquarium and visitor center that are open seasonally.

Grand Canyon National Park: larger than the state of Rhode Island

the driftless region

Viroqua Visitor Center, 220 S. Main St., Viroqua, WI, 54665, 608-637-2575
www.viroqua-wisconsin.com

Glaciers missed this region in northern Wisconsin. The landscape retains mysterious-looking formations that were once part of a prehistoric seabed, like Three

Chimneys Rock (three miles outside Viroqua on Highway 14; turn left on Three Chimneys Road) and the inverted triangle shape of Monument Rock (six miles south of Viroqua on Highway 14).

palo duro canyon state park

11450 Park Rd. 5, Canyon, TX 79015, 806-488-2227
www.palourocanyon.com

Referred to as the Grand Canyon of Texas, this 16,000-acre state park is home to a spectacular range of cliffs, rock towers, and canyons showcasing the geology of the Texas High Plains. On-site horse rentals and guided tours are available.

yellowstone national park, wyoming, montana, idaho

307-344-7381, www.nps.gov/yell

Yellowstone is something of a geological workshop, where the effects of glacial drift, mountain building, and erosion continue to shape the landscape, even today. Half of the planet's geothermal features are clustered in Yellowstone, where water vapor issues from ancient fissures in the earth's surface. Check the park's website for details about park access, which varies by season.

grand canyon

I-40 near Flagstaff, AZ, 928-638-7888
www.nps.gov/grca

Wind and water can shape rock into forms on a scale that no machine can duplicate. The phenomenon is best experienced at the Grand Canyon, long considered one of the wonders of the world. It's also one of the busiest attractions, and families face a dizzying array of options for exploring, from airplane to mule rides. A recommended venue for families with small children, the Grand Canyon Railway (www.the train.com), operates along historic tracks from Williams, Arizona, then offers motorcoach tours along the South Rim.

craters of the moon national monument

18 miles W of Arco, ID 83213, 208-527-1300
www.nps.gov/crmo

Drive and hike across the largest lava field in the United States, evidence of volcanic eruptions more than 2,000 years ago. At the visitor center you can learn more about traveling through the lava fields, and about the ecosystem that has grown up in this unusual terrain.

koke'e natural history museum

Kekaha, Kaua'i, HI 96752, 808-335-9975, www.kokee.org

This small museum is a great starting point for explorations of Waimea Canyon. Trails rim the lush canyon, while tours and exhibits provide fascinating

> The shape of Earth's surface affects nearly every natural process and human endeavor.
> —Dr. John LaBrecque, NASA

history of this spectacular landscape. Mark Twain once called it the Grand Canyon of the Pacific.

valley of fire state park

55 miles north of Las Vegas on I-15, NV, 702-397-2088 http://parks.nv.gov

See rock transformed by natural and human means: Sandstone beehive formations are shaped by eroding winds, while Atatl rock is graced with ancient petroglyphs.

hauser geode beds

Chamber of Commerce
201 S. Broadway, Blythe, CA 92225, 760-922-8166
www.blytheareachamberofcommerce.com

Outside the city of Blythe you can keep a sharp eye for signs leading to this federal land where generations of families have hunted for geodes— ordinary-looking stones that can be split open to reveal sparkling crystals. Stop in Blythe to pick up information about getting to the geode beds (about 2½ hours from Phoenix).

mono lake

Visitor Center, Hwy. 395 & 3rd St., Lee Vining, CA 93541, 760-647-6595, www.monolake.org

Mysterious rock formations appear in and around this salt lake, just east of Yosemite. Revealed as water levels fall, these limestone towers (called tufa) are the result of the lake's naturally alkaline environment.

ten best
family hikes

Include children in plans for mapping out your hike or choosing places to pause along the way.

sky meadows state park, virginia

www.dcr.virginia.gov/state_parks/sky.shtml

Located just an hour outside of Washington, D.C., this is a lovely park with views of the Blue Ridge mountains. Take a short day hike on one of the many nature trails. Settle in with a picnic and enjoy expansive views of the rolling farmland.

chimney tops trail, great smoky mountains, tennessee

www.nps.gov/grsm/

This park contains the world's best example of deciduous forest. Quarter-mile paths, called quiet walkways, stem from the park's roadway. Any one

of them offers access to silent wonder. Near Sugarlands Visitors Center is Chimney Tops Trail, a lovely four-mile hike through old-growth forest up to sheer cliffs.

woodpecker trail, big shoals state park, florida

www.floridastateparks.org/RangerProg.cfm

Located along the Suwannee River and the site of Florida's largest white-water rapids, this park offers 28 miles of trails with beautiful scenic views from the riverside bluffs. A popular trail is the 3.4-mile paved Woodpecker Trail.

ohio & erie canal trail, ohio

www.nps.gov/archive/cuva

Popular with local and visiting families, this historic trail has many points of access. Try the 4.3-mile Boston Store to Station Road Bridge section, which includes the historic Boston Store, several canal locks, and the Station Road Bridge, constructed in the early 1880s. This park is not far from the big cities of Akron and Cleveland.

illinois & michigan canal

www.nps.gov/ilmi/

Less than an hour outside Chicago, near Channahon, is a lovely hike from Lock #6 past Lock #7 to McKinley Woods. Features include a restored lock tender's house, leafy trees, and the Des Plains River.

aspen center for environmental studies, colorado

www.aspennature.org

Wander into this lovely nature center, say hello to Belle the eagle, and sign up little ones for nature classes, where they can hike the beautiful Hallam Lake Trail. The whole family will enjoy the popular, paved Rio Grande Trail nearby, which follows the twisting Roaring Fork River.

muir woods national monument, california

www.nps.gov/muwo/

Located just north of the Golden Gate, this park offers a wonderful Junior Ranger hike through giant coastal redwoods. While parents savor the cool shade and well-marked trail, kids search for clues to the Muir Woods Quest. Before long, the spirited hike will have the entire family discussing boles, hollows, and old-growth forests.

will rogers historic state park, california

www.parks.ca.gov/default.asp?page_id=626

Amble through this beautiful park located in the Pacific Palisades neighborhood of Los Angeles. The famous actor's 186-acre ranch offers a moderate three-mile hike starting at the tennis courts and ending with beautiful views of Santa Monica. Tour the stables and have a picnic on the polo fields.

> Methinks that the moment my legs begin to move, my thoughts begin to flow.
>
> —Henry David Thoreau

horsetail falls trail, columbia river gorge, oregon

www.portlandhikersfieldguide.org

Check this website for great hiking trails all around the Columbia River. Located 45 minutes outside of Portland, Horsetail Falls Trail is a 2.7-mile loop that's a wonderful adventure for families with active kids (as always, excercise caution and keep an eye out for steep drops). The trail offers unforgettable views of three waterfalls: Horsetail, Ponytail, and Oneonta.

hoh rain forest, olympic national park, washington

www.nps.gov/olym/

The Hoh Rain Forest includes several family-friendly nature hikes. To explore this enchanted land, try the Hall of Mosses Trail (0.75 mile) and the Spruce Nature Trail (1.25). Look for Sitka spruce, western hemlock, and huge western cedar. Wander through moss-draped maples and conifers. This temperate rain forest receives up to 12 feet of rain each year.

Water is vital for a hike but heavy to carry. Think about stashing some in hidden spots about a third of the way into your hike, then stopping to quench your thirst on the way back.

ten best
american landscapes

This list comes from Bruce Babbitt, secretary of the interior from 1993 to 2001, governor of Arizona from 1978 to 1987, and attorney general of Arizona from 1975 to 1978.

the american cathedrals

www.nps.gov/yell, www.nps.gov/yose, www.nps.gov/grca

These are three places that each American should see in his or her lifetime. They are unique in the world:

Yellowstone National Park
Yosemite National Park
Grand Canyon National Park

sanibel island, florida

www.sanibel-captiva.org

It is the first place I would take my young kids to see really spectacular birds.

chesapeake & ohio canal national historical park, maryland

301-739-4200

This 184.5-mile-long canal is an irresistible mix of river experience, wildlife, and historical vignettes

The cliff dwellings of Mesa Verde

showing America's westward movement.

cape hatteras national seashore, north carolina

www.nps.gov/caha

The most pristine, free-spirited beachfront in America and my favorite wild seashore.

mesa verde national park, colorado

www.nps.gov/mese

It is the most evocative archaeological landscape in America.

nebraska crane migration

www.rowesanctuary.org

I would take my teenagers to the spectacle on the Platte River in the spring. It is a migratory extravaganza! Up early, cold weather, breathtaking. It happens for only three or four weeks in the spring . . . an awesome experience. More than 500,000 sandhill cranes, plus hundreds of thousands of ducks and geese converge on the Platte. You just can't believe your eyes.

humboldt redwoods state park, california

www.humboldtredwoods.org

They are the biggest and most beautiful trees you will see anywhere. There is a spiritual quality about the place.

glacier bay national park & preserve, alaska

www.nps.gov/glba

Sit on the shore of Glacier Bay with humpback whales spouting in front of you and grizzly bears eyeing you from behind . . . really extraordinary.

appomattox court house, virginia

www.nps.gov/apco

In Virginia, where Lee surrendered to Grant in 1865. Here you will feel the meaning of our Civil War heritage. Robert E. Lee's staff settled on this private home as the appropriate place to tender his army's surrender. It highlights cities where successful conservation policies begin to assure "breathing room" for neighboring wilderness.

books | cities in the wilderness
by bruce babbitt
"A new vision for land use in America," useful for parents who think about the landscapes of the future.

grand staircase-escalante national monument, utah

www.utah.com/escalante

This is Grand Canyon and Zion National Parks without people. The primordial western landscape, and you can be there all alone. Vast, glorious, and untrammelled.

Bruce Babbitt

Secretary of the interior from 1993 to 2001, Babbitt led the creation of the Pacific Northwest forest plan, restoration of the Everglades, passage of the California Desert Protection Act, and legislation for the National Wildlife Rescue system.

As a certified firefighter, Babbitt brought his front-line experience to creating new federal wild land fire policies. He pioneered the use of habitat conservation plans under the Endangered Species Act and worked with President Clinton to create 22 new national monuments including the Grand Staircase-Escalante National Monument in Utah.

ten best
waterfalls

A waterfall marks a point where a stream bed changed—either suddenly as glaciers shifted, or over the course of a long period of erosion.

niagara falls

Niagara Reservation State Park
Buffalo, NY 14303, 716-278-1796
www.nysparks.state.ny.us

The three famous falls intersect the boundaries of the United States and Canada. Bring passports for all family members if you plan to cross the international border. However, it's easier and fun to stay on the U.S. side, ride the elevator to the base of the falls, and step aboard a *Maid of the Mist* boat.

cavern cascade

Watkins Glen State Park, Rte. 14, Watkins Glen, NY 14891, 607-535-4511, http://nysparks.state.ny.us/parks

Walk the paths and bridges of this enchanting park in the heart of a famous upstate New York village. In the course of a 2-mile path, visitors can see 19 waterfalls.

amicalola falls

418 Amicalola Falls Lodge Rd., Dawsonville, GA 30534
706-265-4703, http://gastateparks.org/info/amicalola/

This park is the access point for Springer

Take a waterfall boat tour if you can.

Mountain, location of the southern end of the Appalachian Trail. It's also home to the longest cascading waterfall east of the Mississippi—729 feet. Hike the trails with views near the bottom of the falls. The trek to the top is for experienced climbers only.

falling waters

Falling Waters State Park, State Rd. 77A, Chipley, FL, 850-638-6130
http://floridastateparks.org/fallingwaters

Make sure you call ahead to find out if this northwest Florida waterfall is running. It's fed by underground springs, so if the water table is low—no waterfall! In drought-free conditions, the falls pour into a giant, unmapped sinkhole. No one really knows how deep it is, or exactly where the water goes.

yahoo falls

Big South Fork National Recreation Area
4564 Leatherwood Rd., Oneida, TN 37841
423-569-9778, www.nps.gov/biso

Waterworks here have carved sandstone into mysterious shapes. In the northern reaches of the park, Kentucky's highest waterfall drops more than a hundred feet in a single dramatic spill. The park's scenery and well-marked trails make it ideal for a family hike to the base of the falls.

willow falls

Willow River State Park, 1034 County Hwy. A, Hudson, WI 54016
715-386-5931, www.dnr.state.wi.us

This park's most popular hiking trail leads visitors to the limestone gorge where about 20 cascades create a dramatic waterfall view. You'll hike a little over a mile from the park entrance to reach the base of the falls.

north clear creek falls

Scenic Highway 149 near Spring Creek Pass, CO; Mineral County Chamber of Commerce, 719-658-2374

Visible from a well-marked highway overlook, this waterfall spills out of flat prairie into a quarry canyon more than a hundred feet below, leading to the Rio Grande. The view is a highlight of the Silver Thread Scenic Byway, a 135-mile drive along historic mining regions between Lake City and South Fork, Colorado.

multnomah falls

Visitor Center, Oregon Hwy. 30, Troutdale, OR 97060
503-695-2372, www.fs.fed.us/r6/columbia/recreation/waterfalls

The Columbia River Gorge is home to 13 famous waterfalls, the longest and most famous being Multnomah, with its 620-foot cascade of water fed from underground springs. Water flow is most powerful in winter and spring.

D. H. Lawrence once said, "Water is H_2O, hydrogen two parts, oxygen one, but there is also a third thing that makes it water and nobody knows what that is." It is magic, the kind that can only be found in nature, life, and human possibilities once we are open to them . . .

—**David W. Orr**
author of Ecological Literacy *and* Earth in Mind

bridal veil falls

Milepost 28, Historic Columbia River Scenic Hwy., Corbett, OR, 800-551-6949, www.oregonstateparks.org

See and hear the famous cliff-edge falls where a clear mountain creek streams more than 150 feet straight down to the Columbia River. From the parking and picnic area at the entrance to the small park, take the lower trail to reach the base of the falls for the best viewing. An upper trail offers interpretive signs along with views of the higher reaches of the fall.

wailua falls

Maalo Road, Hanamanlu, Kauai, HI, www.kauai-hawaii.com

Visit in the morning to see the sun shining on the falls. The twin falls spill nearly 80 feet along the passage of the Wailua River. It's best to watch the falls from the highway vantage point; it can be treacherous to hike closer. Ancient myths say that warriors jumped from the top of the falls to prove their bravery. It would be fatal to attempt this, and it is prohibited. The falls were made famous in *Fantasy Island*, a popular television series.

[The Lower Falls of Yellowstone National Park is the longest waterfall in the park, at 308 feet. The park is a treasure trove of beautiful waterfalls.]

ten best
coastal cliffs

America's broadest sandy beaches are created as the ancient inland mountains wear away over millions of years. But the rocky cliffs at the ocean's edge are relatively "new" mountains, and you can observe that beaches there are shorter and rockier.

portland head lighthouse

Fort Williams Park, 1000 Shore Rd., Cape Elizabeth, ME 04107, 207-799-2661 www.portlandheadlight.com

Hike a pebbled path of Maine's fabled rocky coastline and one of its most famous lighthouses. Look near the southeastern shore for rock that looks like wood: It's metamorphic rock developed from ancient sandstone, which now appears to splinter like wood.

cliff walk

Easton's Beach/Memorial Blvd., Newport, RI 02840 800-976-5122, www.cliffwalk.com

This famous cliff walk is full of contrasts, with rocky scrambles near green swaths of lawn to one side and sharp cliff drops on the other. This 3.5-mile walk is a national recreation trail where turn-of-the-20th-century mansions compete with Atlantic vistas for the attention of awed visitors. It's breezy and pleasant here in summer.

Portland Head lighthouse

palisades

Palisades Interstate Park Commission Alpine Approach Rd., Alpine, NJ 07620 201-768-1360, www.njpalisades.org

Imposing cliffs (formed hundreds of millions of year ago) are up to 500 feet high, bordering the Hudson River in New York and New Jersey and extending to the river's mouth on the Atlantic. Check the park commission for the best scenic drives, hiking trails, and picnic areas, all minutes from Manhattan.

calvert cliffs

Calvert Cliffs State Park, 9500 H. G. Truman Pkwy., Lusby, MD, 301-743-7613, www.dnr.state.md.us/publiclands/southern/calvertcliffs.html

On the western shore of the Chesapeake Bay, families can walk along ancient beaches and find fossilized marine life and tiny shark's teeth, left behind nearly 15 million years ago when a warm ocean receded from the area that is now southern Maryland and Virginia.

lime kiln point

San Juan Island, WA, 360-902-8844, www.parks.wa.gov

Dense forests grow right up to the edge of steep rocky slopes here. This state park is still a functioning lighthouse point, but it is also an orca research and whale-watching facility. Take the ferry from Anacortes, then bike or bus about ten miles from Friday Harbor. A hiking trail, picnic sites, and spectacular views are all free here, and guides are on duty during summer months.

sunset bay

Sunset Bay State Park, off U.S. 101, 12 miles SW of Coos Bay, Coos Bay, OR 97420
541-888-4902, www.oregonstateparks.org

Hiking trails connect this former private estate with Shore Acres and Cape Arago State Parks. Sandstone cliffs are wonderful vantage points to see dramatic surf—watch for whales, too. Check the website for scheduled tide-pool walks. The bases of the cliffs are exposed at low tide, allowing glimpses of plant and animal life.

haystack rock

Cannon Beach, OR, 503-436-8060
www.ci.cannon-beach.or.us

Tillamook Head is part of the rocky coastline where Lewis and Clark finally sighted the Pacific Ocean. They harvested whale blubber here at Cannon Beach and would have seen this 235-foot monolith on the shore. The area is a "marine garden." In spring and summer, interpreters educate visitors about the remarkable history of the shoreline.

point loma

Cabrillo National Monument, 1800 Cabrillo Memorial Dr. San Diego, CA 92106, 619-557-5450, www.nps.gov/cabr

This point marks the southernmost tip of the west

> Only as a child's awareness and reverence for the wholeness of life are developed can his humanity to his own kind reach its full development.
>
> —**Rachel Carson**

coast. The environment shifts where cliffs give way to a thriving intertidal zone at the edge of the sea. Caves and tide pools are home to individual ecosystems that exist in synch with the changing tides. It's a beautiful day trip just across the bay from San Diego.

big sur

Point Lobos State Natural Reserve & Julia Pfeiffer Burns State Park, CA, 831-667-2315
www.parks.ca.gov

Choose the famous old coastal road that follows the undulating valleys of this spectacular coastline. Point Lobos is a wonderful hiking spot for families. You'll notice the phenomenon of microclimates: fog and cool air in one curve of the road, hot sunshine just around the bend.

na pali coast

Captain Sundown Na Pali Sightseeing Sail, Kauai, HI
808-826-5585, www.captainsundown.com

These towering volcanic *pali* (cliffs) can be seen during trail hikes through Na Pali Coast State Wilderness Park (www.hawaiistateparks.org). But the view from the ocean brings even more dramatic perspective to their grandeur. This sightseeing company offers three-hour afternoon and evening sails especially suited for families.

ten best
chesapeake bay sites

From Tom Horton, here are ten favorite places to experience the diversity and culture of the Chesapeake Bay.

savage neck, virginia

www.dcr.virginia.gov/natural_heritage/

Located on the lower Eastern Shore of Virginia, north of Cape Charles. Here at the Savage Neck Preserve, see how the bay is shaped by sand brought in by the Atlantic, with miles of beach, high bluffs, and forested dunes up to 80 feet high.

smith island, maryland

www.smithisland.org

A marshy archipelago in mid-bay with one of the estuary's only two offshore inhabited islands. Three towns there welcome tourists by daily ferry from Crisfield. Smith is famous for its watermen's culture, crab cakes, and eight-layer cakes.

tangier island, virginia

www.tangierisland-va.com

Six miles south of Smith, identical on paper, but in reality a very different flavor of the bay from its northern neighbor. Also served by daily boats from Crisfield. Both places are true crabbing cultures, where nature still shapes human enterprise rather than the other way around.

aberdeen proving ground, maryland

www.apg.army.mil

You can't go ashore here as it's full of unexploded ordnance from nearly a century of weapons testing; but Aberdeen's many miles of unspoiled marsh and forest are a remarkable testament to how the military has inadvertently preserved huge gobs of nature. Aberdeen has more bald eagles than most places outside of Alaska.

upper blackwater river, maryland

www.fws.gov/blackwater

A canoe or kayak trip on this part of the Blackwater National Wildlife Refuge is to experience Chesapeake wetlands at their finest. Put in at the Route 335 bridge and paddle west (upstream). Protected waters and gentle currents, loblolly pine forests, bald eagles, ospreys. The ranks of dying pines in places show the vulnerability of this region to sea-level rise.

dragon run, virginia

www.virginiaplaces.org/watersheds/dragonrun.html

This tidal forested creek, best accessed by small power craft or paddling, is one of the most unspoiled nooks of the Chesapeake's 64,000-square-mile watershed.

pocomoke river, maryland

www.dnr.state.md.us/publiclands/eastern/
pocomokeriver.html

This bay tributary on Maryland's Eastern Shore features mile after mile of deep, dark waters that wind through some of the nation's northernmost cypress swamps. Canoeing north from Snow Hill in May is one of the best places to see prothonatary warblers and other migrant songbirds. Nice state parks for camping at Shad Landing and Milburn Landing.

confluence: nanticoke river & marshyhope creek, maryland

www.dnr.state.md.us/greenways/counties/
dorchester. htnl

These unspoiled river corridors resound with owls at night and afford sanctuaries to a variety of waterfowl, including wild tundra swans each winter. Navigable to Federalsburg in Maryland and to Seaford and Laurel in Delaware, these waters remain close to what Capt. John Smith saw when he sailed them in 1608. You can literally use his 400-year-old map to navigate as far up as the confluence. Watching the full moon rise here is an unforgettable experience.

mattawoman creek, maryland

www.dnr.state.md.us/fisheries/recreational/
fwhotlowertidalpotomac.html

Off the Potomac River's northern shoreline, extending into southern Maryland's forests and swamps, the Mattawoman is rated one of the most productive rivers for fish remaining in the mid-Atlantic. It is threatened by development, but that is still on the drawing boards.

ego alley, maryland

www.visit-annapolis.org/index.aspx

The polar opposite of all the above, this is a concrete-walled extension of the Severn River into downtown historic Annapolis, just past the U.S. Naval Academy. Owners of boats large and small, loud and quiet, like to show off their craft here to crowds of tourists. A world sailing capital, seat of Maryland's government, home to the Naval Academy, full of well-preserved colonial architecture, and within easy distance of Baltimore and Washington, Annapolis has something for everyone.

Tom Horton

Tom Horton is a native of Maryland's Eastern Shore, an avid kayaker, and a noted writer. He covered the Chesapeake for the *Baltimore Sun* for 35 years and is the author of several books about the bay, including *An Island Out of Time: A Memoir of Smith Island in the Chesapeake,* which explores the waterman culture and life on the bay.

ten best
botanical gardens

Gardens and grasslands have a cooling effect on the Earth. These destinations draw attention to the beauty and power of green places.

brooklyn botanic garden

1000 Washington Ave., Brooklyn, NY 11225
718-623-7200, www.bbg.org

On Tuesdays in the fall there are drop-in programs for children in the Children's Garden, featuring planting or craft activities. In this beautiful outdoor space within the famous Brooklyn Botanic Garden, you'll find playground equipment, trees, and colorful gardens that create an imaginative play environment. Ask about the history of the Children's Garden and the delightful story of "Patsy's bean."

camden children's garden

3 Riverside Dr., Camden, NJ 08103, 856-365-8733
www.camdenchildrensgarden.org

This park is home to a statue of New Jersey native Walt Whitman, portrayed here with a butterfly perched on his finger. Appropriately, it's installed in the park's butterfly garden. The Storybook Gardens allow children to experience creative play in beautifully planted playhouses and walled gardens inspired by familiar fairy tales and legends. Children will get a bird's-eye view of the garden overlooking Red Oak Run when they enter the Tree House.

morris arboretum

100 E. Northwestern Ave., Philadelphia, PA 19118, 215-247-5777
www.business-services.upenn.edu/arboretum/

Brand new treehouse paths and a tree-to-tree suspension bridge let kids get a canopy view of some of the region's most interesting trees. The state's official arboretum is here on the University of Pennsylvania campus, where you'll also find the Garden Railway, a G-scale train running through imaginative miniature landscapes that change seasonally.

united states botanic garden

100 Maryland Ave., SW, Washington, DC 20001
202-225-8333, www.usbg.gov

America's "national garden" is adjacent to a glass-enclosed conservatory, with background views of capital city landmarks. Across the street is Bartholdi Park, with more gardens, a fountain, and displays to inspire home landscaping.

garvan woodland gardens

540 Arkridge Rd., Hot Springs, AR 71913
800-366-4664, www.garvangardens.org

This wooded garden is surrounded by Lake Hamilton, a world-class botanical showcase maintained by the University of Arkansas. A Razorback Tea

Party is served on the second Tuesday of each month, and a train garden delights young visitors year-round.

morikami museum & japanese gardens

4000 Morikami Park Rd., Delray Beach, FL 33446
561-495-0233, www.morikami.org

The garden walk is almost a mile long, including the Contemplation Pavilion, where visitors are encouraged to "listen with your eyes and see with your ears." Plan to stay for lunch at the Cornell Café. Tea service and menu choices add to a family's multisensory experience of this memorable site.

chicago botanic garden

1000 Lake Cook Rd., Glencoe, IL 60022
847-835-5440, www.chicagobotanic.org

An amazing collection of bonsai trees, an English walled garden, and the pathways of McDonald Woods make a visit to this famous garden an unforgettable family experience. It's located about 20 miles north of Chicago.

mount goliath

Denver Botanical Gardens mountain trail, Mount Evans Scenic Byway, Clear Creek County, CO, 720-865-3585
www.botanicgardens.org

Part of the Arapaho National Forest, this mountain peak is maintained by the renowned Denver Botanical Gardens (with three other

> One touch of nature makes the whole world kin.
> —William Shakespeare

locations in the Denver metro area). Plan ahead to reserve space for a free guided wildflower hike along spectacular Rocky Mountain trails. Family tip: Go to the York Street location to see the children's "secret path" garden.

boyce thompson arboretum state park

Boyce Thompson Arboretum, 37615 U.S. Hwy. 60, Superior, AZ 85273
520-689-2723, http://arboretum. ag.arizona.edu/about_us.html

Imagine a beautiful garden that requires almost no water at all. This desert park showcases one of the world's largest collections of arid-region plants, and kids are amazed by the cactus garden. It's a delightful visit, and the Queen Creek Canyon area is a nice place for resting in the shade.

quail botanical gardens

230 Quail Gardens Dr., Encinitas, CA 92024
760-436-3036, www.qbgardens.org

The Seeds of Wonder children's garden features weekday programs for preschoolers that are really popular with local families. Check out the roof of the rest room—it's a desert plant garden. Everyone in the family will be intrigued by ingenious topiaries and beautiful flower beds throughout the gardens.

ten best
famous trees

All trees take in carbon dioxide and produce oxygen—exactly the opposite of the human respiratory system.

white birches

Rte. 2, Shelburne, NH, www.newenglandforestry.org/forestry/forestdetail.asp?id=25

In the White Mountains of northern New Hampshire, the papery white bark of birch trees seems to glow in the dark. Native Americans used almost every part of white birches, obtaining sugar from their sap and using the bark for shelter and canoe coverings. They're part of the American landscape. You'll pass this area en route to the famous Mount Washington Auto Road in Gorham (www.mount washington.com).

witness trees

Gettysburg National Military Park, 1195 Baltimore Pike Gettysburg, PA 17325, 717-334-1124, www.nps.gov/gett

It's interesting to imagine what's happened near some of North America's oldest trees. These "witness trees" were here when Civil War battles raged around them, and were part of the quiet landscape of Lincoln's Gettysburg Address. A storm destroyed one of the oldest in 2008, but park rangers can direct visitors to the remaining

Trees animate the landscape everywhere.

few. Throughout the country, witness trees are identified at historic sites. Take time to gaze into the branches and consider what has happened nearby.

emancipation oak

Hampton University, Hampton, VA 23668, 757-727-5000, www.hamptonu.edu/about/emancipation_oak.cfm

The Emancipation Proclamation was first announced under the branches of this tree, today a grand specimen with a crown that measures at least 98 feet in diameter. It is rooted in African-American education traditions: Before the Civil War, slave children were secretly taught here. One student, Booker T. Washington, went on to found the Tuskegee Institute.

cypress trees

Great Dismal Swamp, 3100 Desert Rd., Suffolk, VA 23434, 757-986-3705, www.fws.gov/northeast/greatdismalswamp

Mysterious and sinewy-looking bald cypress trees rise up out of the shallow waters of this wetland environment. Prehistoric fossils illustrate the ancient history of the cypress in North America. Hiking and biking trails allow access to great views across the borders of Virginia and North Carolina.

angel oak

3688 Angel Oak Rd., Johns Island, SC 29455
803-559-3496, www.angeloaktree.org

Live oaks are also known as evergreen oaks because they keep their leaves almost all year long. This live oak is believed to be more than 1,400 years old—the oldest living thing east of the Mississippi. Its lowest branches sweep the ground, and Spanish moss festoons the upper reaches—a sight to behold.

mangrove trees

Biscayne National Park, 9700 S.W. 328 St., Homestead, FL 33033, 305-230-7275, www.nps.gov/bisc

Mangrove trees are adapted in unique ways. Some block salt from their roots; others pass salt through their leaves. Their roots form an erosion barrier, and also serve as feeding and living places for critical small ocean life at the base of the food chain.

johnny appleseed legacy

Lynd Fruit Farm, 9090 Morse Rd., SW, Pataskala, OH 43062, 740-927-1333, www.lyndfruitfarm.com

John Chapman planted nurseries to provide saplings for frontier families. An apple tree at the entrance to this pick-your-own farm was propagated from a "descendant" of an original Chapman tree. For the record, the only original "Johnny Appleseed" tree still growing is on private property in Savannah, Ohio. The Johnny Appleseed Heritage Foundation is a tribute to John Chapman's vision. There are many tall tales still told of his adventures.

quaking aspen colony

Fishlake National Forest, 115 E. 900 N, Richfield, UT 84701, 435-896-9233, www.fs.fed.us/r4/fishlake/

A 100-acre colony of quaking aspen trees is known as Pando, a Latin word meaning "I spread." Geneticists study these trees because they reproduce as clones: The entire colony is thought to be a single living organism sharing one root system.

general sherman tree

Sequoia National Park, 47050 Generals Hwy., Three Rivers, CA 93271, 559-565-3341, www.nps.gov/seki

This giant sequoia is the largest tree in the world, with the greatest cubic feet of wood expanse. It also marks the starting point of the Congress Trail, a two-mile walk on a paved path through the Giant Forest portion of the national park.

old-growth coastal redwoods

Muir Woods National Monument, Mill Valley, CA 94941, 415-388-2596, www.nps.gov/muwo

These coastal redwoods are some of the tallest living organisms on the planet—the tallest here is about 258 feet high (clearance under the Golden Gate Bridge is 220 feet).

books | the giving tree
by shel silverstein

A simple and poetic book—at first read, a child's story about the life of an average man. But read it again for life lessons about sacrifice, generosity, and love.

ten best
naturalist's favorites

Some of these destinations represent irreplaceable pieces of nature that are slipping away even as you read this. Others are my own family favorites, part of our lifelong exploration of wild places.
—Rick Ridgeway

big sur coast, california

www.bigsurcalifornia.org

One of the more spectacular coastlines in the world. Pfeiffer State Park has a wonderful camp-ground, with access to stunning hiking trails. You can reach waterfalls and see famous ocean views depending on the trails you choose. You'll want to visit here more than once.

golden trout wilderness of the high sierra, california

http://www.fs.fed.us/r5/inyo/recreation/wild/index.shtml

This wilderness area has some of the easiest access for families to higher altitude backcountry hiking in the High Sierra, because you can drive to the trailhead at a high elevation. There's lakeside camping with great fishing.

The best journeys are the ones that answer questions that at the outset you never even thought to ask.

—Rick Ridgeway

channel islands national park, california

www.nps.gov/chis

Hiking and camping, and it requires a fun boat ride to get there. One of my favorite places in the U.S., it's called the Galapagos of North America—with bird, animal, and plant species native just to the islands.

north rim of the grand canyon, arizona

www.nps.gov/grca

The "undiscovered" side of the greatest canyon in North America. There are small dirt roads you can access right to the rim of the canyon, where you can camp with your family removed from the crowds just across the chasm on the south side.

frank church wilderness area, idaho

www.fs.fed.us/r4/sc/recreation/fcronr/fcronrindex.shtml

A huge wilderness that is infrequently visited, with easy hiking trails to secluded lakes with great fishing. It was here that Lewis and Clark met Sacajawea, the Indian woman who accompanied them on their westward journey. The explorers were astounded by the splendor of this area.

niobrara river, nebraska

www.nps.gov/niob

I love the Sandhills grasslands section of the Great Plains—wide open spaces with small country roads, and wonderful stops for day-hiking, such as the Agate Fossil Beds National Monument. The Niobrara is superb for canoeing and kayaking—really good for families.

grand staircase-escalante national monument, utah

www.utah.com/escalante

A fragile place, and a great one for families. Bryce Canyon and Calf Creek Falls are two famous destinations, and the drive to get here is part of the whole experience.

henry mountains, utah

www.utah.com/playgrounds/henry_mtns.htm

Also in Utah—an excellent place for car camping and hiking, but global warming is already changing the isolated habitats. It's a beautiful part of nearly two million acres of federally managed land in central Utah with ecosystems ranging from desert to forest to mountains.

wind rivers, wyoming

www.wind-river.org

A wonderful place for horse-packing and longer backpack trips—great for families, but again, the ecosystem is threatened by warming. This area is the home of South Pass, the easiest place to cross the Continental Divide.

cabeza prieta, arizona

www.fws.gov/southwest/refuges/arizona/cabeza.html

This was one of my favorite family trips, but that was ten years ago. I'm afraid now it may be a war zone because of the border issues with Homeland Security and the Fence, but worth investigating—it's super-fragile.

Rick Ridgeway

Rick Ridgeway is one of America's best-known climbers and adventurers. For the last 25 years, he has made his passion his vocation, developing books, documentary films, and television programs. He is the author of the highly acclaimed *Seven Summits, The Shadow of Kilimanjaro*, and, most recently, *Below Another Sky*. In 1996 he walked 300 miles from the summit of Mt. Kilimanjaro to the Pacific Ocean, and in 1998 he celebrated Christmas on the first big wall climb ever completed in Antarctica.

ten best
migration airways

America's great airborne migrations are indicators of changing weather patterns, habitat health, and the ancient and unchanging habits of the animals themselves. Breeding and feeding grounds await at the end of the journey.

hawks

Cape May Point State Park
Lighthouse Ave., Cape May, NJ 08212
609-884-2159, www.nj.gov/dep/parksandforests/
parks/capemay.html

In September and October, trained observers are on duty to record the habits of migrating hawks and other raptors. At the end of the summer, the park is also a resting place for migrating dragonflies and monarch butterflies.

buzzards

Makoshika State Park, 1301 Snyder Ave, Glendive,
MT 59330, 406-377-6256, www.makoshika.org

Turkey vultures (also known as buzzards) assist park rangers as natural cleaners in this, the largest state park in Montana. In winter months they migrate as far south as Central America, but they return each spring to great fanfare. On the second Saturday of June, rangers host Montana Buzzard Day with a pancake breakfast, kids' games,

and an 8K run. The park is home to renowned fossil beds and summer cultural events.

turkey vultures

Hinckley Reservation, Hinckley Township,
Medina County, OH
216-635-3200, www.clemetparks.com

A sign of spring in Medina County, Ohio: the return of turkey vultures to the same municipal park. Legend has it that they appear like clockwork on March 15 every year.

hummingbirds

Hummingbird Migration Celebration, Strawberry Plains
Audubon Center, Holly Springs, MS 38635
662-252-1155, www.msaudubon.org

A late summer event marks the migration of ruby-throated hummingbirds. Experts band the birds and sometimes invite visitors to help release them.

mexican free-tailed bats

Congress Avenue Bridge, Austin, TX, 512-416-5700

More than a million bats make their summer home under a famous Austin bridge. They swarm out at dusk to feed on insects and other pests. Watch from the observation hill adjacent to the *Austin American-Statesman* publishing office (305 S. Congress Ave., Austin, TX 78704).

white pelicans

Medicine Lake, 223 North Shore Rd., Medicine
Lake, MT 59247, 406-789-2305
www.fws.gov/medicinelake

Visit in spring to witness the
annual arrival of white pelicans
from the Gulf of Mexico. As many
as 10,000 birds migrate north for
rich feeding grounds on the prairies of Montana. A wingspan of
nine feet makes the bird a sight
to behold.

trumpeter swans

Red Rock Lakes National Wildlife Refuge, Red Rock
Pass Rd., Lima, MT 59739, 406-276-3536
www.fws.gov/redrocks

A number of swans make their year-round homes
here, and as many as 2,000 more arrive in late
fall from colder Canadian waters. Together they
winter where there is a reliable food supply and
warm springs that keep water from freezing.

barn swallows

Mission San Juan Capistrano, 26801 Ortega Hwy.
San Juan Capistrano, CA 92675, 949-234-1300
www.missionsjc.com

Folks in the town of Capistrano take swallows
seriously, protecting the birds' mud nests and
anticipating their annual return around March
19. Here, a Saint Joseph's feast day festival is
held to coincide with the reliable arrival of the
celebrated swallows.

monarch butterflies

Natural Bridges State Beach & Monarch
Refuge, 2531 W. Cliff Dr., Santa Cruz,
CA 95060, 831-423-4609, www.
santacruzstateparks.org/parks/
natbridges

Hike the Butterfly Preserve,
where a trail wends through
parkland that is a winter home
for monarch butterflies. In summer, families can explore delicate
tide-pool ecosystems near the park's
sandy cove. A bicycle path around the
refuge area is open year-round.

golden eagles

Denali National Park, Alaska Rte. 3, George Parks Hwy.
Denali, AK 99755, 907-683-2294, www.nps.gov/dena

In spring, eagles begin to arrive in familiar nesting areas around the park's Polychrome Path, and
golden eaglets hatch before summer. By late fall,
they are ready to migrate along the Rocky Mountains as far south as Mexico. Use binoculars to see
the arriving adults; the migrating juveniles will be
harder to spot.

---

resource | online game

Check out this online game developed by Audubon New York. Players navigate a flock of native
birds in search of food, water, shelter, and space.
In order to win, they must dodge dangers from
both natural and man-made hazards.

http://ny.audubon.org/missionmigration.html

ten best
zoos & animal shelters

When children have an opportunity to get close to animals, they're more likely to be interested in preserving their environments in the wild. These zoos and sanctuaries are especially well known for the quality of staff and ability to share the beauty, power, and vulnerability of the animal world.

The Association of Zoos & Aquariums has a great website: www.aza.org.

bronx zoo

2300 Southern Blvd., Bronx, NY 10460, 718-220-5100
www.bronxzoo.com

The BxM11 express bus goes straight from Madison Avenue to the gates of the zoo. Think of it as your first adventure on a day of discovery. Plan to go nose-to-nose with western lowland gorillas, spot snow leopards, and trek through an indoor rain forest.

tisch children's zoo

64th St. & Fifth Ave., New York, NY, 718-220-5100
www.nyzoosandaquarium.com

Specially designed for children under the age of six, this zoo in Central Park is worth a visit just to see the charming entrance gate. Children love the highly interactive exhibits, where they can pretend to be the animals (as well as see them).

cincinnati zoo & botanical garden

3400 Vine St., Cincinnati, OH 45220, 800-944-4776
www.cincinnatizoo.org

Start with a trip to this zoo's website. They list three different types of self-guided tours with maps you can print out ahead of time. Each provides a unique way of seeing and savoring the best exhibits at this famous zoo, home to the only Sumatran rhinos in the United States, as well as a really great children's zoo area.

brookfield zoo

First Ave., Brookfield, IL 60513, 800-201-0784
www.czs.org

Summer is butterfly season here in Chicago. Hundreds of butterflies are raised and released into the outdoor garden exhibit between June and mid-September. Check out the pupa room, where you might see a butterfly emerge from a chrysalis.

deer forest fun park

6800 Indian La., Coloma, MI 49038, 269-468-4961
www.deerforest.com

Pet tame deer and wooly llamas in this 30-acre park. Storybook Lane adds to the amusement park mood of the place, but the real charm is in the proximity of domesticated creatures in the paths and woodlands.

rabbit sanctuary

8260 Judd Rd., Willis, MI 49810, 734-461-1726 www.rabbitsanctuary.org

This five-acre facility is open for tours by appointment. Visit the adoption area and see the sanctuary's largest outdoor pen, big enough for up to 300 rabbits.

albuquerque biological park

Albuquerque, NM 87104, 505-786-2000 www.cabq.gov/biopark

It's all a stone's throw from the legendary Rio Grande. See Albuquerque Aquarium, Rio Grande Botanic Garden, and Rio Grande Zoo. The BioPark "family" includes as many as 6,000 animals.

olympic game farm

1423 Ward Rd., Sequim, WA 98382, 800-778-4295 www.olygamefarm.com

Where do animals go after they've appeared on TV? Many of them come here, to a sanctuary and visiting area not far from Seattle. Drive through the park to see tigers, zebras, timber wolves, and three species of bear, to name a few. You can also choose to walk the park's trails and pet llamas and buffalo.

> The greatness of a nation and its moral progress can be judged by the way its animals are treated.
>
> —Mahatma Gandhi

california raptor center

1 Shields Ave., University of California, Davis, CA 95616 530-752-6091, www.vetmed.ucdavis.edu/calraptor/onsite.html

About 200 injured birds are brought here each year, and nearly half of them are returned to the wild. The center's free museum is open every day but Sunday.

san diego zoo

Balboa Park, San Diego, CA 92112, 619-231-1515 www.sandiegozoo.org

The 100-acre San Diego Zoo is world-famous, with 4,000 animals and 800 rare and exotic species. It has the largest population of giant pandas in the nation. The monkey trail is one of the most popular exhibits, weaving jungle lore with real-life conservation. The petting zoo, baby animal nursery, and SkyTram may be the most memorable sites for the youngest visitors. It's definitely a full-day destination (maybe two).

books | the very hungry caterpillar
by eric carle

Pages are layered, hole-punched, and printed to create a wonderfully tactile story about a caterpillar, its appetite, and its amazing transformation.

ten best
protected habitats

Wherever you go, respect the habitat and keep your distance. Some of these places are big and dramatic and isolated, and some are close to major metropolitan areas.
—Sara and Chuck Savitt

bald eagles

Great Falls Park, 9200 Old Dominion Dr., McLean, VA 22102, 703-285-2965
www.nps.gov/grfa

It takes a practiced eye to begin recognizing bird species, their habitats, and their habits. This park is a great place to learn the art. Bald eagles, spring bird migrations, and ducks of every variety are here. Look and listen for them.

roseate terns

Great Point, Coskata-Coatue Wildlife Refuge Wauwinet Rd., Wauwinet, MA 02554, 508-228-5646
www.thetrustees.org

Best known for its historic lighthouse, white-sand beaches, and world-class fishing, the refuge is a complex ecosystem of rare habitats, plants, and birds—including endangered roseate terns.

wolves

Mammoth Hot Springs in Yellowstone National Park, WY 82190, 307-344-7381, www.nps.gov/yello

Gray wolves once roamed most of North America, but they were hunted as dangerous predators.

There were no wolves left in Yellowstone by 1926. In 1995, fourteen wolves from Canada were released, and by 2007, more than 170 wolves were roaming in the greater Yellowstone area.

manatee

Merritt Island National Wildlife Refuge, Titusville, FL 32781, 321-861-0668, www.fws.gov/merrittisland

Here you may glimpse a manatee—a slow-moving mammal that surfaces to breathe every three to five minutes. While they have no natural predators, manatees are endangered by boat traffic and habitat loss.

african & asian animals

Wild Animal Park, Escondido, CA 92027, 760-747-8702
www.sandiegozoo.org

Part of the San Diego Zoo system, this is one of the few places in the nation where wild animals are raised. It is home to the endangered California condor, cheetahs, giraffes, lions, and elephants.

red-legged frog

Pinnacles National Monument, 5000 Hwy. 146, Paicines, CA 95043, 831-389-4486, www.nps.gov/pinn

In 1985, this park's reservoir was drained to remove non-native catfish that encroached on the habitat of the largest frog species west of the Mississippi. Red-legged frogs (and other amphibians) are making a slow comeback here.

salmon

Hiram M. Chittenden Locks, 3015 N.W. 54th St., Seattle, WA 98107, 206-783-7059, www.nws.usace.army.mil

Generations of chinook and steelhead salmon travel an intricate path from river to ocean and back. The Puget Sound waterfront community works hard to keep the pathway clear. At these locks, see a glass-paneled fish ladder where salmon move between salt and fresh waters. The U.S. Army Corps of Engineers maintains this site, including providing educational information about salmon habitat preservation.

loggerhead sea turtles

Back Bay NWR, 4005 Sandpiper Rd. Virginia Beach, VA 23456, 757-721-2412, www.fws.gov/backbay

These pelagic turtles come ashore to lay eggs. Fish nets and loss of safe beachfront are major threats. Here, beach trails and a visitor center provide a glimpse of ideal loggerhead nesting ground.

piping plover

Sleeping Bear Dunes National Lakeshore, 9922 Front St., Empire, MI 49630, 231-326-5134, www.nps.gov/slbe

The park's Platte Point area is the best place to view the protected lakefront that is the summer home to these endangered small shorebirds. Volunteers build protective shelters for their nests and observe behaviors. Visitors must watch from a distance—by canoe or kayak is best.

whooping crane

Aransas National Wildlife Refuge Complex, 1 Wildlife Cir., Austwell, TX 77950, 361-286-3559, www.fws.gov

In 1941, there were only 15 whooping cranes left in the world. A last remaining flock from northwest Canada continues to winter here—as many as 236 in 2007.

Chuck & Sara Savitt

Chuck and Sara Savitt met at a nature-writing workshop in Taos, New Mexico. Sara (a poet and freelance writer) and Chuck (president of environmental publisher Island Press) discovered their mutual love of wilderness in the heart of the Sangre de Cristo Mountains. They spend as much time as they can hiking, exploring, and taking road trips to enjoy and observe wildlife and nature. Their seven-year-old daughter Nona is a constant companion as they explore the natural world. They live in Washington, D.C.

ten best
everyday animals

Some familiar creatures are now threatened or endangered. Take a closer look at who is sharing your backyard, parks, streams, and woods. Sometimes the most ordinary animals have the most extraordinary histories and habits!

bullfrogs

James River State Park, 751 Park Rd.
Gladstone, VA 24553, 434-933-4355
www.dcr.virginia.gov/state_parks/jam.shtml

These big amphibians are native to the East Coast, where the males' mating calls are a familiar springtime sound. In the central United States and West Coast, they are considered pests because they encroach on the habitats of native frogs. This beautiful state park is a place to discover the ideal bullfrog habitat.

black squirrels

Princeton University, Frist Campus Center,
Washington St., Princeton, NJ 08544, 609-258-1766
www.princeton.edu/main/visiting/tours/

On Saturdays or Sundays, you can take a free one-hour walking tour of the famous university campus. You'll hear lots of collegiate lore, including observations of the famous black squirrels that make their home here. Fall is a great time to visit this Ivy League campus.

anoles

Wikewa Springs State Park, 1800 Wekiwa Cir., Apopka, FL 32712, 407-884-2008
www.floridastateparks.org/WekiwaSprings

Leafy green in color, this little southeastern lizard can appear brown depending on changes in temperature, environment, or stress levels. In some parts of Florida the native green anole is experiencing a challenge for habitat from a slightly larger species of brown anole. Not far from the Orlando resorts, this state park has natural springs with hiking trails, canoe and kayak rentals, and opportunities to see native animals.

raccoons

All over the country

Like all wild creatures, raccoons should be observed from a distance. They are a true North American native species that has adapted its feeding and denning habits to live in suburban and urban places.

pigeons

Cities everywhere

Pigeons rarely perch in trees. It's because they are the descendants of rock-dwelling birds first brought to North America by 17th-century settlers. Their instincts encourage them to seek out concrete ledges. By the time they can fly, baby pigeons are almost as big as adults. How to tell them apart: Adults have orange eyes, while juveniles' are brown.

armadillos

Lost Maples State Natural Area, 37221 FM 187 Vanderpool, TX 78885, 830-966-3413 www.wildtexas.com/parks/lmsna.php

Originally from Central and South America, armadillos are everywhere in the central south regions. Only the three-banded type can roll into a ball when alarmed. In the United States you'll observe the nine-banded armadillo, which just hustles away. This popular camping and hiking destination is 80 miles from San Antonio.

seagulls

Shorelines everywhere

Look for details that distinguish one species from another. The herring gull can drink seawater and pass salt through holes near its eyes: Look for salt drips on its beak. The laughing gull has a black head during breeding season. The ring-billed gull thrives in inland areas, often drawn by landfills and other feeding opportunities. The closer you look, the more you learn.

prairie dogs

Devils Tower National Monument, Devils Tower, WY 82714, 307-467-5283, www.nps.gov/deto

Black-tailed prairie dogs are the foundation of the Great Plains ecosystem. Their burrows shelter other animals, and they are the only food of the black-footed ferret. Seen as pests, 98 percent of the species was wiped out in the last hundred years. Look for them here near the Belle Fourche River.

honeybees

North Carolina Zoo, 4401 Zoo Pkwy., Asheboro, NC 27205, 800-488-0444, www.nczoo.org

Bee pollination is responsible for as much as 30 percent of the American food supply, yet bees' numbers have decreased by half in the last 50 years. This zoo exhibit, new in spring 2009, features a life-size hive with interactive exhibits, plus weekend visits from working beekeepers. Scientists study honeybees and a recent phenomenon known as colony collapse disorder, hoping to learn more about the habits of these now-endangered insects.

skunks

Arizona-Sonora Desert Museum, 2021 N. Kinney Rd. Tucson, AZ 85743, 520-883-2702 www.desertmuseum.org

These rodents are opportunistic eaters, ridding the forest floor of carrion and insects. They are among the native North American mammals that thrive today in both urban and wild areas. See four different species at this celebrated desert zoo.

Observe all wild creatures from a safe distance, no matter how familiar they may be. Some can carry rabies or Lyme disease. But looking for animals and noticing how they live can tell us a lot about our own environments!

ten best
aquatic life

There's much to be learned from an aquarium visit. Animal and plant life abounds, tidal patterns can be explored, and conservation messages come across loud and clear (or silent and powerful).

new england aquarium

Central Wharf, Boston, MA 02110
617-973-5200, www.neaq.org

The renovated family galleries explore three ocean habitats—the Enchanted Kelp Forest, Coral Reef Kingdom, and Rugged Rocky Shore—and the variety of life within each. The bright exhibit design and dramatic lighting set the gold standard for aquarium design.

national aquarium in baltimore

Pier 3, 501 E. Pratt St., Baltimore, MD 21202
410-576-3800, www.aqua.org

A visit to this aquarium is an intuitive experience, where curving banks of exhibits and ramped, moving walkways lead you from one area to the next. See live feedings by scuba divers, dolphins shows,

a rain forest exhibit, and a towering Australian river valley at this waterfront city destination.

national aquarium in washington, d.c.

14th & Constitution Ave., NW
Washington, DC 20230, 202-482-2825
www.nationalaquarium.com

This tiny jewel of an aquarium is one of the capital city's best-kept secrets. It's an outpost of Baltimore's famous aquarium, located on the lower level of the U.S. Department of Commerce building. It's a cool and tranquil place to visit on a hot day. America's "Population Clock" is located on the main floor of the building.

tennessee aquarium

1 Broad St., Chattanooga, TN 37402
800-262-0695, www.tennis.org

From the world's largest freshwater aquarium, take a high-speed catamaran tour of the Tennessee River Gorge, known as Tennessee's Grand Canyon. Visitors come from all over to see Gentoo and

> " sally, massachusetts | baby & fish We took our six-month-old granddaughter to the aquarium and she loved it! There aren't a lot of places that a baby can really enjoy, but the way the New England Aquarium's tanks are set up, you can get really close. It was fun to watch her gaze at schools of fish.

macaroni penguins, "Ocean Journey" and "River Journey" exhibits, and IMAX films.

shedd aquarium

1200 S. Lake Shore Dr., Chicago, IL 60605
312-939-2438, www.sheddaquarium.org

This beaux arts building is a national landmark, and the exhibits inside are state of the art. A dramatic moon jellies exhibit is not to be missed, along with beluga whales in the Oceanarium, plus lively river otters and lots of sharks. It's centrally located in Grant Park.

downtown aquarium

700 Water St., Denver, CO 80211, 303-561-4450
www.aquariumrestaurants.com

Visit for lunch or dinner and linger over the view of the giant aquarium. Aquarists are on staff to care for the exhibits and animals. It's a fun family destination with a jam-packed gift shop. There are other locations in Texas and Tennessee.

aquarium of the americas

1 Canal St., New Orleans, LA 70130, 504-581-4629
www.auduboninstitute.org

For families, the aquarium's interactive Adventure Island area is a destination in itself. A limited number of visitors can assist with the mid-day stingray feedings here. Plan the whole day around the aquarium, plus visits to the other Audubon attractions: the new Insectarium and Audubon Zoo.

monterey bay aquarium

886 Cannery Row, Monterey, CA 93940, 831-648-4800, www.mbayaq.org

From the sea lions basking on the rocks nearby to the anemones in Pacific tide pools, the aquarium's exterior melds beautifully with the treasures you'll find inside. Galleries feature more than 45 bilingual interactive exhibits, some native to the Califonia coast, and others from far away, like leafy and weedy sea dragons.

sea world san diego

500 SeaWorld Dr., San Diego, CA 92109, 800-257-4268
www.seaworld.com

Visitors aged 13 and older can learn about training marine mammals at "Wild Arctic Interaction." Reservations are required for this personal encounter with beluga whales. Try your hand at training signals, then feed these attentive white whales with the guidance of experienced mammologists. This Mission Bay park is a full-day destination.

seattle aquarium

1483 Alaskan Way, Seattle, WA 98101, 206-386-4300
www.seattleaquarium.org

Discovery goes far beyond the walls of the aquarium itself. Beach naturalists from this aquarium are on duty along local waterfronts to point out unique plants and animals. In summer months, check the schedule for naturalists posted at many parks and beaches along the coast. Don't miss the Puget Sound Orcas Family Activity Center.

ten best
science camps

Working together toward a common goal makes a family stronger. Build a robot . . . sail a boat . . . dig for fossils. It's a good idea for adults to model curiosity and focused interest for their children. Camps and workshops like this are a great start.

atlantic coastal camp

College of the Atlantic, 105 Eden St.
Bar Harbor, ME 04609
800-597-9500, www.coa.edu

Summer nature camps bring families together to kayak, hike, observe wildlife, and look up close at ecosystems from beachfront to forests. This renowned program offers a great way to jump right into an exploration of the wonders of coastal Maine.

family robotics workshop

2 S. Pack Sq., Asheville, NC 28801, 828-254-6373
www.thehealthadventure.org

In summer months, the Health Adventure's Discover Science Camp sponsors a two-day robotics workshop for parents and kids together. Adults and children gain technical acumen and cooperative problem-solving experience as they design and operate their own robots.

u.s. space camp

U.S. Space & Rocket Center, One Tranquility Base
Huntsville, AL 35807
800-637-7223, www.spacecamp.com

Parents can live out their own astronaut dreams at adult space camps while kids conduct experiments and don aviation gear at children's programs that run at the same time. The U.S. Space Camp, Space Academy, and Aviation Challenge are year-round private programs for children, adults, and educators.

family astronaut training program

Kennedy Space Center, FL 32899
www.ksctickets.com/familyatx.html

Two-day family astronaut training programs include space shuttle mission simulation, rocket building, and VIP tours of Kennedy Space Center. The adventure, designed for adult/child pairs, includes accommodations at a nearby Cocoa Beach hotel.

nature day camps

Montana Outdoor Science School, 4050 Bridger Canyon Dr., Bozeman, MT 59715, 406-582-0526
www.outdoorscience.org

Day programs are designed for families with kids of varying ages. Great programs for parents with teens include science illustration and nature journaling, avalanche awareness, and fly-fishing. Guided nature hikes are ideal for families with littler ones. Some programs are offered at the MOSS site; others are free to the public at various locations around Bozeman.

weekend adventure camp

Islandwood, 4450 Blakely Ave., NE, Bainbridge Island, WA 98110, 206-855-4300, www.islandwood.org

Summer adventure camp weekends are designed especially for families. Activities provide fun ways to learn together about environmental stewardship and wilderness exploration.

geology day camps

Geology Adventures, Ravensdale, WA 98051
425-413-1122, www.geologyadventures.com

These rock-collecting trips are guided by experienced geologists. Itineraries are established in advance, and families meet up with guides at appointed locations such as the Cascade and Okanogan mountains, plus locations in Canada.

camp sealab

100 Campus Center, Bldg. 42, Seaside, CA 93955
831-582-3681, www.campsealab.org

One-day family workshops provide a great introduction to the ecosystems of California's central coast. Programs are scheduled throughout the year. Programs cover topics including fish anatomy, navigation, sea turtles and conservation, watershed studies, scientific illustration, and marine mammals.

overnight educational cruise

Ocean Institute, 24200 Dana Point Harbor Dr. Dana Point, CA 92629, 949-496-2274
www.ocean-institute.org

Try a beachfront campfire combined with an overnight cruise on a research vessel staffed by marine biologists. A summer bioluminescence adventure includes lab experiments, dissections, and an onboard study to observe marine animals that glow in the dark.

family archaeology week

Crow Canyon, 23390 Rd. K, Cortez, CO 81321
970-565-8975, www.crowcanyon.org

Here in the Mesa Verde region, this center sponsors week-long summer camps where families participate in the daily activities of a working lab and excavation site. The location is rich in evidence of ancient Puebloan cultures, from tools and pottery shards to bone fragments and fossils.

books | ender's game
by orson scott card

This is a great book for kids interested in science, science fiction, and technology. Ender Wiggins is the young boy chosen to be trained to save the world. He travels to many worlds and into the future. Its sequels, *Speaker for the Dead, Xenocide, Children of the Mind, A War of Gifts,* and *Ender in Exile,* are also excellent.

ten best
places for stargazers

These reflect my memories of watching the night sky from grade school on up. Places with low ambient light are best.
—Capt. Sunita Williams, USN

a parking lot

I think one of the best places I star/spaceship gazed was lying in a parking lot. What made it really special was that my little dog lay down next to me, like that was where we were going to sleep overnight. That was fun!

flying over west texas

We fly trainer jets with glass canopies. Flying over west Texas one evening with all the lights down low in the cockpit allowed me to really see the milkiness of the Milky Way.

on a beach

At Prince Edward Island, you'll see the northern lights (aurora borealis) beginning around the end of August—and other times of the year, depending on conditions. The farther north you go, the brighter the lights and colors will appear.

Capt. Williams holds the record for time spent in space by a woman.

in the mountains

We just ran a 24-hour race from Fort Collins to Steamboat Springs, Colorado, through the mountains and Wyoming. We were running on some dirt roads all through the night in a relay team of six, so everyone had one leg running in the dark. With really no ambient lights around, you could see the Milky Way spanning from one side of the horizon to the other.

a small town

Again, a small town in the mountains, this time in Flagstaff, Arizona. The clear air and low humidity make it easy to look up and see lots of stars. Lowell Observatory is in this area, so I'm not the only one who's noticed that it's a great place to look up at the night sky!

off the coast of cape cod

The flight path of the shuttle on its way to the International Space Station goes over the southern side of the Cape. For that matter, any place on the East Coast will see the space shuttle fly by after evening liftoffs. There is information about liftoff schedules on www.nasa.gov.

camping

We went camping in Canyonlands National Park in Utah. Again, no one around—we only saw one person in ten days, a cowboy herding cattle through the canyons . . . incredible. We lay on the rocks each night and saw shooting stars and satellites fly overhead as well as the infinite number of stars.

from space

On board the International Space Station or the space shuttle, you turn the lights down low and you can see forever.

stargazing in space

The stars don't twinkle when you look at them from space. Without water vapor in the atmosphere to blur your vision, the stars seem like definite points of light.

space walk

Looking through my visor during a space walk . . . being in the blackness of space really made it feel 3-D. It didn't seem like a sphere, more like it just went on forever. Strange sensation. The stars were crystal clear, and being above the northern lights was a little weird but fun. It really puts you in

> Heaven-born, the soul a heavenward course must hold; beyond the visible world she soars . . .
> —Michelangelo

your place when you can actually see with your own two eyes how much energy there is out there in the universe. More than we could ever imagine here on Earth.

Sunita Williams

Sunita Williams is an American astronaut who served as a flight engineer aboard the International Space Station, launching with the crew of STS-116 on December 9, 2006. During her 195 consecutive days in space she was a member of both the *Expedition-14* and *Expedition-15* crews.

Capt. Williams's astronaut training program included scientific and technical briefings, learning about shuttle and International Space Station systems, physiological training, and ground school to prepare for T-38 flight training, as well as learning water and wilderness survival techniques. She has logged over 2,770 flight hours in more than 30 different aircraft.

ten best
science museums

The average family doesn't have a high-powered microscope at the kitchen table, or a walk-in kaleidoscope in the backyard. But science museums make these resources available to everyone, along with educators who know how to present abstract concepts so that everyone can begin to understand.

On display at the National Air and Space Museum

museum of science boston

1 Science Park, Boston, MA 02114, 617-723-2500
www.mos.org

Imagine a child standing still, watching a precisely tuned contraption in perpetual motion. The giant Rube Goldberg machine stocked with colorful pool balls is a centerpiece of this renowned museum in west Boston. It has a great new wing dedicated to the science of engineering, engaging visitors in the problem-solving activities key to innovation.

national air & space museum

Independence Ave. at 6th St., SW, Washington, DC
20560, 202-633-1000, www.nasm.si.edu

The Smithsonian Institution's most-visited museum is home to the Wright *1903 Flyer,* the *Spirit of St. Louis,* and moon rock that you can touch. A second facility is just outside D.C.: the Steven F.

Udvar-Hazy Center (www.nasm.si.edu/udvarhazy) displays the *Enola Gay,* the space shuttle *Enterprise,* and a Lockheed Blackbird.

the franklin institute

222 N. 20th St., Philadelphia, PA
19103, 215-448-1200, www2.fi.edu

Save a whole day to explore this renowned museum. For young children, the "KidScience" exhibit is an especially memorable experience—an introduction to the basic elements of science through storytelling, fictional characters, and compelling superhero tableaux. "Sir Isaac's Loft" combines art and physics with irresistible hands-on experimentation like a light spirograph and the alarming "Bowling Ball of Doom."

discovery place

301 N. Tryon St., Charlotte, NC
28202, 704-372-6261
www.discoveryplace.org

Rat basketball is one of the most popular activities at this fun science museum—including great information on the brain science involved in learning new skills. A new satellite facility for very young children is open in nearby Huntersville.

science museum of minnesota

120 Kellogg Blvd. W, St Paul, MN 55102
651-221-9444, www.smm.org

This innovative museum is built into bluffs overlooking the Mississippi River. The river flows just outside its windows and past ten acres of outdoor exhibits and programming space. Family favorites: nine holes of mini golf exploring changing landscapes, a Dinosaurs and Fossils Gallery (with a *Diplodocus* skeleton discovered by high school students), and hands-on activities in the Experiments Gallery.

hands-on! regional museum

315 E. Main St., Johnson City, TN 37601
423-434-HAND, www.handsonmuseum.org

This small museum is scaled especially for children's interests and abilities. Kids love to switch on the flashing light of a police motorcycle, play giant chimes, create enormous bubbles, and conduct real experiments in the Eastman Discovery Lab.

museum of science & industry

57th St. & Lake Shore Dr., Chicago, IL 60637
773-684-1414, www.msichicago.org

This famous museum's mission is to "inspire the inventive genius in everyone." Check out the six-foot floating globe programmed with constantly changing images of Earth's actual weather patterns, ocean currents, and geological forces at work. The "Networld" exhibit allows you to create a digital image of yourself and explore the inner workings of the Internet.

the aerospace education center

3301 E. Roosevelt Rd., Little Rock, AR 72206
501-376-4629, www.aerospaced.org

Every Friday night is family night at this science center's IMAX theater and EpiSphere planetarium (discounted admission and free popcorn). EpiSphere is a digital dome for astronomy presentations, but it also has great views for presentations on science topics like weather (think swirling tornadoes).

exploratorium

3601 Lyon St., San Francisco, CA 94123, 415-397-5673
www.exploratorium.edu

This is "the museum of science, art, and human perception." Check ahead on reservations for the famous "Tactile Dome," an all-dark exhibit in which visitors must "see" with the sense of touch (it's busiest in summer months). Make time for the new "MIND" exhibits, exploring the cognitive sciences of emotion, perception, learning, and communication. Look for the toilet-bowl drinking fountain.

tech museum of innovation

201 S. Market St., San Jose, CA 95113
408-294-8324, www.thetech.org

Be a Silicon Valley inventor for a day. Check out the "Virtual Test Zone," where real-life science is illustrated using virtual world technology. Get inside the mind of a painter, or explore a stage that shows how digital music works. Changing exhibits are created by leaders and innovators in digital imagery.

ten best
innovators' homes

Why didn't I think of that? See where the geniuses worked and how they lived every day. Celebrate the spirit of innovation by visiting the homes of some of the most famous American creators and scientific thinkers.

samuel morse

Locust Grove, 2683 South Rd. Poughkeepsie, NY 12601 845-454-4500, www.lgny.org

He patented the electromagnetic telegraph and sent the first electrically communicated message. The estate of Samuel Morse is now a historic site with a beautiful Victorian-era home, gardens, and three miles of walking trails. The "Morse Exhibit" highlights the artistic and scientific achievements of this 19th-century innovator.

rachel carson

The Rachel Carson Homestead, 613 Marion Ave. Springdale, PA 15144, 724-274-5459 www.rachelcarsonhomestead.org

This famed 20th-century ecologist grew up in southwestern Pennsylvania, and today families can visit the place that influenced her earliest years. The grounds and garden are open year-round, and the historic house is open for tours by appointment. Nearby trails along the Allegheny River are managed by the Rachel Carson Trails Conservancy (www.rachelcarsontrails.org).

benjamin franklin

The Franklin Institute, 222 N. 20th St., Philadelphia, PA 19103, 215-448-1200, www2.fi.edu

This founding father is buried in Philadelphia (Christ Church, 2nd St., www.christchurchphila.org). Born in Boston, he arrived in Philadelphia at the age of 16 and spent the rest of his life coming and going from here. A great way to explore Franklin's legacy is with a visit to the city's famous science museum, which bears his name. The popular exhibit "Franklin: He's Electric" celebrates his contributions to meteorology, music, electricity, optics, and aquatics. The Benjamin Franklin National Memorial is located in the rotunda of the institute.

benjamin banneker

Benjamin Banneker Historical Park & Museum, 300 Oella Ave., Baltimore, MD 21228, 410-887-1081 www.baltimorecountymd.gov/Agencies/recreation/countyparks/

The son of a former slave, Banneker was an important 19th-century astronomer and mathematician who worked to promote international peace and to abolish slavery. The site of his rural home (midway between Baltimore and Washington, D.C.) is now a public park with museum exhibits detailing his life's work.

thomas jefferson

Monticello, 931 Thomas Jefferson Pkwy.
Charlottesville, VA 22902, 434-984-9822
www.monticello.org

This grand plantation home is known as Thomas Jefferson's "autobiographical masterpiece," built and rebuilt over a period of more than 40 years. In summer months, special 30-minute tours are offered for children and their families, exploring the entwined lives of Thomas Jefferson, his family, and the generations of slaves who lived and worked here. It's southeast of the campus of the University of Virginia.

orville & wilbur wright

Wright Brothers National Memorial, Mile Post 7.5
Hwy. 158, Kill Devil Hills, NC, 252-473-2111
www.nps.gov/wrbr

This breezy beachfront hill is the time-honored location where Wilbur and Orville Wright launched their first successful flying machine. In summer months, programs for children include kite-making and kite-flying workshops, so kids can experience the same thrill of creating and navigating their own wind-worthy creations.

thomas edison, henry ford

Edison & Ford Winter Estates, 2350 McGregor Blvd.
Fort Myers, FL 33901, 239-334-7419, www.efwefla.org

Thomas Edison's New Jersey home is a national historic site, and Henry Ford's Fairlane is a national historic landmark in Detroit. But the two were winter neighbors in southwestern Florida, where Edison maintained a busy working laboratory and

an experimental garden. Their adjacent homes are open for visitors year-round.

amelia earhart

223 N. Terrace St., Atchison,
KS 66002, 913-367-4217
www.ameliaearhartmuseum.org

The famous aviator's birthplace and childhood home is now a museum in a residential area. At nearby Warnock Lake, a one-acre earthworks portrait of Amelia Earhart is sculpted in a field and partly visible from a viewing station. It is, of course, best seen from the air.

henry ford

Fair Lane, 4901 Evergreen Rd., Dearborn, MI 48128
313-593-5590, www.henryfordestate.org

Just outside Detroit, there's something for everyone here: a historic mansion with a great restaurant for visitors, beautiful gardens, and grounds. The centerpiece of a visit is an exploration of Ford's powerhouse, consisting of his generators, research laboratory, and garage.

george washington carver

George Washington Carver National Monument
5646 Carver Rd., Diamond, MO 64840, 417-325-4151
www.nps.gov/gwca

Carver was an agricultural engineer who transformed the science of growing and creating agricultural products. Born into slavery, his life work of scientific exploration began during his childhood on the Moses Carver farm, now a national monument in his honor.

ten best
scientific inspirations

These are some of the places that inspired me as a kid—and continue to inspire me today!
—Dr. Richard Huganir

smithsonian institution natural history museum, washington, d.c.

www.mnh.si.edu

The Natural History Museum is among my most favorite in the country. Where else can you go to see the extraordinary complexity and beauty of the natural world? The museum employs many scientists studying the natural world.

woods hole marine biological laboratory, massachusetts

www.mbl.edu

The Woods Hole Marine Biological Laboratory is an international center for biological research. Located in the sleepy little village of Woods Hole on the coast of Cape Cod, it is a beautiful, inspirational environment to explore nature and to see how scientific research is done. It's a great place to stop and visit if you are taking the ferry to Martha's Vineyard.

franklin institute, pennsylvania

www2.fi.edu

As a kid I loved this Philadelphia museum. It fostered my love of biology and science. I can still remember walking through the giant-size heart, being excited and terrified at the same time. You can learn more about Benjamin Franklin, a brilliant scientist, politician, and philosopher.

northern lights (aurora borealis), alaska

http://fairbanks-alaska.com/northern-lights-alaska.htm

A mysterious and magical natural phenomenon. The colors are so amazing and ephemeral. The light is produced by the interaction of ions in the solar wind with ions in Earth's magnetic fields. Even through we know a lot about the conditions that create the northern lights, they are no less mysterious and extraordinary.

w.m. keck observatory on the summit of mauna kea, island of hawaii

www.ifa.hawaii.edu/mko/

It has two very large telescopes located on the top of Mauna Kea—a dormant volcano (14,000 feet) where you can peer deep into space. From the visitor center at 9,000 feet, you can view stars with portable telescopes.

the salk institute for biological studies, la jolla, california

www.salk.edu

The Salk Institute was established in the 1960s by Jonas Salk, M.D., the developer of the polio vaccine. Salk selected the world-renowned architect Louis I. Kahn to design the institute. Their collaboration produced a facility of unique beauty.

yosemite national park, california

www.nps.gov/yose

It is one of the great natural wonders of the world. It illustrates the power of glaciers and the power of natural forces. It is also the site of many hauntingly beautiful Ansel Adams photographs and a mecca for rock climbers.

arecibo observatory, puerto rico

www.naic.edu

Largest single-dish radio telescope in the world. Here you can listen for radio signals from outer space to detect planets and energy but also to listen for signals from other worlds. It was one of the listening sites in the film *Contact* and was also in the James Bond film *GoldenEye.*

national aquarium, maryland

www.aqua.org

A beautiful glass building right on the water in Baltimore. It exposes you to the possibilities of life underwater through diversity, scale, and scope. Walk down the ramp in the shark tank and see the most formidable predators on Earth up close.

the air and space museum, d.c.

www.nasm.si.edu

Every kid imagines being an astronaut, and where is there a better place to do so than at the National Air and Space Museum in Washington, D.C.? The history of the space programs is inspirational, and the spaceships are extremely cool.

Richard Huganir

Dr. Richard Huganir is a professor and director of the department of neuroscience at Johns Hopkins University, as well as an investigator with Howard Hughes Medical Institute. Dr. Huganir's research has focused on the cellular and molecular mechanisms that encode memories in the brain. He is a member of the National Academy of Sciences. Some of his other inspirational interests are wine, travel, music, and his family.

ten best
factory tours

Celebrate American imagination and industry by visiting and touring America at work. It is fascinating to see how and where things are made.

teddy bears

Vermont Teddy Bear Factory, 6655 Shelburne Rd. Shelburne, VT 05482, 802-985-3001 www.vermontteddybear.com

See teddy bears being made by hand at this factory, open year-round. It's a fun way to see the soft goods manufacturing process, from fabric cutting to stitching, shaping, stuffing, and finishing. About 400 bears are made here each day.

glassmaking

Corning Museum of Glass, 1 Museum Way, Corning, NY 14830, 800-732-6845, www.cmog.org

Glassmaking (and glass-breaking) demonstrations are memorable moments at this upstate New York museum, adjacent to the famed Corning factory. A glassworker is stationed in the museum's GlassWorks gift shop, making glass ornaments like delicate miniature animals or realistic-looking glass icicles that are later available for sale—it's a nice stop for young children who might not be old enough for the longer demonstrations.

potato chips

Utz Quality Foods, 900 High St. Hanover, PA 17331, 800-367-7629 www.utzsnacks.com

Watch the chip-making assembly line from a glass-enclosed gallery, beginning with the preparation of fresh potatoes to finishing and packaging individual bags. At the Utz Factory, it's known as the Chip Trip. After the tour, stop at the factory outlet store located two blocks from the manufacturing plant.

baseball bats

Louisville Slugger Museum & Factory, 800 W. Main St., Louisville, KY 40202, 877-775-8443 www.sluggermuseum.org

This historic company started out making wooden bowling pins, bedposts, and roller skids. Guided factory tours are conducted every day. The bat-making business corresponds to market demand, so some seasons are busier than others. Each visitor receives a miniature baseball bat at the end of the tour.

> " suzy, maryland | **discovery** Hands down, these were the best small kid locations on our San Francisco trip. Number one: the Jelly Belly factory. Number two: Muir Woods. Go there!

fire rescue vehicles

E-ONE, 1601 S.W. 37th Ave., Ocala, FL 34474, 352-861-3524, www.e-one.com

Fire trucks, pumpers, ladders, and rescue equipment are all manufactured here. See rows of giant engines, cabs, and even aluminum ladders being assembled and tested. The cab-painting stop is a real highlight. An emphasis on quality control and workplace safety comes across to even the youngest visitors.

pinball machines

Stern Pinball Factory, 2020 Janice Ave., Melrose Park, IL 60160, 708-345-7700, www.sternpinball.com

Call ahead to schedule a behind-the-scenes tour at the world's only factory still making coin-operated pinball machines. There are about 3,500 parts in a pinball game, and nearly a half-mile of wire. This factory makes up to 55 machines each day. It takes about a year to design a pinball game, bringing together the expertise of game designers, engineers, artists, and many others.

motor home assembly

Winnebago Industries Visitors Center, 1045 S. 4th St. Forest City, IA 50436, 800-643-4892 www.winnebagoind.com

See giant motor homes being assembled. Inside and out, every part of these famous recreational vehicles is manufactured and put together in this gleaming factory. Tours are offered April through October, twice each day.

pennies, nickels, & dimes

The United States Mint, 320 W. Colfax Ave. Denver, CO 80204, 303-405-4761, www.usmint.gov

Find out how coins are made and learn about the life span of a typical coin. Reservations are required for tours, which can be booked up to two months in advance on the mint website; this place is super-busy in summer. A limited number of stand-by tickets may be available. The U.S. Mint in Philadelphia also offers tours.

tea blending factory

Celestial Seasonings, 4600 Sleepytime Dr., Boulder, CO 80301, 303-530-5300, www.celestialseasonings.com

Free hourly tours are available for families with children over the age of five. See the tea leaves being sorted and blended. Smell the wonderful aromas of hibiscus, mint, and chamomile. Taste a sample at the end of the tour—and stay to buy lunch in the Celestial Café.

jelly beans

Jelly Belly Factory, One Jelly Belly La., Fairfield, CA 94533 800-522-3267, www.jellybelly.com

Take a 40-minute guided tour on a catwalk above the factory floor. See "raw" jelly bean ingredients being mixed, flavors and colors being added, and assorted beans being blended and packaged. Don't miss the jelly bean portraits of celebrities!

ten best
feats of engineering

Change the course of a river . . . withstand the enduring push of the ocean . . . connect and protect people and places on their travels and adventures. Innovative engineering is the art of problem solving at its most practical (and often imaginative).

The Hoover Dam, a power source for more than 70 years

hoover dam, arizona & nevada

www.usbr.gov/lc/hooverdam

Located about 30 miles southeast of Las Vegas. Witness water power at work. A dam directs rushing water to spin magnetic rotors past stationary wires, producing electricity. When it first opened in 1939, it was the world's largest hydroelectric plant. Today it's still one of the largest in the nation, generating enough low-cost power to serve 1.3 million people in Nevada, California, and Arizona.

intrepid museum

Pier 86, W. 46th St. & 12th Ave., New York, NY 10036 212-245-0072, www.intrepidmuseum.org

How can 100,000 tons of steel float? And just how does that jet stay up in the air? This museum is home to a World War II aircraft carrier, a Concorde jet, a diesel-powered submarine, and supersonic jet fighters.

gateway arch

Jefferson National Expansion Memorial 11 N. 4th St., St. Louis, MO 63102 314-655-1700, www.nps.gov/jeff

The Gateway Arch memorializes the city's role in westward expansion and is considered a marvel of modern engineering. It is 630 feet high, and also 630 feet from leg to leg at the base. There are 60-foot foundations for each leg; the structure is built to withstand an earthquake, and in 50-mph wind the top will sway about 1.5 inches from the center.

chesapeake bay bridge tunnel, virginia

757-331-2960, www.cbbt.com

This 20-mile trestle-and-tunnel creation crosses the Chesapeake Bay where it meets the Atlantic Ocean, connecting Virginia's eastern shore with South Hampton Roads. It includes four man-made islands and two mile-long tunnels under busy ship channels.

georgia dome

1 Georgia Dome Dr., NW, Atlanta, GA 30313, 404-223-4636, www.gadome.com

This is the largest cable-supported domed structure in the world, home to the Atlanta Falcons football team. The 290-foot-high roof is composed of

130 Teflon-coated fiberglass panels—covering 8.6 acres. The roof's supporting cable totals 11.1 miles, and the dome is as tall as a 27-story building.

lake pontchartrain causeway, louisiana

504-835-3118, www.cityofno.com

For generations, people have invented structures that allow them to live and work in beautiful south Louisiana. The causeway across Lake Pontchartrain is the longest bridge in the world, connecting Jefferson and St. Tammany Parishes. About 42,000 cars cross Lake Pontchartrain every day of the week.

minneapolis skyways

888-676-6757, www.minneapolis.org

Minneapolis has the largest skyway system in the world, linking nearly 80 blocks of downtown attractions, businesses, and hotels. There are eight miles of elevated and enclosed footbridges here (and five miles in neighboring St. Paul).

golden gate bridge, california

415-921-5858, www.goldengatebridge.org

This is the second longest suspension bridge in the nation, located where the San Francisco Bay meets the Pacific Ocean. It's painted "international orange," a color chosen in part because of its visibility in fog. Bridge painting goes on year-round to protect the steel structure from corrosion. At times, the bridge acts as a doorway to fog rolling in from the Pacific, when high pressure causes the vapor to be "squashed" to lower levels.

the skywalk, arizona

877-716-9378, www.destinationgrandcanyon.com

Located at Grand Canyon West on the Hualapai Indian Reservation, the new Grand Canyon Skywalk is a U-shaped cantilevered glass bridge jutting 70 feet past the rim of the Grand Canyon. It's sturdy enough to hold the weight of a dozen fully loaded 747s, and strong enough to withstand winds up to 100 mph. Tickets and advance reservations are required.

trans alaska pipeline system

Milepost 258 Richardson Hwy., Delta Junction, AK 99737, 907-895-5096, www.alyeska-pipe.com

Eight hundred miles long, 48 inches in diameter, the Alaskan pipeline system is one of the world's largest, pumping oil from the North Slope to Valdez, Alaska (the northernmost ice-free port). To protect delicate permafrost, 420 miles of the pipeline is elevated aboveground. More than 15 billion barrels of oil have moved through the system since it was completed in 1977.

books | fantastic feats and failures

by the editors of yes magazine

The creative use of duct tape helped to save *Apollo 13*. This book explores everyday and extraordinary engineering ideas and records both how they worked and how some failed.

traveling to learn
history & the arts

museums, homes, public places, historic sites

There's definitely something in the air. Mathematicians estimate that every breath you take includes oxygen molecules that once passed through the lungs of *brontosauruses*, of George Washington, of Chief Sitting Bull. No matter where we are, we relate to other living things in a very physical way.

These air molecules are infinitesimally small. Imagine how we can connect to others through the gigantic influence of art, music, and literature created by remarkable people. The experience gets even more powerful when we step right into their worlds. We can read Emily Dickinson's poetry as we walk on the pathways of her home. We can gaze at mythical heroes in N. C. Wyeth's paintings, then look to the sky over his studio and see the same Pennsylvania skylines and treetops that he saw each day.

We can help our children make historic connections, too. When we sit together in a splendid concert hall we hear the same notes that made Mozart and Bach celebrities in their lifetimes. We marvel that certain melodies will give you goosebumps—just as they did for the first people

> A jug fills
> drop by drop.
> —Buddha

who heard them more than 200 years ago. We can stand on the outskirts of St. Joseph, Missouri, and feel the thunder of hooves as riders barrel down trails first blazed by prehistoric people (and later by the Pony Express).

When you're planning a trip, try to find out a little more about the history of the place, unusual geographic features, and the cultural influences on literature, art, and music that make it so special. Once you're there, ask around about local tall tales or regional twists on familiar stories. The more you all know, the more you'll appreciate every moment of the journey.

Kids will learn that history is a living art. Stories change every time they're told, flexing or flowing to suit the ear of the listener and the heart of the teller. When we visit remarkable places and see them for ourselves, they become a part of who we are. If our children get a little dirt under their fingernails or dust in their hair along the way, all the better. They're some of the surest signs of a traveler. So take a deep breath, be inspired—and get going!

ten best
authors' homes

This list was compiled by award-winning poet and author Elizabeth Spires.

emily dickinson

280 Main St., Amherst,
MA 01002, 413-542-8161
www.emilydickinsonmuseum.org

For families with young children, a trip to the visitor center followed by an exploration of the grounds and gardens is a memorable experience, especially if you bring along a book of Dickinson's poetry to read along the way.

robert frost

Stone House, 121 Vt. Rte. 7A, Shaftsbury, VT 05262, 802-447-6200, www.frostfriends.org

"Stopping by Woods on a Snowy Evening" was written here, as well as many other poems in Frost's first Pulitzer Prize–winning book *New Hampshire*. You can visit the historic house and see Frost's beloved apple trees, not far from his burial place in Bennington, Vermont.

authors of concord

Concord Visitors Center, 58 Main St., Concord, MA 978-369-3120, www.concordchamberofcommerce.org

Henry David Thoreau lived and wrote at his home about a mile outside Concord, at Walden Pond. His

> There is more done with pens than swords.
>
> —Harriet Beecher Stowe

neighbors included Louisa May Alcott, Nathaniel Hawthorne, and Ralph Waldo Emerson. All of these famous American writers are now buried in the town's Sleepy Hollow Cemetery.

mark twain

The Mark Twain House, 351 Farmington Ave., Hartford, CT 06105, 860-247-0998 www.marktwainhouse.org

At the height of his career, Twain made his home in this mansion. But by the early 1900s it was turned into an apartment building. Twain admirers purchased the house in 1927 and began the process of turning it into a National Historic Landmark.

jack london

Jack London State Historic Park, 2400 London Ranch Rd., Glen Ellen, CA 95442, 707-938-5216

He was the author of *The Call of the Wild, The Sea Wolf*, and more than 40 other stories of outdoor life. London called this place Beauty Ranch.

ernest hemingway

The Ernest Hemingway Home, 907 Whitehead St., Key West, FL 33040, 305-294-1136 www.hemingwayhome.com

The Nobel prize–winning author lived and

worked in this house in Old Town Key West from 1932 to 1940 and produced much of his best work. See the famous six-toed cats, just part of the Hemingway legend here.

edgar allan poe

203 Amity St., Baltimore, MD 21223
410-396-7932 www.eapoe.org

America's first mystery writer lived here in the 1830s, one of the many places he called home during his restless life. It's not far from Poe's grave in Westminster Burying Ground.

paul laurence dunbar

219 N. Paul Laurence Dunbar St., Dayton, OH 45402
937-224-7061, www.ohiohistory.org

Dunbar achieved fame in his lifetime as "the poet laureate for African Americans." The son of former slaves, he lived here at the end of his life. Dayton is also known as "the birthplace of aviation," original home of Orville and Wilbur Wright's bicycle shop.

harriet beecher stowe

77 Forest St., Hartford, CT 06105, 860-522-9258
www.harrietbeecherstowecenter.org

The author of *Uncle Tom's Cabin* lived and worked here, not far from Mark Twain's home. Children's tours are on school holiday afternoons, or anytime by appointment.

> Was it possible that I was a poet? . . . From what secret place had my words come?
> —from *The Mouse of Amherst*

william faulkner

Rowan Oak, Taylor Ave., Oxford, MS,
662-234-3284 www.olemiss.edu

A Nobel prize–winning author, William Faulkner loved this historic (pre–Civil War) homestead, naming it Rowan Oak in 1931. It's now owned by the University of Mississippi.

Elizabeth Spires

Elizabeth Spires is the author of six collections of poetry: *Globe, Swan's Island, Annonciade, Worlding, Now the Green Blade Rises,* and, most recently, *The Wave-Maker.* She has also written six books for children, including *The Mouse of Amherst,* the tale of a white mouse who lives in Emily Dickinson's bedroom, *I Am Arachne,* and *I Heard God Talking to Me: William Edmondson and His Stone Carvings.* She lives in Baltimore and is a professor of English at Goucher College, where she holds a Chair for Distinguished Achievement.

ten best
orchestras

Beginning at a very young age, children can recognize different instruments and interpret "stories" through sound. Orchestras across the country count families among their most important audiences.
—Edward Polochick

atlanta symphony orchestra

Atlanta Symphony Hall, 1280 Peachtree St., NE, Atlanta, GA 30309, 404-733-4900
www.atlantasymphony.org
The ASO Family Concerts introduce children to a stimulating and appealing mix of original and beloved children's tales, with visual humor and award-winning dancers and actors.

boston symphony orchestra

Symphony Hall, 301 Massachusetts Ave., Boston, MA 02115, 617-266-1492, www.bso.org
Here, Youth & Family Concerts include captivating music and interaction between the conductor and the audience. There are activities before and after the concert and Symphony Hall tours.

forth worth symphony orchestra

Bass Performance Hall, 525 Commerce St., Fort Worth, TX 76102, 817-665-6000, www.fwsymphony.org
Bass Performance Hall is located in Fort Worth's historic Sundance Square district. The Fort Worth Symphony performs acclaimed children's programs here all season, and the hall itself is a venue for other famous events, including the Van Cliburn International Piano Competition.

chicago symphony orchestra

Symphony Center, 220 S. Michigan Ave., Chicago, IL 60604, 312-294-3000, www.cso.org
Special concerts for kids and families include Hallowed Haunts, the Vienna Choir Boys, and Jazz for Young People, all appropriate for children five and up. Younger children can attend *Kindermusik* classes.

cleveland orchestra

Severance Hall, 11001 Euclid Ave., Cleveland, OH 44106 216-231-7355, education@clevelandorchestra.com
In addition to family concerts and guest artists visits, the orchestra provides fantastic classroom resources for education concerts, workshops for teachers, and a nationally recognized program, Learning Through Music School Partnership Program.

philadelphia orchestra

The Kimmel Center for the Performing Arts, Broad & Spruce Sts., Philadelphia, PA 19102, 215-893-1999
www.philorch.org
Sound All Around is an energetic program for toddlers and parents that features storytelling combined with musical performances. You can get

tickets for a single session or sign on for a whole series at locations all around Philadelphia.

los angeles philharmonic

Walt Disney Concert Hall, 151 S. Grand Ave., Los Angeles, CA 90012-3034, 213-972-0704
www.laphil.com/education

The LA Phil offers a school partnership program in which musicians and teaching artists collaborate with classroom teachers and students to connect music with the general curriculum.

san francisco symphony

Davies Symphony Hall, 201 Van Ness Ave., San Francisco, CA 94102, 415-864-6000, www.sfskids.org

Music for Families matinees are described as "part performance, part family outing." Each matinee includes a symphony performance, a lively discussion, and extra take-home materials so the exploration can continue. Note: Every year this famed orchestra performs Prokofiev's *Peter and the Wolf* in mid-December.

new york philharmonic

Avery Fisher Hall, 10 Lincoln Center Plaza, New York, NY 10023, 212-875-5656, www.nyphil.org

The New York Philharmonic is the oldest symphony orchestra in the nation, and Lincoln Center is its home base. Teenagers plus a guest (parent or friend) get specially priced Phil Teens tickets to concerts and discussion programs. And on select Saturday afternoons in the fall and spring, families converge here for wonderful children's concerts and preconcert "kidzone" festivities.

national symphony

John F. Kennedy Center for the Performing Arts, 2700 F St., NW, Washington, DC 20008, 800-444-1324, www.kennedy-center.org

Ensembles of the National Symphony Orchestra perform small, seasonal children's concerts in the Kennedy Center's technologically advanced Family Theater. Intimate in size (about 350 seats), with state-of-the-art acoustics, it's a wonderful place for families to experience live performances.

Edward Polochick

Conductor, pianist, harpsichordist, lecturer and panelist, teacher, and mentor, Edward Polochick has been a member of the Peabody Conservatory faculty as director of choruses and associate director of the orchestra since 1979. He was director of the Baltimore Symphony Chorus from 1979 to 1999, and in 1987 he founded Concert Artists of Baltimore. Lincoln, Nebraska, also is delighted to have Edward Polochick as music director of the Lincoln Symphony Orchestra since 1998.

ten best
public sculptures

I am very interested in public sculpture that builds from nature. As a sculptor, the technical aspects of fabrication and engineering also fascinate me. There are many wonderful sculptures to see across the country. I offer a few that stand out as examples of great human achievement in consort with nature, powerfully celebrating what it means to be human in the vastness of our modern world.
—David Hess

"Spoonbridge and Cherry" at Minnesota Sculpture Garden

millennium park, illinois

www.millenniumpark.org

"Cloud Gate" is British artist Anish Kapoor's first public outdoor work in the United States. To create this stunning form in Chicago, a team of technicians actually welded and polished it on-site. The park is also home to Jaume Plensa's "Crown Fountain," a digital fountain with faces that spit water.

mount rushmore national memorial, south dakota

www.nps.gov/moru

The sheer scope of this is unbelievable, and the likeness of the presidents is amazing. It was done by Gutzon Borglum between 1927 and 1941 with dynamite and no computer renderings.

minneapolis sculpture garden

http://garden.walkerart.org

Here you'll find work by Siah Armajani, Tony Cragg, David Nash, and Martin Puryear. It's home to "Spoonbridge and Cherry" by Claes Olenburg and Coosje van Bruggen, tremendous in its simplicity and complexity all at once.

crazy horse memorial, south dakota

www.crazyhorse.org

This ambitious project was started by sculptor Korczak Ziolkowski and the Lakota chief Henry Standing Bear in 1948 to honor the culture, tradition, and living heritage of Native Americans. Still unfinished, the scale is huge and the figure is complex.

st. louis arch, missouri

www.nps.gov/jeff/

Designed by Eero Saarinen, this is one of the most beautiful pure forms of public art in the world. It is an incredible thing. It adds beauty, hope, and magic to the urban skyline. Like the Statue of Liberty, you can actually go inside it.

dia/beacon, new york

845-440-0100, www.diaart.org

This renovated factory in Beacon, New York, shows monumental work. It's a good way to see the work of artists whose creations are also in other parts of the country, like Walter de Maria (his *The Lightning Field* is in western New Mexico) and Michael Heizer (whose Nevada earthworks are .25-mile long mesa carvings).

storm king art center, new york

www.stormking.org

An hour north of New York City, this blue chip collection celebrates the connection between sculpture and nature. Here you'll see work by Andy Goldsworthy, Richard Serra, and Alexander Calder and gain a historical perspective on American sculpture.

vietnam veterans memorial

www.nps.gov/vive

In the 1970s there was a national competition to design a Vietnam memorial. The winner was 21-year-old student Maya Lin, who is today a leading architectural artist. It's on the National Mall in Washington, D.C., truly an important work.

statue of liberty, new york

www.statueofliberty.org

It was designed by Frederic Bartholdi, built in a French warehouse, shipped to the United States, then bolted together. The sculpture becomes truly architectural when you go inside.

olympic sculpture park, washington

www.seattleartmuseum.org

A waterfront sculpture park in Seattle with views of Puget Sound and the Olympic Mountains. This used to be an industrial site, but now it's full of very powerful contemporary sculpture.

David Hess

David Hess's works are installed at locations including the Emerson Corporation in St. Louis, Missouri; Baltimore/Washington International Airport; the Baltimore Museum of Industry; and Mount Vernon Children's Park. He created award-winning installations at the Baltimore Visionary Art Museum, where he is also a ten-year participant in the museum's annual Kinetic Sculpture Race. He's a graduate of Dartmouth College and makes his home with his family outside the city of Baltimore.

ten best
studios & galleries

Are artists neat or messy? Do they live in the country or the city? What kinds of materials do they use, and what makes them feel creative? Find endless answers when you visit homes, studios, or museum exhibits that highlight the way artists work.

norman rockwell's studio

Norman Rockwell Museum, Glendale Rd., Rte. 183 Stockbridge, MA 01262, 413-298-4100, www.nrm.org

Rockwell's actual studio was moved to this museum, complete with his painting materials, books, and letters. The studio is open in the summer and early fall (the museum itself is open year-round). This is said to be the most popular destination in the Berkshires.

the eric carle museum of picture book art

125 West Bay Rd., Amherst, MA 01002
413-658-1100, www.picturebookart.org

Renowned illustrator Eric Carle was a founder of this museum, where the central exhibits are famous illustrations from children's books displayed in formal museum settings. Kids love the art studio with free materials and encouragement to create artwork based on the collection. There's also a library with more than 3,000 illustrated books and daily story-time sessions.

dr. seuss

21 Edwards St., Springfield, MA 01103, 800-625-7738
www.catinthehat.org

How big would you imagine a "life-size" Cat in the Hat to be? Find out at this sculpture garden, home to outdoor bronze statues depicting Dr. Seuss and five of his best-loved characters.

tasha tudor

Marlboro, VT, 802-257-4444
www.tashatudormuseum.org

Plans are underway to create a Tasha Tudor Museum as a destination for the many fans of this iconic storyteller, illustrator, and crafter. In the meantime, the private Tudor family farm is open for ticketed events in June, when visitors can reserve ahead of time to see the family corgis and to tour Tasha Tudor's own gardens.

grandma moses

Grandma Moses Gallery, Bennington Museum
75 Main St., Bennington, VT 05201
802-447-1571, www.benningtonmuseum.org

The city of Bennington's museum houses the largest public collection of the primitive painter whose real name was Anna Mary Robertson Moses. The 19th-century schoolhouse that she and her family once attended was moved from Eagle Bridge, New York, to the museum grounds.

Today it is open as an interactive center for families.

n. c. wyeth

Brandywine River Museum, U.S. Rte. 1, Chadds Ford, PA 19317, 610-388-2700, www.brandywinemuseum.org

His paintings of pirates, cowboys, and outdoor life captured the imagination of turn-of-the-century readers. The museum exhibits original paintings from classics like *Treasure Island* and *Kidnapped*. A shuttle bus takes visitors to N. C. Wyeth's home and studio, located in the nearby village.

N.C. Wyeth's painting for Treasure Island

maurice sendak gallery

Rosenbach Museum & Library
2008-2010 Delancey Pl., Philadelphia, PA 19103
215-732-1600, www.rosenbach.org

In one of this museum's most popular galleries, see original work and the personal collection of the author and illustrator of *Where the Wild Things Are*. This museum houses famous books, letters, and personal belongings of figures ranging from George Washington to poet Marianne Moore.

isabella gardiner museum

280 The Fenway, Boston MA 02115, 617-566-1401
www.gardnermuseum.org

Though not an artist herself, Isabella Gardiner built this museum to house her personal art collection, then lived on the fourth floor until her death in 1924. The museum and its collection are still a trib-

ute to the enduring and influential vision of an advocate of the arts.

georgia o'keeffe

Georgia O'Keeffe Museum, 217 Johnson St. Santa Fe, NM 87501, 505-946-1000, www.okeeffemuseum.org

Located two blocks from Santa Fe Plaza, this is the only museum in the world dedicated to the works of an internationally known woman artist. The collection includes more than 1,000 O'Keeffe drawings, paintings, and sculptures.

charles m. schulz

Charles M. Schulz Museum, 2301 Hardies La., Santa Rosa, CA 95403, 707-579-4452, www.schulzmuseum.org

This museum honors the creator of Charlie Brown and the rest of the Peanuts gang. The Education Room is staffed and stocked with materials for creating comics. Interactive zoetropes let visitors make their own animated cartoons. You can also see Schultz's studio and Wrapped Snoopy House, a tribute from artist Christo.

books | talking with artists *by pat cummings*

You'll recognize the work of these children's book illustrators: Lois Ehlert, Jerry Pinkney, Chris Van Allsburg, and others. In this book you'll find out how they discovered their unique gifts.

ten best
visionary art places

Visionary art is produced by self-taught individuals, usually without formal training, whose works arise from an innate personal vision that revels foremost in the creative act itself. In short, visionary art begins by listening to the inner voices of the soul, and often may not even be thought of as "art" by its creator. It's like love—you know it when you see it.
—Rebecca Hoffberger

"Whirligig" by Vollis Simpson

vollis simpson whirligigs, north carolina

www.wilson-nc.com/Whirligigs.cfm

Simpson's Windmill Farm holds more than 30 of his large-scale, wind-powered, kinetic sculptures. You're encouraged to walk around the field and see for yourself, but also come back at night to shine your headlights on the hundreds of dancing reflective disks.

the watts towers, california

www.wattstowers.us

You must see them—because they're the Watts Towers!! The spiraling towers in Los Angeles (as high as 90 feet) were built without scaffolding or power tools—the creation of Simon Rodia, an Italian immigrant, quarry worker, and railroad man.

the orange show, texas

www.orangeshow.org

Postal workers tend to go "postal" when they make brilliant outside environments. The house, gardens, yard (and now community) in Houston all testify to the transformative vision of postal worker Jeff McKissack and his tribute to the healing powers of the edible orange. Also the headquarters for the best art car parade in the country!

kenny hill's chauvin sculpture garden, louisiana

www.kohlerfoundation.org/chauvin.html

Kenny Hill's biblical, Cajun, angelic, and very personal sculpture garden is adjacent to the Nicholls State University Art Studio, about 90 minutes south of New Orleans. The story is that Kenny is now building a new creation somewhere in Arkansas.

coral castle, florida

www.coralcastle.com

Built by a Latvian recluse who may well have known the secrets of levitation, this castle in Homestead was built of megalithic stones and topiary in tribute to his lost love, "Sweet Sixteen."

salvation mountain, california

www.salvationmountain.us

For salvation, this mountain in Imperial County works better than any TV preacher who ever broadcast. Maker Leonard Wright lives on-site and continues to work on this monument of praise, salvation, and unconditional love.

the underground gardens, california

www.undergroundgardens.info

Photos can't capture it. You simply have to see for yourself. This is the subterranean Mediterranean vision of Baldassare Forestiere. His ten-acre, hand-built underground wonderland in Fresno is complete with terraces, arches, and gardens, some more than 90 years old.

the forevertron, wisconsin

http://heart2art2heart.com/pages/theforevertron.html

Dr. Tom Evermor is a dreamer and a genius who gives us "the world's largest sculpture made of recycled scrap metal"—equipped with an egg-shaped capsule for contemplating the universe. Don't miss his bird orchestra.

the land of pasaquan, georgia

www.pasaquan.com

Ghosts and magic in the South—what could be better? Near Buena Vista, Pasaquan is open to the public only occasionally. The website lists

> Visionary artists don't listen to anyone else's traditions. They invent their own.
>
> —Rebecca Hoffberger

dates of special events including the Fourth of July (birthday of Pasaquan's creator, St. EOM).

the garden of eden, kansas

www.garden-of-eden-lucas-kansas.com

The granddaddy of U.S. environments, all rolled up into one handy biblical, political, historical, and very personal concrete masterpiece—speaking volumes of a longing for personal paradise.

Rebecca Alban Hoffberger

Rebecca Alban Hoffberger is both founder and director of the American Visionary Art Museum—the official national museum for self-taught, intuitive artistry—located in Baltimore, Maryland. Having opened its doors over Thanksgiving in 1995, the museum seeks to promote the recognition of intuitive, self-reliant, creative contribution as both an important historic and essential living piece of treasured human legacy.

ten best
architectural treasures

Buildings house people and things, but architecture creates a symbol that expresses the character and beliefs of a place. Large or small, buildings have a history, and they tell important stories of their creators. Their purpose, the materials used to make them, and the people who use them all communicate who and what buildings are about.

empire state building

350 5th Ave., New York, NY 10118
212-736-3100, www.esbnyc.com

Completed in 1931, the Empire State Building stands 1,454 feet tall, the second tallest building in the United States (Chicago's Sears Tower is the tallest). Tickets are required, and there can be a long wait to get to the observation deck on the 86th floor (there's an additional fee to get to the deck on the 102nd floor). The last elevator goes up at 1:15 a.m.

rockefeller plaza

30 Rockefeller Plaza, New York, NY 10020
212-332-6868, www.rockefellercenter.com

Experience "Radiance" from the 67th floor observation deck at the Top of the Rock. This crystal wall is a 180-foot-wide geode consisting of 600 illuminated glass panels. In the plaza's atrium, you'll see a 14,000-piece chandelier shaped to look like the Rockefeller Center turned upside down.

the washington monument

15th St., SW, Washington, DC, 202-426-6841
www.nps.gov/wamo

Children will like the view from the top. They will see that Washington is a low city, the result of building height restriction. The monument's masonry, construction, and recent renovations are all explained during a visit.

biltmore

Biltmore Estate, 1 Approach Rd., Asheville, NC 28803, 800-411-3812, www.biltmore.com

Four acres of floor space on a 125,000–acre estate: The gilded age era Vanderbilt mansion is the largest individual home in America. Still privately owned, it is a luxury vacation destination in a park setting that is open to the public for tours. It's a wonderful winter holiday destination, with spectacular decorations.

john hancock center

875 N. Michigan Ave., Chicago, IL 60661
888-875-8439, www.hancock-observatory.com

From the 94th-story, open-air Skywalk, visitors can experience spectacular views spanning up to 80 miles and 4 states. The building is shaped like a wedge, creating the illusion that it is even taller. The idea was to balance the need for extra parking/commercial space below and smaller residential areas above.

milwaukee art museum

700 N. Art Museum Dr., Milwaukee, WI 53202
414-224-3200, www.mam.org

It's considered an architectural landmark, composed of three remarkable structures. War Memorial Center is shaped like a floating cross. Quadracci Pavilion features a 90-foot-high glass ceiling and the Burke Brise Soleil, a sunscreen that folds and unfolds twice each day. Outdoors, the Cudahy Gardens are composed of formal, geometric landscapes.

tower of the americas

600 Hemisfair Plaza Way, San Antonio, TX 78205
210-223-3101, www.toweroftheamericas.com

The 750-foot tower offers a panoramic view of San Antonio and the surrounding area. Glass-walled elevators ascend over 500 feet to the restaurant and observation level. The theme structure for HemisFair in 1968, it symbolizes the progress made by the confluence of civilizations in the Western Hemisphere.

taliesin west

12621 Frank Lloyd Wright Blvd., Scottsdale, AZ 85261
480-860-2700, www.franklloydwright.org

Think of American architecture and you'll probably think of Frank Lloyd Wright. He designed hundreds of public and private structures. Here you'll see the skylights, angled walls, dramatic rooflines, and environmental influence that define the Wright school of architecture. This property served as his winter home, studio, and school. It is the headquarters for the foundation that bears his name.

u.s. capitol

Capitol Hill, Washington, DC, 202-225-6827
www.visitthecapitol.gov

The capitol was designed and built with the function of Congress in mind: a place where elected leaders could gather and meet in public to do the work of a democratic government. Although free, reservations are recommended. They are available online or through your senator or representative's offices. Tours depart from the new Capitol Visitor Center on the east side of the building.

the getty

1200 Getty Center Dr., Los Angeles, CA 90049, 310-440-7300, www.getty.edu/visit/see_do/architecture.html

Visit this celebrated museum, where the very architecture provides an introduction to both the nature and the culture of what's inside. Imported Roman stone was used to build the museum; a close look reveals the imprint of ancient feathers and leaves.

 books | round buildings, square buildings & buildings that wiggle like a fish. *by philip m. isaacson*

This personal view of structures around the world takes readers on a personal tour of buildings around the world. Young readers will look at doors and windows, ceilings and stairways in a whole new way.

ten best
prehistoric sites

Think about who walked a path or climbed a hill before you did. What grew here? Who lived here? Prehistoric sites are everywhere. When you visit some of these famous ones, you begin to look at your own surroundings in a new way.

silver mound

Mississippi Valley Archaeology Center at the University of Wisconsin-La Crosse, 1725 State St., La Crosse, WI 54601, 608-785-8463, www.uwlax.edu/MVAC

As long as 10,000 years ago, people gathered here to collect and cut stones. The quartzite found here is very hard, and it's good for making arrow points and other sharp or pointed tools.

indian mounds

Natchez Trace Parkway, 2680 Natchez Trace Pkwy. Tupelo, MS 38804, 662-680-4025, www.nps.gov/natr

The native inhabitants of the southern Mississippi River Valley were known as mound builders, makers of earthen constructions created a little more than 2,000 years ago. The mounds were used for burial, and also as platforms for important people in the community. You can see them in historic sites along the parkway—at first glance they appear to be small hills.

ashfall fossil beds

University of Nebraska State Museum, Royal, NE 68773, 402-893-2000 www.ashfall.unl.edu

A volcano erupted about 12 million years ago and blanketed this prairie in ash. Without grazing areas, the animals died off—prehistoric elephants, sabretooth deer, and giraffe-like camels. Since 1971 there's been an ongoing dig to recover many of their fossils.

wahkpa chu'gn buffalo jump

U.S. Hwy. 2, west of Havre, MT 59501, 406-265-6417 www.buffalojump.org

Native Americans used this cliff as a hunting ground by herding buffalo right over the edge. Today it's an important site for learning about the cultural history of people who used this site between 600 and 1,200 years ago.

the great plains dinosaur museum

405 N. 1st St. E, Malta, MT 59538, 406-654-5300 www.maltachamber.com/dinosaurs.htm

In the region east of the Rockies, this state is home to the Montana Dinosaur Trail (http://mtdino trail.org/), with 15 separate museums and field stations that help families explore the wealth of prehistoric artifacts found here. The Great Plains Dinosaur Museum is centrally located on the statewide trail (about three hours from Billings).

dinosaur quarries

Museum of Western Colorado, 462 Ute Ave., Grand Junction, CO 81501
970-242-0971, www.wcmuseum.org

The Rabbit Valley Research Natural Area is part of the museum's grounds, where fossilized remains of eight different species of dinosaurs have been found. In summer the museum hosts one-day and five-day paleontology digs (called Dino Digs) for families with children ages five and older.

cliff dwellings

Mesa Verde National Park, Mesa Verde, CO 81330
970-529-4465, www.nps.gov/meve

There are 600 cliff dwellings in this park, once home to the ancestors of the ancient Puebloan people. They carved and dug these graceful spaces between 700 and 1,400 years ago. The dwellings are marvels of beauty and function: An underground apartment (or kiva) maintained the same temperature of 50°F year-round.

painted desert and petrified forest

1 Park Rd., Petrified Forest, AZ 86028, 928-524-6228
www.nps.gov/pefo

People come from all over the world to see fossilized remnants of petrified trees and dinosaur bones (some dating back 225 million years). But it's also a landmark site for discovering prehistoric human

> History is philosophy teaching by examples.
>
> —Thucydides

history, with fragments of ancient pottery or rock paintings left behind by the ancient Puebloan, Mogollon, and Sinagua people.

john day fossil beds

Clarno Palisades, Hwy. 218, Fossil, OR
541-987-2333, www.nps.gov/joda

Three different visiting areas make up this national monument site, where the layered landscapes provide a breathtaking visual history of the region. The Clarno Palisades is an ancient mud tower that holds fossilized palm trees and bananas.

utah field house of natural history

496 E Main St., Vernal, UT 84078, 435-789-3799
www.utah.com/stateparks/field_house.htm

See T-Rex in the great outdoors! Gardens are a main attraction here, where 17 life-size models are posed in natural environments. The Field House is a highlight along the Dinosaur Diamond highway, a 512-mile loop that crosses the border of Utah and Colorado as it leads visitors to some of the country's most fascinating prehistoric sights. At the south end of the highway loop, see the massive rock art panel at Arches National Park. There are tons of dinosaur fossils.

ten best
frontier places

What would inspire you to pack up all of your belongings, leave your friends behind, and set out on a perilous journey to a land you'd only heard about? American settlers and frontier families of the 18th century had their reasons: the possibility of owning land, escape from crowded cities, and even the promise of gold.

laura ingalls wilder historic home & museum

3068 Hwy. A, Mansfield, MO 65704, 417-924-3626, www.lauraingallswilderhome.com

Pioneer exhibits and the letters of the famous *Little House* author are displayed here. Exhibits trace the adventures of the Ingalls family on their westward journeys to Wisconsin, Minnesota, Kansas, and South Dakota. The stories (and exhibits) parallel Wilder's own family travels, beginning with her 1867 birth in a log cabin in Wisconsin.

meramec caverns

I-44, Exit 230, Stanton, MO 63079
573-168-3166, www.americascave.com

It's the largest cave system west of the Mississippi, famous as the hideout of outlaw Jesse James. These caverns are some of the most accessible for family visits. Historic exhibits trace activity in Meramec to the time of the native Osage people. Also in the area

is the Patee House Museum, headquarters of the Pony Express.

national frontier trails museum

318 W. Pacific Ave., Independence, MO 64050, 816-325-7575
www.ci.independence.mo.us/NFTM

Between 1840 and 1860, about 400,000 people headed west on one of the major American trails. Some of these frontier "highways" had been native migration and hunting routes since prehistoric times. Exhibits here are great introductions to the Lewis and Clark Corps of Discovery expedition, along with the Santa Fe, Oregon, and California Trails.

national cowboy and western heritage museum

1700 N.E. 63rd St., Oklahoma City, OK 73111
405-478-2250, www.nationalcowboymuseum.org

The Rodeo Hall of Fame is here—for kids, it's the centerpiece of a colorful museum with lots of beautiful paintings and powerful sculptures of cowboys, Indians, and scenes of the Wild West. Founded in 1955, the museum has welcomed more than 10 million visitors. Its collections, educational programs, and research inform and inspire the legacy of the American West.

boot hill museum

Front St., Dodge City, KS 67801
620-227-8188, www.boothill.org

This museum is set in a meticulously reconstructed 19th-century frontier main street, complete with historical arti-facts. During the summer season, staged gunfights, saloon shows, and a chuckwagon dinner make it a day-long destination. While in town, trek the Dodge City history trail and see a statue of its most famous resident, Wyatt Earp.

custer battlefield museum

I-90 Exit-514, Garryowen, MT 59031, 406-638-1876
www.custermuseum.org

The Battle of Little Big Horn began here, where Sitting Bull and his native warriors defeated a 700-man federal army led by Lt. Col. George Custer. The museum tells the story of the epic battle, but also guides visitors to an understanding of life on the frontier—for settlers, for the American army, and for the Lakota and Cheyenne people.

fort phil kearny

528 Wagon Box Rd., Banner, WY 82832, 307-684-7629
www.philkearny.vcn.com

Of the thousands of people emigrating west in the mid-19th century, nearly ten percent did not survive, succumbing to exposure, starvation, and disease. The threat of attack by native people was relatively small. But this army fort on the Bozeman Trail was the site of some dramatic frontier battles.

buffalo bill historical center

720 Sheridan Ave., Cody, WY 82414
307-587-4771, www.bbhc.org

One-stop discovery opportunity for an array of western interests, research, myths, and legends, all located at Yellowstone National Park's east gate. This complex is home to the Buffalo Bill Museum, the Plains Indian Museum, the Cody Firearms Museum, and the Whitney Gallery of Western Art.

elfego baca

Reserve Chamber of Commerce, Reserve, NM
575-533-6116, www.catroncounty.org

A true story: Elfego Baca is the hero of this small and historic town in central New Mexico. At the age of 19, he appointed himself sheriff and sin-gle-handedly defeated a gang of rogue cowboys in a legendary shootout (sometimes known as the Frisco Shootout). His statue stands on Main Street.

tombstone

OK Corral, 3rd & 4th Sts., Tombstone, AZ 85638
520-457-3456, www.ok-corral.com

The city of Tombstone (not far from Tucson) is home to the famous corral where the Earp brothers (and their friend Doc Holliday) squared off against the Clanton and McLaury gang. You can tour the famous neighborhood, see a gunfight reenactment, and check out the free newspaper museum, which prints souvenir copies of the original newspaper report of the shootout.

ten best
colonial landmarks

In the 17th and 18th centuries, Europe looked to the new world as prize property. Kingdoms sent emissaries to explore, settle, and claim the rich and mysterious land . . . with enduring results.

boston's freedom trail

Visitor Center, Tremont St., Boston, MA
617-357-8300, www.thefreedomtrail.org

The 2.5-mile walk takes you through the streets of Boston for an on-the-spot history lesson about English rule and the famous revolutionary ideas of the colonists. The red brick trail marks 16 historic sites, including Boston Harbor and the Old North Church. Before you go, download a narrated guide from the Freedom Trail website to listen while you stroll.

plimoth plantation

Rte. 3, Plymouth, MA 02360, 508-746-1622
www.plimoth.org

The *Mayflower II* is a full-scale reproduction of the famous ship. Here you can also visit a Wampanoag homesite, illustrating the life of indigenous people at the time of the pilgrims' arrival.

richmond town

441 Clarke Ave., Staten Island, NY 10306
718-351-1611, www.historicrichmondtown.org

Dutch colonists were the first people to settle the island that is now Manhattan. They ceded their ownership of the land to England in 1664, but their influence is still felt today. Ride the free Staten Island Ferry and take the S74 bus to this museum showcasing 17th-century architecture and life in colonial New York.

jamestown

Jamestown Rd., Jamestown, VA, 888-593-4682
www.historyisfun.org

In 1607, an expeditionary party of men and boys arrived here and established the first English settlement in North America—16 years before the pilgrims arrived in Plymouth. They were British subjects assigned the difficult task of settling the unknown land. A colonist's fort, Powhatan village, and sailing ship reproductions make this a memorable family destination on the James River. Visit it as part of the Historic Triangle, which also includes Colonial Williamsburg and the battlefields of Yorktown.

"

sally, massachusetts | nice visit A little museum in Lexington, Massachusetts, gets rave reviews: the National Heritage Museum. It's a good stop on the way to Minuteman Park in Concord.

huguenot street

Visitor Center, 18 Broadhead Ave. New Paltz, NY
12561, 845-255-1660 www.huguenotstreet.org

This 300-year-old village was established by the
Huguenots, religious refugees from southern Bel-
gium and northern France. They purchased 40,000
acres from the native Esopus people and established a colony here, including the first European-
style street in America.

fort christina state park

E. 7th St., Wilmington, DE, 302-652-5629
www.visitdelaware.com

The queen of their nation was a 12-year-old girl when
Swedish settlers arrived in the Delaware Bay in 1638.
They built a fort near what is now Wilmington and
named it after her: Fort Christina. New Sweden
was an active colony until William Penn acquired this
territory in 1681. A Swedish-style log cabin is on the
grounds of this state park, site of the 1638 landing.

st. mary's city

18751 Hogaboom La., St. Mary's City, MD 20686
800-762-1634, www.stmaryscity.org

Peer over the shoulders of archaeologists at work
around St. Mary's City, where ongoing digs help to
fill in the blanks about life in 17th-century Maryland.
See the *Maryland Dove*, a full-scale sailing repro-

> The colonization of North America
> was a kind of "space race"
> among distant world powers.

duction of the original ship that brought building
supplies to Maryland's first colony in 1634.

the cabildo

701 Chartres St., New Orleans, LA 70116
504-523-3939, www.friendsofthecabildo.org

French explorers were the first Europeans to travel
the Mississippi, and in 1682 they claimed the whole
waterway for France and named the region after
King Louis XVI. In colonial times, the castle-like
Cabildo was the seat of government. Walking tours
around this area are free for children accompanied
by a parent.

mission san diego de alcala

10818 San Diego Mission Rd., San Diego, CA 92108
619-281-8449, www.missionsandiego.com

Generations of Spanish explorers and missionaries
arrived in California in the mid-1700s, and between
1769 and 1823 they established 21 churches
between San Diego and Sonoma. This was the
very first. The website above offers information
about all of the mission churches, as well as other
notable examples of Spanish architecture and
construction in the state.

natchez grand village

400 Jefferson Davis Blvd., Natchez, MS 39120, 601-
446-6502, http://mdah.state.ms.us/hprop/gvni.html

A museum, traditional Natchez home, and original
burial mounds are the starting points for exploring
this historic southwest Mississippi site. The history
of the area is intertwined with the arrival of French
colonists at the turn of the 17th century.

ten best
living history sites

Imagine being part of a moment in history. It can happen. Historical reenactments and living history programs bring to life the milestone moments, events, or lifestyles that defined a long-ago time.

astors' beechwood mansion

580 Bellevue Ave., Newport, RI 02840
401-846-3772, www.astorsbeechwood.com

Step back in time at the Astors' opulent Beechwood Museum. The Beechwood Theatre Company brings to life the Astor family, their friends, and their servants. There are daily tours of the early 20th-century mansion given by living history performers.

gettysburg national military park

97 Taneytown Rd., Gettysburg, PA 17325
717-334-1124, www.nps.gov/gett

The most epic battle of the Civil War was fought here on July 1, 2, and 3, 1863. Confederate troops attempted their second invasion of the North at Gettysburg, not far from the state lines of Maryland and West Virginia. Union soldiers pushed back—at a cost of more than 7,000 lives. Five months later, Lincoln delivered his Gettysburg Address here. Reenactments are regularly scheduled.

Gettysburg National Military Park

colonial williamsburg

101A Visitor Center Dr., Williamsburg, VA 23187 757-229-1000, www.history.org

Duke of Gloucester Street and the reconstructed governor's mansion are the centerpieces of this re-created historic city depicting the best of British colonial life in the New World. Shop for authentic toys, wear a tricorn hat, and return the greetings of costumed barristers, shopkeepers, and servants.

middleton place plantation

4300 Ashley River Rd., Charleston, SC 29414
800-782-3608, www.middletonplace.org

Experience a taste of the Old South, with the benefit of a view from the 21st century. This carefully preserved low-country plantation is now a resort, working farm, and historic garden area—and a beautiful family destination. Staff members here are characters who introduce you to life on a 19th-century southern rice plantation.

castillo de san marcos

1 Castillo Dr. S, St. Augustine, FL 32084
904-829-6506, www.nps.gov/casa

This fort was built in 1672 to protect Spain's footprint on the North American continent. Reenactments and weapons demonstrations are regularly scheduled, and rangers are on hand.

conner prairie

13400 Allisonville Rd., Fishers, IN 46038
800-966-1836, www.connerprairie.org

A renowned living history museum, farm, and learning center where families can explore 19th-century life of the American Midwest. It's divided into four main areas: a homestead, a prairie town, a farm, and a Lenape camp. Events are planned every weekend, including storytelling, traditional arts, farm experiences, and more.

oliver h. kelley farm

15788 Kelley Farm Rd., Elk River, MN 55330
763-441-6896, www.mnhs.org

Be a Minnesota farmhand for a day. Try churning butter and weaving a straw hat, and see oxen and horses at work in the fields. Dressed as farmers and field hands, staff members show families how a 19th-century farm was run. Seasonal activities and daily chores provide a hands-on view of daily farm life and early American agriculture.

pony express re-ride

1202 Penn St., Saint Joseph, MO 64503, 816-232-8206
www.stjomo.com/ponyexpress.aspx

This annual event commemorates the founding of the Central Overland and California Pikes Peak Express Company, also known as the Pony Express. In June, teams of horses and riders ride the original trail from Missouri, with handoffs along the way in Kansas, Nebraska, Colorado, Wyoming, Utah, Nevada, and then across California to Sacramento. The ride begins at the original Pony Express head-quarters, now a Missouri museum. Families can mail a letter that will be carried along the route.

flint hills overland wagon train

El Dorado, KS 67042, 316-321-6300
www.wagontrainkansas.com

Experience life on the pioneer trail with an overnight covered wagon journey in the Flint Hills, an unspoiled tallgrass prairie that was once a pathway to the American frontier. Traditional entertainment and chuckwagon-style meals are provided, with a campfire and sleeping under the stars at night. You can bring your own horse and ride along.

george ranch

10215 FM 762, Richmond, TX 77469, 281-343-0218
www.georgeranch.org

This historic park has been in one family for four generations. It includes a mansion home, working ranch, and seasonal crops that visitors can help to harvest. Schedule your visit for a Saturday and plan on having an authentic 19th-century-style meal at one of five different venues around the park.

books | the red badge of courage *by stephen crane*

A celebrated 1895 war novel, in which a young man faces the reality and consequences of war. In it, personal experience overpowers a soldier's preconceived ideas of war and bravery.

traveling to learn
culture & values

Family life is something like the art of a framer. We have this tremendous opportunity to turn our child's attention to what we think is important and interesting. Intuitively or directly, the experiences we offer become permanent installations in the gallery of a child's imagination and memory.

In most parts of the United States, we can begin introducing our children to the sights and sounds of other cultures without going far from our own communities. Depending on where we live, we may hear a different language spoken, meet children wearing culturally traditional clothing, or smell new foods—all in an outing to the grocery store or a shopping mall. When our children see us meet these moments with openness and respect, they will do the same.

America is indeed a melting pot—but at the same time, it's a place where people can hold fast to the cultural identities that make them who they are. Bring your children to a Chinese New Year parade and look around: Cultural uniqueness makes our national diversity all the more interesting.

Science and technology revolutionize our lives, but memory, tradition, and myth frame our response.
—**Arthur Schlesinger, Jr.**

Our cultural identities are also tied to our shared political and economic heritage. Try to add this layer to your family travels. Along the way, consider how the neighborhoods, communities, or regions have evolved over the past 50 (or 500!) years. How? Why? What's next? Answers to many of these questions may inspire your travel plan, too.

Finally, think about what your family will leave behind. We have souvenirs, scrapbooks, and lots of other ways to share and remember the stories of our trips. But it's also interesting to think about how you'll be remembered. Many organizations offer service programs that allow you to work as a family team and tutor, serve, build, or create together. Take a picture of yourselves while you're there and frame it—literally and figuratively. You'll be glad you did. Chambers of commerce and local history museums are ideal sources of information.

ten best
old world fêtes

Inspired by European cultures, these are just a few of the events around the country that celebrate and share old-world heritage, foods, arts, and people.

grecian festival

102 Russell Street, Worcester, MA 01602
508-791-7326, www.grecianfestival.org

For more than 30 years, the Saint Spyridon Grecian Festival has celebrated the richness of Greek culture, with Greek music and dance demonstrations, tasty cuisine, art displays, interactive theater, and a popular festival area for kids—held in June.

irish festival

Waterfront Park, 1A Prince St., Alexandria, VA 22320
703-237-2199, www.ballyshaners.org

This suburb of Washington, D.C., is known for its Irish-themed shops and restaurants. In August, an Alexandria-based Irish cultural group hosts a day-long festival on the banks of the Potomac. Expect traditional food, arts offerings, plus dance and live music performances. Bring lawn chairs. The same group hosts the famous St. Patrick's Day Parade held on the cobblestone streets of the city—usually more than a week before the actual holiday. Tip for families: Get there early for good viewing spots and see the pre-parade classic car show.

heidi festival

418 Railroad St., New Glarus, WI 53574
800-527-6838, www.swisstown.com

New Glarus is America's Little Switzerland, with rolling hills, pastoral towns, and close-knit communities that resemble Glarus, Switzerland. Take part in a unique summer festival that offers the sights, sounds, and smells of Swiss culture: wagon rides, street dances, and, of course, a Heidi play.

bastille day

60th St. from 5th to Lexington Aves.
New York, NY, www.fiaf.org

A giant street fair with hot, salty *pommes frites*, Belgian waffles, and crepes galore. There is a stationary bicycle version of the Tour de France and art activities for children. It's all to commemorate the famous storming of the Bastille prison in Paris on July 14, 1789.

danish film festival

Rich Theatre, Woodruff Arts Center, 1280 Peachtree St., NE, Atlanta, GA 30309, 404-733-5000
www.danishfilmfestival.com

The Danish Arts Society supports this renowned January festival that features some of the best in Danish cinema. The films were selected by the local Danish American Chamber of Commerce.

The last day of the festival features movies for children.

german-american heritage center

712 W. 2nd St., Davenport, IA 52802
www.gahc.org, 563-322-8844

Built in 1868 as a German guesthouse, this historic building is now home to a museum exploring German-American culture from colonial times to the present day. It includes artifacts brought over by German immigrants, trunks, glassware, and other unique items.

florida scottish highland games

407-426-7268, www.flascot.com

Organized and hosted by the Scottish-American Society of Central Florida, the games are held by such societies throughout the nation. But the central Florida society says theirs are the best. Held in January, they feature athletics, highland dance, and many forms of entertainment from Scots tradition.

fort ticonderoga

Lake Champlain, NY 12883, 518-585-2821
www.fort-ticonderoga.org

Discover a unique part of French history at the park three hours north of New York City. It reveals the life of the early French who came to the area and established their own society of New France, then used their fortified regiment to defend the

area from the northern advance of British colonists and soldiers—an army five times their size—at the Heights of Carillon in 1758. Visits include guided tours of the fort, daily musket demonstrations, and a fife and drum corps that reenacts the sounds of the 18th century.

julius meinl austrian café

3601 N. Southport Ave., Chicago, IL 60613
773-868-1857, www.meinl.com.

Discover the best in Austrian cuisine at this kid-friendly restaurant. In addition to savory choices in the café (from sandwiches to strudels), visitors can take home such tastes of Austria as roasted plum preserve, chocolate powder, and pumpkin seed oil.

polish fest

Summerfest Grounds, 200 N. Harbor Dr., Milwaukee, WI 53202
414-529-2140, www.polishfest.org

A three-day festival draws families from all over the country. Listen to accordian music, eat pierogi, and learn the traditional arts of *wycinanki* (paper cutting) and *wianki* (flower wreaths). Children can register to participate in the annual Chopin Piano Competition, a festival highlight. A "nonstop polka stage" keeps the energy level high all weekend, and a children's stage area features plays, music, and magic shows. This June tradition is said to be the largest Polish festival in the nation.

ten best
african gatherings

The history of African Americans in the United States began in 1619, when a Dutch ship brought the first people from Africa to the shores of North America. Of all ethnic groups, African Americans were the only ones to arrive on these shores against their will.

west african drum class

PMT Dance, 69 W. 14th St., New York, NY 10011, 212-924-5694
www.pmthouseofdance.com

Learn the fundamentals of playing colorfully crafted Wula drums to pulsating African beats. The program is run by Youssouf Koumbassa, a Guinean-born artist and former member of the National Ballet of Guinea. Breakdance and hip-hop workshops are also held here.

ethiopian dining

Lalibela, 415 W. Thompson La., Nashville, TN 37211 615-332-0710

One of several Ethiopian restaurants in the Nashville area, it serves up hot, spicy, flavorful dishes from the East African nation.

algerian cuisine

Couscous Café, 1195 20th St., NW, Washington, DC 20036, 202-689-1233, www.couscouscatering.com

Try some of the best in Algerian cuisine in the nation's capital. Among the more popular treats: falafel (garlic, chickpeas, and fava beans formed into a ball and deep fried) and baklava (a sweet pastry).

tunisian cultural & information center

168 Madison Ave., New York, NY 10016, 212-991-9933
www.tunisiancenterusa.com

Learn about the history, culture, tourism, and art of Tunisia at this unique center that is a block from Manhattan's Empire State Building.

the south african food shop

Fullwood Plaza, 11229 E. Independence Blvd. Matthews, NC 28105, southafricanfoodshop.com

This is the place to go to experience foods that are popular in grocery stores in South Africa. The shop offers everything from spicy Durban curry to custard powder to hard-to-find chocolates.

books | nelson mandela's favorite african folktales

by nelson mandela

Storytelling traditions come alive with this beautifully illustrated volume collected by Nobel Laureate for Peace Nelson Mandela. Some familiar, some new, they all represent a spectrum of African culture.

all nigerian soccer festival & tournament

Washington, DC, 202-841-8809

Nigerian soccer is annually one of the best programs in the world. With one of the largest diaspora of any African nation, Nigerian teams from throughout the United States celebrate their heritage and sports prowess with the All Nigeria Soccer Festival/Tournament at various locations during Columbus Day weekend.

ethiopian sports federation festival

www.esfna.net

An Ethiopian soccer tournament draws an international cadre of teams and players for a hugely popular sporting event. A cultural festival coincides with it, with music by Ethiopian artists, dance demonstrations, traditional foods, and a children's talent show. Originally hosted in Houston, the tournament and festival were held in Washington, D.C., in 2008 and in Chicago in 2009.

---

resource | african american history month

African American History Month celebrates the role African Americans have played in U.S. history. This website shares stories of contributions that African Americans have made to society: *www.loc.gov/topics/africanamericans*

african film festival, new york

www.africanfilm,ny.org

Various locations throughout New York City, including Central Park in Manhattan and Carona Park in Queens. The annual outdoor summer series showcases some of the best in African films, which are not only energy packed and entertaining but also full of glimpses of nations rarely seen in American media.

south african cuisine

Ten South, 4183 Roswell Rd., Atlanta, GA 30342, 404-705-8870, www.10degreessouth.com

Calamari grilled and seasoned with peri-peri sauce. Grape leaves stuffed with rice and ground beef and served with yogurt sauce. Chicken curry made with traditional South African spices. These are a few of the delicacies at a restaurant that fuses some of the more popular tastes of the nation that has origins in Portugal, Malaysia, and Germany.

african dance

Tapestry Dance Company Studio, 2302 Western Trails Blvd., Austin, TX 78745, 512-474-9846
www.tapestry.org

Can't dance? No problem. Beginners of all ages are encouraged to learn these energetic dance moves—for workouts or for serious students of the art. They're taught by Jean-Claude Lessou, a former professional dancer in Côte D' Ivoire who has taught students in several U.S. colleges and universities.

ten best
hispanic experiences

Latin American cultures include all Spanish-speaking and Portuguese-speaking countries in the American continents. From South America come the ancient traditions of the Aztec, Maya, Inca, and Toltec. Mexican, Cuban, and Caribbean communities add their own flavors and heritage. These friendly celebrations offer traditions and rituals, foods and cultural arts that provide perspective on another way of life.

mexican american art

The National Museum of Mexican Art
1852 W. 19th St., Chicago, IL 60608, 312-738-1503
www.nationalmuseumofmexicanart.org

See ancient Mayan and Mezcalan artifacts, contemporary folk art, and masterpieces of Mexican painting and textile design. The museum also has a new performing arts space. Check before you visit for schedules of festivals, family activities, and community events. Día del Niño (Day of the Child) is a traditional Mexican holiday, celebrated here each spring.

capoeira

The Afro-Brazilian Capoeira Association
2609 Aldrich Ave., Minneapolis, MN 55408
612-354-7022, www.abcapoeira.com

Learn and see one of the most visually stimulating martial arts experiences. Capoeira began as a form of self-defense created by Brazilian slaves. It has since become a widely popular form of dance and visual expression that inspired the 2003 action film *Only the Strong*.

peruvian festival

The Peruvian Festival of Virginia
15345 Lord Culpeper Ct., Woodbridge, VA 22191
703-981-7805, www.festivalperuanodevirginia.com

An annual destination for families of Peruvian descent, located in the suburbs just outside Washington, D.C. Highlights include a paso horse show, Peruvian dishes, a music concert, and Peruvian folklore dancers.

venezuelan dishes

La Casa de Pedro, 343 Arsenal St., Watertown, MA
02472, 617-923-8025, www.lacasadepedro.com

Enjoy scrumptious Venezuelan dishes in this colorful restaurant along Boston's Charles River. Hot

books | the tortilla factory *by gary paulsen* The story of the "life cycle" of a tortilla, from seed to flour to oven. This thoughtful and vibrantly illustrated picture book comes from an author best known for his young adult novels.

arepa is a kind of corn bread, and a great way to introduce children to this distinctive cuisine. It's especially fun for kids at lunchtime.

tango

Argentinian Tango Lessons and Festival: Denver Turnverein Ballroom, 1570 Clarkson St., Denver, CO 80218 303-831-9717, www.denverturnverein.org

Learn how to step, saunter, and sway like the professional tango dancers. Or simply master a few moves while listening to the tantalizing tango rhythms. Teens love these lessons.

calle ocho

S.W. 8th St., Miami, FL, www.carnavalmiami.com

Carnaval is the Latin American equivalent of Mardi Gras, and this Little Havana celebration is the largest of its kind in the United States. Four blocks are reserved as a KidZone with great food and entertainment. Calle Ocho translates to "8th Street." Sunday is the biggest and busiest of the festival's ten days. Midweek and early evening forays are often best for families.

cinco de mayo

Cinco de Mayo Celebrate Culture Festival: Civic Center Park, Broadway & Colfax Ave., Denver, CO 80203 www.denver.org/metro/features/cinco-de-mayo

Attracting as many as 400,000 people, the two-day festival offers Latin, salsa, and jazz music as well as Tex-Mex food. Cinco de Mayo commemorates a Mexican battle victory over the French in 1862. It is celebrated on May 5 all over North and South America.

brazilian food

Bossa Nova Restaurant, 7181 W. Sunset Blvd., Los Angeles, CA 90046 323-436-7999, www.bossafood.com

From delectable entrées to tasty desserts to a fine assortment of teas, Bossa Nova has some of the best Brazilian cuisine. Try the traditional fried yucca or *coxhina,* a hot shredded chicken specialty. Four locations in L.A.

chilean food

Rincon Chileno, 4354 Melrose Ave. Los Angeles, CA 90029, 323-666-6075

Chilean art and traditional music provide just the right ambiance for this popular restaurant that features chicken and seafood dishes. It's a casual place with a television, with an especially fun atmosphere when international soccer games are televised.

guyana folk festival

Guyana Cultural Association of New York 1368 E. 89th St., Brooklyn, NY 11236, 718-209-5207 www.guyfolkfest.org

All Caribbean cultures come together in the performing arts festival. It's a ten-day festival: Kids are free on Family Day.

ten best
asian events

At first glimpse, America's Asian cultures are indeed a melting pot. Yet from the Far East to the Middle East, people bring distinctive traditions of food, music, art, and celebration, all shared at events like these.

festival of india

Various locations, 336-593-8108
www.festivalofindia.org

An extraordinary traveling festival tour that offers glimpses of India from a spiritual, social, and historical perspective. Programs have explored protecting cattle (sacred in India), vegetarianism, and reincarnation. Past festival sites include Washington, D.C., New York, Tampa, Dallas, and Seattle.

the national japanese american memorial

Washington, DC, 202-530-0015, www.njamf.com

Located off the National Mall on Louisiana Avenue, NW, the triangular grounds that include a marker, trees, shrubbery, and stone honor Japanese patriotism during World War II. The memorial commemorates the sacrifice of Japanese Americans who fought and died in the war, despite the fact that many of their families and countrymen were placed in U.S. concentration camps two months after the start of the war.

afghan cuisine

Bamiyan Afghani Restaurant, 358 Third Ave., New York, NY 10016, 212-481-3232
www.bamiyan.com

Begin with a traditional lentil soup. Try the *aushak* appetizer: steamed scallion dumplings topped with yogurt-mint sauce. And for the entrée, select the *kabuli palow* with lamb (browned baked basmati rice with tender pieces of lamb, topped with shredded carrots). And save some room for *malai-e* dessert, Afghan homemade ice cream with rose water and honey.

korean american film festival

Korea Studies in Media Arts, San Francisco State University, 1600 Halloway Ave., San Francisco, CA 94132, www.mykima.org

What began as an impromptu gathering of film enthusiasts at San Francisco State University in 2001 has become a much-anticipated annual event. With a variety of film genres, the festival gives movie-goers a unique glimpse into Korean culture, featuring some of the finest Korean-American filmmakers.

asian american festival

Richard J. Daley Center, 50 W. Washington St. Chicago, IL 60602, www.aacchicago.org

Hosted by Korean American Community, the springtime event brings together cultures and experiences from throughout the Asian diaspora. It's a cultural celebration held in a fun street fair environment with great food, entertainment, costumes, and workshops.

the chinese american museum

125 Paseo de la Plaza, Suite 400, Los Angeles, CA 90012, 213-485-8567, www.camla.org

The museum gives Chinese Americans a unique place to tell and relive their stories. Past exhibits have included a collection of dolls brought from China by children and a photographic display of early Chinese-American neighborhoods.

lao culture

1940 N. Fresno St., Fresno, CA 93703 www.laoamerican.org

For Lao families, there are free weekly classes to preserve Lao literacy and to learn traditional dance. Founded in 2001, the Laotian American Advancement Center educates many aspects of the nation's culture and the lives of those who have made America home.

seattle international district

Hing Hay Park, 423 Maynard Ave., S, Seattle, WA 98104 206-382-1197, www.cidbia.org

This park is a gathering place at the heart of Seattle's vibrant Pan-Asian community of shops, restaurants, and galleries representing Chinese and Japanese, Filipino, and other Southeast Asian cultures. Summer "night markets" celebrate traditional dance, martial arts, storytelling, and great food, plus outdoor movies just after the sun sets.

filipino american library

135 North Park View St., Los Angeles, CA 90026 213-382-0488, www.filipinoamericanlibrary.org

What better place to learn about Filipino culture than a library dedicated to it? Since 1985, the library has given its community a chance to explore Filipino culture and history in depth. It also features an annual Summer Reading Club for children.

nisei week

Japanese American Cultural & Community Center, 244 San Pedro St., Los Angeles, CA 90012, 213-628-2725 www.jaccc.org

Honoring the first American-born Japanese, the summer festival that's more than 60 years strong highlights Japanese-American culture and history.

Korean First Birthday
A traditional party game: The honored baby is presented with an array of objects. The first one she reaches for is a sign of her future.

ten best
down under happenings

Aboriginal or European-influenced, Australia's traditions of art, sport, and celebration are endlessly fascinating for American families. Here are a few places to join in the fun without crossing the Pacific.

> That great America on the other side of the sphere, Australia.
> —Herman Melville

I. Teens would enjoy seeing the film *Gallipoli* in advance of attending an event like this.

meat pies

Australian Bakery Café, 48 South Park Sq., Marietta, GA 30030, 678-797-6222, www.australianbakery.com

Traditional meat pies are the highlight here: ground beef with gravy and a pastry crust. It's family-run and frequented by Australians who crave familiar food, including Christmas pudding and lamingtons (sponge cake with chocolate and coconut).

fiji festival usa

Fiji American National Association, 26250 Industrial Blvd., Hayward, CA 94545, 510-780-9699 www.fijifestival.com

Have a *lovo* feast, play netball (similar to basketball but with a lower hoop and no backboard), and taste food from the islands at this extraordinary festival.

anzac day

Various locations, New York, NY, www.nyfooty.com

An annual, festive party celebrated by Australians and New Zealanders who honor members of the Australian and New Zealand Army Corps (ANZAC) who fought in Turkey during World War

melbourne cup telecast

Emerald Downs Racetrack, 2300 Emerald Downs Dr., Auburn, WA 98001, 253-288-7000 www.emeralddowns.com

Watch the Melbourne Cup, Australia's premier thoroughbred horse race, at Emerald Downs with a live, Australian broadcast feed.

rugby fans

Richmond Arms Pub, 5920 Richmond Ave., Houston, TX 77057, 713-784-7722, www.richmondarmsonline.com

How often does an American sports fan enter a sports bar and witness pastel-clad fans watching a stirring match between the All Blacks (New Zealand's national rugby team) and the Wallabies (Australia's national rugby team)? Not to miss.

papua new guinea sculpture garden

Cantor Center for Visual Arts, Stanford University 328 Lomita Dr., Palo Alto, CA 94305, 650-723-4177 www.stanford.edu/~mjpeters/png

Located on the Stanford University campus, these wooden sculptures of people and animals were created by ten master New Guinean carvers.

They worked together with a team of American and New Guinean landscape architects to create this special place. Bring a sketchbook and encourage children to draw what they see—it's unlike any other sculpture garden in the country.

australian river gorge

National Aquarium in Baltimore, 501 E. Pratt St.
Baltimore, MD 21202, 410-576-3800, www.aqua.org

Handprint cave paintings and the sounds of didgeridoo music add to the experience of flood and drought at an Australian river gorge—right in an American city. See native creatures like a laughing kookaburra and pignose turtles. One exhibit, "Animal Planet Australia: Wild Extremes," has its own beautifully designed wing at the celebrated aquarium.

g'day usa

Various locations, Tourism Australia
310-695-3213, www.australia-week.com

The showcase of Australian culture, food, wine, and tourism has been the calling card for this, one of the nation's premier Aussie festivals. Hosted in major U.S. cities including Los Angeles, San Francisco, and New York, the festival draws tens of thousands.

women's footy

www.womensfooty.com

Australian rules football is a physically challenging sport that's similar to rugby and American football. Yet in this country (as in most others), the sport called "footy" is played by women, too. With teams across the country, the U.S. Women's Australian Football League features such teams as the Orange County Bombshells, the Atlanta Lady Kookaburras, and the Minnesota Morrigans.

pacific rim children's chorus festival

Pacific Rim Music Resources, 159 Laimi Rd.
Honolulu, HI 96817, 808-595-0233
www.pacrimfestival.org

Children's choirs from more than 20 countries gather in Hawaii to learn the music and choral traditions of Pacific Rim cultures. Participants learn chants, try ethnic dances, and make simple Polynesian musical instruments. The July festival culminates in two evening performances that are free and open to the public.

books | children from australia to zimbabwe

by maya ajmera & anna rhesa versola

This photographic book takes small children on a virtual world tour—in alphabetical order. Find basic facts about new places, and discover how much you may have in common with faraway families. It's the first in a series of internationally themed books produced by the Global Fund for Children.

ten best
native american ways

Spiritual celebrations or ceremonies are often deeply personal and private in Native American communities. But other venues are designed to welcome the curiosity and questions of visiting families. Here are a few ways for families to experience a taste of native culture in communities across the country.

national museum of the american indian

4th St. & Independence Ave., SW, Washington, DC 20560, 202-633-1000, www. nmai.si.edu

It is the first national museum dedicated to the life, cultures, and history of this land's original people. The NMAI features extraordinary records, artwork, sculptures, and exhibits, all housed in a striking museum that dominates the National Mall. Send free e-postcards from the museum's library, and find out about the building's remarkable symbolic architecture. The café features foods inspired by a diversity of indigenous cultures.

explore navajo interactive museum

10 N. Main St., Tuba City, AZ 86045, 928-283-5441 www.explorenavajo.com

Just east of the Grand Canyon's South Rim, this interactive museum is a good starting point for families interested in visiting the Navajo Nation.

You'll learn about the history of the nation and some tips for touring. The nation owns three hotels, including a Quality Inn in Window Rock, Arizona.

corn dances

Santo Domingo Pueblo, Santo Domingo, N.M. 87052 505-465-2214, www.newmexico.org/native_america/ pueblos/santo_domingo.php

August 4 is St. Dominic Annual Feast Day's world-famous dance ceremony. The pueblo is located near ancient turquoise mines.

pipestone national monument

36 N. Reservation Ave., Pipestone, MN 56164 507-825-5464, www.nps.gov/pipe/

Only American Indians can extract pipestone from the quarries here—a permit is required, and there is a lengthy waiting list. In summer months, visitors can meet Native American pipe makers and observe their work of carving sacred stone pipes.

aquinnah cliffs

Aquinnah Cultural Center, 35 Aquinnah Cir., Aquinnah, MA 02535, 508-645-7900, www.wampanoagtribe.net

These red clay cliffs are sacred to the Wampanoag people, whose earliest ancestors were here as long as 10,000 years ago. A visitor center and nearby Wampanoag-owned shops and restaurant are open from late spring to mid-October. The tribal office on Black Brook Road is open year-round and offers additional visitor information and area maps.

moundville native american festival

Moundville Archaeological Park, Moundville, AL 35474, 205-371-2234, http://moundville. ua.edu/festival.html

The hills in this park are the remains of earthern pyramids made by the people who lived here more than 800 years ago. Each October, the University of Alabama hosts a festival on the grounds, with Native American art, music, foods, and special exhibits.

american indian exposition

Hwy. 8, Anadarko, OK 73005, 405-247-5661 www.indiancityusa.com

The weeklong August festival features 15 Native American groups and includes horse and greyhound races and the World Championship Fancy Dance Competition.

hawaiian paniolo

Parker Ranch, Blacksmith Shop, Pukalani Rd., Kamuela, HI 96743, 877-885-7999, www.parkerranch.com

More than 160 years ago, an AWOL British sailor introduced the idea of raising cattle near Mauna Kea. Paniolo are Hawaiian cowboys, and visitors (over the age of seven) can ride the trails with them and hear stories of the cattle industry in Hawaii.

annual festival of iroquois arts

Iroquois Indian Museum, 324 Caverns Rd. Howes Cave, NY 12092, 518-296-8949 www.iroquoismuseum.org

This museum has a year-round schedule of events, lectures, and special exhibits. This late-summer arts festival includes an arts market, children's activities, and archaeology and wildlife workshops.

alaska indian arts

Haines, AK 99827, 907-766-2234 www.haines.ak.us

Alaska native culture permeates villages and towns across Alaska. There are ten totem poles located throughout this historic town, and the nearby Alaska Indian Arts Center is a place to see native carvers at work. The renowned Chilkat Dancers storytelling group performs in summer months at a traditional Tlingit tribal house.

Let's Talk About . . .
The American Repatriation Foundation is a non-federally funded, not-for-profit organization founded in 1992 by Elizabeth Sackler. The foundation assists in the repatriation of ceremonial materials to American Indian people. For more than 15 years, it has educated students and the public about the importance of repatriation.

ten best
folklife spots

Folklife describes the way that families and communities use their unique resources to celebrate heritage, honor milestones, and share stories and ways of life from one generation to the next.
—Peggy A. Bulger

mt. pleasant & st. helena island, south carolina

www.basketmakers.org
www.penncenter.com

As a key part of the newly designated Gullah-Geechee Heritage Corridor, the sweetgrass basketmakers of Mt. Pleasant and the Penn Center on St. Helena Island are preserving the unique African traditions still practiced by the Gullah-Geechee people of coastal South Carolina, Georgia, and North Florida. Descendants of slaves brought to the sea islands from Sierra Leone, these basket makers, singers, and storytellers are living cultural resources for us all.

washington, d.c.

www.folklife.si.edu, www.loc.gov/folklife

Home to the Smithsonian Folklife Festival (held annually on the last week of June and the first week of July) and the American Folklife Center at the

Handmade sweetgrass baskets

Library of Congress, which is the largest folklife archive in the country.

new york city

www.citylore.org, www.CTMD.org

CityLore is located here, with a mission to "foster New York's—and America's—living cultural heritage." The website of the Center for Traditional Music and Dance alerts you to performances of the city's diverse ethnic communities.

elko, nevada

www.westernfolklife.org

The Cowboy Poetry Gathering is held here each winter. It's a nationally known event that highlights the artistic traditions of the American West. The event, hosted by the Western Folklife Center, includes arts workshops for children.

whitesburg, kentucky

www.appalshop.org

The traditions and cultures of Appalachia are celebrated by Appalshop, a grassroots cultural center and media production house. Each June it hosts Seedtime on the Cumberland, a spirited extravaganza of live music, film screenings, and arts activities.

galax, virginia

www.oldfiddlersconvention.com
www.blueridgemusiccenter.org

Home to the oldest fiddlers' convention (held annually in August) and the Blue Ridge Music Center. The Fiddler's Youth Competition is an annual highlight at the eight-day convention.

memphis, tennessee

www.southernfolklore.com, www.
bealestreet.com, www.tourgraceland.com

Come here to visit the Center for Southern Folklore, the historic Beale Street music corridor, and (of course) Graceland!

jonesborough, tennessee

www.storytellingfoundation.net

The International Storytelling Center resides here, and the National Storytelling Festival is held annually in September.

elkins, west virginia

www.augustaheritage.com

At the Augusta Heritage Workshop, families can sign up for weeklong workshops to learn traditional music, dance, crafts, or storytelling.

middlebury, vermont

www.vermontfolklifecenter.org

Youth Radio Vermont is one of the programs of this cultural center. Local teens are trained to produce radio documentaries that are aired locally and available online. The center hosts innovative cultural exhibits year-round.

additional sites:

Greek-American neighborhoods of Tarpon Springs, FL
www.spongedocks.net

Little Havana Cuban community of Miami, FL
www.miamiandbeaches.com

Faulkner's home and southern culture in Oxford, MS
www.olemiss.edu

Civil rights heritage in Montgomery, AL
www.arts.state.al.us

Peggy Bulger

Peggy A. Bulger is director of the American Folklife Center at the Library of Congress. She is the author of *South Florida Folklife*, with Tina Bucuvalas and Stetson Kennedy, the editor of *Musical Roots of the South*, and producer of videos and recordings including *Music Masters & Rhythm Kings* and *Deep South Musical Roots Tour*. A native of New York, she earned her Ph.D. from the University of Pennsylvania. Bulger has been documenting folklife and developing and managing folklife programs for more than 30 years.

ten best
places to stay current

Visit the places where news originates. Children feel engaged and empowered when they see the work that goes into producing a news program, passing a law, or launching a space shuttle!

watch weather

Mount Washington Observatory, NH, 603-356-2137
www.mountwashington.org

Located at the summit of Mount Washington, the highest point in New England, visitors can monitor weather conditions as well as catch one of the most spectacular views on the planet.

united nations

Visitor's Entrance, 1st Ave. & 46th St., New York, NY
10017, 212-963-8687, www.un.org

Eighteen acres in the heart of New York is not U.S. territory. The United Nations campus is international property belonging to all UN members. Tour guides are young people from 20 nations who conduct tours in 15 different languages. See the General Assembly Hall, meeting place for representatives of 192 nations.

launch into space

John F. Kennedy Space Center, FL 32899, 321-449-4444
www.kennedyspacecenter.com

Be there for what is always a one-of-a-kind moment in American history: a scheduled rocket or shuttle launch into space. Sign up online for updates about rocket launch schedules. There are several options available, ranging from launch viewing at the Visitor Complex to special access for the closest possible viewing location—about six miles from the launchpad. There is sometimes an extra option for a buffet-style meal with an astronaut.

lawmakers at work

United States Capitol, 100 Constitution Ave., NE
Washington, DC 20002, 202-225-6827, www.aoc.gov

Watch the nation's lawmakers carve out (or drag out) legislation. The capitol is open to the public for guided tours only, Monday through Saturday, and on all federal holidays except Thanksgiving Day and Christmas Day.

U.S. Capitol

go behind the scenes

30 Rockefeller Center, 30 Rockefeller Plaza, New York, NY 10012, 212-332-6868, www.rockefellercenter.com

Be at the hub of activity in the nation's financial and cultural center and one of the most historic locales in the world for news and entertainment. In addition to being the location of Radio City Music Hall and a breathtaking observation deck, the 22-acre, 19-building center is also the home to NBC Studios and is where live studio tapings of the *Today Show* are held.

fight crime

National Museum of Crime & Punishment 575 7th St., NW, Washington, DC 20004 202-393-1099, www.crimemuseum.org

The museum not only houses some of the nation's most renowned artifacts in its efforts to fights crime (including Al Capone's jail cell and Bonnie and Clyde's automobile), but also is the home of the nationally televised show *America's Most Wanted,* where tips about the nation's most notorious criminals come in live on the national switchboard.

ship out

111 East Loop North, Houston, TX 77029, 713-670-2416, www.portofhouston.com/samhou/samhou.html

Watch activity at the nation's busiest port, courtesy of the Sam Houston Boat Tour. Passengers view international cargo vessels and operations at the port's Turning Basin Terminal. The boat is the property of Houston's Port Authority, and the tour

Every event has a unique final cause.

—Aristotle

cruise is free; however, reservations must be made in advance. You can do this online.

break camp

NFL Team Training Camp, various sites, www.nfl.com

What's possibly more fun than watching an NFL game? Watching one's favorite team prepare for the season during training camp, most of which, unlike the games, are free. See the grueling workouts, the schematic plays, and the occasional skirmish.

live news

CNN Center Tour, 190 Marietta St., NW, Atlanta, GA 30303, 404-827-2300, www.cnn.com/tour/atlanta

Experience world news live, and watch how some of the leading anchors and reporters deliver it to the world. Purchase tickets in advance for this 55-minute tour. Your ticket stub will get you discounted admission at several other Atlanta destinations. Check the website for details.

lights, camera, carpet

Oscar Awards Red Carpet at Kodak Theatre 6801 Hollywood Blvd., Hollywood, CA 90028 323-308-6300, www.kodaktheatre.com

Only 300 tickets are issued (online) for the bleacher section to witness stars of film and television walk along arguably the nation's most coveted rug while photographers flood the area with flashbulbs. Guided tours are available every day. It's part of the Hollywood & Highland complex that is home to Grauman's Chinese Theatre.

ten best
civil rights landmarks

Travel in the American South means opportunities to walk in the footsteps of 20th-century heroes.

howard law school

2900 Van Ness St., NW, Washington, DC 20008, 202-806-8000
www.law.howard.edu

The school, its Founders Library, and its law school provided legal strategy for ending "separate but equal" policies in American public schools. Arguments presented before the U.S. Supreme Court by graduate Thurgood Marshall and the NAACP Legal Defense Fund led to monumental decisions in the *Brown* v. *Board of Education* case ending public school segregation. Marshall went on to become the nation's first nonwhite U.S. Supreme Court justice.

sitting in at woolworth's

The International Civil Rights Museum, 301 N. Elm St. Ste. 303, Greensboro, NC 27401
336-274-9199, www.sitinmovement.org

The museum began as a Woolworth's Five & Dime. On February 1, 1960, four college freshmen took vacant seats at the "whites only" lunch counter. They were not served. They departed, but returned each following day, joined by more students—both black and white. By the end of the week the four had swelled to 400. The result:

In Atlanta, the gravesite of Rev. Martin Luther King, Jr.

The lunch counter was integrated by the summer, and 32 other southern cities followed suit.

tougaloo

Tougaloo College, 500 West County Line Rd., Tougaloo, MS 39174, 601-977-7700
www.tougaloo.edu

During the 1950s and 1960s, the historically black school was a center for civil rights activities in racially turbulent Mississippi. Students at the school, located ten miles north of the state capital of Jackson, led an effort to end racial discrimination in the capital.

bloody sunday on the edmund pettus bridge

Edmund Pettus Bridge, Selma, AL
www.nps.gov/nr/travel/civilrights/al4.htm

In a watershed moment, marchers led a Selma-to-Montgomery march for voting rights, but on March 7, 1965, they were attacked by state and local lawmen with tear gas and billy clubs just shy of the bridge. The result: Reverand Dr. Martin Luther King, Jr., led a march to the bridge two days later. Later that month, 25,000 marchers reached the state house in Montgomery. Some traveled 12 miles a day on foot to reach the final destination.

the orangeburg massacre

All Star Bowling Lane (now All Star Triangle Bowl)
1543 Russell St., Orangeburg, SC 29115, 804-534-4844

The city's only bowling alley was a segregated venue (at a time of the 1960s when most venues were integrated). Students gathered at majority black South Carolina State University on Feb. 8, 1968. A police confrontation followed; three students were killed and 27 injured. It was one of the first police-student conflicts on campus that led to deaths.

central high school

1500 Park St., Little Rock, AR 72202, 501-447-1400
www.lrcentralhigh.org

At this national historic site, nine African-American students integrated the school for the first time on Sept. 23, 1957. They stood up to a crowd of angry protesters in a moment that was broadcast live around the world.

juanita craft civil rights house

2618 Warren Ave., Dallas, TX 75215, 214-670-8637
www.dallasculture.org/juanitaCraftHouse.cfm

Juanita Craft (1902–85) advised Dr. Martin Luther King and President Lyndon B. Johnson on civil rights matters and played a major role in integrating the 1954 Texas State Fair, theaters, and restaurants in Dallas. Her home is open by appointment only.

howard thurman home

614 Whitehall St., Daytona Beach, FL 32114, 386-258-7514

A site on the Florida Black Heritage Trail and the U.S. National Register of Historic Places, it is the home of Howard Thurman (1900–81), a renowned theologian, educator, and civil rights leader whose book *Jesus and the Disinherited* laid much of the philosophical groundwork for the civil rights movement.

civil rights memorial

400 Washington Ave., Montgomery, AL 36104
334-956-8200, www.splcenter.org

The black-granite Civil Rights Memorial honors those who lost their lives during the civil rights movement. It's located across the street from the Southern Poverty Law Center office building.

ebenezer baptist church

407 Auburn Ave., Atlanta, GA 30312, 404-688-7300
www.historicebenezer.org

Founded in 1887 by Rev. John A. Parker, a former slave, the church was a hub of the civil rights movement and is best known for having been pastored by Rev. Martin Luther King, Jr., and his father. Today it is a museum chronicling civil rights for African Americans tracing back to the first slaves brought to the nation in Virginia in 1619.

books | milton's secret
by eckhart tolle, robert s. friedman & frank riccio
A children's book with wisdom for all ages. Milton is a boy who learns to deal with bullies and to overcome fears familiar to children everywhere.

ten best
service opportunities

Ask kids about what they'd like to do to make changes in the world. The whole family benefits when everyone pitches in.

americorps

202-606-5000, www.americorps.org

Volunteers age 17 and older can register to participate in many state and national volunteer programs, including helping hurricane victims in the Gulf Coast and flood victims in Iowa.

citizen corps

www.citizencorps.gov

This is a program of the U.S. Department of Homeland Security. Their "Ready Kids" campaign promotes ways for children and parents to prepare for emergencies, and support local disaster relief and community safety.

feeding america

800-771-2303, www.feedingamerica.org

Formerly known as Second Harvest, this agency has programs in communities across America. The website shows opportunities for adults and older teens to assist in repackaging and distributing surplus food or to tutor in local Kids' Cafes. The whole family can participate in September's Hunger Action Month activities, which vary by state. There are also fundraising opportunities to support the agency at a national or local level.

habitat for humanity

800-422-4828, www.habitat.org

Search their website by location, then find out when and how your family can participate in building and rehabilitating simple, decent houses with the help of the homeowner (partner) families. Since its founding in 1976, HFH has provided more than one million people with shelter.

cityyear

617-927-2500, www.cityyear.org

The national service programs for ages 17 to 24 bring together people of diverse racial, cultural, and socioeconomic backgrounds for a full year of community service.

interamerican workshop

414-377-4590, www.interamericanworkshop.org

This group's Fellow Travelers Project allows contributors of all ages to gather and share online information about travel and service abroad.

The information helps to spread cultural awareness.

u.s. army corps of engineers volunteer clearinghouse

800-865-8337
www.lrn.usace.army.mil/volunteer

The U.S. Army Corps of Engineers Volunteer Clearinghouse's toll-free number offers volunteer opportunities throughout the nation. Parents provide information about their family's talents, interests, and desired location and they get a volunteer assignment suited for them, possibly including campground host, trail maintenance, or wildlife habitat building.

nicodemus

www.wildernessproject.org

The Nicodemus Wilderness Project provides opportunities for youth to learn leadership skills that can in turn be used to save and maintain the natural environment. Reserve the first Sunday in

> With both my children and my grandchildren, I have encouraged them to reach high—not to think about what somebody else is doing but about what should be done. And I have always told them that the only way to do it is to start within yourself first. And then your family. And then just spread out!
>
> —Anna Mae Dickson
> *community leader, Grimes County, TX,*
> *Southern Exposure*

June, when everyone comes to help out on National Trails Day.

learn and serve america

202-606-5000, www.learnandserve.org

An organization that supports learning programs from kindergarten through college, Learn and Serve America involves nearly one million youngsters in public safety, education, and the environment.

youth for service

212-598-0973
www.ysop.org

Founded in New York City by Quakers in 1983, the project challenges young people to take part in addressing the problems in today's society. Project sites are located in the New York City and Washington, D.C., metro areas. Student and adult programs are available.

once a year

For a very young child, autumn comes as an amazing surprise. The leaves turn yellow! They fall off the trees! There are parties and costumes—a robot here, a princess there. The months go by, and when October rolls around again, there is extra delight in anticipating the spectacle, the fun, and the rituals that are unique to this time of year.

Annual traditions are like bookmarks in the passage of our families' lives. We can measure ourselves by the way we change and grow from one summer vacation to the next, or recall vivid memories of what it was like to be together at a single, wonderful moment in time.

Maybe it's the most stirring countdown you'll ever utter, standing among tens of thousands at New York's Times Square on New Year's Eve, as the big, bright sphere slowly drops just before the new year ushers in.

Perhaps it's awe you'll experience during the opulent light displays of Fiesta Flambeau once the sun goes down over Fiesta San Antonio, an annual, ten-day event that draws more than 3.5 million people each spring.

Rituals and traditions are essential to a child's sense of time, memory, and family heritage. When it comes to special celebrations and holiday events, there's so much to be said for simply being there.

These are among the nation's once-a-year, seasonal events. Since much family travel is planned around certain times of the year—taking into account school vacations, holidays, and changing seasons—these are events that make for memorable family getaways, traditions, and rituals year-round.

Some events, like the Tournament of Roses Parade in Pasadena, California, in early January, last just a few hours. Others, like the Colorado Balloon Classic in Colorado Springs during Labor Day weekend, last a few days. Events like the Cherry Blossom Festival in Washington, D.C., in the spring last more than a week depending on the weather!

Such seasonal attractions are not only fun for the entire family, but also remind us how our rich culture evolved and how it can be experienced from one time zone to the next in all seasons. The events draw visitors from all over the world and offer a chance to sample amazing regional music, cuisine, art, and history. And one of the unique things about seasonal celebrations is that they come only once a year.

chapter four
seasonal celebrations

It's the most wonderful
time of the year . . .

ten best
autumn

annual oyster festival
www.theoysterfestival.org
Classic October waterfront event in Long Island, New York, with tall ships, carnival rides, and oyster-shucking contests.

sheep & wool festival
www.sheepandwool.com
Marvel at sheepdog demonstrations and see a leaping llama contest in early October in Rhinebeck, New York.

italian american festival
www.italianamericanfestival.com
An annual Mercer County event with food, music, rides, and all things Italian in West Windsor, New Jersey.

autumn moon festival
www.sanfranciscochinatown.org
In Asia this is a traditional children's holiday. In mid September see the famous Lion Dance parade and sample mooncakes in San Francisco, California.

the black family reunion celebration
www.ncnw.org/events/reunion.htm
Storytelling, music, great food, and dancing are all part of a September gathering in Washington, D.C., that honors African-American families.

national apple harvest festival
www.appleharvest.com
Two-weekend event celebrating everything apple, with kids' offerings, in Arendtsville, Pennsylvania.

head of the charles regatta
www.hocr.org
Watch from the Anderson Bridge: A crew race is the largest fall spectator sporting event in New England. Boston is beautiful at this time of year.

the keene pumpkin festival
www.pumpkinfestival.com
Annual effort to display the world's largest collection of illuminated jack-o-lanterns in Keene, N.H.

oktoberfest-zinzinnati
www.oktoberfest-zinzinnati.com
America's biggest German festival, with the world's largest chicken dance, in Cincinnati, Ohio.

northern plains indian art market
www.npiam.org
Each market day begins with a Lakota blessing ceremony, held in late September in Sioux Falls, South Dakota.

ten best
fall foliage

maine
www.state.me.us/doc/foliage
Colors begin to change around Labor Day in northern Maine's hills and coastal forests.

vermont
www.vermontvacation.com
Fall is a very busy season here. Visit a local park for great autumn color everywhere you look.

new hampshire
www.visitnh.gov
September and early October may be the best months to hike the Appalachian Trail in this state.

massachusetts
www.massvacation.com
Density and intensity of color increases with each minute traveling out of Boston.

new york
www.iloveny.com
The whole state is famous for foliage, and Manhattan's Central Park is an oasis of autumn color.

alabama
www.800alabama.com
When the weather finally turns cooler, fall color lasts into mid-November.

michigan
www.dnr.state.mn.us
This state's natural resources website posts a foliage report. Try a scenic lakeside visit.

wisconsin
www.travelwisconsin.com
Try the Great Divide Scenic Byway, 29 miles through the Chequamegon-Nicolet National Forest.

colorado
www.colorado.com
Quaking aspen leaves turn a deep golden color all around the Rockies.

intermountain region
www.fs.fed.us/r4/conditions/fallcolors.shtml
The U.S. Forest Service reports on foliage in Nevada, Utah, Idaho, Wyoming, and California.

books | look what i did with a leaf!
by morteza e. sohi
Children can follow illustrations to make amazing collage art with autumn leaves.

ten best
halloween

salem haunted happenings
www.hauntedhappenings.org
In this historic Massachusetts town, a full month of spooky events leads up to Oct. 31.

sea witch halloween & fiddler's festival
www.beach-fun.com
Hear scary stories around bonfires on the beach in Rehoboth, Delaware.

new york's carnival
www.halloween-nyc.com
In Manhattan, anyone in a costume can march in this Greenwich Village parade.

zoo party
www.louisvillezoo.org
Toddlers dressed like monkeys can see real monkeys in Louisville, Kentucky.

ghost & vampire tour
www.neworleansghosttour.com
Bring your teens to New Orleans for gruesome and historic tales of the city. Some of them are true!

anoka halloween
www.anokahalloween.com
Celebrate in the Halloween Capital of the World, in Anoka, Minnesota.

day of the dead festival
www.meca-houston.org
Across Texas, these Mexican celebrations are in honor of loved ones who have passed on. Check out the one in Houston.

halloween harvest festival
www.halloweenharvestfestival.com
A six-week festival with a haunted house and hay rides in Woodland Hills, California.

halloween & costume carnival
www.visitwesthollywood.com
Join in the largest Halloween street party in the country in West Hollywood, California.

halloween in lahaina
www.visitlahaina.com
Starts with a children's parade at this Mardi Gras of the Pacific, a Hawaiian event for all ages.

> **joy, connecticut | halloween tip** Let kids see others putting on costumes, wigs, or crazy makeup. They're less likely to experience a "clown crisis" when they know it's a regular person under the getup!

ten best
thanksgiving parades

america's hometown parade

www.usathanksgiving.com

Plymouth, Massachusetts, is home to a "living history" parade with historically accurate costumes, music, and floats, plus community events.

parade spectacular

www.stamford-downtown.com

Held the Sunday before Thanksgiving, with dramatic Saturday evening balloon illumination, in Stamford, Connecticut.

macy's thanksgiving day parade

www.macys.com/campaign/parade/parade.jsp

Spectators get to Manhattan as early as 6:30 a.m. for a viewing spot between 77th and 81st Streets. Or see the Wednesday night pre-parade.

thanksgiving day parade

www.gophila.com

Philadelphia claims the oldest Thanksgiving Day parade in the country, held here since 1910.

carolinas' parade

http://carrouselparade.org

A southern tradition to welcome the start of the holiday season in Charlotte, North Carolina.

holiday lights! parade

www.gahannaevents.com

Held in Gahanna, Ohio, on the Saturday evening after Thanksgiving.

mcdonald's parade

www.chicagofestivals.org

Bundle up and sip hot cocoa at Chicago's biggest parade of the year.

america's thanksgiving parade

www.theparade.org

Arrive before the parade to see costumed runners in fun 5K and 10K races in Detroit, Mich.

h-e-b holiday parade

www.wamuparade.com

Houston hosts the best of Texas marching bands, making this an anticipated family event.

jacksonport parade

www.jacksonport.net

A lighthearted family celebration where parade watchers join in the fun in Jacksonport, Wisconsin.

[Does your family have a Thanksgiving blessing? Make one up together on your way to the parade!]

ten best
winter

christmas craft festival & gingerbread house competition
www.bostoncentral.com

Celebrated Boston chefs build amazing gingerbread houses for entry in a citywide contest.

holiday train show
www.nybg.org

See famous New York landmarks in a great train layout at the New York Botanical Garden. It's a wonderful Bronx destination and an annual favorite for visiting families.

manhattan shop windows
www.iloveny.com

In December, downtown window displays heighten holiday anticipation in New York, New York.

neighborhood light display
www.christmasstreet.com

Amazing cooperative lighting effort by 34th Street rowhouse residents in Baltimore, Maryland.

national gingerbread house competition
www.romanticasheville.com

With more than 300 entries, it's one of the largest cookie architecture events in the nation, in Asheville, N.C.

festival of lights
www.ccprc.com

At James Island County Park in Charleston, South Carolina, indoor and outdoor light exhibits are on display from mid-November to early January.

ice sculpting
www.cincyzoo.org

The Cincinnati Zoo's annual Festival of Lights includes demonstrations of ice sculptures created with power saws. An Ohio favorite.

highland park carriage rides
www.visitdallas.com

See a beautiful high-profile shopping district and a giant pecan tree all lit up for the holidays, in Dallas, Texas.

model train festival
www.washingtonhistory.org

Beautiful train displays are a winter highlight at the Washington State History Museum in Tacoma, Washington.

holiday lights train
www.roaringcamp.com

This train chugs through holiday displays in a Fulton, California, giant redwood forest. It's part of a wonderful winter lights festival here.

ten best
winter solstice

winterlight

www.mos.org

Look up! A really popular Museum of Science Planetarium program explores the stars and symbols of the solstice night sky in Boston, Massachusetts.

chanukah/winter solstice

www.telshemesh.org

In New York City, a unique celebration of light, storytelling, and cultural sharing combine the traditions of Chanukah and the coming of winter.

new york revels

www.nyrevels.org

Join in a real once-a-year celebration of international music and dance in honor of the returning sun. New York City locations vary each year.

helicon concert

www.kenkolodner.com

Beautiful performance tradition with compositions featuring the hammered dulcimer, in Baltimore, Maryland.

winter solstice festival

www.whatsonwhen.com

There is less than four hours of sunlight in Fairbanks, Alaska, on December 21. Folks here know how to celebrate the solstice.

red butte garden

www.redbuttegarden.org

Crafts and music at the University of Utah official gardens in Salt Lake City, Utah.

winter solstice concert

www.stmarkscathedral-ut.org

This free concert is an annual tradition for families in Salt Lake City, Utah.

children's day

www.boulder.shambhala.org

A children's blessing day coincides with the winter solstice at this meditation center in Boulder, Colo.

muir woods winter solstice

www.nps.gov/muwo

Giant redwoods are aglow with luminaria on the longest night of the year in Mill Valley, California.

winter solstice festival

www.downtownfairbanks.com

The folks here are ready to celebrate the return of daylight in Fairbanks, Alaska.

Since ancient times, people have gathered on the shortest days for warmth and kinship.

ten best
christmas

advent wreath making

www.cccambridge.org

Make your own with fresh greens at Christ Church in Cambridge, Massachusetts.

st. patrick's cathedral

www.saintpatrickscathedral.org

Try the lovely Christmas day celebration at 1:00 p.m. in New York, New York.

washington national cathedral

www.cathedral.org

Children's concerts, traditional music, and caroling are all on the schedule here in the nation's capital. Check the website.

las posadas

www.missionsanjose.org

A traditional nine-evening Mexican Christmas procession led by children in San Jose, California. Celebrate the holiday season with song.

lighting the living tree

www.cape-fear.nc.us

Through December, see the lights on an ancient live oak in Wilmington, North Carolina. It's billed as the largest Christmas tree in the world.

crèche exhibit

http://udnativity.org

In Ohio, the University of Dayton has an annual display of more than 1,300 nativity scenes.

handel's messiah singalong

www.messiahsingalong.org

All are welcome to St. John's Episcopal Church in Boulder, Colorado. Everyone knows the words to the Alleluia Chorus, but songsheets are provided.

christmas at the palace

www.palaceofthegovernors.org

A one-evening celebration of Hispanic, European, and Native American holiday traditions in Santa Fe, N.M.

living christmas tree

www.knoxtree.org

In Knoxville, Tennessee, singers stand in a large tree and accompany a nativity play.

drive-through nativity pageant

www.fcc-connection.com

See eight live Christmas scenes from the comfort of your car in Huntington Beach, California.

"
amy, virginia | caroling We do our caroling in the car. We sing together on our way to school, church, and yes, Grandmother's house.

ten best
chanukah

community theater
www.sabesjcc.org
Near Minneapolis, Minnesota, a radiant holiday show is a December highlight.

world's largest menorah
www.iloveny.com
See a 32-foot menorah being lit from a cherry-picker truck in New York City.

jewish film festival
www.wjff.org
Wonderful for teens—an early December festival of movies with Jewish themes in Washington, D.C.

national menorah lighting
www.nationalmenorah.org
See a giant menorah illuminated in front of the White House in Washington, D.C.

klezmer concert
www.jewishmuseum.com
A high-spirited evening of traditional klezmer music—great for kids—in Miami Beach, Florida.

chanukah bowl
www.jewishinstlouis.org
An evening of bowling, latkes, and the lighting of a menorah in St. Louis, Missouri.

candle making and olive press
www.chanukahinhouston.com
Visitors are welcome to hand-dip menorah candles and press olives for oil in Houston, Texas.

chanukah on the river
www.chabadsa.com
A family evening out, with a lively riverboat cruise including a magic show and menorah illumination, in San Antonio, Texas.

chanukah on ice
www.thechabadhouse.com
An evening of free ice-skating, traditional Jewish music, and a menorah carved from ice in Westminster, Colorado.

contemporary jewish museum
www.thecjm.org
This is only museum in the city that's open on Christmas Day, even when Chanukah falls on December 25, in San Francisco, California.

[An eight-day celebration on the 25th day of Kislev, this ancient Jewish celebration commemorates a biblical battle and a miraculous oil lamp.]

ten best
kwanzaa

new england storytelling
www.afroammuseum.org
The Museum of African American History has art and storytelling events in Boston, Massachusetts.

capital city celebration
www.danceplace.org
Dance Place is a festive gathering location for this family celebration located in Washington, D.C.

kwanzaa craft workshop
http://oha.alexandriava.gov/bhrc/
Before and during Kwanzaa, events are hosted by the Black History Museum in Alexandria, Virginia. Make *zawadi,* traditional Kwanzaa gifts.

carolina illumination
www.hayti.org
Evening candle lighting for families and friends for the first six nights at the beautiful Hayti Heritage Center in Durham, North Carolina.

cary kwanzaa celebration
www.townofcary.org
A children's village is a central feature, along with performances and workshops, in Cary, N.C.

celebrate kwanzaa
www.shape.org
The active S.H.A.P.E. community center hosts Kwanzaa family activities in Houston, Texas.

christmas/ kwanzaa expo
www.phoenixblackmba.org
A one-day event honoring traditions of two cultural celebrations in Phoenix, Arizona.

winterfest
www.seattlecenter.com
Kwanzaa celebrations are part of the multicultural fun in Seattle, Washington.

kwanzaa gift show
www.kwanzaagiftshow.com
This African-American holiday crafts event in Oakland, California, is free for kids.

kwanzaa celebration
www.worldbeatcenter.org
The World Beat Center in San Diego, California, preserves African and indigenous culture.

[
Kwanzaa means "first fruit" in Swahili. It's an African-American celebration of heritage and hope.
]

ten best
eid-al-fitr

open mosque days

www.shuracouncil.org

Once a year in southern California, select mosques are open to visitors to learn more about Islamic culture.

empire state building

www.esbnyc.com/tourism/tourism_lightingschedule.cfm

See New York's iconic Empire State Building lighted green for Eid-al-Fitr.

mall of america

www.mallofamerica.com

After a month of fasting, many Muslim families in the Twin Cities unofficially converge at one of the world's largest shopping malls.

eid in the nation's capital

www.dceid.org

Come for rides, games, bazaar, and food, all in the Convention Center in Washington, D.C.

islamic treasures

www.asia.si.edu

View Islamic art at the Freer Gallery of Art and

A fast ends with feasting: depending on the lunar calendar, Eid-al-Fitr occurs in different seasons.

the Arthur M. Sackler Gallery in Washington, D.C.

north carolina eid

www.nceidfestival.org

An American holiday with music, dance, and food in Cary, N.C.

international museum of muslim cultures

www.muslimmuseum.org

In Jackson, Mississippi, see exhibits of international textiles, arts, and ancient texts. A fascinating way for families to explore the diversity of Muslim culture and traditions.

islamic center of america

www.icofa.com

This Dearborn, Michigan, mosque and education center is open to the public for tours.

festive eid menu

www.andalous.com

Andalous Restaurant in Chicago serves a festive Moroccan holiday menu in honor of Eid-al-Fitr.

muslim family days

www.icna.org

Annual gathering near the time of Eid-al-Fitr, held recently at large theme parks across the country.

[Eid-al-Fitr begins at the sighting of the new moon after Ramadan. Eid-al-Adha falls about ten weeks later.]

ten best
new year

first night boston

www.firstnight.org

A citywide celebration planned especially for families in Boston, Massachusetts.

new year's eve ball

www.timessquarenyc.org

Join in the countdown as the ball drops in Times Square in New York, New York.

first night seaside heights

www.seasideheightstourism.com

Boardwalk attractions stay open to ring in the new year in Seaside Heights, New Jersey.

mummers parade

http://mummers.com

Inspired by the ancient Druid practice of noise-making to drive away spirits in Philadelphia.

Philadelphia's 2008 Mummers Parade

new year's parade

www.comericabankparade.com

It's the city's official "welcome" event before the Cotton Bowl football game in Dallas, Texas.

east meets west

http://goldwest.visitmt.com

Butte, Montana's parade dragon was a gift from the people of Taipei.

provo first night

www.provo.org

Teen dance contests, music, food, and revelry all around the downtown area in Provo, Utah.

chinese new year festival

www.sanfranciscochinatown.com

Be there for the night of the illuminated parade in January or February in San Francisco, California. The date depends on phases of the moon.

tournament of roses parade

www.tournamentofroses.com

You've seen it on TV—now be there in person in Pasadena, California.

first night st. petersburg

www.firstnightstpete.com

A great family celebration topped off with waterfront fireworks in St. Petersburg, Florida.

ten best
martin luther king day

day of service
www.mlkday.gov
This website features volunteer opportunities for a day of service in all 50 states.

lincoln memorial
www.mlkmemorial.org
Visit the site of the famous "I have a dream" speech in Washington, D.C.

king memorial gardens
www.king-raleigh.org
Highly regarded multicultural events are held year-round in Raleigh, North Carolina.

mlk festival in the park
www.sarasotagov.com
Mid-January weekend festival—great food, and great weather, too, in Sarasota, Florida.

museum of racist memorabilia
www.ferris.edu/jimcrow
Ferris State University's exhibit has great early-January events in Big Rapids, Michigan.

mlk dream classic
www.mlkdreamclassic.org
A high school basketball and drumline competition

Martin Luther King Jr. was born on January 15, 1929.

in January in Chicago, Illinois.

mlk wonderweekend
www.cmhouston.org
Start with hands-on activities at the Children's Museum of Houston in Houston, Texas.

rodeo of champions
www.billpickettrodeo.com
A reknowned rodeo explores how black cowboys and cowgirls influenced the American West, in Denver, Colorado.

yerba buena gardens
www.yerbabuenagardens.com
Visit this powerful waterfall memorial inscribed with King's words, a place of reflection and inspiration in San Francisco, California.

kingdom day parade
www.lacity.org
A two-mile parade that is said to draw more than a million people is one of the nation's biggest commemorative events, in Los Angeles, California.

Martin Luther King, Jr., gave voice to America's civil rights movement beginning in the middle of the 20th century.

ten best
st. patrick's day

st. patrick's day parade
www.bostoncentral.com
In South Boston, going strong for more than a hundred years.

irish memorial
www.irishmemorial.org
This monument at Penn's Landing honors the Irish immigrants of Philadelphia.

fun dog show
www.ballyshaners.org
A canine event the morning of the famous Old Town Parade in Alexandria, Virginia. Festivities are usually two weeks before the "real" St. Patrick's Day.

st. patrick's day mass
www.irishatlanta.com
Visit Christ the King Cathedral to mark the start of the city's weekend festivities in Atlanta, Georgia.

st. patrick's day parade
www.clevelandirishparade.org
This high-spirited event is one of the first signs of spring in Cleveland, Ohio.

[
America's first St. Patrick's Day parade was held in New York in 1762 when Irish militiamen marched to breakfast singing traditional songs.
]

chicago river
www.greenchicagoriver.com
The river turns green and city bridges are great vantage points in Chicago, Illinois.

irish museum
www.irishmuseum.org
Take a train to Union Station and follow the crowd to the museum and Irish cultural center on the lower level, in Kansas City, Missouri.

irish channel parade
www.irishchannelno.org
The Irish Channel neighborhood hosts its own parade and party in New Orleans, Louisiana.

world's largest shamrock
www.oneillchamber.org
A fun run and parade where a giant shamrock's painted in the road in O'Neill, Nebraska.

leprechaun race
www.keepaustinfun.com
Before the parade, see "leprechauns" compete on a tricky obstacle course in Austin, Texas.

ten best
easter

greek orthodox cathedral

www.thecathedral.goarch.org

Easter services (in Greek and English) are held on the orthodox dates for Easter Saturday and Sunday in New York, New York.

easter egg roll

www.whitehouse.gov

Traditionally held on or near the White House lawn, with egg races, in Washington, D.C.

sunrise service

www.bandshell.org

On the beach in Daytona Beach, Florida, a historic bandshell constructed of natural coquina rock is the site of an early Easter morning service.

bunny hop easter tour

www.puddinhill.com

Puddin Hill candy shop shows off its celebrity Easter eggs in Greenville, Texas.

stations of the cross

www.costilla-county.com/stationsofthecross.html

Life-size sculptures of the last moments in the life of Jesus are on a mesa in San Luis, Colorado.

arizona easter pageant

www.easterpageant.org

The Easter story performed outdoors, in English and Spanish, in Phoenix.

easter parade

www.sresproductions.com

There are also kids' rides and games, a petting zoo, pony rides, and much more in San Francisco.

glory of easter passion play

www.crystalcathedral.org

Live animals, great music, and special effects make this an Orange County Easter tradition in Garden Grove, California.

haute dog easter parade

www.hautedogs.org/easter.html

Attend a parade featuring dogs in hats, bonnets, and other costumes in Long Beach, California.

easter services

www.lakeshrine.org

Lake Shrine is a Sunset Boulevard park recognizing five principal world religions in Pacific Palisades, California.

> **molly, new york | parade** At the annual Easter Parade on 5th Avenue here in N.Y. City, everyone wears homemade bonnets and other crazy hats. Fun and festive.

ten best
rites of spring

fairy festival
www.rockportfairyfestival.com

Dress up, eat fairy cake, and take a mermaid cruise in early June in Rockport, Maine.

kinetic sculpture race
www.kineticbaltimore.com

There are witty awards at the hilarious (and serious) race of human-powered sculptures on land and in the harbor in May in Baltimore, Maryland. The prize is for arriving in the middle.

cherry blossom festival
www.nationalcherryblossomfestival.org

In mid-March see blooming trees, a gift to the United States from Tokyo, in Washington, D.C.

annual lighthouse festival
www.staugustinelighthouse.com

In mid-March climb in the lighthouse near the oldest U.S. fort, in St. Augustine, Florida.

kayak & wildlife festival
www.charlottecountyfl.com

A mid-April nature event in Port Charlotte, Florida, with kayak races and a fishing tournament.

juneteenth
www.freedomcenter.org

A lively family festival marks the June 17 signing of the Emancipation Proclamation, in Cincinnati, Ohio.

spring planting festival
www.nps.gov/biso/planyourvisit/springplanting.htm

A popular late April event at a national recreation area in Big South Fork, Kentucky and Tennessee.

azteca cinco de mayo
www.aztecadegkc.org

A family-friendly Mexican celebration around May 5 in Kansas City, Kansas. There are Cinco de Mayo events in communities all around the country.

beach kite party
www.kiteconnection.com

A beachfront event in March with professional kite flyers in Huntington Beach, California.

lei day
www.co.honolulu.hi.us/parks/programs/leiday

Make leis at the Hawaiian version of May Day, celebrated since 1928, in Honolulu, Hawaii.

> **kevin, maryland | horse race** Spring means the beginning of horse racing season. It's fun to take the kids, like my dad took me.

ten best
mother's day

duckling day parade
www.friendsofthepublicgarden.org
Kids dressed up as ducks follow the Harvard University March-ing Band in the Public Garden in Boston, Massachusetts.

5K family run & walk
www.ournewportschools.org/
mothersdaywalk.html
See mansions and Atlantic coastline at a fun Mother's Day race along scenic Ocean Drive in Newport, Rhode Island.

mother's day singalong
www.prospectpark.org
Afternoon event (with ice cream) at Leffert's His-toric House in Prospect Park in Brooklyn, N.Y.

mother's day at mount vernon
www.mountvernon.org
A day of festivity at George Washington's home, including garden walks and a guest appearance by Martha, at Mount Vernon, Virginia.

medieval times
www.medievaltimes.com
Mothers visiting with families get in free on Mother's Day in several states.

a garden symphony
www.bellingrath.org
First visit the acclaimed rose gardens, then unpack a picnic supper at the youth orchestra concert in Bellingrath Garden in Theodore, Alabama.

herb sale & tea party
www.aswp.org
Peruse wildflowers and herbs, and plan to walk the lovely trails at the Beechwood Farms Reserve in Pittsburgh, Pennsylvania.

riverboat cruise
www.chattanoogariverboat.com
Take a relaxing two-hour cruise along the Ten-nessee River, a good midday or evening option in Chattanooga, Tennessee.

art fair
www.laumeiersculpturepark.org
Held every Mother's Day weekend, with food, music, and eclectic art at a wonderful open-air museum in St. Louis, Missouri.

garden tour
www.parks.sonoma.net/burbank.html
Corsages for moms at the Luther Burbank Home and Garden in Santa Rosa, California.

ten best
summer

shakespeare in central park

www.publictheater.org

Free plays each summer—and not always Shakespeare—in New York, New York.

cowtown rodeo

www.cowtownrodeo.com

A professional rodeo with weekly shows in Pikestown, New Jersey.

twilight tattoo ceremonies

www.nps.gov/fomc

Drum event at Fort McHenry, home of the national anthem, in Baltimore, Maryland. Stay to see the lowering of the flag in the old walled fort.

pony swim & pony penning

www.chincoteague.com/pony/ponies.html

See the wild pony roundup—and bring bug spray—at Chincoteague Island, Virginia.

georgia peach festival

www.worldslargestpeachcobbler.com

Usher in summer at this late June extravaganza with music, dancing, and, of course, peaches, in Peach County, Georgia.

national blueberry festival

www.blueberryfestival.com

Come for a lively parade, live music, magic shows, and blueberry pancakes in South Haven, Michigan.

sheffield garden walk & festival

www.sheffieldfestivals.org

Tour neighborhood gardens and explore fun activities for children at the kids' corner in Chicago, Illinois.

renaissance festival

www.renaissancefest.com

Jousting, jesters, and late summer fun at one of the country's largest Renaissance events in Shako-pee, Minnesota.

solstice phenomenon

www.phoenixpubliclibrary.org

The first sunlight of summer passes through skylight lenses to create the illusion of flames. It happens at Burton Barr Library only on June 21, in Phoenix, Arizona.

seafair milk carton derby

www.seafair.com

Homemade boats compete in this kickoff event at Seafair, Seattle's high-energy summer festival.

ten best
memorial day

memorial day parade

www.memorialdayparade.org

It's one of the largest Memorial Day parades in the country, in Douglaston, Queens, New York.

soldiers national cemetery

www.nps.gov/gett

Quiet observances are scheduled at the site of Lincoln's Gettysburg Address in Pennsylvania.

national memorial day choral festival

www.kennedy-center.org

Choirs from across the nation perform at the Kennedy Center in Washington, D.C.

national memorial day concert

www.pbs.org/memorialdayconcert

This free event is held on the West Lawn of the U.S. Capitol in Washington, D.C.

national memorial day parade

www.nationalmemorialdayparade.com

The parade travels along Constitution Avenue past the White House in Washington, D.C.

wreath-laying ceremony

www.arlingtoncemetery.org

This annual Memorial Day event is held at the

Tomb of the Unknowns. A concurrent event is held in Arlington National Cemetery's amphitheater.

chicago memorial event

www.centerstagechicago.com

A prelude to a very popular parade, held at the Eternal Flame at Daley Plaza in Chicago, Illinois.

veterans memorial day tribute

www.coloradoveteransmonument.org

A parade and tribute ceremony are held near the state capitol, in Denver, Colorado.

memorial day parade

www.canogaparkmemorialdayparade.com

Equestrians, fun marching units, and classic cars make this a parade to remember in Canoga Park, California.

pearl harbor memorial

www.nps.gov/usar

At the site of the U.S.S. *Arizona*, an annual commemoration event honors veterans and victims of World War II in Honolulu, Hawaii.

[A day to recognize Americans who died in the service of the nation.]

ten best
sand castle competitions

master sand sculpting
www.hamptonbeach.org
A week of serious professional construction in June in Hampton Beach, New Hampshire.

sand castle competition
www.ci.mashpee.ma.us
Children and parents only at this South Cape Beach event in Mashpee, Massachusetts.

annual contest
www.nantucket.plumtv.com
On Jetties Beach, in Nantucket, Mass., in August, families vie to have the best-named creation.

new jersey sand castle contest
www.njsandcastle.com
A great July contest for kids at the Jersey Shore in Belmar, New Jersey.

sandsculpting championship
www.neptunefestival.com
Held during the Neptune Festival in September in Virginia Beach, Virginia.

aia sand castle
www.aiasandcastle.com
Professional architects gather in early June each year for a very serious competition of sand construction and design. Kids can look and vote, but not build. Winners claim the Golden Bucket award.

sandfest
www.texassandfest.com
In April on Mustang Island in Port Aransas, Texas, you'll enjoy this sand sculpture festival.

sandsations
www.funbeach.com
Family castle building combine with the Sand Flea Pet Parade, in July in Long Beach, Washington.

sand castle day
www.sandcastleday.bravehost.com
Held in June, with highly artistic entries from "masters." Kids are "sand fleas" in Cannon Beach, Ore.

u.s. open
www.usopensandcastle.com
Children can participate, then check out the work of the professionals, in Imperial Beach, California.

> ## aidan, massachusetts | contest
> We make a row of castles. The winner is last to wash away. Last summer another family thought it looked like so much fun that they joined the contest, too.

ten best
father's day

amusement park
www.canobie.com

With kids, dads get free admission at Canobie Lake Park in Salem, N.H.

catch in the park
www.redsox.com

Post-game on Father's Day (depending on the home schedule) in Boston, the Red Sox invite dads and kids onto Fenway field to toss around soft baseballs.

saratoga automobile museum
www.saratogaautomuseum.org

There's free admission for dads on Father's Day. Come see historic cars in Saratoga Springs, New York. Pretend you're choosing one to take home.

pig roast
www.foursisterswinery.com

A working vineyard in Belvidere, New Jersey, is the site of an annual Father's Day afternoon party, featuring live music and a pit-roasted suckling pig. Wine cellar tours are also available.

fishing derby
www.buckscounty.org/departments/parksandrecreation

Kids get to fish and dads can help at this annual Father's Day event in Doylestown, Pennsylvania.

hershey gardens
www.hersheygardens.com

Dad's ticket is free on Father's Day. Located in Hershey, Pa., the Children's Garden is worth a visit, too.

car show
www.libciviccenter.org

Vintage and custom Corvettes are on display at a local auto dealership in Libertyville, Illinois.

r/c air show
www.flintaerorcclub.com

Radio control airplane hobbyists race and fly their prize models. It's a Flint, Michigan, Father's Day tradition hosted by the local hobby club.

santa fe southern railway
www.sfsr.com

Ride the *Atchison Topeka & Santa Fe* train on its historic route into Lamy, New Mexico, and stop for a special Father's Day barbecue lunch. It's a leisurely 120-mile round-trip from Santa Fe.

surf & beach party
www.surfclubs.org

Combined with the annual Menehune Surf Classic, it's billed as the World's Largest Father's Day Celebration with father/son and father/daughter events. Held at Moonlight Beach in Encinitas, California.

ten best
fireworks

east river
http://nycgo.com

A good place to watch is from South Street Seaport; the show synchronizes with music on 1010 WINS radio in New York, New York.

u.s. capitol lawn
www.kennedy-center.org

Fireworks are scheduled together with a free annual concert, A Capitol Fourth, in Washington, D.C.

mount vernon
www.mountvernon.org

From George Washington's home, see fireworks reflected in the Potomac River in Alexandria, Va.

duke of gloucester street
www.history.org

Fireworks illuminate cobblestone streets and the Governor's Palace in Williamsburg, Virginia.

snowshoe mountain
www.snowshoemtn.com

Ski resort turned holiday festival July 2–6, with fireworks on the 4th in Snowshoe Mountain, W. Va.

stone mountain park
www.stonemountainpark.com

Laser shows with fireworks set against the mountain backdrop on July 3, 4, and 5 in Atlanta, Georgia.

over the arch
www.stlouisriverfront.hyatt.com

Book a room at the Riverfront Hyatt in St. Louis, Missouri, and ask for a fireworks view. Tune in to local radio for musical accompaniment.

mount rushmore
www.nps.gov/moru

See fireworks on July 3, and illumination of the presidential sculpture on July 4, in Keystone, S.D.

gas works park
www.wamufamily4th.org

An all-day enormous event culminating in awesome fireworks set to popular music in Seattle, Wash.

port of san diego
www.marriott.com

From a bay-facing room at Marriott Hotel & Marina, you can see most of the California city's display.

"laurie, california | fireworks We took our niece to see fireworks when she was two, and the sound was a little too much for her. The next time we made a trip to see fireworks, she was eight years old and the explosions were suddenly so exciting, not scary!

ten best
state fairs

vermont state fair
www.vermontstatefair.net

A great family value, with extensive entertainment (opening Labor Day weekend), in Rutland, Vermont.

the big e
www.thebige.com

Begining in mid-September, the Eastern States Exposition is the largest fair in the Northeast, in West Springfield, Massachusetts.

state fair of virginia
www.statefairva.org

Late September event held at the Richmond Raceway Complex in Richmond, Virginia.

ohio state fair
www.ohiostatefair.com

Don't miss the wonderful butter cows and other dairy sculptures. This famous midsummer (early August) fair in Columbus, Ohio, features a Saturday spelling bee.

iowa state fair
www.iowastatefair.com

This classic destination in Des Moines, Iowa, was the inspiration for the novel and 1962 film *State Fair*.

minnesota state fair
www.mnstatefair.org

In August, with daily podcast from Minnesota Public Radio in St. Paul, Minn.

state fair of texas
www.bigtex.com

A September/October fair with a famous mascot. Big Tex is a 52-foot cowboy statue in Fair Park, Texas.

wyoming state fair & rodeo
www.wystatefair.com

Experience rodeo culture—early August each year in Douglas, Wyoming.

oregon state fair
www.oregonstatefair.org

Cool fair: Enter the watermelon seed spitting or duct tape contest in Salem, Oregon.

california state fair
www.bigfun.org

A state tradition since 1853, with horse racing and great shows, in Sacramento.

[Originally an agricultural gathering, the annual fair is a yearly celebration of a state's unique resources, history, and (of course) food and music.]

international travel

For years, the family has talked about a once-in-a-lifetime trip to Egypt's Pyramids of Giza, China's Great Wall, Brazil's Sugarloaf Mountain, or Zambia's Victoria Falls. Then the opportunity to go arises, and suddenly preparation brings a plethora of questions:

What's the best age for global travel with little children? It all depends on a parent's appetite for adventure . . . and a child's developing capacity to adjust to new places and people.

- What's the difference between passport and a visa?
- Where can one exchange U.S. dollars for Zambian kwacha or Chinese yuan?
- What's a value added tax?
- Why are shots required for entry?
- Can you pay a country's exit fee with a credit card?

Such questions can bog down a trip before even venturing to an airport's international terminal. That's why when traveling abroad—particularly with young children—it pays to plan. Research a country. Learn about its history, its culture, its people, and its expectations of those who visit.

Traveling abroad is a valuable learning experience, offering families an opportunity to probe the world beyond America's shores, to understand a bit more about how others live, and to share the commonalities and appreciate and enjoy the many differences. It is also a chance to see some of the world's great natural and human-made wonders. Be amazed together by more than 800 cheeses made in France . . . to the rain forests of Costa Rica . . . to the canals of Amsterdam and the Great Barrier Reef of Australia.

These lists comprise only basic information about visiting the continental expanses beyond North America. Think of them as an aerial view of some trips you'll eventually take after you begin to scratch the surface of the opportunities that await—here, there, and everywhere.

More than any generation that's gone before, our children are part of an ever-changing global family. Together, learn all you can about the world's ever-closer people, places, histories, and resources. Eventually, inevitably, and fortunately, they make up the landscapes of our families' futures.

chapter five
see the world

I believe in freedom, creativity, and conversation.
And I believe that tourism is the handmaiden of them all.
—Lars-Eric Lindblad, founder, Lindblad Travel

mexico: yucatán peninsula

Its history stretches back to ancient civilizations, before the arrival of Europeans to modern-day Mexico. Many cultures and customs endure, along with a growing tourism industry.

mayan riviera

www.visitmexico.com

The area south of Cancún International Airport is one of the world's most fascinating destination spots, with tropical beaches, ancient ruins, and the Great Mayan Reef—the largest coral reef in the Western Hemisphere.

chichen itza

http://whc.unesco.org/en/list/483

One of the most visited Mayan ruins, about 125 miles from Cancún. It features step pyramids, temples, and buildings with elaborate carvings. El Castillo is the famous pyramid here. Keep an eye out for rainbows and other amazing effects of sunlight and shadow at this ancient pilgrimage site.

The seven countries of Central America are part of the North American continent. South America is home to 14 nations.

isla holbox

www.holboxisland.com

The island west of Cancún is known for watching one of the ocean's largest fish, the whale shark, a filter feeder with a mouth that measures up to nearly five feet.

ek balam

www.xaac.com/playacar/ekbalam.htm

This ancient Mayan city has more than three dozen structures with elaborate carvings and inscriptions and a pyramid 100 feet high and more than 500 feet long. It is an active archaeological site, with evidence of human civilization dating back to 100 B.C. About three hours from Cancún.

xcaret

www.xcaret.com

A Mayan theme park that is a youngster's paradise. It includes a reenactment of a traditional Mayan ballcourt game, traditional dance and music, and a water theme park. Just south of Playa del Carmen.

> **michelle, virginia | memory** When my twin sister and I were small, we flew with our parents from Brazil to Colombia. We were escorted to the cockpit to meet the pilot, since it was considered good luck to have twins aboard. We felt very special.

costa rica

This Central American nation is among the few places with active volcanoes, great surf, and an endless variety of wildlife (more than 1,200 species of butterflies alone).

arenal volcano national park

www.arenal.net/arenal_volcano_national_park.htm

Just north of the Tilarán Mountains, Arenal is one of the world's most active volcanoes. Its flowing lava makes for spectacular viewing. See it at night while bathing in a naturally heated hot spring.

la paz waterfall gardens park

www.waterfallgardens.com/lapaz-waterfall gardenspark.html

Rain forests, exotic birds, abundant flowers: The park features a butterfly haven with more than 20 species and an enclosed frog exhibit. About 20 miles from the San José airport.

zapote bullfight

www.costaricabureau .com

First thing's first: No bulls are harmed. It is actually more like Spain's Running of the Bulls, as men run out into a ring to engage the bull in a high-energy chase. This is one of many carnival-style events in Zapote's annual festival week, just after Christmas in San José.

brazil: rio de janeiro

Rio is a world center for culture, history, music, art, sports, and architecture. Portuguese is the official language.

sugarloaf mountain

www.bondinho.com.br

Cable cars travel up this 1,300-foot coastal mountain. Climbers scale the vast rock, delighting crowds with their dexterity. Option: View the mountain from the ancient Fort Santa Cruz da Barra at the entrance of the Bay of Guanabara.

tijuca national park

www.braziltour.com

In addition to serving as the area's natural air conditioner, the park is home to 30 waterfalls, 300 plant species, and 100 animal species.

christ the redeemer

www.corcovado.com.br

The 130-foot-tall statue of Jesus with outstretched arms atop Corcovado mountain is known as one of the new seven wonders of the world.

maracana stadium

www.braziltour.com

Brazil is a hub of international soccer, and Maracana Stadium is the Yankee Stadium of the nation. To get a sense of the passion that soccer brings out in the people, watching a game here is a must.

see the world
latin america

belize

This Central American nation is home to the world's second longest coral reef system, lush rain forests, and ancient Mayan ruins—some restored and some claimed by jungle overgrowth. Its hotels and tourism infrastructure make it a popular destination for families.

hol chan marine reserve

www.holchanbelize.org

From San Pedro you can ride a charter boat out to Hol Chan for a day of snorkeling, swimming, or scuba diving (a basic boat ticket costs less than a movie and popcorn in the United States). Shark Alley is here, known for the nurse sharks and rays that gather to be hand fed by guides and visitors.

monkey river float trip

www.belize-vacation.com/belize/monkey-river.htm

From Placencia, journey along the Monkey River to a jungle hiking trail. Howler monkeys are known to populate the trees here. On the quiet float trip you're likely to spot manatees, dolphins, and toucans in and around the mangrove-lined waterway.

waterfall zipline

www.hotelvistagolfo.com

This mountainside hotel in Tajo Alto offers horseback riding and zipline rides over eleven waterfalls in its "adventure park." Zipline rides are available for visitors as well as hotel guests.

beach bonfire

Check with hotels: many will help you charter a fishing boat, then arrange an evening bonfire on the beach to cook your catch. Sometimes fishing guides offer special advice about preparing fish for meals.

cockscomb basin

www.belizeaudubon.org

With high rainfall and density of oxygen-producing plant life, rain forests are known as our planet's "air conditioners." This wildlife sanctuary near Maya Center is also a jaguar preserve, home to five species of wild cats: jaguar, puma, margay, jaguarundi, and ocelot. Short self-guided trails are open to visitors; some longer hikes require permits and experienced guides.

ecuador: quito

This mountainous country is on the Pacific coast of South America, and it captures the imagination of travelers at any age. It's home to the Galápagos Islands, the Cotopaxi active volcano, and the planet's most active bird-watching sites. Plan to stay a while!

stand on the equator

In Quito, you can visit two different sites to mark this city's location on the Equator. At high noon here, you're closer to the sun than at any other point on Earth. Mitad del Mundo is a more historic site, though the Intinan Solar Museum is the more geographically correct location. Pick your spot and stand with one foot in each hemisphere.

galápagos expedition

www.nationalgeographicexpeditions.com

Endemic: a species found nowhere else on Earth. In the Galápagos, 9,796 of the reptiles are endemic—just the beginning of a long list of truly unique life forms and landscape features. Here is where Darwin began to form the idea of evolution. Lindblad Expeditions in partnership with National Geographic offers guided naturalists' visits, with weeklong explorations of the terrain and seascapes of this legendary place. Expeditions are scheduled year-round aboard ships equipped with wetsuits and snorkel gear and staffed by teams of experienced naturalists.

argentina: tierra del fuego

"The end of the world" is the southernmost tip of Argentina, and South America ends here. It borders Chile near Ushuaia, the southernmost city in the world.

tierra del fuego

www.patagonia-argentina.com

This national park has great self-guided trails, exhibits about the native people of the region, and guided tours for visitors. It's a beautiful place where forests and mountains meet the ocean, with breathtaking landscapes in every direction.

the beagle channel

Here is the place where the Atlantic and Pacific Oceans meet, named for the ship that first carried Darwin to the Galápagos. It's in Ushuaia, right on the border between Argentina and Chile.

the end of the world train

www.trendelfindelmundo.com.ar

Ushuaia was once the end of the line for prisoners who helped to build the station here. Today, it's a compelling destination for explorers (and railway fanatics) of all ages. The authentic and historic trains travel every day to Tierra Del Fuego National Park. The region offers beach fun and swimming in December and skiing in July!

canada

quebec: montreal

Montreal is known for its French influence and people fiercely passionate about the city's ties to the European nation (French is the city's official language).

old montreal

www.vieux.montreal.qc.ca/eng/accueila.htm

One of the oldest urban places in North America, the once-walled-in area is home to narrow cobblestone streets and breathtaking architecture.

parc jean drapeau

www.parcjeandrapeau.com

The site of the 1967 World's Fair, the grounds are a summer haven for outdoor music on Sundays as well as for bicycle rides around the Circuit Gilles Villeneuve race track on Île Notre-Dame. It's on the St. Lawrence River, with a beautiful wetlands trail and dragon boats.

> Notice the tagline on Quebec license plates: *Je me souviens.* The English translation is "I remember." It's a reference to the province's historic loyalty to French language and customs.

See the world without crossing an ocean. Passports are needed for travel to Canada and reentry to the U.S.

montreal international fireworks competition

www.internationaldesfeuxloto-quebec.com/en

Held in La Ronde amusement park, the festival features fireworks displays accompanied by orchestral music.

mount royal

www.montreal.com/parks/mtroyal.html

A quality stop for those who enjoy the urban outdoors. The park sits above downtown and offers picturesque views of the city. It's a place for cycling down scenic paths in the summer and skiing, sledding, and ice-skating in the winter.

the just for laughs festival

www.hahaha.com

One of the world's largest comedy festivals, Just for Laughs features 2,000 performers and 1,300 free outdoor shows, as well as street entertainers and stand-up comedians.

the montreal biodome

www2.ville.montreal.qc.ca

Four natural environments of both North and South America: a tropical forest, a Laurentian forest, a marine ecosystem, and Antarctic climates.

ontario: toronto

Toronto is less than two hours from Buffalo, New York, with a uniqueness and charm that can only be found across the border.

the cn tower

www.cntower.ca

It's the world's tallest freestanding structure, visible from virtually everywhere in the city. It includes a glass-floor observation deck.

black creek pioneer village

www.blackcreek.ca

This 19th-century village is a living history site filled with ducks, horses, sheep, and costumed actors portraying villagers of the period.

bata shoe museum

www.batashoemuseum.ca

The four-story structure features hundreds of pairs of shoes from all over the world, conveying changing trends in the fashion industry.

hockey hall of fame

www.hhof.com

Hockey is Canada's pastime, so this is a fitting place for the sport's hall to honor the game's legends.

british columbia: vancouver

This seaport city set before a mountainous backdrop regularly ranks as one of the cleanest cities in the world.

hsbc celebration of light

www.celebration-of-light.com

The largest fireworks competition in the world, with four nights of displays in July and August.

kids' market

www.kidsmarket.ca

Spend a shopping, eating, and playing day at this kids' paradise located at the entrance to Granary Island. All shops are geared for children, including toys, fashion, a hair salon, and a special boutique and deli for kids and their pets. Visit at Christmastime for extra fun.

the grouse grind

www.grousemountain.com

Hike this famous trail or take a tram to the top for panoramic views of the city. See grizzly bears at the Refuge for Endangered Wildlife and lumberjack demonstrations in the summer.

> **mike, maryland | vancouver memory** Unbelievably fresh food. Just-caught seafood. Vegetables and herbs from gardens just outside the restaurant. Edible flowers. Fresh-baked breads and scones. Amazing juice bar. Thick slices of toast, always buttered. White or brown bread? I miss it.

see the world
europe

england: london

London is steeped in cultural, literary, political, and social history, with centuries-old Gothic buildings, double-decker buses, and narrow streets.

shakespeare's globe theatre

www.shakespeares-globe.org

Come to the place not far from where Hamlet, Macbeth, and Romeo and Juliet came to life for the first time. This re-creation of the famous theater stands about 700 feet from the original. "Groundlings" can stand in the yard to see performances; tickets are sold on the day of show. There's also an exhibition hall here.

bbc experience

www.bbc.co.uk/tours

The nation's multimedia network is also a tourist attraction, as it offers visitors an interactive look at the media, from reading a weather forecast on TV to commenting on a football game. The two-hour tour requires reservations and is open to visitors over the age of nine.

Big Ben's minute hand is 14 feet long.

madame tussaud's & the london planetarium

www.madametussauds.com/London

The venue offers two opportunities to see stars. The first is life-size, lifelike figures of such entertainment icons as Brad Pitt and Naomi Campbell. The second is gazing at celestial objects in simulated nighttime.

big ben

www.parliament.uk

This is the famed clock tower of England's Houses of Parliament. A light just above the clock face is illuminated when Parliament is in session.

british museum

www.britishmuseum.org

More than 250 years old, the museum of United Kingdom history and culture occupies more than 500,000 square feet and has more than 12,000 items. Children can borrow a magnifying glass from the information desk.

> Europe is the most densely populated continent. That's why there is international cooperation to protect the rare and ancient fields and forests here.

france: paris

The City of Lights is widely regarded as the world's most popular when it comes to style, elegance, and artistic expression.

louvre museum

www.louvre.fr

The "Mona Lisa" draws huge crowds—as does Alexandros of Antioch's "Venus de Milo" and other works that are the most celebrated in artistic history. Start with a visit to the bookstore to pique kids' interest in the details of this remarkable place.

the eiffel tower

www.tour-eiffel.fr

Don't go to Paris without visiting one of the most recognizable structures in the world. Once the world's tallest tower at 1,063 feet, the structure offers spectacular views of the city from the observation level. It is painted in three shades to complement the color of the Paris sky. Walk to the southwest area of the Luxembourg Gardens and look for the small statue resembling the Statue of Liberty.

The Louvre's glass pyramid was added in 1989.

books | paris to the moon *by adam gopnik*

What would it be like to raise your family in Paris? Read an American writer's perspective on living and working here from 1995 to 2000.

paris music festival

www.parismusicfestival.com

Held every June 21, the street music festival is one of the most eagerly anticipated events in the country, as hundreds of musicians converge on Paris and offer free performances playing everything from jazz to hip-hop.

batobus

www.batobus.com

Nix the tour bus and hop aboard a water taxi that rides up and down the Seine River, stopping off at such locales as the Louvre and the Eiffel Tower.

carousels

www.paris.fr/portail/english/Portal.lut?page_id=8118

Among the more popular attractions for children are the jewel-like carousels, which are ideal highlights in this walking-friendly city. What's more, they are scattered throughout the city's famous parks and gardens.

bastille day celebrations

http://en.parisinfo.com/shows-exhibitions-paris/festivals-and-fun-1

The nation commemorates the storming of the Bastille on July 14, 1789, with celebrations throughout the country. For historic perspective, see *Les Miserables* (a 1998 film based on the novel by Victor Hugo) or *The Count of Monte Cristo* (2002, based on the novel by Alexandre Dumas). Catch fireworks at the Eiffel Tower.

see the world
europe

italy: rome

Ruins from the ancient Roman Empire set the stage: See the remains of massive, elaborately decorated buildings, structures, and public terraces.

Fifteen member states of the European Union use the euro as their currency. The design of paper bills reflects major architectural periods.

colosseum

www.italiantourism.com

First opened in A.D. 80, it is the most ancient of Roman monuments. Gladiators once roamed these corridors and pathways. Prepare for the visit by reading the classic comic *Asterix the Gladiator*.

circus maximus

www.italiantourism.com

"Circus" is a Latin word for a ring or racecourse. A colossal structure that held more than 200,000 people, this was the site of thrilling chariot races.

bioparco zoo

www.bioparco.it

Visitors can interact with the animals: Picnic while feeding ducks, see elephants up close. The zoo is a quality educational experience, offering knowledge on everything from tortoises to stray cats.

germany: berlin

It was known best for its wall—a solid barrier between the socialist and democratic regions of historic Berlin. The landmark 1989 collapse of the socialist regime made the area a new world symbol for freedom as the wall came tumbling down.

fez-berlin

www.fez-berlin.de

It's something like an artsy YMCA, a metro center where families flock for theater, music, and sports activities. Come for puppet shows, live theater, and a children's museum.

berlin wall & checkpoint charlie

www.mauermuseum.de

Learn about the history of the wall that separated East and West Germany until 1989 and the notorious gateway, Checkpoint Charlie.

sachenhausen concentration camp memorial

www.germany-tourism.de

Learn about the darkest moments in modern world history, at the site of a primary concentration camp of 20th-century Nazi Germany.

europa center

www.europa-center-berlin.de

The high-rise building complex features a shopping center and panoramic viewing of the city on the 20th floor. See the "Clock of Flowing Time" with moving vials of liquid that illustrate the passage of seconds, minutes, and hours.

domain dahlem

www.domaene-dahlem.de/index2_e.htm

Billed as "Germany's only working farm with subway access," this open-air museum has great programs on growing, harvesting, and preparing food. See farm animals, tour the organic farm, and check out the tool collection chronicling the region's agricultural history.

zoologischer garten

www.zoo-berlin.de

Berlin's zoo and aquarium is home to a giant panda and more than 4,000 animals and insects. Its architecture is intriguing, including a colorful Chinese archway.

eating | street food

"Street food in Berlin is all about *imbisse*—[meaning] everything from sidewalk stalls that sell *currywurst* (sliced sausage smothered with curry powder and ketchup) to holes in the wall that serve Turkish *döner* kebabs (thick pita sandwiches stuffed with shaved meat, salad, and yogurt sauce)."
—Gisela Williams, *New York Times*, 11/12/2006

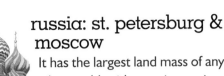

Moscow is home to St. Basil's Cathedral.

russia: st. petersburg & moscow

It has the largest land mass of any nation in the world with terrain ranging from the isolation of Siberia to the metropolis of St. Petersburg.

the hermitage

www.hermitagemuseum.org

In St. Petersburg, you can see the treasures of Russia's fabled royalty. Once the Winter Palace of Empress Elizabeth Petrova, it was expanded to house the storied international art collection of Catherine the Great. This place is the destination of a lifetime for visitors of any age.

moscow metro

www.moscow-taxi.com/sightseeing/metro.html

Chandeliers, marble columns, and colorful frescoes enliven the historic stations of Moscow's elaborate subway system. The lavish décor is a hallmark of original Communist goals of sharing the wealth of the nation in public spaces.

the kremlin and red square

www.moscow.info/red-square/index.aspx

Come to Moscow to see the streets and buildings once known as the center of Soviet policy. St. Basil's Cathedral is here, with its colorful and swirling domes and turrets, commissioned by Ivan the Terrible in the 1500s to celebrate a victory over the Mongols. The Kremlin houses a museum of Russian artifacts.

australia: melbourne

It's one of the world's largest planned cities, but don't let its rectangular shape and organized grid of angled streets fool you. It's a lively destination for fans of culture, history, and outdoor activity.

colonial tramcar restaurant

www.tramrestaurant.com.au

Dine while journeying through historic Melbourne in what is billed as the first traveling tramcar restaurant in the world: a converted 1927 tram.

surf coast

www.surfcoast.vic.gov.au

For many visitors, the Great Ocean Road starts in Torquay, winding inland toward rain forests and out again to quaint villages. This laid-back surf city is known for its friendly atmosphere and beautiful views. Take a surf lesson here.

suga

www.suga.com.au

Ever see how hard candy is made? Here's your chance. See the elaborate process around lunchtime, when free samples are doled out. At the Royal Arcade location, chocolate is made next door at Koko Black.

Australia and New Zealand are part of the Oceania region. New Guinea and hundreds of small South Pacific islands are also part of this geographic family.

federation square

www.federationsquare.com.au

This cultural hub and public meeting ground is known for such cultural institutions as the Australian Center for the Moving Image.

scienceworks and planetarium

www.museumvictoria.com.au

A family delight that works all five senses: gadgets to push, pull, and spin, live demonstrations, tours, and activities. Don't miss the Lightning Room, with the giant Tesla coil, capable of producing two million volts of electricity.

captain cook's cottage

www.melbourne.vic.gov

Located in the famous Fitzroy Garden, this was Capt. James Cook's 18th-century family cottage, moved here (brick by brick) from England in 1834. It commemorates Cook's "discovery" of Australia in 1770.

royal arcade

www.royalarcade.com.au/home.htm

Built in 1870s, it is Melbourne's oldest shopping mall. Come for Victorian architecture and great shops.

australia: sydney

Remember that it is summer here when it's winter in the Northern Hemisphere. Come to Sydney for sunny Christmas vacations on the beach.

oceanworld

www.oceanworld.com.au

Not as large and imposing as the Sydney Aquarium, it's an enjoyable experience for children, featuring daily shark-feeding sessions and a delightful seal show.

bondi beach

www.bondivillage.com

One of the most accessible beaches in the area and one of the most popular in the hemisphere. The beach draws tourists from as far away as Japan and the United Kingdom. For those avoiding waves, the beach features enclosed swimming baths.

sydney harbor bridge

www.sydney.com.au

One of the most popular pastimes is to climb one of Australia's most famous landmarks, particularly at sunset, to watch the city's illuminated skyline.

It took 14 years to build the Sydney Opera House.

new zealand: auckland

Volcanoes, lagoons, harbors, bridges, and skyscrapers: That's Auckland, home of lush parks, bustling urban landscape, and inviting shores.

mount eden

www.aucklandnz.com

The dormant volcano is the highest point in the area. Climb to its summit to see panoramic views of the city's skyline.

bay of islands

www.bay-of-islands.nz.com

One of the most popular holiday sites in the country, the bay lures with fishing, diving, sailing, and other water-sport opportunities.

the auckland domain

www.aucklandcity.govt.nz/whatson/places/parks/domain.asp

An expansive park in the center of the city that's loaded with gardens, playing fields, and glass houses with tropical plants. It's kind of like Central Park, Kiwi-style.

" john, virginia | **penguins** In New Zealand, the yellow-eyed penguin reserve on the Otaga Peninsula was unforgettable. Got to see penguins come home at sunset, watching from a beach bunker.

see the world
africa

south africa: cape town

When South Africa ended generations of violent rule with its first democratic elections in 1994, it assumed a rightful reputation as a nation of unparalleled beauty and wonder. Cape Town is its crown jewel, a mountainous, seaside metropolis with spectacular landscapes.

table mountain

www.sanparks.org/parks/table_mountain

A breathtaking sight: With two cone-shaped peaks at each end of its flat top, the 3,563-foot mountain resembles a table with two chairs. When clouds drift over, it appears that the "table" is draped with a cloth. See it from any spot in Cape Town.

the cango ostrich farms

www.tourismcapetown.co.za

See the tall, winged creatures up close and personal, from watching the eggs and chicks in

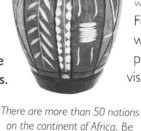

There are more than 50 nations on the continent of Africa. Be prepared: A family's visit here will be a life-changing experience.

incubators to feeding the birds by hand to riding one.

robben island

www.robben-island.org.za

For nearly 400 years this island outpost was one of the world's most notorious prisons. Today it is a museum, a mecca for visitors who come to see the prison cell of Nobel Laureate Nelson Mandela, the nation's first democratically elected president.

khayelitsha township

A sprawling settlement between Cape Town's airport and the downtown area. It's filled with outdoor markets that sell one-of-a-kind, handmade items.

two oceans aquarium

www.aquarium.co.za

At the southern tip of the continent where the Atlantic and Indian Oceans meet, this aquarium is home to more than 3,000 living sea animals.

> **joe, virginia | fast food** Fish and chips are to South Africa what hamburgers are here. The most popular place for fish and chips in Cape Town is called Snoekies, in Hout Bay. They serve a naturally flavorful fish called king clip. Most folks eat the fish and chips with vinegar; ketchup would be improbable to find.

south africa: kalahari

National parks provide introductions to the spectacular wilderness of this sub-Saharan desert, grassland, and river landscape. Guides and tours are a family's best bets for exploring the region's rich geological and archaeological environments.

kgalagadi transfrontier park

www.sanparks.org/parks/kgalagadi

One of the largest conservation spaces in the world, this wildlife area comprises Kalahari Gemsbok National Park (South Africa) and Gemsbok National Park (Botswana)—a total of nearly nine million acres. Safaris will seek out views of famous black-maned lions, Gemsbok antelope, and popular meerkats. The park is large enough for animals to follow natural migration routes here. Look forward to seeing the nests of sociable weavers. These nests are the largest in the world, and some are said to be more than a hundred years old.

augrabies falls national park

www.sanparks.org/parks/augrabies

The black rhino has recently been reintroduced to the wilds of this park after an absence of more than a hundred years. Here, the Orange River spills 183 feet into a deep gorge, visible from several different vantage points. Look for the Cape otters in the river, and the rock hyrax that make their home in the canyons.

wonderwerk cave

www.museumsnc.co.za

Ancient rock paintings and even older tools are just a few signs of very primitive human development found in this cave, known as the oldest in the world. Tours can be arranged through the McGregor Museum, which has many other exhibits dedicated to important archaeological finds of South Africa.

spitskop dam

In summer (December–March), this is a busy destination point for birds traveling south from Europe and Asia. It's also a breeding ground for native spoonbills, egrets, and herons.

tswalu kalahari reserve

www.tswalu.com

This safari and game reserve is known for accommodating families with young children. It's a luxury resort with a spa, restaurant, and pools, but also the starting point for wonderful game drives and bush walks.

> The most widely spoken language in Africa is Arabic (150 million people), but it's limited primarily to North Africa. In sub-Saharan Africa it's Swahili (95 million), but it's mainly spoken in the eastern portion. There are 11 official languages in South Africa.

see the world
africa

tanzania: serengeti

The Serengeti region is largely composed of the Serengeti National Park, with other regions and national parks bordering all around. You'll see animals and spectacular desert and volcanic scenery at almost any time of year except for the traditionally rainy autumn months of April and May.

volcano that is now a naturally protected animal conservation site. It borders the Serengeti National Park on the north and the west, and is home to the nomadic Maasai people. Plan to hike around the mineral-laden soda lake of Empakaai crater, a gathering place for flamingos.

serengeti national park

www.serengeti.org

The world's largest concentration of lions are here, and the Serengeti is the starting point for the famous migration of hoofed animals like wildebeest and zebras. An almost unlimited number of companies host caravans and safaris in the region; check with a travel agent for outfitters who are experienced in touring with children.

ngorongoro conservation area

www.ngorongoro-crater-africa.org

The Ngorongoro Crater is about 12½ miles across, the remnant of a massive prehistoric

olduvai gorge museum

www.leakey.com

Located in the Ngorongoro Conservation Area, this small museum tells the story of important discoveries made near here, especially by the famed Leakey family of paleoanthropologists. See casts made from a trail of early hominid footprints dating back 3.6 million years.

masai mara

www.masaimara.org

The southwestern reaches of the Serengeti extend into Kenya. Here, the grasslands of this national reserve are the destination for wildebeest migrating from the Serengeti plain, which reaches a peak between July and early October. Tsavo National Park is here, home to bat-eared foxes and rare topi antelope. Year-round rainfall makes this a temperate place to visit.

morocco: marrakech

This North African nation offers an exciting, enduring glimpse into Arab culture that is both traditional and modern. One of its oldest cities, Marrakech is a busy hub of culture and trade.

djemaa el-fna

This busy urban square and marketplace in Marrakech features rows of mouthwatering foods as well as lively entertainment, including jugglers, storytellers, and snake charmers.

ourika valley
www.marrakech-cityguide.com

A lush, green valley at the foothills of the Atlas Mountains. It is a walker's paradise that includes seven waterfalls and opulent bio-aromatic gardens.

the marrakech film festival

Held between September and December, this festival showcases Arab and African cinema and brings out some of the most popular names in world entertainment. The festival honored Leonardo DiCaprio in 2007.

[More than half of all Moroccans speak at least two languages.]

egypt: alexandria & cairo

From Africa's most densely populated city (Greater Cairo, with 17 million people) to the breathtaking pyramids of Giza to the seaside city of Alexandria, a blend of ancient history and modern technology is showcased in a vibrant culture.

pyramids of giza
www.touregypt.net

These ancient monuments comprise the world's first architectural skyline, believed to have been built around the 25th century B.C. Among them: the Great Sphinx and 455-foot Great Pyramid, the only remaining member of the Seven Wonders of the Ancient World.

alexandria
www.alexandriaegypt.com

Water is important here. See Egypt's largest seaport and Fort Qaitbey, built with stone from the former Alexandria Lighthouse. It was one of the Seven Wonders of the Ancient World.

port ghalib
www.discoverportghalib.com

Located along the southern Red Sea coast, this upscale tourist venue includes a port large enough to hold a thousand yachts—as well as rolling hills, sand dunes, and underwater coral reefs. It's buoyed by 23 hotels, a golf course, and retail shops.

see the world
asia

india: delhi

Unforgettable colors, spicy smells, sights, and sounds bring to life a mix of centuries-old traditions seen in rural living and high-tech modernization.

connaught place

www.connaughtplacemall.com

The shopping center is shaped like a horse because its designers figured it would bring luck to shoppers and storekeepers. It is one of the area's most popular gathering places, with markets, stores, and theaters.

delhi cuisine

Delhi is known for spectacular street food. Try *samosas* (deep-fried potato pastries), *pakora* (vegetable fritters), or *aloo chat* (cold, spicy potato salad).

qutub complex

www.exploredelhi.com/qutub-minar/index.html

The UNESCO World Heritage site is home to historic monuments, a mosque, and a 13th-century tomb. The grounds are a nice picnic and recreation spot with an evening light-and-sound show.

Asia makes up one-third of Earth's land mass, and it's where human civilization began.

the red fort

www.exploredelhi.com/red-fort/index.html

One of the top tourist sites in Delhi, this imposing, red sandstone fort was completed in 1648. Today it's surrounded by lush gardens.

national railway museum

www.nationalrailmuseum.org

The museum marks the nation's impact on the world's railway history with a collection of Indian trains from yesterday to the present. It includes a small train for children, the *Faerie Queen*, and a café with great food.

taj mahal

www.taj-mahal.net

Before you visit this iconic shrine, take the virtual tour on the website noted above. It provides panoramic views of the interiors. The Taj Mahal is located in Agra, about 125 miles from Delhi.

hong kong

This nation is a "special administration region" of China, with its own currency, customs rules, and immigration policies.

spring lantern festival

www.discoverhongkong.com

On the last day of the Chinese New Year, the city glows with brightly colored lanterns strung throughout the city.

the peak/tram

www.thepeak.com.hk

In use since 1888, the tram takes riders to the Peak, where they can tour Madame Tussaud's Waxworks Museum (featuring likenesses of Jackie Chan and Bruce Lee). There are great nature trails near the summit.

dolphin watch

www.hkdolphinwatch.com

Ever see a pink dolphin? Hong Kong's humpback dolphins *(Sousa chinensis),* which dart, dive, and swim in the Pearl River Delta, are indeed that color.

ferry rides

www.starferry.com.hk/tour.html

Hong Kong's green and white tub-shaped ferries have traveled back and forth from Hong Kong to Kowloon Peninsula for more than 100 years.

ocean park

www.oceanpark.com.hk

A plethora of attractions, Ocean Park is just the thing for a family looking for water fun and thrills. Its Ocean Theatre showcases dolphins and seals and its giant fish tank with hundreds of species.

museum of tea ware

www.lcsd.gov.hk/ce/Museum/Arts/
english/tea/intro/eintro.html

The beverage popularized here centuries ago is exhibited in the museum, which also displays the evolution of the manufacturing process.

golden bauhinia

www.discoverhongkong.com/eng/attraction/
at_most_expo.jhtml

Witness an enduring tradition up close with the national flag-hoisting ceremony each morning.

kowloon

www.discoverhongkong.com/eng/index.jsp

Not far from Hong Kong Island is the Kowloon Peninsula, a popular venue for shopping, eating, and cultural attractions.

repulse bay

www.discoverhongkong.com/eng/attraction/
at_most_repb.jhtml

Annually one of the most popular white-sand beaches in Hong Kong; tourists and locals alike flock to the bay each summer.

japan: tokyo

This is an electric city, especially at night, when neon lights and gadgetry illuminate well into the horizon. Yet everywhere there is evidence of rich and influential human history.

tsukiji fish market

www.tsukiji-market.or.jp/tukiji_e.htm

Treat your palate to some of the most unique seafood offerings—more than 1,500 stalls that house such goodies as blue fin tuna, deep sea crabs, eels, and salmon.

hama-rikyu garden

www.tokyo-park.or.jp/english/park/detail_04.html

The public walking gardens house a breathtaking landscape of flowers, trees, and a tea house set on a small island in the middle of a pond.

tanabata festival

www.stcb.or.jp/eng/

The Japanese take part in this tradition twice each summer, writing their wishes on small, colorful strips of paper and hanging them on bamboo branches. The Asagaya district hosts an amazing parade with floating paper creations.

Japanese Kenji character for the word "family."

anime center

www.animecenter.jp

The Akihabara district is anime capital of the world, home to this gallery with interactive exhibits. Expect to see young people dressed as their favorite anime characters or personal avatars.

don quijote

www.donki.com

One of the most unusual discount chain stores on the planet. Patrons shop 24 hours a day for everything from wigs to vinyl pants to live fish to food to electronics. There's one whole floor of costumes. Here, the word "depart" is slang for "department store."

kasai seaside park

www.city.edogawa.tokyo.jp/foreign/e/4/parks.html

An expansive beach park that includes a domed aquarium with penguins, plus tuna swimming in a giant ring-shaped tank. Kasai also houses a bird sanctuary and the tallest Ferris wheel in Japan.

sumo wrestling

www.sumo.or.jp

Sumo matches are often only a few seconds long, but the excitement lasts for hours. Major tournaments occur here in January, May, and September.

see the world
checklist

international travel

Going abroad is all about preparation and planning. Anticipation, of course, is part of the fun.

1. learn to say hello

It's fun to pick up some basic phrases. Try a software-based language program, or attend a language camp like the one offered by Concordia Language Villages in Minnesota (see Chapter Two).

2. get inoculations

www.cdc.gov/travel

The Centers for Disease Control has a great website with complete lists of required shots. It's also updated constantly about health alerts in every region of the world.

3. get a local perspective

Call the foreign embassies located in the United States. For example, the Japanese Embassy will send information for families preparing to visit.

4. register as a traveler

http://travel.state.gov/travel/tips/registration/registration_1186.html

Consider registering with the State Department. You can stay in touch with American embassies in case of emergencies.

5. get your passports early

It's exciting for children to know that they're always prepared for international travel.

6. learn about money

Let kids become the experts on international currency and exchange rates. Check daily reports to see how money is always changing.

7. check current events

http://travel.state.gov/travel/travel_1744.html

The State Department has a website with ongoing security postings to give you an idea of what to expect at your destination.

8. make a communication plan

Your cell phone may not work outside the United States. Check with your service provider. In any case, have a backup plan for communication.

9. think about souvenirs

Find out about the culture and resources of the places you'll visit. Research the best markets or regions for finding good mementos.

10. go to the library

Read novels or see movies that are set in different countries. You'll absorb new ideas about geography, languages, and history.

[PART THREE]

chapter six
travel wish lists
our way

chapter seven
family memories
we remember

chapter eight
resources
tell me more

our way

Every family loves the thrill of discovery—finding the out-of-the-way place, learning the best time to arrive at the theater, stumbling upon the one-of-a-kind shop. Even better: coming home to share the story of your find with another family. It's the way we make travel plans when we're traveling with children—checking with folks who have been there before so we're sure to make the most of our time.

The best travel advice comes from families who share their travel stories.

Families from all over have compiled itineraries that you can use when you're planning your next adventure. They share the big obvious points and the little details: what they ate, what they avoided, and what made the most lasting impressions.

Their lists cover geographic, historic, ethnic, and cultural highlights for some of the places that families visit most—cities with big sports teams and regions with beautiful beaches, national parks with famous monuments and quiet country roads where the clock seems to have stopped a century ago. Some convey the pleasure of exploring new sites far from home, while others want you to know about all that their hometowns have to offer. Imagine that you had a good friend who wanted to help you plan a perfect family vacation. That's what you'll find in the pages that follow.

Traveling with children often means that you stop at the familiar, even clichéd destinations. You rush, sometimes, through historic landmarks, then linger a little longer than you'd like around the gumball machine. You might pass by the famous exhibits or scenic views because the schedule just didn't work out the right way. But together with children, you might also take the time to stretch your legs in a community park, or to peek around the corner of a neighborhood ice cream stand to discover a little-known museum or historic site. Given friendly advice from families who have gone before you, you can be alert to more opportunities. It's all part of the recipe for discovery . . . a little more of this, a little less of that.

Check out a few itineraries that might just work for you. And then send us your own (see Chapter 8 for details). Because when it comes to traveling with your family, the story never really ends!

travel wish lists

I've been everywhere, man.
Crossed the deserts bare, man.
I've breathed the mountain air, man.
Of travel I've had my share, man.
I've been everywhere.
—Geoff Mack

a walk along
the freedom trail

The Freedom Trail is an actual red line that is painted (or sometimes set in brick) on the sidewalks through Boston. It takes you by the most historical and important parts of the city.
—Malcolm Fouhy

chinatown

www.boston.com

Starting at the Boston Common visitor center, take a right on Tremont Street and you reach China-town after about two blocks. There are a lot of fun stores and cultural attractions. For example, there is this great thing called bubble tea that is a lot like iced tea, but has bubble-like tapioca balls in it.

the granary burial ground

www.thefreedomtrail.org/visitor/park-street-church.html

Just up Tremont Street from the Boston Common is the Granary Burial Ground. Among the people buried there are Samuel Adams, John Hancock, Paul Revere, and Mother Goose.

boston common/swan boats

www.thefreedomtrail.org

The Swan Boats are a very popular activity. They are man-powered paddleboats that seat about 20 people for a 15-minute peaceful cruise on the pond. There is not a lot to eat around the Boston Common; there are much better places elsewhere.

faneuil hall

www.faneuilhallmarketplace.com

This was a historic meeting place during the Revolutionary War. Now it's one of the best places to eat. Quincy Market ($) gives you many choices. For sit-down service try Durgin Park ($$) or McCormick & Schmick's ($$$).

boston's north end

www.northendboston.com

Here you find a lot of American history and some Bostonian culture. The famed Old North Church is where Paul Revere had the lanterns put up so he could ride around the surrounding areas and warn of British attack ("One if by land. Two if by sea . . . "). His house is open to the public.

Eat in the North End. You'll find (arguably) the best pizzeria in Boston, Pizzeria Regina. There is almost always a long line, but it moves fast. For desserts, Mike's Pastry is the place to go. You have to be a little pushy to get through the crowd.

u.s.s. constitution

www.ussconstitution.navy.mil/

This ship was in actual naval battles during the

Revolutionary War, and it got its name from the way cannonballs bounced off its sides. Take the tour! Sailors give it, and they have their own funny anecdotes.

bunker hill monument (charlestown)

www.nps.gov/bost/historyculture/bhm.htm

This is a great place to view the city. A little effort is required to climb the 294 steps to the top, but the scenery is rewarding.

water taxi

www.roweswharfwatertaxi.com

It leaves from Pier 3 near the *Constitution* at the waterfront. If you walk to Charlestown it can be a long walk back, and this is a relaxing way to shorten the trip and to see some Boston Harbor activity. It is free for kids under 11.

the new england aquarium

www.neaq.org

Located just off the Freedom Trail and on the other side of Faneuil Hall. It is home to a selection of sharks, penguins, seals, and other fish. Whale watches and ferries from Charlestown and Cape Cod leave from the aquarium.

fenway park

http://boston.redsox.mlb.com

Not on the Freedom Trail, but still in the heart of Boston, Fenway is the home of the Boston Red Sox. Take a tour. They're offered up to 3½ hours before

The Constitution *is the oldest commissioned ship in the world.*

game time. It is *almost* impossible to get game tickets, unless you want to talk to the hundreds of scalpers around the stadium.

one more thing . . .

Look up at the grasshopper weathervane on the top of Faneuil Hall. We've heard it was originally misdirected to the College of William and Mary in Virginia, which really wanted a butterfly. It is the only original bit of the first building still there. It was grasshopper-napped in 1974, but we can't find any more details about that story . . . yet.

Malcolm & Aidan Fouhy

Contributor Malcolm Fouhy (16) lives in Boston. While he was recovering from surgery following a soccer injury, his brother Aidan (14) scouted these locations to ensure the accuracy of this list.

an adventure in the
adirondacks

The lakes and mountains of upstate New York are wonderfully accessible for families, whether you're looking for hikes, history, or just time together breathing the crisp, clean air. It's refreshing in summer, cozy in winter, and beautiful all the time.
—The Eff-Fairhalls

adirondack museum
www.adkmuseum.org

The region's biggest museum, it's worth a day trip to Blue Mountain Lake. There are daily events for families, special events, and permanent exhibits on the crafts, arts, traditions, and history of the region.

wild center
www.wildcenter.org

Formally named the Natural History Museum of the Adirondacks, it opened in 2006 in Tupper Lake to educate and entertain about the diversity of life in the park. Hundreds of live creatures, high-definition films, guided walks around the 31-acre property, and special events are among the attractions.

sagamore
www.sagamore.org

One of the "great camps" built for the rich, this 1,500-acre estate on Sagamore Lake was a summer retreat for the Vanderbilt family. Now it's a popular stop for visitors who come for tours and programs, and sometimes to stay and dine at the rustic, 27-building national historic landmark.

the "other" sagamore
www.thesagamore.com

This grand hotel and resort on Lake George has its own golf course, spectacular waterfront, and affordable dining for day trippers who just want to gawk.

seagle music colony
www.seaglecolony.com

Who would believe that the works of Puccini, Mozart, Sondheim, and other masters of opera and musical theater can be heard at a venue in Schroon Lake? Famous baritone Oscar Seagle created this center in 1915 to nurture young, gifted singers and to entertain the public.

oscar's
www.oscarssmokedmeats.com

Those hankering for some good smoked meat or cheese make a beeline for Oscar's Adirondack Smoke House in Warrensburg.

fort ticonderoga

www.fort-ticonderoga.org

A national historic landmark, the fort tells significant chapters of the stories of the Revolutionary War and the French and Indian War. Its strategic location on Lake Champlain ensured that whoever controlled the fort controlled the region.

high peaks region

www.adirondacks.com

The 46 mountains ranging as high as 5,344-foot Mount Marcy aren't just for climbing. You can enjoy the spectacular mountainscapes by car. One of the best routes takes motorists west from Exit 30 of the Northway on Route 73, winding through the picturesque Keene Valley on the way to Lake Placid.

cascade mountain

www.apa.state.ny.us

Six miles east of Lake Placid, this Adirondack High Peak (4,098 feet) is the most frequently climbed. And for good reason: It's comparatively easy and offers wide-open vistas.

essex county fair

www.essexcountyfair.org

In much of the Adirondacks, it's hard to find local produce. But agriculture endures in the valleys, and this fair in Westport honors the industry in mid-August. Tractor and truck pulls, a demolition derby, and 4-H demonstrations are part of the entertainment.

The Eff-Fairhall Family

Elaine Eff is an award-winning oral historian, folklorist, filmmaker, and author of *You Should Have Been Here Yesterday*, a handbook for those who want to learn how to use oral history and other methods to record the history of their communities. John Fairhall is a career journalist whose experience as an editor and writer informs his passion for travel and adventure. He fell in love with the Adirondacks while attending Albany State University.

books | adirondack cookbook

by armand vandestigche & robert e. birkel

Funny, simple, easy-to-make recipes from a wildly beautiful part of the country.

a weekend in
philadelphia

The City of Brotherly Love is a great destination for a day trip, or, even better, a whole weekend. Philadelphia is close to New York, Washington, D.C., and the Atlantic Ocean, making it a great home base for East Coast visitors. The Liberty Bell and the President's House will be on everyone's list of things to see. These sites will bring you even closer to the people, the history, and the real spirit of the city.

Imagine who might have walked the old cobblestone streets here.

Start with two great community festivals where everyone—elders to infants—comes on out and has a great time . . .
—Debora Kodish

odunde

23rd & South Sts., www.odundeinc.org

African-American festival on the second Saturday of June: There's a procession to the Schuylkill River and offerings to Oshun. Incredible music and dance on two stages, plus an African marketplace.

mid-autumn festival

10th & Arch Sts., www.aaunited.org

Organized by Asian Americans United on a Saturday in September

(depending on the moon): a wonderful lantern procession led by lion dancers and Chinese cultural performances underneath the Chinatown Arch.

john heinz wildlife sanctuary

www.fws.gov/refuges/profiles/index
.cfm?id=52570

Out by the airport. A postmodern wildlife preserve: wetlands within view of oil pipelines and freeway—but beautiful! You can see ospreys, herons, and more on a three-mile loop.

bartram gardens

www.bartramsgarden.org

America's oldest botanical garden, home of an 18th-century naturalist. Take the 34 trolley to the entrance, and then wander through the historic house. Follow pathways right down to the Schuylkill River.

fingcropan

www.fpaa.org/pa_map.html

Jody Pinto's work in Fairmount Park is just one of the great public artworks we have here. I also love Martin Puryear's Treehouse in West Fairmount Park. The Fairmount Park Art Association has an online map.

These artworks represent a small number of the pieces of art that are all over the city.

city markets

Two great urban markets: Reading Terminal Market. A train shed full, at 100-plus years old it's a great market. Or go to 9th Street/Italian Market (which now includes Vietnamese and Mexican provisioners as well). Stop at John's Water Ice at 8th and Christian Streets, get cheese at Claudio's or DiBruno's—and be entertained by the line (www.phillyitalianmarket.com). Take a bit of a detour over to the original Termini's bakery on 8th Street for great treats. It's an 80-year-old family business (www.termini.com).

stroll some of our avenues

www.visiteastpassyunk.com

Passyunk Avenue in South Philadelphia from 9th to Broad includes lots of family businesses and plenty of cheesesteak options, and go to Baltimore Avenue from 43rd to 50th for great immigrant shops and restaurants—Francophone West African, Eritrean, Lao, Vietnamese, Nigerian, and more.

smith memorial playground

www.smithplayhouse.org

One of our famous Fairmount Park Houses has a giant slide for kids that is a blast. The slide was added in 1905 and rebuilt in 2005. The playground is open to the public free of charge. (Editor's note: see more information about the playground in Chapter One, page 26.)

the wagner free institute

www.wagnerfreeinstitute.org

An amazing 19th-century science museum with meticulously arranged displays of fossils, shells, and other geologic treasures. Children's programs are offered weekly; reservations are required.

spiral q puppet theater

www.spiralq.org

Giant puppets used in community pageants and protests, on display in their living loft. Check the schedule for puppet parades, community workshops, and performances. If you come in October, march in their Peoplehood procession and pageant winding through West Philly to Clark Park (and a great farmer's market!).

Debora Kodish

Debora Kodish is the founder and director of the Philadelphia Folklore Project, where she has worked for 21 years with local grassroots community groups and artists on cultural heritage issues. She serves on the Advisory Council of the Smithsonian Center for Folklife and Cultural Heritage, and the board of the Folk Arts – Cultural Treasures Charter School. She and her partner are the parents of two daughters, now 18 and 21, who grew up going to the ODUNDE and Mid-Autumn Festivals.

pennsylvania
dutch country

We have four children and live in Baltimore, Maryland. After vacationing at the beach with a toddler in diapers, we decided our next vacation would not include sand. We planned a four-day vacation in Lancaster, Pennsylvania, that included amusement parks, trains, and fun—less than two hours from home. When we took this trip our children were nine, seven, three, and one.

—Ellen Neff

willow valley resort

www.willowvalley.com

This is a great hotel for a family because there are activities to do and a great buffet for dining. We bought a package that included a room to fit our family of six and meals where children eat free. The buffets were great because the food was good, there were healthy choices, and our children didn't eat chicken nuggets and French fries every day. We all loved the variety of foods, plus the fun of making different choices. The place has a real resort feel for families.

golf & pool

At the resort Dad could play one round at their golf course. Meanwhile, Mom and the children went through their corn maze and swam at their indoor pool and mini-water park.

dutch wonderland

www.dutchwonderland.com

This amusement park is geared toward younger children, ten and under. We loved the little rides, shows, and water park.

hersheypark

www.hersheypark.com

This was a 30-minute drive from Willow Valley and well worth it. This park is great for families, with adult rides right near children's rides so we could stick together. The boardwalk here was huge, with slides, a water roller coaster, and a wave pool. We spent several hours there. Later we thought it would be even better to go to Hersheypark for two days. We'd have a day for dry rides and one for the boardwalk, plus a few shows.

strasburg railroad

www.strasburgrailroad.com

A 45-minute steam engine train ride through Amish country. The children loved it. Nearby was the Choo Choo Barn, a miniature train display. It was the biggest miniature train display we had ever seen. We were there for over an hour looking at all the details.

route 340

We saw lots of different farms, markets, and roadside stands. Depending on the time of year you can buy flowers, vegetables, ice cream, or crafts right out of people's front yards.

amish farmhouse

www.amishfarmandhouse.com

This area is home to the country's oldest Amish community. You can visit the Amish Farm and House, with exhibits about these very private families and their farm traditions.

amish buggies

www.abesbuggyrides.com

We've heard about a real Amish family that takes people on horse-drawn rides in the community, called Abe's Buggy Rides. You'll recognize the Amish men by their  black hats and long beards. The women wear long, old-fashioned dresses and caps that cover their pinned-up hair. The children wear simple, plain clothes, too.

smorgasbord-style restaurants

www.bird-in-hand.com

Pennsylvania Dutch cooking is a labor of love. There are several popular and plentiful smorgasbord-style restaurants to choose from. We liked Bird-in-Hand Family Restaurant, right on Route 340 in Bird-in-Hand, Pennsylvania.

cherry crest adventure farm

www.cherrycrestadventurefarm.com

A great fall destination, though it's open May through November. It has kind of a farm-style amusement park atmosphere that folks around here are really proud of. There's a potato festival in September, with races, games, and a very funny potato hunt (same idea as an Easter egg hunt).

The Neff Family

Ellen and Marty Neff are the parents of Becca, Emma, Drew, and Jenna. They love to make day trips from their home in Baltimore, and they also enjoy everyday adventures in their own neighborhood.

a dad's favorite places in
washington, d.c.

Each family member has his or her own preferences when it comes to visiting the nearest big city. Here are a few places that one D.C. suburban dad enjoys time after time (or year after year) when he takes his daughters "in town" to visit the nation's capital.

christmas trees on the ellipse

www.nps.gov/whho/national_christmas_tree_program.htm

In addition to the National Christmas Tree, each state and U.S. territory has its own decorated tree. Each year we look forward to visiting the trees that represent the places where my daughters and I were born (New Jersey for me, Massachusetts for my older daughter, Virginia for my younger daughter).

open-air bus sightseeing

www.dctours.us

The double-decker buses resemble those popularized in London. We board the second deck and see Georgetown, Independence Avenue, and Union Station from an entirely different perspective. While riding from the roofless second deck, be sure to duck for low branches and power lines.

The National Mall is the main point of reference for most forays into Washington, D.C.

gravelly point

A grassy public area just shy of the Reagan National Airport runway. It's one of the coolest places for kids and families in the area; folks ride bikes, skate, play soccer, have picnics, or simply watch planes take off and land.

the nutcracker, capital style

www.washingtonballet.org

Performed by the Washington Ballet with D.C. scenes and settings, the timeless holiday classic features Washington-area youngsters among the cast extras. The stage is set in Georgetown and features George Washington as the Nutcracker and England's King George III as the Rat King.

smithsonian institution

www.si.edu

So vast and full of historic treasures that there's no way a family can see everything in one visit. Some of our favorites are the Natural History Museum, where there's a great children's hall, and the Museum of American History, which has the first ladies' inaugural gowns. Plan on several days!

gifford's ice cream and candy

www.giffords.com

There are six locations in the D.C. area, including one at 555 11th Street, NW, which is adjacent to many popular attractions. It's a great place to break for sweets: Gifford's features ice cream flavors of the month and a wide selection of hot drinks and smoothies, but the chocolate ice cream shake is to die for.

international spy museum

www.spymuseum.org

Upon entering, visitors assume a secret identity and then they must remember their personal details while they embark on a journey filled with intrigue. The state-of-the-art museum includes a secret passage made from air-conditioning ducts.

newseum

www.newsmuseum.org

It's a museum dedicated to news media, so it's naturally informative. Yet it's also an in-depth, often entertaining look at how news events shaped world history. Among the most popular exhibits are a slab of concrete and a lookout tower from the former Berlin Wall.

alexandria waterfront

www.visitalexandriava.com

One of the most popular waterfronts in the National Capital area, it is a charming, family-friendly venue that hosts many outdoor events year-round. The waterfront includes the famous Old Town section, which offers eclectic shopping and dining as well as a water taxi to the National Harbor.

the national mall

www.nps.gov/nama

The main area of this vast, grassy park, between the U.S. Capitol and the Washington Monument, is the hub of the district. It is flanked by some of the nation's finest museums and art galleries.

The Burris Family

Joe Burris is a 22-year veteran journalist for the *Nashville Tennessean,* the *Boston Globe,* and the *Baltimore Sun.* He has written stories in 13 states and 4 foreign countries. He has covered the Winter Olympics and post-apartheid South Africa and has profiled many newsmakers. Joe lives in Alexandria, Virginia, with his wife Mpho and daughters Nyaniso and Onalenna.

colonial & contemporary
williamsburg

Colonial Williamsburg is the biggest attraction in our city of Williamsburg. But everyone here has a 21st-century life, too. Here are some of the places you'll love in our hometown.
—The Evertzes

the historic triangle
www.historictriangle.com

Williamsburg is the most famous re-creation of a colonial settlement. Jamestown is the site of America's very first European colony. And Yorktown is a colorful landmark of both the Revolutionary and Civil Wars.

best photo op
www.colonialwilliamsburg.com

It may seem touristy, but every local Williamsburger does it, so why not you?! Walk right down to DOG Street to the courthouse and take some hilarious family photos in the wooden stocks.

daily parades
www.visitwilliamsburg.com

In the streets of Colonial Williamsburg, the Fifes and Drums Corps is world renowned. Most members are signed

The Governor's Mansion is the centerpiece of Colonial Williamsburg.

up for it when they are born and begin training in fifth grade. Check the visitor center for parade times.

colonial kids

The historic area is full of shops, homes, and interesting places that take you on a trip through time to the colonial era. Lots of families like to get costumes, toys, and other things to play with when they're here. The website has more information: www.history.org.

best times to visit
www.colonialwilliamsburg.com

Revolutionary City programs in the summer and Drummer's Call weekend in May. Yorktown Day in October. Grand Illumination, right before Christmas. Check the CW website for details about dates.

busch gardens
www.buschgardens.com

Save a day for the amusement parks. We love Busch Gardens—there's a reason that it's been named the Cleanest Park in America over ten times in a row. Go after 4:30 p.m., when it's less crowded and much cooler. If you're here in the fall, don't miss Howl-o-Scream. Water Country USA is nearby for all those kids who might be missing the pool back home. Go on the Aquazoid.

autumn drive
Fall in Williamsburg is so picturesque. CW is beautiful then, and you can admire the fall foliage with a drive down Colonial Parkway.

go to a "tribe" football game at william & mary
www.wm.edu

Most of the time, you can get in free after halftime. This college was founded in 1693.

sno-to-go
www.sno-to-go.com

This place is open only in summertime. Sno-to-Go is the place to be! From your standard strawberry and bubblegum flavors to Frog in a Blender and Beetlejuice, they have everything your heart desires. They do sell ice cream, but the snow cone is irresistible. If you must have the best of both worlds (and trust us, you do), you'll get it "stuffed"!

favorite local food
Eat where we do. Try Food for Thought (ribs, shrimp, po' boys, pad thai, great skinny fries), Green Leaf (great for dinner, our beloved local spot), Peking (near K-Mart, great feng shui interior and all-you-can-eat Chinese buffet), Gazebo (order the "Plantation Breakfast"), and, last but not least, pizza or burgers at Paul's Deli (near

William & Mary, a real local hangout). They're all in the phone book. In CW, order ahead for the best sandwiches from the Cheese Shop.

one more thing . . .
www.anoccasionforthearts.org

Caroline and her mom want you to be here for Occasion for the Arts, the annual fall arts festival held in Colonial Williamsburg.

local slang
CW—Colonial Williamsburg
DOG Street—Duke of Gloucester Street
The Tribe—Mascot of the College of William and Mary

The Evertz Family

Caroline, Paul, and Kurt have lived in Williamsburg almost all their lives with their mom and dad, Jane and Hubert. Hubert is a native of Germany and is a lifetime member of the Karneval marching group, Prinzen Garde Köln.

the ultimate
florida keys vacation

Key Largo's climate is different from any place we've ever been—tropical, yet with wonderful ocean breezes. We planned this week to have quality time together and have a truly adventurous and educational vacation. Here's what we loved best.
—Deb Kirkland

staying at key largo

www.manateebayresort.com

We loved the Key Largo Resort at Manatee Bay. It's really close to the John Pennekamp Coral Reef State Park. A charter service is on the resort grounds, so it's convenient for scheduling ecotours, kayak rentals, and pretty much anything we wanted to do. There are restaurants in easy walking distance, most of them casual and laid-back, which was perfect for our family.

jules' undersea lodge

www.jul.com

This is like a submerged condo, with chef service. It's actually an underwater research lab that was converted into a lodge, moored in a Key Largo lagoon. You can stay overnight or opt for the three-hour Innerspace experience (complete with lunch). Scuba gear and unlimited breathing tanks are included.

The Seven Mile Bridge connects the keys to the Florida mainland.

swimming with dolphins

www.dolphinscove.com

The three of us swam with dolphins, and it was an incredible experience. Later, the boys swam with sea lions. They also have a Dolphin Wade, where these beautiful mammals slide into shallow water so smaller kids can touch them without swimming.

hand-feeding the rays

www.theaterofthesea.com

There are dolphin and sea lion shows at the Theater of the Sea in Islamorada. We also hand-fed the rays and snorkeled with them in shallow pools. You can swim with dolphins here, too. This lagoon is an old quarry!

snorkeling a coral reef

www.pennekamppark.com

We'll always remember seeing a barracuda while snorkeling out on this coral reef state park. A boat goes out between three and eight miles for snorkeling and scuba. There's also a glass-bottom boat that goes out to another reef a little farther out.

airboat ride

www.everglades.com

This was one of the Alligator Farm activities. For kids looking for amusement park-type thrills, this fits the bill. The airboat starts like a wildlife tour, but ends with high-speed 360s and everyone getting soaking wet.

alligator show

www.everglades.com

Trainers helped us to hold alligators, and we saw some great shows and feeding demonstrations. There are also snake shows, and trainers carry them around the park for a closer look.

duval street

www.delsol.com

This is Key West's "main street," and we loved looking in all of the shops. One of our favorites was the Del Sol store, where all of the items change color when they're in the sun!

key west sunset

We got henna tattoos in Key West, then watched Mallory Square entertainers right up until the moment of the beautiful sunset (better than a three-ring circus). Key West is about 100 miles from Key Largo.

next time . . .

www.robbies.com

We did everything we had planned except tarp feeding at Robbie's Marina in Islamorada on the way to Key West. One of the local dive masters said it is a huge attraction and kids love it.

end of A1A

www.keywest.com

We drove out to the southernmost tip of the United States, where we discovered a huge painted marker noting the distance to the next neighbor to the south (Cuba: 90 miles). This marks the end of the famous A1A highway, running down the east coast of Florida parallel to the Atlantic Ocean.

The Kirkland/Mendelson Family

Deb Kirkland and her sons Ben (11) and Max (8) love to go on vacation together. They point out that they love the big Orlando resorts, but also make time for indoor skydiving, which is as much fun as Disney. Other favorite vacations have included Mexico, the Caribbean, Arizona, and the Canadian side of Niagara, complete with a helicopter ride, a cruise on the *Maid of the Mist*, and dinner at the famous rotating restaurant.

a grandmother's guide to
sanibel, florida

I love to spend time here in Sanibel with my grandchildren. Here are a few things that I know other grandparents and kids like to do, too!
—Virginia Fleming

sanibel recreation center

www.mysanibel.com

Fabulous, with four pools for different levels—one is just fun with spouts and sprays. There are a huge basketball gym and a workout room with state-of-the-art equipment, skateboard park, and tennis courts. A wonderful addition to the community, and local kids go there daily for the Sanibel rec program.

big arts (barrier island group for the arts)

www.bigarts.org

There are great arts and crafts summer camps. Three of ours went for a week this summer and loved it. For grade schoolers there are rotating schedules of dance, pottery, music, and such. Older kids can try a fine-arts apprenticeship.

sanibel sea school

www.sanibelseaschool.org

Number one on the list because everyone loves it and the kids want to go back and back again. The barrier island environment is a setting for hands-on education for adults and children alike.

schoolhouse theater

www.theschoolhousetheater.com

The summer kids' program is a delight. They put on a production at the end—something different every year. The theater itself hosts professional productions for audiences of all ages in addition to the summer program for kids.

bailey matthews shell museum

www.shellmuseum.org

It's the only shell museum in North America and a little gem, with a year-round kids' game room, touch tank, museum hunt for prizes, and summer kids' session.

tarpon bay kayak trails

www.tarponbayexplorers.com

Rent a kayak or take a guided canoe or kayak tour. This outfitter is located in the J. N. "Ding" Darling National Wildlife Refuge, famous as a protected area for spectacular birds. It's also possible that you'll see alligators, manatees, or dolphins.

biking anywhere for breakfast

When the kids are here we bike up to Over Easy Café every morning. The bike trails are great: 24 miles on the 11-mile-long island. There are several bike rental shops on the island—you can't miss them. Everyone wears a helmet!

great restaurants

These are all institutions and easy to find in the local phone book. Doc Ford's—lots of tropical dishes and a big sports bar . . . Island Cow for the kids . . . Schnapper's Hots for hot dogs and burgers . . . plus Timbers, Trader's, the Bean (for coffee), and the Lighthouse Café on east end—the same family has owned it for many years, and it's a "must do" for breakfast.

off-island

www.efwefla.org

Take a day to visit the Edison and Ford homes on McGregor Boulevard in Fort Myers. It's a great plan for inclement weather, but worth the trip even if it isn't raining! There are children's programs offered in the summer, such as experiments in Edison's Lab. The gardens and surrounding homes are lovely as well.

day trip to useppa island

www.captivacruises.com

Go on the "big boat" with lunch on one of the old island restaurants. On Useppa there is a wonderful Calusa museum. The old Collier Inn there is full of history and great old photos. Try Captiva Cruises, from McCarthy's Marina.

Virginia Fleming & grandchildren

Virginia Fleming makes her home in Sanibel Island on Florida's Gulf Coast. She is a world traveler who has a great family tradition. When each of her 11 grandchildren reaches the age of 10, he or she gets to choose a destination that they'll visit together. That way she can enjoy special time with each before they're all grown up. A recent trip was with three grandsons, ages 10, 11, and 12. This time, the "three amigos" decided that they wanted to visit Alaska together with their grandmother.

a local family's guide to
memphis

Memphis, Tennessee, is located on a massive bluff on the mighty Mississippi River, the largest river in the nation. The river itself is an awesome sight, but there are lots of things to do and see in Memphis. The MATA trolley line is a fun way to get around downtown.
—Maryanne Lessley

See the Mississippi by riverboat.

mud island
www.mudisland.com
A River Museum and a cool reproduction of the Mississippi River from beginning to end. You can walk along, splash around, and imagine the actual depths of this amazing body of water.

national civil rights museum
www.civilrightsmuseum.org
Take an emotional tour and witness the very spot where Dr. Martin Luther King, Jr., was assassinated. The museum offers an in-depth history of the civil rights movement, a must-see in Memphis.

the peabody hotel
www.peabodymemphis.com
Even if you don't stay there, take a break from walking around downtown in the lobby with a refreshing drink or a warm cup of coffee. Don't miss the Peabody Ducks swimming around in the fountain.

beale street
www.bealestreet.com
Take in the energy, the sights, and the sounds of the Home of Blues and the Birthplace of Rock-and-Roll. It is a hopping place in downtown. If you are lucky, the Beale Street Flippers will be around performing their gymnastic feats for tips.

the memphis farmers market
www.memphisfarmersmarket.com
Open every Saturday May to October. Take a stroll through the largest open-air farmers market in the area. Meet local growers and artisans and pick up some souvenirs and healthy snacks.

our favorite places to eat
Downtown—Try the Arcade for breakfast, anytime. Gus's Fried Chicken for lunch and dinner at the Rendezvous (famous for their ribs, which are shipped all over the country) or McEwen's on Monroe. A fine-dining experience at the Inn at Hunt Phelan would be a real treat. Midtown—You must have a burger from Huey's,

and Bosco's brews their own beer. For dinner, visit the Cooper-Young area for several eclectic, trendy restaurants. Café 1912 and Tsunami are favorites.

memphis zoo

www.memphiszoo.org

You'll need a car to get around Memphis. The Memphis Zoo is an absolute must-see. It is one of the country's top-rated zoos. The Northwest Passage and the Giant Pandas are the newest exhibits, but Cat Country is still a favorite.

graceland

www.elvis.com

Well, you're in Memphis! You simply must visit the home of the King of Rock-and-Roll, Elvis Presley. Walk inside and you are thrown back in time. If you are a big Elvis fan, August is your time to visit. Elvis week is celebrated in a big way. The official website has a children's activity book that you can download before your visit. This might help explain to children what all the excitement is about.

the children's museum

www.cmom.com

A fun place for younger kids. It is a great place for hands-on learning in math, science, health, and art. Don't miss the cool vertical maze and the working beehive. The museum is open seven days a week. It's a great place for birthday parties.

the pink palace museum

www.memphismuseums.org

You'll know it when you see it because it is literally a pink palace. Amazingly, it was originally built to be a residence. However, now along with the museum of Memphis and mid-South History, it is home to a planetarium and an IMAX theater.

The Lessley Family

The Lessleys are lifelong Memphians. Bo and Maryanne were high school sweethearts and have been married for 16 years. Maryanne loves to cook, especially with local produce, and is the manager of the Memphis Farmers Market in downtown Memphis. Bo enjoys golf and fishing and is part-owner of Signs Now in Memphis. The girls are avid recyclers, great students, and active in school sports. As a family, they love to be outdoors together, grilling out, gardening, hiking, or riding bikes.

family and friends in
san antonio

We have a lot of visitors, but we also love to make quick trips around town with our two little boys.
—Tiffani Schoenberger

the alamo
www.thealamo.org

We take all of our out-of-town visitors here for a little bit of history. Davy Crockett and 188 other "freedom fighters" died here in a battle for Texas' independence from Mexico. The grounds are beautiful, the kids can run around, and it is close to Riverwalk and downtown restaurants.

tower of the americas
www.toweroftheamericas.com

The water garden and the playground are favorite places for the kids to take a break and play. There's a 4-D theater on the first floor and an observation deck at the top of the tower.

natural bridge caverns/natural bridge wildlife ranch
www.wildliferanchtexas.com
www.naturalbridgecaverns.com

These are on our list of places to visit.

The Alamo is an old mission church right in San Antonio.

I know the kids will love spending the day at the Safari Park!

san antonio zoo
www.sazoo-aq.org

Most of the animals are close enough for the kids to see and hear. They love the new Africa exhibit, the Petting Farm, and the Tiny Tots nature spot. We usually end the day with a ride on the Eagle Train and a bag of popcorn!

witte museum
www.wittemuseum.org

The kids love to play in the H-E-B Science Treehouse at this colorful history museum. You can get here aboard the Eagle Train from the zoo.

enchanted springs ranch
www.enchantedspringsranch.com

Here in nearby Boerne, Texas, we met our first real cowboy and saw a buffalo close up. The kids loved exploring the western town, watching a cowboy duel, and riding the pony.

sea world
www.seaworld.com

We spend the day at the Lost Lagoon or going to shows. There is an area for smaller kids to climb and play, and some rides too! Our favorite thing to do is feed the dolphins.

botanical gardens

www.sabot.org

The Botanical Gardens has great children's exhibits and lots of room for the kids to explore. Check out the Old Fashioned Garden, the Rose Garden, Kumamoto En Garden, and the Sensory Garden. Then take a walk on the Texas Native Trail, with unique local characteristics.

riverwalk & river taxi

www.thesanantonioriverwalk.com

The river taxi is a wonderful way to see downtown San Antonio from a different perspective. The guides are full of information about the history of the area.

day trips

We go to Austin to visit the state capitol, Texas State History Museum, and LBJ Library and Museum. Family members have day-tripped to Fredericksburg to see the National Museum of the Pacific War. The Nimitz Museum is a wonderful museum about World War II.

places to eat!

1. Rudy's BBQ—off I-10 on the way to Enchanted Springs Ranch. Stop there to pick up a picnic lunch or to get a bite on the way home.
2. La Fogata—wonderful Mexican food with a great atmosphere.
3. Alamo Café—close to the zoo and the Botanical Gardens.
4. Boudros Riverwalk—on the Riverwalk, a great place to eat when visiting the Alamo, Tower of the Americas, and Riverwalk.
5. Scenic Loop Café—off I-10. Great food, and it has a play area to keep the kids busy while you eat.

The Schoenberger Boys

Todd and Tiffani Schoenberger have two sons, Landon and Colton. The family is originally from Annapolis, Maryland, and currently resides in south Texas. All four are avid vacationers who love the beach. They also enjoy watching sporting events, especially Baltimore Ravens football.

from mount rushmore to
little big horn

We moved back East in the summer of 2008 and took our time crossing the country with two cars, a trailer, two recently acquired cats, and a lot of stuff that did not make it into the moving van. What a great trip! Here is a two-day highlight of a very memorable point along the way.
—Kim & Frank Donovan

Mount Rushmore, South Dakota

mount rushmore

www.nps.gov/moru

This is a truly incredible monument to American ingenuity and pride during the Industrial Age. We were fortunate to have as our guide a Native American park ranger who compared the four presidents with four famous Indian leaders of the time. The Junior Ranger program helps children (and parents) gain appreciation for Gutzon Borglum and his ability to scale his original sculpture to the side of the mountain.

rapid city

www.visitrapidcity.com

This South Dakota city has a walking tour around life-size statues of American presidents. La Quinta Inn is a nice motel that takes pets; attached to it is the state's largest indoor water park, with large tube slides and play pools.

little big horn

www.4uth.gov.ua/usa/english/travel/npsname/index235.htm

At this famous Montana battlefield, pick up Junior Ranger booklets and tour the visitor's center to find answers to the questions.

see the movie

www.4uth.gov.ua/usa/english/travel/npsname/index235.htm

Don't miss the film on the Battle of Little Big Horn shown in the visitor's center theater.

the indian memorial

www.nps.gov/libi

This is a modern memorial that recognizes the courage of the Indian warriors who fought and died at Little Big Horn.

last stand hill

www.nps.gov/libi

Look south across the Little Big Horn River and imagine an encampment with more than 7,000 Indians less than a mile away. This is where Lt. Col. George Armstrong Custer and 41 troopers of the Seventh Cavalry made their last stand on the afternoon of June 25, 1876. Look for the white memorial markers where each soldier fell, including Custer's brother, Tom.

the custer national cemetery

www.cem.va.gov/CEMs/nchp/ftcuster.asp

A review of the gravestones will reveal a history of the settlement of that part of Montana. There is lots of shade here—a nice place for a picnic.

Note the dates on old headstones.

reno-benteen battlefield

www.nps.gov/libi

Here a sub-element of Custer's command attempted to outflank the Indians and was repulsed. The event set the stage for Custer's final defeat later the same day. The drive will also allow the family to enjoy the incredible Montana scenery.

Note: Bring a picnic. Compared to the concessions at other national parks, Little Big Horn can seem a bit stark.

wall drug

www.walldrug.com

It has a great collection of old photos on the walls. Our favorite is a photo of the horse Comanche—the only Seventh Cavalry survivor at Little Big Horn. He was owned by Captain Keogh—a Civil War Irishman we tracked across country from Little Big Horn to Gettysburg, where he originally fought with the Union Cavalry. Mortally wounded, Keogh chose not to shoot his horse (contrary to common practice), and the story goes that when the rest of the Seventh Cavalry made it to Little Big Horn a day after the battle, Captain Keogh still had Comanche's reins in his hands.

The Donovan Family

The Donovans are a Marine Corps family that loves to travel. Their adventures began when Frank and Kimberly met in Crete in 1992. Today, Margaret and her mom are accomplished riders and Brendan loves to see the world, especially with his dad. They all enjoy reading, playing soccer, and making the most of their time together.

a family adventure
national parks of the west

In the summer of 2006 we took advantage of some extended vacation time to make a big driving trip to the great national parks of the West. Our children were 8, 10, and 14. This was one of the best decisions we have made! Our family was able to experience firsthand our country's amazing natural resources and beauty set aside for our enjoyment and wonder.
—Julie Backous

Bryce Canyon arch

Originating from our hometown of Seattle, our three-week loop route encompassed nine states and ten national parks/national recreation areas, as follows:

sand dunes national recreation area, oregon

www.fs.fed.us/r6/siuslaw/

We enjoyed a "rush" riding in dune buggies driven by professionals, and photographed the kids mid-air as they jumped off sand dunes.

redwood national park, california, & oregon caves national monument, oregon

www.oregoncaves.com

Hiking among the "granddaddy" redwood trees, we felt small. We experienced chill and darkness as we ventured into the Oregon Caves.

zion, bryce canyon & grand canyon national parks (north rim)

www.utahszionandbryce.com

We stayed at Zion Ponderosa Ranch Resort just outside Zion and took three day trips to national parks. Leaving early morning each day, we went on a day hike, returning to the resort in time for fun activities such as archery and trail riding.

death valley national park, california & nevada

www.nps.gov/deva/

We drove through the park at dusk, watching the stars emerge and experiencing the extreme heat even after sundown.

yosemite national park, california

www.nps.gov/yose/

We tent camped within the park, surrounded by large boulders that were perfect for the kids to climb and explore; we hiked to a waterfall and swam in a river.

grand teton national park, wy.

www.nps.gov/grte/

Day hiked to Jenny Lake to enjoy a picnic and swimming.

yellowstone national park, wyoming, montana, idaho

www.nps.gov/yell/

Tent-camped at Gibbons Creek; fly-fished and caught and released numerous fish in a creek that winds through a grassy meadow; revisited Old Faithful after not seeing it for 35 years!

some helpful points:

- We enjoyed at least one day hike at each national park, getting us away from any crowds; we tent-camped three nights at a time to minimize hassles of setting up/taking down camp.
- We divided up the driving with stays at hotels, tent-camping, and homes of friends. This accommodated the need for laundry and showering.
- Rather than staying at the national park lodges, we instead tent-camped in the park and had breakfast at each lodge. We found that the lodges are beautiful old structures worth visiting.
- Our long driving days were divided by staying multiple nights at our destinations.
- We didn't hesitate to stop at national historic markers or other fun places along the way, even if it meant extending the driving day.
- We started our days early, putting kids in the car in pajamas, and stopping several hours into the drive for breakfast.

one more thing

The animated movie *Cars* is a great one to watch before, during, or after this trip since it highlights canyons, landforms, and small towns of the West. Our family watched the movie after our trip and enjoyed it probably more than most.

The Backous Family

Julie and Doug Backous make their home in Seattle, Washington, with their children Taylor, Jonathan, and Lindsey. They all agree that this was the trip of a lifetime!

books | national parks of america
by stewart udall, james udall, david muench (photographer)

Beautiful photographs that will take your breath away and inspire you to visit these parks.

local family favorites in
portland, oregon

Rain or shine, Portland is great for families and perfect for entertaining visitors with kids. Here are a few of our favorite urban adventures and day trips.
—Amy Brown

Portland: an environment-friendly city

cycle the city

www.portlandonline.com

Portland is bursting with bike lanes, bike paths, bike boulevards— even bike paths on bridges. For safe and easy urban cycling, jump on Portland's Eastbank Esplanade and Waterfront Park pathways.

aerial tram

www.portlandtram.org

See everything in the city! This new aerial tramway whisks passengers 3,300 feet above the city in sleek, silvery pods.

saturday market

www.portlandsaturdaymarket.com

This colorful open-air arts and crafts market—open on Sundays, too—shares a glimpse of Oregon's hippie culture. Find one-of-a-kind souvenirs and treasures, from tie-dye to impressive arts and crafts. There is a kids' activities area, music main stage, and wonderful international foods. Great for people watching, too!

forest park

www.forestparkconservancy.org

We feel like we've escaped to the mountains when we hike the trails of this 5,000-acre urban forest, located in view of the city's center. Seventy miles of hiking and mountain-biking trails await.

mount tabor

http://vulcan.wr.usgs.gov/Volcanoes/Oregon BoringLavaField/VisitVolcano/mount_tabor.html

We love this park for its towering firs, bike route, picnic areas, great play structure, and knowing that we're playing atop an extinct volcanic cinder cone! It is part of the Boring Lava Field, with at least 30 cinder cones and small shield volcanoes. The entrance is located at S.E. 60th and Salmon St.

jamison square

www.portlandonline.com

A full city block with the most amazing interactive fountain that attracts hundreds of families and children on warm weekends. Located in the hip Pearl District. Surrounded by shops and eateries. Start at 819 N.W. 11th Ave.

multnomah falls

http://trips.stateoforegon.com/multnomah_falls/

This is the granddaddy of Oregon's waterfalls and just minutes from downtown. We love to hike the 1.2-mile zigzagging path to the top.

pacific city (day trip)

www.pacificcity.org

Kites and beach toys in hand, we head to the fishing village of Pacific City. Scale the huge sand dune of Cape Kiwanda, explore tide pools, go crabbing or whale watching, and watch surfers. Oregon's rugged coastline makes for an unforgettable day.

fort clatsop (day trip)

www.nps.gov/lewi/planyourvisit/fortclatsop.htm

The kids relive the epic journey of explorers Lewis and Clark at Fort Clatsop in Astoria, the oldest American settlement west of the Rockies.

powell's city of books

www.powells.com

This is one of the world's great bookstores. Grab a map once inside and navigate the store's nine color-coded rooms, housing more than 3,500 different sections. A book lover's paradise! It's at 1005 W. Burnside Street.

locally owned restaurants that local families love:

- Laughing Planet Cafés
  www.laughingplanet.com
- McMennamin's Pubs
  www.mcmenamins.com

- Burgerville Retaurants
  www.burgerville.com
- Pastini Pastaria
  www.pastini.net
- Hot Lips Pizza
  www.hotlipspizza.com
- Daily Café
  www.dailycafe.net
- Grand Central Baking Company
  www.grandcentralbakery.com

The Brown Family

The Brown family lives in Portland and loves the city's great green culture. Matt is an urban planner and landscape architect, and Amy's "homegrown" firm Seed PR represents organic foods and agricultural businesses. Together with their sons Jake (11) and Ben (8), they take advantage of the area's temperate climate and fascinating geography with frequent family hikes.

taking your time in
san francisco

Expectations are high when you first set foot in this famous city. There's so much to see and do—but where to begin? We'd like to share some of our favorite places to visit.
—Charlotte Jacobs

start here
www.exploratorium.edu
www.nps.gov/goga/
From the Exploratorium at the Palace of Fine Arts, cross the street and you could walk along the Marina or bike, walk, or drive across the Golden Gate Bridge.

waterfront
www.maritime.org, www.ghirardellisq.com
Fisherman's Wharf is along the waterfront as well—farther east a couple of miles. You can walk the distance and stop off at the Maritime Museum, take a tour of the Jeremiah O'Brien, and then walk up a block and walk around Ghirardelli Square and watch chocolate being made.

eat here
www.fishermanswharf.org, www.rainforestcafe.com
Once at Fisherman's Wharf you can get a bite to eat at one of the local restaurants. Clam chowder in a French bread bowl is a big hit, along with some fresh crab. The kids would probably like to eat at

the Rain Forest Café, which is usually very crowded.

tour & attractions
www.ripleys.com, www.waxmuseum.com
www.nps.gov/alcatraz/
Continue on the waterfront and you will see Ripley's Believe It or Not and the Wax Museum (a bit expensive). Farther along you will see street vendors and entertainers and a place to purchase Alcatraz tour tickets. While waiting for the tour you can walk to Pier 39. Make sure you stop and watch the harbor seals at the end of the pier.

at&t park
http://sanfrancisco.giants.mlb.com/
sf/ballpark/tours.jsp
Take the AT&T Park tour and see the home of the San Francisco Giants. If the Giants are in town you will not be able to have the tour, but you can purchase game tickets instead. The tour takes about an hour and a half.

chinatown
www.sanfranciscochinatown.com
The gates of Chinatown are located on Grant and Bush. Chinatown is a must-see but tends to be

very busy on the weekends. While on Grant Street you may walk into Old St. Mary's Church, one of the oldest churches in the city. Walk up a block to Stockton and you will also see a very busy street with produce for sale on the sidewalks. Cooked duck, squab, and pork hang in the windows for sale. While walking around don't forget to go through the little alley. Ross Alley is where they make fortune cookies; the ladies still make each one by hand. Waverly Place has a small temple up a few flights of stairs that you may walk into and pay your respects. While in Chinatown you need to try some dim sum on Grant Street.

cable cars

www.sfcablecar.com

Grant Street is about a block east of Powell and Market and the cable car turnaround is located there. When you finish walking around Chinatown, you can leave the gates and head for the cable cars to view the city from a different perspective.

best views

www.onlyinsanfrancisco.com

You must drive to . . . Coit Tower, a beautiful spot to view the city. Drive (or walk) down Lombard Street—the famous crooked street—and then drive to Twin Peaks for another beautiful lookout area to view the city.

golden gate park

www.nps.gov/goga/

A day at Golden Gate Park can keep you busy . . .

the California Academy of Sciences, Children's Playground, and Japanese Tea Garden are here. Look at the buffalo, and even rent a rowboat at Stow Lake. The San Francisco Zoo is also nearby.

more places we love to eat

Mel's Diner is kid-friendly (the original is on Geary Street, one on Lombard and the other on Van Ness), House of Prime Rib (Van Ness), North Beach Pizza (Italian section of the city—North Beach, just west of Chinatown).

The Jacobs Family

Charlotte and Tom Jacobs and their sons Trevor (14) and Bryant (13) live in Pacifica, California. This quaint coastal town (located just 20 miles south of San Francisco) is an ideal starting point when out-of-town family and friends come to visit. The Jacobses enjoy using the local beach as a recreational outing for surfing, boogie boarding, fishing, and relaxing before they take on the big city.

ten wonderful places in
santa cruz & monterey

Once you visit this magical coastline, you might never want to leave!
—Patti Bond

Ride the wooden coaster.

the boardwalk & main beach

www.beachboardwalk.com

A half-mile-long historic amusement park and mile-long beach with rides and attractions including a historic roller coaster and carousel. It's a day's worth of entertainment. About an hour before dinner in downtown Santa Cruz, be sure to take a leisurely stroll along Pacific Avenue. It's alive with street musicians, art galleries, and shops.

butterflies

www.santacruzstateparks.org/parks/natbridges/

Natural Bridges State Park and Monarch Refuge is a refuge for wintering monarch butterflies. The park also has a sandy cove and tide pools. The best time to see monarchs in the park is usually from mid-October to late January.

beautiful science

www2.ucsc.edu/seymourcenter/

Seymour Marine Discovery Center and Long Marine Lab is a working marine laboratory with exhibits plus tours to the marine mammal research overlook and vistas of the Monterey Bay National Marine Sanctuary.

henry cowell state park

www.santacruzstateparks.org/parks/henrycowell/

Take a one-mile, self-guided nature walk through a redwood grove as well as Douglas fir, madrone oak, and a stand of ponderosa pine. The tallest tree is about 285 feet tall and about 16 feet wide, and the oldest trees could be 1,400 to 1,800 years old.

roaring camp railroad

www.roaringcamp.com

You can journey back in time on a one-hour trip aboard an old steam locomotive, chugging up a narrow-gauge track through the Big Trees to Bear Mountain. Or you can ride on the diesel beach train down the scenic San Lorenzo River to the Santa Cruz Beach Boardwalk and back. Lunch is served!

saturday breakfast

www.montereybayfarmers.org

Have breakfast at the Monterey Bay Certified Farmers Market at Cabrillo College in Aptos, the premier farmer's market on the Central Coast.

capitola

www.capitola.com

Find quaint seaside shops and a popular surfing beach with board rentals and tide pooling. Rent a rowboat or kayak to glide in the kelp beds among seals and otters, or get a one-day fishing license and cast a line. Get ice cream at either Café Violette or Souza's. For dinner, try Shadowbrook, with a cable car that carries guests from street level to the restaurant on the creek. The bar has a lower-priced menu.

scenic drive

www.monterey.org

Drive from Carmel to Monterey on the scenic 17-mile road through Pebble Beach, an hour's drive. Be sure to visit Monterey Bay Aquarium. Today the surrounding area is a marine sanctuary and is home to a large resurgent population of sea lions. Have lunch at Portola House in the aquarium or Louie Linguini's at 660 Cannery Row.

the best playground

www.monterey.org

Dennis the Menace Playground was our children's favorite playground of all time and the city's most famous. The park opened in 1956 with a donation from Mr. Hank Ketcham, creator of Dennis the Menace. It's located just a few blocks from Cannery Row. Cannery Row, a historic waterfront district made famous by John Steinbeck, provides tons of fun things to do for the entire family.

carmel

www.carmelcalifornia.com

Famous for its white sandy beach, fascinating residential architecture, superb dining, and visual and performing arts. Clint Eastwood was the mayor from 1986 to 1988. Explore the many public pathways that will take you to delightful hidden courtyards and gardens and fairy-tale cottages. Try a walking tour like Carmel Walks (www.carmelwalks .com). Then cool your feet at the beach. Not far is Point Lobos State Reserve, a beautiful wild place with hiking trails.

The Bond Family

After moving from the East Coast to the West Coast, the Bond-Beech family has been enjoying exploring the beautiful state of California and its many diverse areas. Favorite family activities are camping, playing music around the campfire, and playing a card game named Up and Down the River.

adventure for everyone
southern california

For an outside-loving family, everything depends on tides, cloud cover, wind conditions, and day of the week. The week day/weekend consideration is important because *everything* is a bit less fun on weekends because of the crowds. Still, there always seems to be room for everyone at Balboa Park!
—Grace Stedje-Larsen

The Hotel del Coronado makes a great backdrop for family photos on the beach.

coronado beach
www.hoteldel.com

Walk on the beach in Coronado to look for sand dollars—the earlier the better. Go from the beautiful Hotel del Coronado toward North Island and you will surely find some sand dollars if you know how to look for them. Purple ones are still alive. White ones are dead and bleached by the sun. During the week and certain weekends you will probably see Navy SEALs candidates training in the water or running down the water line (very exciting and inspiring to any boy ages 4 to 34).

breakfast
www.binoscoffees.com

Eat breakfast at Bino's, a European-style coffee and crepe café near the Hotel del Coronado. Perfect for people watching, kid-friendly, and delicious.

Two water fountains nearby occupy little ones while the order awaits.

low tide
www.nps.gov/cabr/

If it's low tide . . . go to Point Loma's Cabrillo Monument and tide pools. See the incredible individual ecosystems in each little tide pool. You may see a tiny octopus if you are lucky. Limpets, crabs, sea stars, trilobites, sea slugs, tiny fish, and anemones abound. The monument and visitor's center offers spectacular views of San Diego (May and June could provide too much cloud cover) and the Pacific Ocean, so beautiful. You may see the migratory whales during spring and fall. Warning: Low tide tends to be a bit stinky (kelp and such on the shore).

seal pups
www.sandiego.gov/lifeguards/beaches/cove.shtml

Also at low tide, La Jolla Cove is small and pretty. See Children's Beach, now off-limits to people because seals have claimed it as a birthing area.

torrey pines
www.torreypine.org

After lunch, hike in Torrey Pines State Natural Preserve. There is a kind of twisty maritime chaparral that grows here and nowhere else on Earth. It gets moisture from the fog rolling in from the sea.

lunch views

http://flytorrey.com

Lunch in La Jolla: Go to the GliderPort in nearby Torrey Pines. Order a sandwich and watch people jump off the cliff with their colorful gliders or parachutes.

balboa park

www.balboapark.org

When the tide is high: Balboa Park! It's our favorite inland place. Our favorite thing to do is to look for all of the things we see in the book *Carl's Afternoon at the Park*. The book was set here! One Saturday we saw all of the things illustrated in the book (the carousel, the children's train, the painters, the balloon artists, the ice cream man . . .). On the way out we actually saw a lady walking a rottweiler like Carl near the big fountain (true story). Mom was the most excited of all!

eating with children

www.balboapark.org

Have lunch at the park in the sculpture garden (Waters Cafe). The kids can run around and examine the sculptures while you wait for your food. I love this café. If it's dinnertime, go to the Corvette Diner in Hillcrest. The waiters throw straws on the table and crack jokes, plus pass out bubble gum to all of the kids. It's a riot.

petco park

http://sandiego.padres.mlb.com/sd/ballpark/index.jsp

Home of the San Diego Padres. You can get here by water taxi. Buy the cheap field tickets and sit on the grass. This area has a ball field on it, and the kids play baseball during the game.

city farmers nursery

www.cityfarmersnursery.com

This garden store is my best-kept secret, with ancient play equipment, a giant fish pool, two gigantic tortoises, some random farm animals, and a huge bin of shallow dirt to dig your own compost worms. I love this place. So does my daughter, but my son wants to wash his hands after everything we do there.

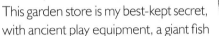

The Stedje-Larsens (plus grandparents)

Grace and Eric Stedje-Larsen live in Coronado, California, with their three young children. They love to visit family in Wyoming, New York, Virginia, and North Carolina, and they always find plenty to do in their own backyard.

brothers' road trip:
seattle to ketchikan

A few years ago I persuaded my brother Neil and his son Dane to accompany me on a road trip from Seattle to Ketchikan. I hoped to show him how warm and sunny even Alaska could be in the summertime. Here's the route we followed.
—Bill Shigley

Ferry travel: essential in Alaska

fraser river

www.chrs.ca/Rivers/Fraser/Fraser_e.htm

Our route followed the Fraser River upstream. The dense rain forest and rugged mountains of the coast range meant that most roads simply went along the larger rivers as they cut through the mountains. The Fraser River is the largest river in British Columbia and the longest river in the CHRS. It is also reported to be the greatest salmon river in the world.

hope & hells canyon

www.advenalaska.com/hope/, www.fs.fed.us/hellscanyon/

We passed by the town of Hope and a few hours later through Hells Canyon. This area had seen a large gold rush in the 1850s as prospectors explored farther north from the gold mines in California. Our goal on the first day of our trip was the town of Prince George—a short drive of 600 miles.

william's lake

www.britishcolumbia.com

Naturally we didn't make it, and we stopped a few hours early at William's Lake. This area was drier than I had expected and looked more like Montana; it seemed that the coastal mountains had blocked the big Pacific storms and kept the rainfall on the coast. The towns in this part of British Columbia first developed around the trading posts of the Hudson Bay Company and those of the native peoples—the First Nations as they are called in Canada. Prince George lies between two great river systems, the Fraser and the Skeena. The latter river descends through the mountains to the Pacific. For thousands of years this ecosystem has offered a rich supply of salmon to Indian tribes is this area—the Haida, the Tshimshian, and the Tlingit.

ferry to ketchikan

www.tourismprincerupert.com

That evening we arrived at Prince Rupert, British Columbia's largest coastal port. In the morning we boarded the Alaskan state ferry for the ten-hour trip to Ketchikan. This area on the coast is abundant in fish and wildlife and for thousands of years has been the historic homeland of the coastal tribes.

It has one of the Northwest's largest native artwork collections. During our stay in Ketchikan we visited the native village of Saxman and watched traditional wood carving.

skeena river

We followed the Skeena River the next day, continuing our drive through the mountains. It was a land of dramatic beauty with few signs of humans. It reminded me of the great rivers farther south such as the Skagit and Columbia. Here you will find five different types of salmon from the second longest river in British Columbia, Canada.

prince of wales island

www.princeofwalescoc.org

The next day our friends took a day off from work to take us fishing along Prince of Wales Island. The day was warm, if not hot, and sunny, and seemed to be not so different from parts of the California coastline. We spent the day dropping baited pots in 400 feet of water and were rewarded by literally buckets of spot prawns.

clarence strait fishing

www.visit-ketchikan.com

Our last day in Ketchikan saw us fishing for halibut in Clarence Strait, again in sunny weather. We came back into port that evening so that we could take the night ferry south to Prince Rupert.

Inukshuk: symbol for the 2010 Winter Olympics

to the pacific

We retraced our route as we headed south, except that we turned off at the native village of Lillooet for Pemberton and the Whistler valley. We drove to Garibaldi Provincial Park and again met the Pacific at Horseshoe Bay and Vancouver.

sleeping on deck

www.alaskaferry.com

Aboard the return ferry we rolled out our sleeping bags on the recliner chairs on the back deck. That night we crossed the border, passed Mount Baker, and were soon back in Seattle.

back home

It was a great trip, and I think that Neil and Dane were glad to experience the natural beauty and magic of the Northwest, as well as the gentle, moderate influence of the Pacific along our western coastline.

The Shigley Brothers

Bill Shigley is an avid outdoorsman and has had some amazing adventures—including a stay in a secret mountaintop cave house, built by a friend who carried up building materials one board at a time. He won't say where. His brother Neil is a California-based painter and sculptor, father of sons Dane, Hunter, and Laith.

local family favorites in
hawaii

We got together and came up with our favorite destinations among all of the main islands here in Hawaii (beginning with our own great children's museum at the top of the list, of course). We're a pretty diverse group, so you'll find a little bit of everything here. Aloha!

—Hawaii Children's Discovery
Center staff

Hawaiian monk seal

hawaii children's discovery center

www.discoverycenterhawaii.org

Step into the world-class, hands-on educational galleries at the Hawaii Children's Discovery Center, designed to inspire the young and young at heart, and discover the wonder of learning through creative play!

beaches & parks

www.co.honolulu.hi.us

For no cost and many wonderful memories, visit the natural environment at Hawaii's unique beaches and parks. A top spot for families is Ala Moana Beach Park, where children and grownups can enjoy a picnic under the coconut trees, dig and pour mounds of sand, and splash along the shoreline, which is protected by the reef.

hawaii nature center

www.hawaiinaturecenter.org

Since 1981, more than 800,000 children and adults have participated in environmental education programs at the Hawaii Nature Center, the only organization in the state of Hawaii solely dedicated to educating children about the native environment in the outdoors. Offerings include hands-on field programs for preschoolers through elementary school-age children, community programs for families, and guided hikes.

keiki zoo

www.honzoosoc.org

Children delight in seeing many familiar farm animals face-to-face at the Keiki Zoo, where they can crawl through a tunnel to the center of an aquarium, pet four different types of domestic animals, and climb inside real animal habitats.

hawaiian waters adventure park

www.hawaiianwaters.com

Designed to appeal to all ages and featuring a unique variety of age-appropriate rides and amenities, from the Keiki Kove to a thrilling six-story drop in a lush resort-like atmosphere, Hawaiian Waters

Adventure Park is one of the largest water theme parks in the world.

the bishop museum

www.bishopmuseum.org

Explore at the Science Adventure Center, where families participate in the interactive lab activities, explore the interior of a volcano, and climb up to the tree house and get a bird's-eye view of an erupting caldera.

polynesian cultural center

www.polynesia.com

Take part in authentic activities, games, and crafts and even sample food from Samoa, Aotearoa (Moari New Zealand), Fiji, Hawaii, Marquesas, Tahiti, Tonga, and Rapa Nui (Easter Island).

hawaii volcanoes national park

www.nps.gov/havo

Located on the Big Island, Hawaii Volcanoes National Park is the only spot in the world where families can see the results of 70 million years of volcanism, migration, and evolution—processes that thrust a bare land from the sea and clothed it with unique ecosystems and a distinct human culture.

waikiki aquarium

www.waquarium.org

Located in Honolulu, the aquarium features over 2,500 organisms representing more than 420 species of aquatic animals. A great place to see the Hawaiian monk seal, a family favorite!

maui ocean center

www.mauioceancenter.com

This is the largest tropical reef aquarium in the Western Hemisphere. Travel from the rocky surge zone to the edge of the deep reef, and participate in presentations by marine naturalists.

hikes

www.hawaiistateparks.org

Hike to the Makapu'u lighthouse, where families can see breathtaking panoramic views of the east side of Oahu and, perhaps, catch a glimpse of migrating whales in the ocean waters or one of the outer islands on a clear day.

Staff of the Hawaii Children's Discovery Center

We are educators, artists, child specialists, party planners, membership organizers, and more. We all live here near Honolulu, but we have roots all over the islands of our beautiful state. Come visit and we'll tell you more. Mahalo!

we remember

Dad prefers photo albums, a treasure trove for the choice offerings from his 35mm camera. Mom opts for scrapbooks, where she attaches everything from show ticket stubs to the autograph from the television star the family ran into at a restaurant. The kids, however, are into technology. They store memories on cell-phone cameras and Internet photo-sharing sites.

Nowadays, there are many ways for a family to store highlights from a family vacation. Allowing each person to choose his or her own method ensures that everyone is involved. Family vacation moments can be featured prominently on a video-sharing site or in a photo album. They can also go in your wallet, on your television set, on your Mp3 player, or cell phone, or in many other places

Families can express unique styles. Some pose in front of sunset backdrops or popular landmarks. Others capture videos of the family cheering wildly as the home team belts a winning run. Or, it could be audio of the family giggling uncontrollably while singing (read butchering) a song at a karaoke contest. The act of recording and saving your stories is essential to your family. It is a powerful affirmation that the people, places, and moments

Your journeys continue with keepsakes that share your stories.

are worth remembering and sometimes can provide sustenance when needed. Keep photo albums and scrapbooks in places of honor on a family bookshelf. When we look at them together we're honoring the best of our shared memories.

When everyone plays a part in telling and remembering the family's story, the memories are more colorful, compelling, and collaborative. It's funny how sometimes we remember things the same way and other times quite differently. The more varied, the better; it allows a family to see how the same moment is seen through different eyes.

There's another trick for capturing vacation highlights in a special way. One family calls it the "memory camera." When you notice a very special moment unfolding, stop and concentrate on what makes it so beautiful and important. Take in the sight, the sound, even the smell of the air around you and really commit it to memory. Encourage children to do the same. You can even hold up your hands and "frame" the scene with your fingers, like a director in an old-time movie. Because one of the very best places to store your favorite travel memories is (of course) in your own free, flexible, portable, high-capacity memory.

chapter seven
family memories

Memory makes us who we are.
—Rick Huganir

paper
scrapbooks

Scrapbook making is a timeless tradition. Dating back centuries, families have held memories of adventures in personalized books.

do some research

If you're a beginner, check scrapbook sites, go to the library, or visit a local craft and hobby store.

tell a story

Many people organize their travel scrapbooks chronologically. Some other ways include a geographic journey or special themes.

create the first look and feel

There are many products to help you create the perfect design. Think about the size of your scrapbook, style of "wallpaper" pages, types of pens, symbols, words, letters, and sayings, all in hundreds of styles and looks.

choose an album

Create a design that suits your concepts, vision, and sense of organization. There are many scrapbooks available in a variety of sizes and paper choices. There are also scrapbooks that use different fabrics and textures on the cover.

There is nothing as satisfying as organizing your memories, thoughts, and dreams in the highly textural media of scrapbooks, photo albums, journals, and sketchbooks.

design ideas

Everyone has a vision of how a scrapbook should look. These ideas come from serious "scrappers:"

- Stamping is a fun and easy technique. Create an accent or border. Try coloring images with pencils or markers.
- Use artwork from your family. This makes the best background for photographs and is a lasting treasure.
- Add texture. Try sandpaper, burlap, fabric from an old shirt, a table cloth, felt, or even a napkin from a restaurant.
- Layer images, illustrations, words, quotes, or headings and other keepsakes on top of backgrounds.
- Hand stitch or appliqué. The best way to achieve this look is to hand stitch the title or other images on a piece of fabric with embroidery floss. You can stitch on paper, too.

add the extras

Create meaning and depth by finding a perfect place for all the little pieces of paper you have brought home. Keep your plane, train, or boat ticket. Hold on to a napkin from a favorite restaurant. Try ribbons, paper luggage tags, hotel stationery, or even dried flowers from a roadside.

page layout

You are the graphic designer. Do you want a double-page spread, or do you want to work in single layouts? Will you use the same type throughout or change it around? What colors do you want to use? How about black and white photos or store-bought art? Get ideas from magazine pages or advertisements that catch your eye.

design a cover

Be creative! What about a photograph of your entire family in a favorite location? Or try creative lettering with the title of your adventure: "Our Alaska Trek." Sometimes it is easier to decorate the cover after you have designed the inside pages.

make it a family project

Before your trip, talk with everyone in the family about creating a scrapbook. Ask them to collect photographs, postcards, and keepsakes. When you get home, have a scrapbook night. Here are some guidelines:

The art of art, the glory of expression and the sunshine of the light of letters, is simplicity.

—Walt Whitman

- Order pizza. Then talk about how to organize the story.
- Have everyone share their collections.
- Create a storyboard. This helps everyone figure out what goes on each page.
- Give everyone a page to work on.
- Display and share your great finished scrapbook. Bring out scrapbooks on birthdays, graduations, or other celebrations. They are wonderful conversation starters. When they're out and on display, you can add a few pages or mementos every year.

don't worry if it takes you a while to start

Celebrate the fact that your scrapbook is really a never-ending project. Work on it a little at a time, the way you'd write in a journal or address holiday cards. First, find a box to hold all of the special memories, tokens, photographs, and other materials you have collected. A shoebox is fine. Mark the outside of the box with the name and date of the trip. Put small items in zipped plastic bags and lay them flat in the box. An old backpack or briefcase is good for storage, too—anything that helps you protect your mementos until you're ready to arrange them.

paper
journals & diaries

Writing in a journal helps you capture a moment in time. In years to come, kids delight in these memories and relive adventures with a fresh perspective.

start when you get up

First thing in the morning, write down your thoughts and feelings. Often we process information as we sleep. When you wake up, you may find you have a clearer view of the past. You can also plan ahead. Use your journal to create an itinerary for your family. Over breakfast you can discuss the plans. Add dates to your entries.

write about how your family experienced an event or visit

These will become lasting keepsakes. How did each person experience the adventure?

[
Always carry a blank or lined book and a couple of pens. Unlined books are nice if you want to add sketches; lined pages make your writing look neater.
]

There are so many ways to create a great journal.

What did you learn about your family? What insights did you gain? Read these to your family or keep them for a special time.

start a circle journal

Here's an idea that works: One person writes an entry and passes it on to the next family member. By the end of the trip everyone has added perspectives and views. Another family assigns a different person to be scribe for the day. Interviews, observations, and biased opinions are encouraged.

hear it, write it

Record what you hear (and overhear). Casual remarks can be so memorable. It is amazing how many quotations you can gather along the way. In museums there are always interesting things being spoken aloud. Often these get at the heart of a person's thinking. You can also make a habit of writing down the funny things children say. Add dates and place names.

make room for other stuff

Some journal writers allow room for drawings, photos, and even keepsakes that can be glued or easily taped in place. Tie your journal with a ribbon or a fat rubber band if it gets very full of stuff.

put a map in your book

Download a printout and paste it to the inside cover. Track different parts of your journey. Highlight different points along the way—places you have been, things you have done.

paste an envelope on the back cover

You can stuff things you have gathered along the way or things you want to use. There are lots of premade journals and diaries on the market. But you can make one using a three-ring binder and loose-leaf paper.

be prepared

Carry a plastic bag with calligraphy pens, crayons, glue stick, tape, pencils, ballpoint pens, colored pencils, and felt-tip pens. You can put anything you

> Travel involves my ears, my eyes, my nose, my tongue, and my touch in surprising ways. My body yearns to record all the new stimuli lest I forget what it feels like to be so engaged with the world.
>
> —Kelly Westhoff

want in your journal and use any type of material. If you don't have journal supplies on hand, scribble notes on napkins or envelopes and tuck them into your journal later on. Or you can transcribe more neatly when you have time.

let others make entries

Ask people you meet along the way to write you a letter or postcard to include in your journal. Ask them to create lists for you, such as their favorite place, activity, embarrassing moment, meal, or song. Different stories and handwriting will make your journal extra interesting.

write in letter form

You could write to yourself, to a family member, or to a dear friend. Or write from someone else's perspective: What would a baby say? Or what would your car tell if it could talk? Include quotes, poetry, sayings, or song lyrics that capture your feelings. Excerpts from your journal make great holiday letters. Or add journal entries to your scrapbook!

" **susan, maryland | power of words** As I reread a post-vacation essay, it is hard to believe that six years have passed. Family life is always changing, isn't it? When we vacationed, our days were carefree—we read on the beach, snorkeled, and played Scrabble at night. Fortunately, those memories have been captured in words. Pictures are visual images. Words go deeper.

paper
sketchbooks

Creating sketchbooks or visual journals, as they are sometimes called, is such a great way to experience a vacation. You don't have to be an artist to do it!

get a sketchbook
Make sure your sketchbook is big enough to work easily for any age. A sturdy cover and back are also very helpful. Put your sketchbook in a backpack with a range of art supplies for ease of use.

let everyone participate
Have everyone draw a portrait of other family members. Encourage your family to write as well as draw

Remind children to sign and date their sketches.

in the sketchbook. Captions, cartoon bubbles, quotes, and stories all add to images. Another fun activity is to have each person be on the lookout for something eye-catching, then rapidly sketch the scene for 30 or 60 seconds. Sign and date every sketch.

experiment with sketches and styles
Try drawing people, landscapes, wildlife and nature, animals, or even a still life. What about a minimalist perspective, an abstract drawing, or using colors to create a mood? Use tracing paper to copy illustrations you like, and then add your own colors and details.

experiment with interesting materials
There are some awesome drawing materials on the market. Try using pen and ink, charcoal, colored pencils, and even watercolor. *Plein air* watercolor painting is done outside, capturing landscape or scenery in a fresh way. Use heavy watercolor paper for best results. A variety of paper stocks and perforated pages make a sketchbook most practical. Look for sketchbooks that let you tear out pages with a clean, straight edge.

Fact: Leonardo da Vinci always kept a sketchbook with him to write down ideas or to draw things that caught his eye. At his death he left more than 8,000 pages of sketchbooks, including scientific projects, inventions, architectural designs, and more. Many of the notes da Vinci made in his sketchbooks were written backward and could only be read if held up to a mirror.

so maybe you can't draw . . .

How about making a collage? This form of art is a simple way to express yourself. Find maps, magazines, brochures, photographs, letters, or other items that symbolize your subject. Cut or tear them into pieces and layer them on the page with glue. Embellish these using other art materials or your own photos.

check out websites

There are tons of websites on sketchbooks and techniques for creating different styles and types of drawings. Depending on your level of skill and interest, there is something for everyone.

let your thoughts wander

Don't limit your sketchbook to your physical travels. Draw on your imagination. Your family may have a great idea for an invention, experiment, poem, or project. Use your sketchbook to illustrate your hopes and dreams.

make a sketchbook for a friend

This is a great way to share the story of your journey. Get a small 4 x 6 inch sketchbook. Decorate the cover and draw a title page, dedication page, and your own illustrations. If you are making

this for a child, you might consider choosing a regional folktale or fairy tale.

frame the good stuff

When you get home, choose the piece of art that is most memorable and frame it. You will be amazed how memories will continue to flow from this simple act. You can also give framed art as gifts to family and friends. Try making your own frame by gluing on pebbles or scraps from your trip.

start a library

Reserve space on a bookshelf for your self-published work. This could include scrapbooks, journals, sketchbooks, recipe books, and more. This is a great way to give the authors and artists in your home a special place.

books | ed emberley's drawing book: make a world

by ed emberley

If you can make a circle, a line, and a squiggle, you can draw anything. This book is fun for parents and kids together.

paper
autograph collecting

A small signature can make a big memory. Here are some ways to think about an autograph and a few guidelines for collecting them.

how to ask for an autograph

It is exciting to recognize someone famous in a public place. Show your children how to make an appropriate request. Introduce yourself first. "Hello, my name is Ben. I apologize for disturbing you, but are you X?" If they are who you think they are, you can simply say, "I am a big fan and would appreciate having your autograph." If they say yes, be ready with a pen and your autograph book. If they say no, be gracious and say, "Thanks anyway."

Autographs make great travel souvenirs.

anything can be autographed

You can use a notepad, index cards, baseball hat, T-shirt—you name it. Many people like to use a small 3 x 5 inch book with blank pages. Often these have a spiral binding for ease in turning the page and storing the pen.

make everyone a star

Collect the signatures of people you meet on your journeys. Ask them to sign their name and write a favorite saying or slogan. You will end up with a book full of useful words of wisdom.

plan an autograph outing

Go to a baseball game, a concert, or a museum—and bring your autograph book. Bookstores have authors sign books all the time, and there are also

> **karen, new york | special signatures** I still remember my daughter walking around Disneyland with her Disney autograph book. She spent all day tracking down her favorite characters, then asking them to sign her book. In the end she had over 25 autographs! It is fun now to look back and see Goofy, Mickey, Minnie, and Donald's signatures.

trade shows to meet celebrities. You can also ask for autographs after a lecture or speaking engagement.

make a written request
Send a letter requesting an autograph. If you're contacting an author, send it to the publisher of her latest book. An athlete? Send it to the team headquarters.

when requesting autographs by mail:
Make it easy to respond by including:
- a self-addressed and stamped manila envelope
- a letter of introduction, explaining why you would like an autograph
- a thank-you note when the autograph arrives

try this at home
Think about creating an autograph book at home. You could collect autographs from friends, family, teachers, and coaches. Ask them to share their favorite thing about you. Use different colored pens to make every page look unique, and add your owns notes and memories about the signer.

make a display
Once you have done the hard work of getting an autograph that you really want, show it off. You can put it in a simple frame and border or include it with a photograph and the autograph below. These make great gifts, too.

> Smile when you ask for an autograph. It helps!

set a goal
Can your family collect one autograph from a person in each state? Or one from each cast member of a favorite movie? Since autographs can be very valuable, you might want to go to specific signature-collecting events and figure out how to acquire or trade some special ones to round out your collection. Keep a log or journal listing each autograph and where you got it.

caring for autographs
Once you have done all the work of collecting autographs, you really need to protect and care for them. Because they are written on paper, they will fade with time. Use acid-free holders to protect your autograph. They're available in office supply stores or online. Use pencil to write dates or other notes.

books | the point is
by ruthie chong
The subtitle of this book is *Handwriting Analysis, 101 Fun Facts with Stories*. Bring it along to see what your autographs reveal.

paper
creating photo albums

It's the one thing everyone says they'll grab if the house is on fire. Photo albums are very special. So many memories are born out of everyday photographs—and those we take on our journeys. Here are some ways to create special photo albums along the way.

Order a digital album or glue together a traditional one.

start with the camera
Challenge your family to find the most beautiful landscape. If you can, bring a spare camera, such as a disposable or inexpensive digital version.

make photo assignments
Find the most beautiful landscape. Capture the best sunset. Take a shot of wildlife. Look for the most interesting people. It is so fun to see through the eyes of another.

get a family picture
People are really nice and thoughtful in framing a shot with your camera. Try to do this wherever

you go. You will be amazed at how others see your family.

make special critter photographs
Take pictures of your children's favorite stuffed animals in a variety of locations. Why not bring along a cuddly buddy and photograph it along your travels, with your family, with new friends, in front of monuments, on horseback . . . the sky is the limit. Keep them together in one album.

organize your images
Online or in photo boxes? Either way, categorize your shots for easier album making:

- individual children
- mom's family
- vacations
- holidays
- dad's family
- friends
- animals
- family milestones

Once you have created categories, you are ready to sort your photographs in chronological order. Take your time and enjoy this phase. Keep a box

maura, maryland | tradition Every summer we go to Martha's Vineyard. Before we leave, we take pictures of the kids at John Belushi's grave. It's a little quirky, but the kids look forward to it, and now we have eight years' worth of these pictures!

handy and sort just 10 or 20 photos at a time.

convert old photos

Scan old photos to create digital copies that will last much longer. The images often have faded colors or a soft focus that add nostalgic elements to digital collections. Pair them with newer shots for dramatic effect.

make a digital album

Most online photo shops offer distinctive albums that you can personalize with text and sturdy covers. Snapfish, Kodak Gallery, and iPhoto are popular choices that are easy for beginners to use. Add text to tell a story.

make a traditional album

If you have lots of prints on hand, arrange them in a book bound with plastic sleeves, or a scrapbook-style paper album with photo corners and glue. Choose acid-free papers and fixatives to help preserve your images.

> A family's photo albums are precious possessions. Each page makes memories come alive.

make a special memories book

A mom recently shared that she created a photo album for her son in the military. She found a small album and filled it with pictures of people and places he loved. He told her it kept him feeling close to home.

album debut

Plan an evening to share your work. Have everyone tell a story about the events surrounding the pictures. Sharing stories with each other brings you closer. You begin to see others in your family in a different light when you realize they don't always remember things the same way. Better yet, they remember things that you forgot!

digital
tips for great photos

Photography is a science as well as an art. Handling your camera and learning to frame the best shot are skills that improve with practice and experimentation.

take close-ups

Zoom in to find interesting details and features of your subject. What does the texture of a fence look like? Can you get the pollen on a flower? Capture the light, colors, and lines of the objects you are taking, whether they are people, places, or things.

lighting is always illuminating

Lighting changes a subject's mood and emotion enormously. What is the mood you are trying to capture? Is the light right? Also remember that light from behind will block the details in your subject. Cloudy days are always great for pictures. Try taking pictures at different times of day and see what you like best.

Take plenty of pictures, and then edit to save only the keepers.

alter your point of view

Many people shoot photographs at a 45-degree angle. Try experimenting with other angles. For example, try looking up or down at a subject. Tilt your camera frame at different angles. Lie flat on your stomach or flat on your back, or stand on a chair to get interesting perspectives. Practice on your own, so folks don't get impatient when you're trying to get an unusual shot later on.

get lots of exposures

Try the "sports" or "action" settings on your camera to take multiple exposures of a single scene—even if it's a family shot on the beach. You'll get a variety of expressions and details.

tell a story

Think like a photojournalist. Take a sequence of pictures that tells a story. On museum and other

> " **danielle, virginia | in the details** I save almost all of my pictures, even the ones that don't look so great at first glimpse. Sometimes there's something great in the background, like a funny dog or a child running by. I can zoom in on that part of the picture and enlarge it later, or cut it out and use it for a big collage. I make detailed collages that seem to be everyone's favorite Christmas gift.

tours it is great to try to capture the story of an exhibit or the feel of a place. Remember to shoot details, like the front doors of a museum or street signs near a historic hotel.

all about the weather

Emphasize the environment. Weather is a great mood setter. Historic tours and museums are designed to share information in a clear way. Try to capture the essence of the message or experience with a series of photos.

change your focus

Every picture needs a focal point. But it does not always have to be in the center of the frame. Think about the way you arrange people in your pictures. At historic sites, take pictures of children looking at monuments instead of standing in front of them.

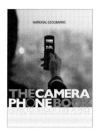

books | the camera phone book
by aimee baldridge & robert clark
This National Geographic title gives you great ideas for capturing great photos (and even making mini movies) with the camera on your cell phone. It also provides a helpful primer for learning about how to store, edit, and send images.

> A good photo preserves a moment in time.

This draws attention to the spirit and meaning of a place.

improve your images

We have all had the experience of taking a photograph of our children's eyes beaming against a beautiful blue sky, only to get the picture back and be disappointed. Experiment with your camera's editing function, or try a product like Digital Image Pro or Photoshop Elements.

cropping for clarity

Another great feature of digital photography is the ability to crop. You can pull in on a picture, deleting specific parts of an image. Or you can move the focus slightly to create additional drama. You can change the focus of the whole picture to a detail that was originally in the background.

backup plan

Save your digital images to a thumb drive or some other backup device. It's a great idea in case your computer malfunctions.

> Don't underestimate your camera's wrist strap. Use it to prevent an all-too-simple slip of the hand that results in a broken or lost camera.

digital
movie/video ideas

Put yourself in the role of a documentary filmmaker. What do you want your family to remember when they watch these movies in 6 months, 6 years, or 16 years?

Everyone in the family can have a turn behind the camera.

keep a video diary

This is a great way to start your travel video. Make sure you set the recorder to show the date or speak into the microphone to record it. You can film the events of the day that are important to you. These might include getting the kids out of bed, planning the day, being in the car, arriving at a destination, exploring a sight, observations after a visit, or dinner conversations.

time is of the essence

In film a minute can feel like a lifetime. Shoot for the short shot. Ten to fifteen seconds is all you need for the best effect. A lot can happen in just a few seconds of "movie time."

[Sometimes you just need to keep the film rolling and other times you need to wait for that perfect moment.]

it's all in the lighting

Digital cameras don't have much lighting control. Opening blinds or filming outdoors will help you create a better video. If faces seem shadowed, turn the focus of the scene so light is coming from the side or from behind the camera. Avoid having people look straight into the light. Move your position so they can face you at an angle.

backgrounds make a difference

Is the background part of the story? Or is ultimately going to be a distraction? Create settings that are neutral or that enhance your story. If you are shooting someone who is about to get on a horse, set the stage by showing horses in the background.

documentary or feature film

Do you have a message or theme for your video? If so, before you hit the "on" button, think about how the pictures you are about to take will fit in. Travel videos are generally documentaries, so be sure you include the entire cast of characters to get the full picture. Or encourage the family to be actors and play roles to tell the story.

narrate if needed

This can be a great and very funny technique. Narrate the events as they are happening or have someone else do the voice-over. It is amazing how people see what is happening in such different ways. Sometimes you can even engage the subject to talk directly to the camera and answer some questions. Other times you may be recording speech or music that does not require narration.

kids are naturals

Encourage the kids to be part of the video making. Let them use the camcorder as well as be in front of the camera. Have them tell the camera where you are and what is happening. Make them the stars that they already are.

spur-of-the-moment shots

The best and most memorable shots come when you least expect them. So make sure you always

> Try to imagine how your recording will look to people who see it in 50 years.

have your video camera nearby. Compact cameras will fit easily in a backpack, purse, or glove compartment. Keep the battery charged up!

keep your video simple

Don't distract your audience. Pans and zooms are great, but when you use them, move very slowly. This will help the viewer get accustomed to the changing point of view. Mimic the formats of favorite television programs or films. Try creating a music or dance video, a skit, or a top-ten feature—all styles that use brief "cuts" to engage the viewer.

editing is the answer

There are some easy-to-use video editing programs available, including Movie Maker and iMovie, that enable you to modify your video, adjust quality of images, and add music. You can also create digital copies of old VHS movies using a variety of products on the marketplace. Their creativity, involvement, and excitement will lead to deeper and more meaningful memories for all of you.

> " karen, massachusetts | family films My dad took the camera everywhere. On Lumaha'i Beach he taped me singing and dancing, belting out "I'm gonna wash that man right outta my hair" from the same spot Mitzi Gaynor sang in *South Pacific* (only to be horrified years later when I realized my father still had the videotape). I wonder if he's had it digitally converted!

digital
sharing your story

Telling your story becomes a journey of its own. Over time, you can try lots of different paths for capturing, saving, and sharing your memories.

create a digital scrapbook

Using your computer, you can download photographs directly into premade scrapbook pages and add stories, quotes, and other keepsakes. Then just push a button, and you can order a beautifully bound book or print it out and make your own. You can also go to many of these site for interesting fonts, embellishments, or designs that you can download and print for use. There are services and tools to preserve, retouch, and share your vintage photographs.

publish your story

Publish your journal. Make copies and share your travel adventures with others. Whether it is a day-

Share the fun! There are lots of ways to tell the story of your family adventures.

journal entry book or a story, there are many programs available to help you publish your work. You can also use word processing to write your journal. This relatively simple tool will enable you to quickly cut and paste text for your journal or book. Use extra photos or scraps to make bookmarks.

make stuff

These days it is possible to put your images on cards, calendars, mugs, T-shirts, key chains, mouse pads—you name it. Use your amazing travel photographs again and again. They make wonderful gifts, holiday cards, or everyday reminders of your great trips together. A good idea: Plan your order, then double-check all of the details before you actually place the order. Choice of photos or spelling errors can't be changed after you hit "place order." You can usually see the virtual finished product first.

> " **mary, maryland | learning as we go** I've heard it said that our children are digital natives, but parents and grandparents are immigrants when it comes to the land of technology. I can learn so much from my kids when we play around with our travel pictures. It's a fun way for us to spend time together.

use digital frames

Program digital frames with different themes. Create a silent movie effect by downloading a digital text frame (like PowerPoint) and placing it with your photos. Or color-code a series of pictures. A whole collection of black and white images can make a powerful statement on a changing screen.

invent beautiful e-cards

It's so easy. Choose an e-card design; add your own photos, videos, music, and words; and then email, blog, or print it out! Send an announcement before you travel in case friends have tips or destination ideas to share. Or make "Bon Voyage!" cards.

design a family website

This is a great way to share travel experiences with everyone in the family. You can post videos or photographs, tell stories, start a family journal, or create a blog for ongoing communication.

go social

Social networking sites focus on building online communities with people who share interests and activities. This is a great way to share your mutual love of travel. Create a web page to share your travel history and interests, invite friends and family to see your adventures, or suggest other things to experience. "Virtual" adventures can inspire wonderful real-life travels.

> Library programs help adults learn about all kinds of digital technology.

cook up a digital recipe book

Collect recipes for foods you all enjoyed on your adventures. Download them into a book, add some information about where you had the food, and add tidbits about the chef and a sprinkle of photographs.

create a photo album on your phone

Download your photos to your phone and create an instant photo album. Then when you are anywhere and someone asks, "How was your vacation?" you can "show and tell." It is also great to be able to send photos from your phone in an instant.

make a slide show

A nod to the old days, when the family would gather to see slides from the family vacation: Create a digital version and play it on your TV screen. Make a night of it by preparing food and drinks inspired by your travels. Keep the remote handy so you can pause for especially great photos!

> Check blogs from digital hobbyists for up-to-the-minute ideas about changing technology.

sounds
soundtracks

Here are a few family favorites for car music or video soundtracks. Make your own mix, roll down the windows, and hit the road!

country
1. I've Been Everywhere: Johnny Cash
2. We Shall Be Free:
   Stephanie Davis & Garth Brooks
3. Love Can Build a Bridge: The Judds
4. Key Lime Pie: Kenny Chesney
5. Thank God I'm a Country Boy:
   John Denver
6. Mountain Music: Alabama
7. On the Road Again: Willie Nelson
8. Hey Doll Baby:
   Sweethearts of the Rodeo
9. Ready Set Don't Go:
   Billy Ray & Miley Cyrus
10. Southern Nights: Glenn Campbell

hip-hop
1. Throughout the Years: Kurtis Blow
2. Magic's Wand: Whodini
3. Release: Timbaland
4. Summertime: DJ Jazzy Jeff & The Fresh Prince
5. Freedom: Grandmaster Flash
   & the Furious Five
6. Lyte As a Rock: MC Lyte
7. Rock Box: Run DMC
8. U Can't Touch This: MC Hammer

9. Double Dutch Bus: Frankie Smith
10. Jump: Kris Kross

rock & pop
1. Old Time Rock and Roll:
   Bob Seger, Thomas Jones, George Jackson
2. I Love Rock and Roll:
   Joan Jett & the Blackhearts
3. A Horse with No Name: America
4. Shipping Up to Boston: Dropkick Murphys
5. Dancing Queen: Abba
6. Pocketful of Sunshine:
   Natasha Bedingfield
7. Rocket Man: Elton John
8. We Will Rock You: Queen
9. Life Is a Highway: Rascal Flatts
10. It's My Life: Bon Jovi

r & b

1. Respect: Aretha Franklin
2. Cupid Shuffle: Cupid
3. Bounce, Rock, Skate, Roll:
   Vaughan Mason & Crew
4. Flashlight: Parliament
5. Disco Nights (Rock Freak): GQ
6. Just Fine: Mary J. Blige
7. Movin': Brass Construction
8. Good Times: Chic
9. Ain't No Stopping Us Now:
   McFadden & Whitehead
10. Pon de Replay: Rihanna

classical

1. Butterfly's Day Out: Yo Yo Ma
2. Thunder and Lightning:
   The English Brass Ensemble
3. *Indiana Jones* Theme: John Williams
4. Fleurs Du Mal: Sarah Brightman
5. *Star Wars* Cantina: John Williams
6. Ride of the Valkyries: Richard Wagner

books | from sea to shining sea

by amy cohn

This essential family book includes music and lyrics for classic American songs, along with beautifully illustrated stories that go along with each. It's a great read-aloud (and sing-aloud!).

> When music changes, so does the dance.
> —**African proverb**

7. The Prayer: Andrea
   Bocelli & Celine Dion
8. Classical Gas:
   Vanessa-Mae
9. Gonna Fly Now
   (Theme from *Rocky*):
   Bill Conti, Carol Connors
10. My Favorite Things:
    Rodgers and Hammerstein

novelty

1. Disco Duck: Rick Dees & His Cast of Idiots
2. YMCA: Village People
3. Tootsee Roll: 69 Boyz
4. Macarena: Los del Rio
5. Hot, Hot, Hot: Buster Poindexter
6. Monster Mash: Bobby "Boris" Pickett
   & the Crypt-Kickers
7. The Purple People Eater: Sheb Wooley
8. Who Let the Dogs Out: Baha Men
9. Eat It: "Weird Al" Yankovic
10. Don't Worry, Be Happy: Bobby McFerrin

best singalongs

1. 100 Bottles of Pop on the Wall
2. I've Been Working on the Railroad
3. This Land Is Your Land
4. Mr. Frog Went a-Courtin'
5. Eric Canal
6. Bingo
7. Row, Row, Row Your Boat
8. The Wheels on the Bus
9. Oh Susannah!
10. Wimoweh

digital
ways to save stories

There is something very satisfying about hearing the voices of people you have met along your way, interviewing your family, or just recording the sounds around you.

daily audio journal

Bring a digital audio recorder in the car and encourage kids to keep a daily taped journal. Assign a child to be a reporter for the day. Suggest questions about how far you've traveled, interesting sites, unique people, landscapes, and regional foods.

one-on-one interview

Find a quiet place to sit down with a family member or interesting new friend. Ask them if you can interview them about their thoughts, experiences, or expertise. Schedule these storytelling moments as you go on your way. Be sure to record the name of your subject and the date and location of the interview.

create a story-round

This is great fun to do in the car. Start a story by saying something like "Today was a special day. We visited an ice cream factory." Then give the recorder to the next person. They continue: "I have never seen so many flavors of ice cream." Then the next person: "The chocolate was made from candy bars!" Let it go on and on until the story feels complete. You will have created a beautiful mosaic.

capture the sounds

Audio is such an amazing medium. It enables you to capture the smallest and most interesting sounds. Begin by taping some sounds you hear: crickets, owls, bees buzzing. Fill the tape with these sounds of nature or other things. In a journal, write down what you have taped. Use these to make a soundtrack for your family films, or download them to make unique ringtones for your cell phone. You can make a game of it: Play

" susan, maryland | **storytelling** Several years ago we recorded my 99-year-old grandmother fresh from a tour of her hometown of Crisfield, Virginia, and asked her to share the "family secrets" along the way. We have three amazing hours of stories and insights that we have shared with her great-grandchildren. We've made copies for everyone, and the plan is to use parts of the recording as the background for a digital slide show with photos from her wonderful life.

snippets of familiar sounds and challenge kids to identify them.

radio explorer
Pretend you and your family are on assignment and are recording a radio program. Talk about the story you want to tell and make a script. Interview folks in your story. You will be surprised how much you learn and how much fun you have together.

changing voices
Spend a little time and energy to record each of your children's voices, ideas, stories, and opinions over the years. You'll have created an archive of their voices. It is so great to be able to hear the curiosity and delight in a child's voice, to hear the cracking as it changes, and ultimately to hear the adolescent and adult voices of your children.

create audio stories and poetry
Record a story you or your family wrote during a trip. Or retell something that happened that you don't want to forget. Add to this over the years. It will make a lovely archive.

play your recordings
Plan a time to play the recordings you have made with your family. This is great fun. Try playing them in the car or at home.

> It takes a thousand voices to tell a single story.
> —**Native American proverb**

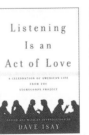

preserve sounds
Audio files are treasures, just like your favorite photos, books, and souvenirs. Many families have old cassettes with saved-up stories or song mixes. There are several tools on the market to convert cassettes or vinyl to CDs or Mp3 format. Create backups for one-of-a-kind recordings or mixes and circulate them to family members so everyone can hear the stories, songs, and sounds.

create a cd case
Use the liner of a CD case to trace the shape you'll need to make your own case cover. Decorate with photos, markers, and scraps. Add a title and date, and even make liner notes on the inside panel. Or use a permanent marker to write directly on the CD, adding names, dates, and even your own hand-drawn embellishments.

books | listening is an act of love *by david isay*
StoryCorps encourages people to record their private and personal stories together with someone they care about. This book is a collection of some of the best.

Listening
Is an
Act of Love

A CELEBRATION OF AMERICAN LIFE
FROM THE
STORYCORPS PROJECT

DAVE ISAY

sensory
hands-on memories

When it comes to sharing travel memories, the sky's the limit.

make a photo quilt

Follow the directions on a package of photo transfer paper, available at craft stores. Enlarge your prints using a copier and make a quilt block from each photo. Piece the quilt blocks together yourself, or take them to a local sewing shop and ask for tips. Sew on buttons, shells, or other small keepsakes from your trip.

Quilt squares are enduring mementos of your family's journeys together.

memory stones

Along your journey you can pick up wonderful stones from different parts of the country. Use a permanent marker to identify each one with a location and date. Put them in a wooden bowl or woven basket for others to enjoy. Or glue a circle of felt to the bottom and use it as a paperweight.

mapping the moments

Maps are fantastic tools and keepsakes. Use a map of a recent trip or favorite destination and write your favorite memory. It could be a date you visited, an event you attended, or something special you remember. You can frame the map and come back to it again and again as your memories build.

keepsake frame

There are many ways to use photographs in unique frames. A favorite idea came from a daughter who made her parents a simple framed picture of the three of them on a trip to the Grand Canyon. Over the picture she glued small pieces of paper with thoughts about her parents: "You are the best. Thank you for sharing the world with me. My love for you is deeper than the canyons."

bowls of beauty

Seashells, rocks, pine cones, and fossils make great objects for display in baskets and bowls. This is a simple but very elegant solution to having your travel memories around you all the time. Try different types of containers to show off your stuff. Like all great art collections, it can change depending on the season or occasion.

mosaic memories

At the end of every trip there are always pockets full of stuff that everyone has collected. You know: bottle caps, shells, stones, beach glass, sticks, and other keepsakes that find their way back home. Try memorializing them in mortar. Go to your local craft store and purchase mosaic grout and a small bottle of wood glue. Arrange your keepsakes on a wooden object like a mirror frame or cigar box. Glue them in place. Let dry for several hours. Mix the grout according to the instructions, apply it around your keepsakes, and wipe it before it dries. You have created an heirloom!

> The days are long but the years are short.
>
> —traditional adage

snow globes

Start with a ready-made snow globe kit. Add a photo from your trip. You can add the name of the place, a quote, or a funny saying. Turn it over and do the same thing on the other side. This makes a great desk accessory and a great gift, too! Most globes allow you to change the pictures so you can update them on your next trip.

make a travel capsule

Like the old-fashioned time capsule, this is a great way to hold all the special pieces of your family trip to revisit at a later time. The key to a good travel capsule is making it personal and interesting. One idea is to have everyone write a favorite thing about the trip and put it in an envelope. Do this for every trip you take. Add tickets, maps, and keepsakes that are special. Decide together on the best time to open the capsule.

pressed flower bookmarks, gift tags, ornaments, and cards

What do you do with the beautiful pressed flowers you carefully brought home? Place them between sheets of adhesive-backed plastic, press out air bubbles, and cut it into bookmark or gift tag shapes. Use a hole punch to add ribbon.

cookbook of favorite travel recipes

While on your trip, don't be shy about asking for recipes from cooks and chefs. You will be surprised how people love to share their creations. Once you have collected your recipes, host a dinner with all your favorite travel foods!

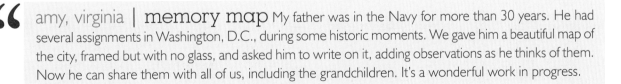

amy, virginia | memory map My father was in the Navy for more than 30 years. He had several assignments in Washington, D.C., during some historic moments. We gave him a beautiful map of the city, framed but with no glass, and asked him to write on it, adding observations as he thinks of them. Now he can share them with all of us, including the grandchildren. It's a wonderful work in progress.

tell me more

So now the ideas are out there. You're ready to back your bags (or at least a backpack) and hit the road together. But travel really starts at home—around the dinner table, at story time, or during the homework hour. Together, your family can discuss places you want to go. Read about epic journeys. Encourage your children to let their thoughts wander and follow where they lead.

Talk about the places you want to go.

Fortunately, a great trip lasts much longer than a few days or weeks. Preparation is definitely part of the adventure: drawing up lists, choosing accommodations, making reservations. The time to travel grows closer, and you make plans to alert the neighbors, stop the paper, and batten down the hatches at home.

Kids can learn a lot from the steps you take to organize and plan for travel. Very small children can think about seasons, and they can count down days on a calendar.

Older children can gather and sort brochures or help parents research destinations on the Internet. Involve teenagers in budgeting, comparing costs of accommodations, or designing the scrapbook that will chronicle your adventure.

Participation brings extra meaning to a child's sense of anticipation. Their creativity, involvement, and excitement will lead to deeper and more meaningful memories for all of you.

Think about the way children see family attitudes about travel. Are you eager and excited about an upcoming trip? Or are you rushing around packing suitcases at the last minute? Either way, children are watching and, as always, they will learn travel skills and habits from you.

Use the following pages to make the whole process easier and more fun. Use the index for easy geographic information. Checklists and planners are easy to photocopy. Stick a "wish list" on the refrigerator and add a few lines each week. Make extra copies of contact pages or medical information so everyone has their own. When vital statistics are at your fingertips, it's easier to get up and go.

Write your own top-ten list and family biography on pages 464–65. Make copies of the pages and start your own travel book, adding photos and highlights as you go. Your family has its own personal geography, and your story deserves to be told!

chapter eight
resources

Your adventure begins at home . . .

ten best
packing tips

The secret to any great vacation is preparation. Needs change according to destination and children's ages, but some tips are timeless.

start early

Designate a box for travel provisions. As you come across things you'll need for your trip, stash them here until you're ready to start packing. Have a "vacation fashion show" a few weeks before you go. Try on special occasion clothes, bathing suits, or hiking gear. It's a great way to take note of what you still need.

make lists

Have children make a list of what they want to take, including clothes, toys, and books. Use your itinerary, a calendar, and even a weather report to help you plan the list. The list on page 460 is easy and fun for children to fill out. It's also handy when you're packing to go home. You can check to be

sure you're returning with everything you took.

pack light & smart

Make sure everyone is not taking too much. Can the family share a single tube of toothpaste? Talk about making choices and looking ahead. You can't take six stuffed animals. Which one will be best to take on a trip? How many shirts do you need if you wear two shirts each day, and you'll be gone for four days?

pack neatly

Folded clothes take up less space than balled-up ones. Fold things as flat as possible, and then roll them tightly to prevent wrinkling.

wear shoes & socks

Shoes take up a lot of suitcase room. Pack your sandals or flip-flops and wear your shoes so you don't

> " suzy, maryland | sleepy When my boys turned two we gave them soft kids' sleeping bags. You can even get them with their names on them. We put them in the crib and they usually slept on top of them. They loved their bags. Whenever we traveled we'd roll them up with their stuffed animal and blanket. At our travel destination we'd unroll their bag and they felt just like home. It made traveling a lot easier and more fun.

have to stuff them in a bag. When traveling, it is safer to wear sturdy, comfortable shoes that protect your toes and heels. If you do need to pack shoes, save space by stuffing socks inside them.

bring your old stuff
One family brings their oldest socks and underwear on trips. Instead of bringing it home dirty, they just throw stuff away as they go. Just remember to have new underwear waiting when you arrive at home!

medicine mom (or dad)
An adult should carry any needed medications or medical supplies in one bag. Remember allergy medicine, inhalers, over-the-counter pain or fever medicine, and waterless alcohol-based hand wipes. Always keep medicine in carry-on bags. Optional: comfort items like chamomile or peppermint tea bags (useful for an upset tummy or handy as compresses).

first-aid kit
It's a good idea to carry one in the car, and certainly take one on longer trips. The basic version includes antiseptic, antibiotic ointment, and bandages. Add insect repellent, sunblock, and a clean plastic bag that you can use as an ice pack.

toiletries
Everyone can pack their own small containers of shampoo, lotion, or other liquids. For very small children, it's exciting to carry their own supplies. It's also necessary if you're flying with carry-on luggage: The Transportation Safety Administration allows you to take only up to three ounces of any liquid aboard a plane.

day pack
A flat-bottomed canvas bag with pockets makes a nice travel caddy. Pack it with maps, itineraries, sunscreen, spare sunglasses, and a pad of paper and pencils. Add some empty plastic bags to use as trash receptacles. Make sure it is not too heavy to carry.

resource | airline carry-on
For updated information about airline carry-on restrictions, check the website of the Transportation Safety Administration: *www.tsa.gov*.

ten best
car trip tips

For many of us, the family car is a home away from home. Whether the trip is across country or across town, you can take steps to make the journey safer and more enjoyable for everyone.

be safe

The National Highway Traffic Safety Administration posts information about child safety and car seat requirements, including locations for car seat safety stations across the country. Visit their website at www. nhtsa.dot.gov, or call 888-327-4236.

drive right

From an early age, children form ideas about safe driving by observing their parents. Use time in the car to point out traffic signs and to talk about the responsibilities that come with the privilege of car travel. Even more important, model good habits

of cell phone use, driver etiquette, and general safety.

eat light

Pioneers had to carry weeks' worth of provisions with them. In general, we do not. Keep a small cooler in the car to carry perishables, and remember that there are grocery stores almost everywhere you'll travel.

eat smart

If your trip includes a mealtime, pack a picnic and plan to stop and eat along the way. Check maps or travel planners for a historic site or a place with a famous view. If you really need snacks while moving, bring crumb-free choices like dried or fresh fruit, carrot sticks, shelled nuts, or cheese sticks.

stretch your legs

If your trip is a long one, plan to stop every two or three hours (or more often, if needed). If possible,

> " mary, massachusetts | car trip Vacation spot, vacation spot, how do I love thee? A simple question easily determined by calculating how willing you are to suffer to get there. With children, lengthy travel is often hellish and 18 hours in a car qualifies as deadly. However, when the destination is heaven on Earth, the ride is a small price to pay.

switch places with older children from time to time for a change of vantage point.

bring a permanent marker

Label water bottles so everyone can identify his or her own as you go. This way there are no unfinished "mystery bottles." Along the way you can mark belongings for easy identification and sorting, like T-shirts, towels, socks, and sandals.

entertainment

Bring books, magazines, journals, or sketchpads along for the ride. Store them in flat baskets that can slide under a seat. Bring music to share, plus extra batteries and earphones for Mp3 players or handheld games. Think about choosing books or music related to your travel destination.

stay organized

There are some great car organizers that hang on the back of driver and passenger seats. Choose one with pockets for a water bottle and individual spaces to store markers or pencils. Details like this are endlessly fascinating for backseat riders.

potty emergency

Help children stay calm in case of a sudden need to relieve themselves. Always accompany a child to a public rest room. If one is not available, find a roadside spot that will allow you to make

an easy return to the roadway. Plan ahead by keeping a roll of toilet paper and some extra plastic bags in the trunk. One family swears by a big empty plastic peanut butter jar with a good lid. Kids are always welcome to relieve themselves in it if necessary, but the idea is usually met with willingness to wait for a "real" rest room.

the return trip

Pack away a few new games or activities to hand out at the beginning of the trip home. It helps to ease back into the long and now-familiar ride.

resources

National Highway Traffic Safety Administration
www.nhtsa.dot.gov

Governor's Highway Safety Association
www.ghsa.org

National Organizations for Youth Safety
www.noys.org

Safe America Foundation
www.safeamerica.org

[
Sounds Like Fun
Check out pages 440 and 441.
You'll find lists of great singalong songs and creative music to travel by.
Make up your own songs, too!
]

ten best
precautions & remedies

Most children make easy transitions to new places, foods, and environments. With preparation, parents can usually deal with the inconvenience of travel-related illness, and also know where to turn if more help is needed.

necessities
Keep medical information on hand: location of nearby care, child's blood type, immunization records, and copies of prescriptions (medical and optical). Copy the list on page 459 for complete details.

homesickness
Scent is powerful. Put a bar of your regular soap brand in an old sock and drop it in your child's bag. Everything will smell just right. Carry along comfort items like a favorite blanket or toy. Familiar things ease transitions to new places.

boredom
This catch-all term describes hunger, tiredness, or a craving for attention. Try to see the moment through your child's eyes and take a casual and creative tone: "I wonder what would happen if the dinosaur skeleton started walking around. I wonder how many people have looked at this monument in the past one hundred years."

crankiness
Meltdowns are inevitable. A parent's anxiety is contagious. Practice relaxation techniques like deep breathing or meditation, and encourage your child to try it, too.

getting lost
When you travel, tape your name and cell phone number to the back of your child's clothing. Learning your cell number is a great exercise in memorization and a fun car activity.

ear pressure
During airplane takeoff, it's common for kids to experience temporary ear discomfort caused by changing pressure in the middle ear. This can be a scary experience for kids. To ease the pain:
- Swallow, yawn, or chew gum.
- Infants can nurse or use a pacifier.
- Explain to children that this is a temporary condition, and that it is happening to adults, too.

travel sickness
The Children's Hospital of Philadelphia (www.chop.edu) describes symptoms including nausea, dizziness, vomiting, pallor, and cold sweating.

Travel sickness can happen anywhere, but most often on boats, planes, buses, and cars. To minimize symptoms:

- Feed a child a light meal before a trip.
- Don't eat on short trips. On longer trips, try small snacks of bland foods like crackers or bananas, and sip drinks.
- Allow frequent stops for walks and fresh air.
- Look outside at distant and still objects, like trees and buildings. This helps to orient vision and hearing.
- Minimize head motion with a pillow or headrest.

jet lag

Our internal clock needs time to catch up with changes in time when we travel. The results are symptoms including tiredness, upset stomach, and even insomnia.

- If possible, ease your family into the day/night schedule of your destination. In the days before your trip, wake up a little earlier (if you're heading east), and stay awake a little later (if you're going west).
- Drink plenty of water before, during, and after a flight. Avoid caffeine. It is a diuretic and causes you to eliminate water, possibly leading to dehydration.
- Exercise. During a long flight you can stretch cramped muscles. Allow children to walk around the plane if possible. You can't lose them!
- Encourage kids to be active outside or in brightly

lit areas during daylight hours to keep their bodies on a familiar day/night schedule.
- Follow the local times as soon as you reach your destination. Keep kids awake until dark and make this their usual bedtime while you're there.

stomach trouble

This can be common during travel, when the body reacts with a message that something is different. Other causes are bacteria or germs in the digestive system, often from contaminated food or water. Symptoms can include diarrhea and constipation, which can be serious problems for young children and infants. Try these precautions when you travel:

- Drink only unopened bottled water.
- Use purified water for making infant formula or brushing teeth.
- Wash hands frequently.
- Use alcohol-based hand sanitizer.
- Rinse pacifiers and toys with purified water.
- Wash, peel, and cook fresh foods with purified water.

more resources

American Academy of Pediatrics/Parent Corner
www.aap.org

The Center to Prevent Lost Children
www.preventinglostchildren.org

Centers for Disease Control and Prevention
www.cdc.gov/travel

U.S. State Department travel website
www.travel.state.gov

getting there

Most reservations are placed at centralized locations that handle nationwide calls. Ask for the phone numbers of individual hotels and call ahead to get specific information about the location and nearby attractions for families.

Inn by Wyndham, Travelodge, Baymont Inn & Suites, and Howard Johnson.

Marriott
888-236-2427, www.marriott.com
Properties include JW Marriott Hotels, Renaissance Hotels, Courtyard by Marriott, and Fairfield Inns.

hotels

Starwood
888-625-5144, www.starwoodhotels.com
Properties include Four Points Sheraton, Sheraton, W Hotel, Westin Hotels, and aloft Hotels.

Intercontinental Hotel Group
800-315-2621, www.ihg.com
Properties include Crowne Plaza Hotels & Resorts, Hotel Indigo, Holiday Inn, Holiday Inn Express, Staybridge Suites, and Candlewood Suites.

Wyndham Hotels and Resorts
877-999-3223, www.wyndham.com
Properties include Ramada Hotel, Days Inn, Wingate

Hyatt
888-492-8847, www.hyatt.com
Properties include Grand Hyatt, Hyatt Regency, Park Hyatt, Hyatt Place, and Hyatt Summerfield Suites.

Hilton
800-HILTONS, www.hilton.com
Properties include Double Tree Hotels, Hilton Garden Inn, Hampton Inn & Suites, Homewood Suites by Hilton, and Embassy Suites.

Best Western
800-780-7234, www.besternwestern.com
Locations nationwide.

" **meg, west virginia | why travel** One-on-one time with each parent enables our son to open up in ways he wouldn't in the normal course of daily activities as a family. These are special times when he feels he can be heard and speaks what's on his mind with no distractions of ringing phones or boiling pots on the stove.

Recreation vehicle rental companies have in-depth support services, including help with mapping and planning your trip and website reports from other traveling families.

rv rentals

Cruise America
480-464-7300, www.cruiseamerica.com

GetRV.com
888-438-7844, www.getrv.com

USA RV Rentals
866-814-0253, www.usarvrentals.com

Convertible? Sport utility vehicle? Minivan? Choose a rental car to match the "personality" of your trip. Check for the availability of vehicles with built-in car seats or other safety features.

car rentals

Alamo
800-462-5266, www.alamo.com

Avis
800-331-1212, www.avis.com

Budget
800-527-0700, www.budget.com

Dollar
800-800-3665, www.dollar.com

Enterprise
800-261-7331, www.enterprise.com

Hertz
800-654-3131, www.hertz.com

National
800-227-7368, www.nationalcar.com

Thrifty
877-283-0898, www.thrifty.com

All-encompassing vacation services make cruises an increasingly popular choice for reunions and extended family gatherings. Check for off-season rates that make cruises even more affordable.

cruise lines

Carnival
888-CARNIVAL, www.carnival.com

Celebrity
800-647-2251, www.celebritycruises.com

Disney
800-951-3532, http://disneycruise.disney.go.com

Holland America
877-932-4259, www.hollandamerica.com

Lindblad Expeditions
800-EXPEDITION, www.expeditions.com

Norwegian
866.625.1166, www.ncl.com

Princess
800-PRINCESS, www.princess.com

Royal Caribbean
866-562-7625, www.royalcaribbean.com

getting there

Get to know a city by visiting its mass transit website. Most have interactive planners with detailed maps to print out plus fare information.

mass transit

Phoenix, AZ
www.ci.phoenix.az.us/PUBTRANS/pubtridx.html
Service includes bus and light rail.

Los Angeles, CA
www.metro.net
Service includes bus and metro.

San Diego, CA
www.sdcommute.com
Sevice includes trolley, bus, and train.

San Francisco-Oakland, CA
www.bayareatransit.net
Service includes bus, rail, subway, ferry, and cable car.

Washington, DC
www.wmata.com
Service includes bus and train.

Miami, FL
www.miamidade.gov/transit
Service includes bus, train, and metromover.

Tampa-St. Petersburg, FL
www.gohart.org
Service includes bus and trolley.

Atlanta, GA
www.itsmarta.com
Service includes bus, subway, and rail.

Chicago, IL
www.yourcta.com
Service includes bus and rapid transit train.

Boston, MA
www.mbta.com
Service includes bus, subway, train, and boat.

Baltimore, MD
www.mtamaryland.com
Service includes bus, train, light rail, and subway.

Detroit, MI
www.detroitmi.gov/ddot/index.html#
Service includes bus.

Minneapolis-St. Paul, MN
www.metrotransit.org
Service includes bus and train.

New York, NY, NJ, CT
www.mta.info
Service includes train, bus, and subway.

Philadelphia, PA
www.septa.org
Service includes bus, subway, trolley, and train.

Dallas-Fort Worth, TX
www.dart.org
Service includes bus, light rail, and train.

Houston, TX
www.ridemetro.org
Service includes bus and train.

Seattle, WA
www.soundtransit.org
Service includes bus, train, streetcars, ferries, light rail, and monorail.

Estimate costs, check out special deals, and find out how other families plan their trips.

online travel planning

AAA
www.aaa.com
Membership-based travel planning services.

Breezenet.com
www.bnm.com
Known for low rates on rental cars.

Christian Travel Finder
www.christiantravelfinder.com
Faith-based vacation and service trips for families.

Expedia
800-397-3342, www.expedia.com
Search engine for travel and accommodations.

FamilyStories
www.familystories.org
Share family travel experiences.

Gorp
www.gorp.away.com
For adventure and outdoor travel planning.

GrandTravel
www.grandtrvl.com
Vacations for grandparents and grandchildren.

Home & Abroad
www.homeandabroad.com
Links to Expedia for planning itineraries.

Hotels.com
800-346-8357, www.hotels.com
Good location for comparing rates.

MenuPages
www.menupages.com
Lists menus of over 25,000 U.S. restaurants.

National Geographic Trip Planner
www.nationalgeographic.com
Point-to-point mapping and links to local websites.

National Park Service
www.nps.gov
Portal to all national park sites.

Orbitz
888-656-4546, www.orbitz.com
Search engine for travel and accommodations.

Priceline
800-774-2354, www.priceline.com
Search engine for travel and accommodations.

R Family Vacations
www.rfamilyvacations.com
Gay and lesbian family vacation planning site.

Sidestep
203-899-3100, www.sidestep.com
Search engine for travel and accommodations.

Transitions Abroad
www.transitionsabroad
Travel, study, and volunteer opportunities for students and families.

Travelocity
888-872-8356, www.travelocity.com
Search engine for travel and accommodations.

Travel Zoo
www.travelzoo.com
Weekly newsletter with travel deals in your area.

XE
www.XE.com
Current currency exchange rates for 180 different currencies.

trip planner

where we're going

destination: _____

_____

accommodations: _____

_____

geographic coordinates: _____

_____

when we're going

season: _____

_____

date: _____

_____

how long we'll stay: _____

_____

why we're going

the main reason for our trip: _____

_____

what's special about this place. _____

_____

whose idea was this? _____

_____

how we'll get there

our plan for traveling: _____

_____

time it takes to get there: _____

_____

getting around at our destination: _____

_____

what we'll see & do

_____

_____

_____

_____

_____

resources:

people we know: _____

_____

books and movies about this place: _____

_____

more: _____

_____

Make a copy for every trip you plan.

vitals

parent name: _____

_____

child name: _____

_____

child's social security number: _____

_____

address/city/state/zip: _____

_____

_____

home phone: _____

cell phone: _____

child's blood type: _____

_____

last tetanus shot: _____

_____

allergies: _____

_____

medications & home pharmacy contact

information: _____

_____

_____

prescriptions (medical and optical):

_____

_____

_____

personal physican name & contact information:

_____

_____

_____

health insurance carrier & policy number:

_____

_____

destination hospital/pharmacy: _____

_____

_____

emergency contact (name and phone number):

_____

_____

_____

_____

_____

_____

Make a copy to keep on record for each child.

packing list

destination & dates: _____

- ☐ ☐ address book
- ☐ ☐ art supplies
- ☐ ☐ batteries
- ☐ ☐ book
- ☐ ☐ camera
- ☐ ☐ cash
- ☐ ☐ cell phone charger
- ☐ ☐ cold weather gear
- ☐ ☐ compass
- ☐ ☐ flashlight
- ☐ ☐ footwear
- ☐ ☐ hair care
- ☐ ☐ hat
- ☐ ☐ jewelry
- ☐ ☐ journal
- ☐ ☐ keys
- ☐ ☐ laundry bag
- ☐ ☐ maps
- ☐ ☐ _____
- ☐ ☐ _____
- ☐ ☐ _____
- ☐ ☐ _____

- ☐ ☐ music
- ☐ ☐ outerwear
- ☐ ☐ paper towels
- ☐ ☐ rain gear
- ☐ ☐ sandals
- ☐ ☐ socks
- ☐ ☐ special occasion clothes
- ☐ ☐ sports equipment
- ☐ ☐ stamps
- ☐ ☐ sun protection
- ☐ ☐ swimsuit
- ☐ ☐ toilet paper
- ☐ ☐ toiletries
- ☐ ☐ trash bag
- ☐ ☐ umbrella
- ☐ ☐ underwear
- ☐ ☐ vitamins
- ☐ ☐ water bottle
- ☐ ☐ _____
- ☐ ☐ _____
- ☐ ☐ _____
- ☐ ☐ _____

Copy this list and check off as you pack.
Check off again as you pack to go home.

details

before we go

- [ ] clean out refrigerator
- [ ] return library books
- [ ] stop mail
- [ ] stop/donate newspapers
- [ ] hide spare key
- [ ] arrange pet care
- [ ] make bill payments
- [ ] check security system
- [ ] finish laundry
- [ ] check answering machine
- [ ] arrange yard care
- [ ] ______________________
- [ ] ______________________
- [ ] ______________________
- [ ] ______________________
- [ ] ______________________
- [ ] ______________________
- [ ] ______________________
- [ ] ______________________
- [ ] ______________________
- [ ] ______________________
- [ ] ______________________

while we're gone

how to reach us: ______________________

____

____

if you can't reach us: ______________________

____

____

____

____

____

when we'll be home: ______________________

location of electric breaker box: ______________________

____

location of main water valve: ______________________

____

____

our home address: ______________________

____

____

our home phone number: ______________________

additional information: ______________________

____

____

Copy and cut in half. Share the right side with your house sitter or neighbor.

wish list
united states

Here are places we want to go, why we want to go there, and good times to make the trip.

1. _____
_____
_____
_____

2. _____
_____
_____
_____

3. _____
_____
_____
_____

4. _____
_____
_____
_____

5. _____
_____
_____
_____

6. _____
_____
_____

7. _____
_____
_____

8. _____
_____
_____

9. _____
_____
_____

10. _____
_____
_____

Copy this page and keep a running list.

wish list
abroad

Here are places in the world that we want to see together, along with our ideas for getting there.

1. _____
_____
_____
_____

2. _____
_____
_____
_____
_____

3. _____
_____
_____
_____
_____

4. _____
_____
_____
_____

5. _____
_____
_____
_____

6. _____
_____
_____
_____

7. _____
_____
_____

8. _____
_____
_____

9. _____
_____
_____

10. _____
_____
_____

Copy this page and keep a running list.

ten best

1. _____

2. _____

3. _____

4. _____

5. _____

6. _____

7. _____

_____

_____

_____

_____

_____

8. _____

_____

_____

_____

_____

9. _____

_____

_____

_____

_____

10. _____

_____

_____

_____

_____

1. Copy these two pages to start your own "ten best" book.

2. Add a title and photo on the left-hand page.

3. Fill in the spaces with your own "ten best" destinations.

4. Add a family photo here, and write your own biography or travel memory below.

5. Send your pages to www.familystories.org.

_____

_____

_____

_____

_____

_____

_____

journey's end . . .

Our work here is dedicated to the memory of Jane Evertz—friend, sister, and intrepid traveler. Her spirit of independence and fun reminds us that family life is a gift, full of potential for remarkable moments.

Working on this book has been like taking a very big family trip. As the saying goes, "Every journey begins with a single step." In this case, that step was a single word: yes.

Nina Hoffman, President, Books Publishing Group, and Executive Vice President of the National Geographic Society, called and said, "We want to add a family travel book to our "10 Best" series. Do you want to do it?" It took me about two seconds to reply. And so the journey began.

I believe that travel is one of the most important ways to help children explore and truly understand the world they live in, and I love traveling with our family. But the task of developing this book was a lot to consider. The first big question: How do you organize materials about travel—for families with kids of all ages—that is meaningful, relevant, and most importantly, fun?

This is where my traveling companions, Mary Bonner and Lisa Hamm, enter the picture.

Mary, Lisa, and I have worked together for more than 20 years. We first worked to develop Curiosity Kits, creating hands-on learning activities for children in arts, sciences, and world cultures and designing more than 600 award-winning projects.

Then in 2007 we launched FamilyStories, a resource for families. FamilyStories invites families to share their stories about moments that matter in their lives, and to listen and learn from other families. FamilyStories gathers experiences from a variety of venues, including our website, our workshops, family reunions and get-togethers, personal interviews, festivals, and any other places for families. The stories inspire further research into the art and science of family life, ranging from new studies about child development and education to recipes for Peruvian hot chocolate or the best bedtime stories.

The FamilyStories model of collecting ideas was a natural for gathering information for *The 10 Best of Everything Families: An Ultimate Guide for Travelers*. We worked for over a year to develop a structure, outline, and graphic approach for the book that harmonized with the ways families think and plan. National Geographic provided great editorial and graphic guidance to create a book that is resourceful and enjoyable to read.

From here, we talked with many, many families all over the country about what they wanted and needed in a contemporary family travel book. Their top recommendations about everything from favorite ice cream spots to scrapbooking strategies, children's museums to waterfalls, and hundreds of other topics were collected, sorted, and reviewed. For months our team checked out ice cream shops, farmer's markets, ranches, camps, hotels, bike shops, and literally a thousand other places to find out what makes them so special and to get more details.

We also talked to people we admire, and asked them to share their personal family travel experiences. We were gratified by the response: Explorer Rick Ridgeway gave us his list of fragile natural landscapes and destinations that are not to be missed. Acclaimed poet Elizabeth Spires offered a selection of American writers' homes for families to visit. Across the board, remarkable people responded to our request in remarkable ways.

At a certain point, the book took on a life of its own. When Hurricane Ike hit, we checked back on the Gulf Coast entries—for editorial purposes, but also out of concern for the people and places that had become familiar to us. We breathed a sigh of relief to learn that the whooping crane nesting areas had been spared and that Hank's was still scooping great ice cream in Houston. All of us involved in the development of this book feel that we have made new friends and gained amazing new insights.

We live in a staggeringly beautiful and diverse country. Geographic contrasts are so striking: from beaches to plains, farmlands to deserts, canyons to mountains. Fascinating and unpredictable weather patterns account for 120°F temperatures in Arizona, three feet of snow in North Dakota, and hurricanes in the Gulf. Families who live across this country have such a variety and depth of cultural heritage and history. These wonderful mixtures of land, climate, and people provide the ingredients for the bounty of rituals, traditions, and stories we share and enjoy everywhere.

In the end, *The 10 Best of Everything Families: An Ultimate Guide for Travelers* offers thousands of voices to help your family create your own unforgettable travel experiences. It is a celebration of our country and a remembering and rediscovering of our amazing selves.

So while this first edition is complete, the journey never really ends. We hope this is only the beginning of some great new trips with your family. We invite you to share your own recommendations on our website and to learn more about traveling together for a lifetime of discovery and adventure.

www.familystories.org

with gratitude

It has been a privilege to work with the professional and seasoned staff of National Geographic Books, including Elizabeth Newhouse, Marianne Koszorus, Al Morrow, and Gary Colbert. Deepest thanks go to Melissa Farris for her outstanding design; her superb talents are seen throughout these pages. Nina Hoffman continues to amaze me with her instinct for refining and redefining what geography is and how it makes a profound difference in our everyday lives.

I am eternally thankful to Mary Bonner and Lisa Hamm, who have carefully and joyfully woven together the details of this book to create a lasting reference. Mary's lovely spirit and words combined with Lisa's firm and friendly managing gifts to make this book a reality. And to their families that made the trip with us—waiting for supper and waiting for us to get off the phone, but also inspiring us with enthusiasm and ideas—thank you.

Contributing editors Joe Burris and Sara Savitt were influential at every stage, and I owe them deep gratitude. Their attention to detail, creativity, and knowledge helped to shape our work. I know we could count on their instincts to bring something perfect to the book.

Our editorial interns and research team include Natalie Forte, Shelley Goldstein, Mara James, Katherine Lashley, Grace Sheahan, Nina Kamooei, and Lindsey Thomas. From core content research to fact checking and contact review, they worked to ensure accurate, reliable information. Extra perspective came from trusted advisors in all areas, notably Chuck Savitt of Island Press and Kathryn Goldman of Goldman & Minton.

Our initial graphic design began with concepts from longtime partner in creativity, Julia Evans. The work evolved with the help of Nikki Huganir, Carly Reis, and Nicole Clark. A very special thanks to principal designer Lotta Olén. Her good nature and adventurous spirit carried us through countless rounds of reviews, and her attention to getting it right was unwavering.

There are too many families, friends, teachers, students, shop owners, park rangers, farmers, advisors, and other experts to thank here by name, but you all know who you are. You made this book sing. Your stories brought context, and excitement to our everyday work.

To my mom, Patsy, who includes travel on her personal job description; to my sisters, who never stop exploring; and to Granny, who started it all, I love you all.

And finally to my kind and generous family—Rick, Ben, Sam, Nikki, and Adam—thank you for appreciating how much I have loved the adventure of this book. And thank you for indulging me in so many rambling stories that have no endings.

Susan H. Magsamen is an award-winning writer, educator, and advocate on family and children's issues. Her books and programs have been called "a beautiful celebration of family life," empowering parents and children to connect—with each other, with other families, and with the world around them. Susan's work is widely recognized as fostering and enhancing the ways we learn, play, create, and grow as individuals, families, and communities.

Susan is the founder of FamilyStories, a multimedia resource for families featuring a five-part book series, workshops, a website, and radio programs. In addition, she is chair of the Editorial Advisory Council for *Wondertime,* an award-winning monthly child development magazine. She is the co-director of the Johns Hopkins University School of Education Neuro-Education Initiative, fostering dialogue, research, and communication among educators, researchers, and key stakeholders. Susan was founder of Curiosity Kits, a hands-on learning company in the arts, sciences, and world cultures. She is also a board member of the American Visionary Art Museum. Susan has developed successful family, parent, child, and school partnerships and collaborations with organizations including Barnes & Noble, United Way of America, XM Radio, Families and Work Institute, Scholastic Inc., National Geographic Society, Sylvan Learning Systems, Public Broadcasting Company, Discovery Channel, Metropolitan Museum of Art, Smithsonian Institution, Chicago Art Institute, and the Walt Disney Company.

Her body of work has earned hundreds of national awards and recognition from child development experts and parenting associations including Oppenheim Awards, Parent's Choice, Family Fun, National Association of Parenting Publications, Hearthsong, and the Canadian Toy Council.

Recent publications:

- *My Two Homes: Practical & Hopeful Wisdom for Families, from Families, When Parents Separate or Divorce*
- *Family Night!: Activities, Games & Great Ideas for Family Fun*
- *Nighty Night: Tried-and-True Bedtime Traditions and Tales for the Whole Family*
- *Making Spirits Bright: New Ways for Your Family to Enjoy the Simple Pleasure of the Holiday Season*
- *Tooth Fairy Time: Everything You Need to Know About Losing a Tooth and the Magic That Follows*

ten best
index

Illustration & Photo Credits

This book was created with contributions from hundreds of resources.

Fairmount Park, courtesy of Melissa McMasters, 27 • Dolcezza Italian Ice, courtesy of Dolcezza, 31 • Cheesesteak, ⓒiStockphoto.com/dirkr, 32 • Nine Layer Cake, courtesy of Smith Island Cake, 33 • Water Ice, ⓒiStockphoto.com/duckycards, 33 • Girl on Swing, ⓒiStockphoto.com/mevans, 36 • Bird, ⓒiStockphoto.com/ElementalImaging, 37 • Peach Basket, ⓒiStockphoto.com/GeoffBlack, 39 • Girl with Shell, ⓒiStockphoto.com/Maica, 46 • Storyland Playground, courtesy of New Orleans City Park, 47 • Cafe du Monde and Beignets, courtesy of Burton E. Benrod, Jr., 52 • Como Park, courtesy of Como Park Zoo & Conservatory, 77 • Ravin' Red, courtesy of Sprecher Brewing Company, 82 • Chicago Hot Dog, courtesy of Portillo's Hot Dogs, Inc., 83 • Sunflowers, courtesy of Bill Lubing, 84 • Farmers Market, courtesy of Carly Ries, 88 • Family Circus comic, courtesy of Bill Keane and the Family Circus Family, 130 • Bikes on Beach, courtesy of Carly Ries, 184 • Grand Canyon, ⓒiStockphoto.com/SoopySue, 240 • Elizabeth Spires, courtesy of Jerry Bauer, 295 • David Hess, courtesy of Eric Salsbery, 299 • girl with binoculars, ⓒiStockphoto.com/ericmichaud, 376

Text Acknowledgments

"My advice to you is not to inquire why or whither, but just enjoy your ice cream while it's on your plate." Excerpt from THE SKIN OF OUR TEETH by Thornton Wilder. Copyright © 1942, 2008 The Wilder Family LLC. Reprinted by permission of The Wilder Family LLC. All rights reserved. Page 41.

Excerpt from DEATH COMES FOR THE ARCHBISHOP by Willa Cather. Copyright © Willa Cather 1927, renewed by the Executors of the Estate of Willa Cather 1955. Reprinted by permission of Random House Inc. and Virago Press. Page 85.

"Seeing is deceiving. It's eating that's believing." Excerpt from FURTHER FABLES FOR OUR TIME by James Thurber. Copyright © 1956, 2008 Rosemary A. Thurber. Reprinted by permission of Rosemary A. Thurber. All rights reserved. Page 113.

Excerpt, reprinted from PRESENT MOMENT, WONDERFUL MOMENT (1990) by Thich Nhat Hanh with permission of Parallax Press, Berkeley, California, www.parallax.org. Page 145.

Excerpt from public speech and MY EXPERIMENTS WITH TRUTH by Mahatma Gandhi, 1993 Beacon Press. Copyright © 1993 Navajivan Trust, Ahmedabad, India. Used with permission. Pages 201 and 271.

Excerpt from LOST WOODS: THE DISCOVERED WRITING OF RACHEL CARSON by Linda Lear. Copyright © 1998 by Roger Allen Christie. Compilation, introduction, and text other than Carson's writing copyright © 1998 by Linda Lear. Reprinted by permission of Beacon Press, Boston. Page 259.

Excerpt from THE CYCLES OF AMERICAN HISTORY by Arthur M. Schlesinger, Jr. Copyright © 1986 by Arthur Schlesinger, Jr. Reprinted by permission of Houghton Mifflin Harcourt Publishing Company. All rights reserved. Page 315.

The 10 Best of Everything Families

Susan H. Magsamen

Published by the National Geographic Society

John M. Fahey, Jr., *President and Chief Executive Officer*
Gilbert M. Grosvenor, *Chairman of the Board*
Tim T. Kelly, *President, Global Media Group*
John Q. Griffin, *President, Publishing*
Nina D. Hoffman, *Executive Vice President;*
    President, Book Publishing Group

Prepared by the Book Division

Kevin Mulroy, *Senior Vice President and Publisher*
Leah Bendavid-Val, *Director of Photography Publishing*
    and Illustrations
Marianne R. Koszorus, *Director of Design*
Barbara Brownell Grogan, *Executive Editor*
Elizabeth Newhouse, *Director of Travel Publishing*
Carl Mehler, *Director of Maps*

Staff for This Book

Elizabeth Newhouse, *Editor*
Melissa Farris, *Art Director*
Al Morrow, *Design Assistant*
Nikki Clapper, *Proofreader*
Bridget A. English, Barbara A. Noe, *Contributors*
Connie D. Binder, *Index*

Jennifer A. Thornton, *Managing Editor*
R. Gary Colbert, *Production Director*

Manufacturing and Quality Management

Christopher A. Liedel, *Chief Financial Officer*
Phillip L. Schlosser, *Vice President*
Chris Brown, *Technical Director*
Nicole Elliott, *Manager*
Monika D. Lynde, *Manager*
Rachel Faulise, *Manager*

Staff for FamilyStories

Susan Magsamen, *Editor*
Mary Bonner, Joseph Burris, Lisa Hamm, Sara Savitt, *Contributing Editors*
Lotta Olen, *Principal Designer*
Julia Evins, Nicole Stanton Clark, Nikki Huganir, *Designers*
Shelley Goldstein, Lindsey Thomas, *Fact-checkers*
Natalie Forte, Mara James, Katherine Lashley, Grace Sheahan,
    Nina Kamooei, *Interns*

Founded in 1888, the National Geographic Society is one of the largest non-profit scientific and educational organizations in the world. It reaches more than 285 million people worldwide each month through its official journal, *National Geographic*, and its four other magazines; the National Geographic Channel; television documentaries; radio programs; films; books; videos and DVDs; maps; and interactive media. National Geographic has funded more than 8,000 scientific research projects and supports an education program combating geographic illiteracy.

For more information, please call 1-800-NGS LINE (647-5463) or write to the following address:

National Geographic Society
1145 17th Street N.W.
Washington, D.C. 20036-4688 U.S.A.

Visit us online at www.nationalgeographic.com

For information about special discounts for bulk purchases, please contact National Geographic Books Special Sales: ngspecsales@ngs.org

For rights or permissions inquiries, please contact National Geographic Books Subsidiary Rights: ngbookrights@ngs.org

Library of Congress Cataloging-in-Publication Data available upon request

ISBN: 978-1-4262-0394-7

Printed in USA